The Yale Anthology of Twentieth-Century French Poetry

The Yale Anthology of
Twentieth-Century

French
Poetry

EDITED BY
MARY ANN CAWS

YALE UNIVERSITY PRESS   *New Haven & London*

Cet ouvrage, publié dans le cadre d'un programme d'aide à la publication, bénéficie du soutien du Ministère des Affaires étrangères et du Service Culturel de l'Ambassade de France aux Etats-Unis.

This work, published as part of a program of aid for publication, received support from the French Ministry of Foreign Affairs and the Cultural Services of the French Embassy in the United States.

The Florence Gould Foundation provided additional funding for the publication of this work.

Epigraph, page v: "Let There Be Translators!" from *Days of Wonder: New and Selected Poems* by Grace Schulman. Copyright © 2002 by Grace Schulman. Reproduced by permission of Houghton Mifflin Company. All rights reserved. The list of acknowledgments for permission to reprint previously published works appears at the back of this volume, beginning on page 617.

Designed by James J. Johnson and set in Minion type by Keystone Typesetting, Inc.

Printed in the United States of America.

The Library of Congress has cataloged the hardcover edition as follows:

The Yale anthology of twentieth-century French poetry / edited by Mary Ann Caws.

 p. cm.

English and French on facing pages.

Includes bibliographical references and index.

ISBN 0-300-10010-8 (cloth: alk. paper)

 1. French poetry—20th century—Translations into English. 2. French poetry—20th century. I. Title: Yale anthology of 20th-century French poetry. II. Caws, Mary Ann.

PQ1170.E6Y35 2004

841'.9108—dc22   2004040695

 ISBN 978-0-300-14318-8 (pbk. : alk. paper)

A catalogue record for this book is available from the British Library.

The paper meets the requirements of ANSI/NISO Z39.48-1992 (Permanence of Paper). It contains 30 percent postconsumer waste (PCW) and is certified by the Forest Stewardship Council (FSC).

10 9 8 7 6 5 4 3 2 1

Let There Be Translators!

And the Lord said, "Behold, the people is one and they have all one
language. . . .
Go to, let us go down, and there confuse their language, that they
may not understand one another's speech."
—GENESIS XI: 6, 7.

When God confused our languages, he uttered,
in sapphire tones: "Let there be translators!"
And there were conjurors and necromancers
and alchemists, but they did not suffice:
they turned trees into emeralds, pools to seas.

God spoke again: "Let there be carpenters
who fasten edges, caulk the seams, splice timbers."
They were good.
　　　　　God said: "Blessed is the builder
who leaves his tower, turns from bricks and mortar
to marvel at the flames, the smith who fumbles
for prongs, wields andirons, and prods live coals,
who stokes the hearth and welds two irons as one."

Praised was the man who wrote his name in other
handwriting, who spoke in other tones,
who, knowing elms, imagined ceiba trees
and cypresses as though they were his own,
finding new music in each limitation.

Holy the one who lost his speech to others,
subdued his pen, resigned his failing sight
to change through fire's change, until he saw
earth's own fire, the radiant rock of words.

—Grace Schulman

Contents

2. 1916–1930: Dada and the Heroic Period of Surrealism

3. 1931–1945: Prewar and War Poetry

4. 1946–1966: The Death of André Breton, the Beginning of *L'Éphémère*

5. 1967–1980: The Explosion of the Next Generation

6. 1981–2002: Young Poetry at the End of the Millennium

Editor's Note

Compiling a major volume such as this one is, of necessity, a highly subjective process. In considering the many poets writing in French in the twentieth century and just after, I have given less attention to the number of poems and pages per poet than to the more important goal of including as many poets from as many countries as a single volume permits. My aim has been to create a truly international anthology, one that represents the diversity and changing nature of French poetics during the century just past, giving sufficient space to the voices of the living, while not letting them overwhelm those of the past. Every effort has been made to include poems that seem to have been most crucial to their own time as well as those from the present that demand to be read.

The brief biographies of the poets that precede their works convey only the most basic information. Critical analyses of their works are not possible in such limited space. These small biographical notes do not include the many major prizes awarded to these poets, nor do they reference English translations of their works. The volumes of poetry cited as principal works are in some cases supplemented by significant prose works, and occasionally by smaller works whose titles seem particularly indicative of an individual way of seeing or thinking.

Not wishing to privilege any country in an international anthology, I have opted to include both the city and country as the poet's birthplace, despite the apparent redundancy of, say, Paris, France, or Montreal, Canada.

Previously published translations have been faithfully reprinted here as they first appeared (except for corrections of what seemed obvious misprints or spelling errors). The many translations commissioned for this volume do reflect, of course, the voice of each translator. As in all bilingual editions, the translation is meant to draw attention to the original on the facing page.

The editor is enormously grateful for help received from so many quarters. This publication would never have been possible without generous funding from the Florence Gould Foundation, the French Ministry of Foreign Affairs, and the Cultural Services of the French Embassy in the United States. My thanks to Yves Mabin and Agnès Young, of the Division de l'écrit et des médiathèques at the Ministère des affaires étrangères, and in particular to Olivier Brossard; to John Young, of the Florence Gould Foundation; and to the Research Foundation of the City University of New York. At Yale University Press, the ongoing enthusiasm of my editor, John Kulka, proved crucial at every point, as was the assistance of Karen Gangel, Mary Traester, and Lauren Shapiro. My warm thanks to Maggie Nelson for her comments on contemporary American poetry, and to the French poets who have made me feel at home in their poems over so many years. Mariana Shackne, here in New York, deserves thanks for her tireless efforts and patience. Above all, I am grateful to all the poets, publishers, and rights holders, whose contributions were invaluable. Of course the labor, time, and generosity of the translators far exceed any remarks or mention I can offer here. What to say but thank you.

Introduction

The poem is what has neither name, nor rest, nor place, nor dwelling: a fissure moving towards the work. JACQUES GARELLI, "Excess of Poetry"

T his anthology responds to the often expressed need for a large-scale bilingual representation of twentieth-century French-language poetry as a whole. In the tumult of our time, poetry offers itself as a borderless country in which we can all reside, at least temporarily. It is in this belief that I have undertaken this massive volume. For the first time, as inhabitants of a brand-new century, we can look back at the twentieth century. Our evaluation, of course, will change with our reading as the years go on. Nothing is presumed about the lasting nature of any attempt to gather what seems important at the moment, except the goodwill of this team of translators and advisers, every one of whom has my deep gratitude.

Many of the translations in this volume have been previously published—some appeared in books, some in journals—and many others have been commissioned specifically for this book. The choice of translators was crucial; I often consulted them about which writers—and then which poems—should be presented. I also listened, gratefully, to the counsel of Francophone and Anglophone friends. But finally, of course, as editor, I had to make my own choices, as intuitive as they were reasoned and often difficult, of both poets and poems.

The bilingual presentation notwithstanding, I have tried to keep in mind the perspective of the non-French-speaking reader. Writing of the decision by the *New York Review of Books* not to retain him as a reviewer, the art historian Michael Fried described his way of being and seeing. Here he might well be speaking of my involvement with this volume. Fried was recognized, he says, as "someone whose primary commitment

was to certain works and artists and whose criticism and scholarship would invariably foreground that commitment in ways that would only imperfectly harmonize with prevailing styles of doing intellectual business both outside and within the academy."[1] This anthology, when it reaches the bookstore shelves, may well go against whatever styles of anthologizing are currently in vogue. My commitment is to a wide reach of works, with all the risk that entails, and to the judgment of the translators I have called upon. The deliberately extensive range of poets includes several who are well known, or even better known, in other genres: Georges Bataille, Samuel Beckett, Louis-René des Forêts, Andrée Chédid, Yves Bonnefoy, Annie Le Brun, and Michel Houellebecq, among others. Here they are considered only as poets—I do not think they would object.

The presentation of poems in this anthology is largely chronological. As we move closer to the present, the proportion of female to male artists changes dramatically; additionally, the female voice takes on increasing assurance as various feminisms develop in France. In French feminisms, especially in the 1970s, the most visible and general approach was heavily psychoanalytic—for example, the work of Hélène Cixous, Julia Kristeva, and Luce Irigaray. In France, as in the United States, feminist agendas would become increasingly associated with the social sciences, relating domains formerly isolated from one another in the universities and public life. As Terry Eagleton says, the temper of the time was not only intellectually exciting, but it made room for much that had been excluded by male enthusiasts of what we call high theory.[2] For Jane Gallop, feminist writing in France (*l'écriture féminine*) is perfectly represented by the formative texts of Hélène Cixous, as in "Le Rire de la Méduse" (The Laugh of Medusa), characterized by a close relation to the body and sexuality; a multiplicity of sources, outlooks, and applications; and an appeal to the common woman (on the model of Virginia Woolf's "common reader"). The focus on the personal and political, on what is generally termed identity politics, is far more often crucially felt in the poetic work of American feminists.[3] In the present anthology, more than a fourth of the poets and a third of the translators are women, a far greater percentage than is found in past anthologies of French poetry.

Francophone poetry also came into its own in the twentieth century— hence the wide-ranging selection of Francophone writers. This international dimension encourages the cross-fertilization of various origins, tongues, and poetic approaches. What the Lebanese Francophone poet Vénus Khoury-Ghata claims about being doubly nourished by two languages could be attributed to many Francophone poets. For years, she says, her first drafts were written in both Arabic, read from right to left, and French, from left to right.[4] The crossing of such linguistic paths— metaphoric, psychological, and material—often results in the most ar-

resting poetic work. The Francophone selections in this volume are from African, Canadian, and West Indian sources—each with its unique heritage and context. The celebrations and authorial conditions of national independence are of crucial importance. Independence was won by Tunisia and Morocco in 1956, and by Algeria in 1959, and by the Central African Republic in 1960. During the 1960s in Africa and the Caribbean, in spite of independence, writers continued, for financial reasons, to write in French, the language of the former colonizer, which entailed psychological conflict or, at the very least, a dose of ambivalence.

In the 1930s, Aimé Césaire, Léopold Senghor, and Léon-Gontran Damas founded the influential *négritude* movement, which sought to restore the cultural identity of colonized Africans. The Martinican Aimé Césaire coined the term *négritude* in an article written for the student newspaper *L'Étudiant noir.* After taking his exams in 1935, the poet spent the summer in his homeland, a sojourn that inspired what is probably the best-known epic poem of return in French literature: *Cahier d'un retour au pays natal.* Returning once again to Martinique in 1939, this time for an extended period, Césaire expounded his theory of the image, in the same aesthetic spirit as André Breton and the Surrealists, who defined the theory of the image, after the poet Pierre Reverdy, as the clash between elements from different fields, providing a powerful jolt to the creative spirit. As Césaire claims in the celebrated essay "Poésie et connaissance" (Poetry and Cognition), "It is through the image, the revolutionary image, the distant image, the image which overturns all laws of thought, that man finally breaks through the barriers."[5] That influential essay first appeared in the journal *Tropiques,* edited by Césaire, his wife Suzanne Roussy, and others. (It was by chance that Breton, in Martinique on his way to the United States from Marseilles, saw the first issue of *Tropiques* in a shop window—a Surrealist coincidence, like his famous spotting of Giorgio De Chirico's painting *The Child's Brain* in a gallery window in Paris, at which sight he leapt off the bus to take a closer look.)

In the meantime, Léopold Senghor and Léon-Gontran Damas were working in Paris, where, in the 1950s, they contributed to the journal *Présence africaine,* founded by the Senegalese philosopher Alioune Diop. African writing was now well enough established to support both a journal and the anthology *Nouvelle somme de la poésie du monde noir.* Albert Memmi's highly influential essay "The Colonizer and the Colonized" appeared in 1957. Little by little, the countries of the Maghreb (Algeria, Morocco, Tunisia) gained their independence.[6] The relation of Francophone literature of negritude (such as Césaire's work, Senghor's *Chants d'ombre* of 1945, and the journal *L'Étudiant noir*) to the black literature of the Harlem Renaissance, especially to the writings of Countee Cullen, Langston Hughes, and Claude McKay, is well documented.

In each of the countries where colonial rule was overthrown, independence brought its own problems. After Quebec declared cultural independence from anglophone Canada in 1977 with the passage of controversial Bill 101 (which made French the official language of the province), anglophone businesses relocated outside the province. In addition, Quebec's language and firmly Catholic tradition stood out more starkly than it had before against the Protestant majority in other parts of the country; freed from English, the Québecois language quickly returned to its native state. The successors to the famous École de littérature de Montréal are two celebrated Canadian writers, Anne Hébert and Gaston Miron.[7]

Organization

This anthology is divided into six chronological parts, reflecting major trends in French poetry during the twentieth century. Within the divisions, poems appear under an alphabetical listing by poet. Poets' dates of birth, not the dates their first books were published, determine the placement of their work. In the short essays preceding each of these sections, poets are discussed by generation—though, when speaking of contemporaries, the discussions are not strictly limited by birthdates. The present organization highlights six crucial pressure points in modern French poetry. They are the emergence of Dada in 1916; the changeover of the journal *La Révolution surréaliste* to *Le Surréalisme au service de la révolution* in 1930; the end of the war and André Breton's return from his exile in New York to France in December of 1945, along with a number of other Surrealists; and then Bréton's death in 1966, the same year the journal *L'Éphémère* was founded by Yves Bonnefoy, Jacques Dupin, Louis-René des Forêts, and Gaetan Picon. The penultimate division ends with 1980, the year Marguerite Yourcenar became the first female member of the Académie française—a major event, as important, certainly, as the publication, in 1975, of the first issue of *L'Arc* to be devoted to a woman (that issue carried the title "Simone de Beauvoir et la lutte des femmes," or "Simone de Beauvoir and the Struggle of Women").

Because poetic endeavors between the 1960s and the current era feel so intensely present, and to some extent continuous, my initial temptation, in the ultimate section, was to separate these forty or so years into two parts, alphabetically by poet: A through K and L through Y. But 1980 stood out for another reason besides Yourcenar's admission to the Académie française. That watershed year marks the beginning of an international exchange between French and American poets—the publication of Jacques Roubaud and Michel Deguy's anthology *Vingt poètes américains*. I have therefore chosen 1981 as the starting point for contemporary poets at the end of the twentieth century.

Wishing, above all else, to underscore the arbitrary nature of any such divisions, however, I think it valuable to bear in mind Charles Baudelaire's three-part definition of modernity: that which is fleeting, transitory, and contingent. The same defines any attempt to anthologize, including this one.

Inclusions

This collection represents the work of as many poets as possible, including poems by more than a few poets who, according to the cliché of prevailing wisdom, have not yet stood the test of time. That is not the only risk taken here, as a quick glance at the table of contents confirms. Many poets are represented by several poems, others by just one—an editorial decision that runs counter to another commonplace view, namely, that it is impossible to get the feel of a poet's work from a single selection. The choices were made with several criteria in mind, some of them made explicit in this introduction, some of them left implicit: all of us who have worked so hard on this volume hope that our best intentions will be met by those of our readers.

Poetic Forms

In addition to expected poetic forms—rhymed, unrhymed, free, and formal verse—I have included songs, dialogue poems, and a large selection of prose poetry. The interrelation of prose and verse earns the prose poem a respectful place among other forms of twentieth-century French poetry. Between 1915 and 1917 the prose poem came to the fore through the work of Max Jacob and Pierre Reverdy. For Jacob, the prose poem conveyed a feeling of closure, of completeness—the style and the situation removing it from everyday life and setting it off as a sort of perfect object. Here Francis Ponge's *objeu* and *proêmes* would find their antecedent. For Reverdy, on the other hand, the prose poem exemplified an openness of form, an undecidability, as well as a kind of uncertainty, both impersonal and obsessive, at once attractive and disquieting. The impact of French prose poetry on contemporary American poets cannot be overstated and is overtly present in the works of John Ashbery, Michael Palmer, and Gustaf Sobin (who are among the translators in this volume).

This intoxicating mix of genres started in France with Aloyisius Bertrand's *Gaspard de la nuit* and was followed in English-language poetry by the prose poems of Gertrude Stein (mainly those written between 1915 and 1917, e.g., *Portraits* and *Tender Buttons*) and, later, by those of W. S. Merwin (*The Miner's Pale Children*). More recently, the works of Ron Padgett and Anne Carson come to mind, as do those of Leslie Scalapino

and Lyn Hejinian. That this tradition spans so many epochs in twentieth-century poetry gives encouragement to those who would claim, as I do, that the prose poem (distinct from the high merge of prose and poetic writing, as in William Carlos Williams's *Spring and All*) represents at its best an ultimate grandeur of poetic form.

In Rupture

The idea of rupture—with past traditions, with the past in one-self, with the world around one—is not a modern one. After all, the Pre-Raphaelites had every reason to think of themselves as a rupture from Raphael, and, long before that, Rome was itself in rupture. The notion of a break is delightfully romantic in the broad sense and allied to Romanticism in a more restricted sense. The endurance of the idea is, like Louis-René des Forêt's prolonged use of the term *ostinato*—the basso continuo or sostenuto underlying the melody or musical construction above it—just as sustaining and continuing and obstinately inescapable as the idea of progress.

Did modern French and Francophone poetry break from the past? Certainly it did from the poetry of, say, Hugo and Verlaine, though less so from a past represented by Baudelaire, Rimbaud, and Mallarmé. But continuity, like discontinuity, is in the eye of the beholder. The declamations found in some of Paul Claudel's work (think of his *Cinq grandes odes* and even his plays, such as *Le Soulier de satin* and the sublime *Partage de midi*) and in much of Saint-John Perse's poetry (*Anabase*, *Éloges*, and why stop there?) are not necessarily in a different key from those of Victor Hugo—perhaps it's only in their modulation that they differ significantly, with no "hélas" needed.[8]

Baudelaire's splenetic laments, Rimbaud's illuminating vision and re-vision, and Mallarmé's abstraction, idealism, and typographic revolution find equivalents not only in the early part of the century but in an undying present. Why not? Poetry is large enough to absorb innovation as it goes along.

Re-Viewing

In all ages of French literature, poetry has found itself reinvigorated by constraints, possibilities, and re-visioning, as in the mode of the poets of OULIPO (Ouvroir de Littérature Potentielle, or Workshop of Potential Literature).[9] This literature finds its freedoms and attendant pleasures in rules and rigorous constraints. The Oulipian Georges Perec wrote *La Disparition* (translated as *A Void*), a nearly three-hundred-page

lipogrammatic novel in which the letter *e* never appears. Instead of reducing creative possibilities, as such constraints might seem to, they actually increase them. In a seemingly irrational way, such careful attention to the material word challenges, refashions, and enhances thought. Claude Berge, a founding member of OULIPO, is primarily responsible for the Oulipian use of combinatory structures. One example of his work takes a famous sonnet by Ronsard as its starting point:

> Quand vous serez bien vieille, au soir, à la chandelle,
> Assise auprès du feu, dévidant et filant,
> Direz chantant mes vers, en vous émerveillant:
> Ronsard me célébrait du temps que j'étais belle.
> Lors vous n'aurez servante oyant telle nouvelle,
> Déjà sous le labeur à demi sommeillant,
> Qui au bruit de mon nom ne s'aille réveillant,
> Bénissant votre nom, de louange immortelle.
>
> Je serai sous la terre et, fantôme sans os,
> Par les ombres myrteux je prendrai mon repos;
> Vous serez au foyer une vieille accroupie,
> Regrettant mon amour et votre fier dédain,
>
> Vivez, si m'en croyez, n'attendez à demain:
> Cueillez dès aujourd'hui les roses de la vie.[10]

Berge rewrites it here in Fibonaccian style. Note the humor, concision, and irony:

> feu filant,
> déjà sommeillant.
> bénissez votre
> os
> je prendrai
> une vieille accroupie
>
> vivez les roses de la vie!
>
> (spinning fire
> already nodding
> bless your
> bones
> I shall take
> an old woman crouching
>
> long live life's roses!)[11]

In this rewritten structure—new, alarming, and fascinating—all the possibilities of verse and thought are called upon, not by the poet-writer but almost by the poem itself.

It would be relatively easy to draw comparisons between the works of contemporary French-language poets represented here and those of their American counterparts of roughly the same ideological and formal outlook (the philosophical and morally oriented brilliance of John Ashbery; the "deep image" poetics of Robert Bly and W. S. Merwin and the richly cosmopolitan style of Richard Howard, John Hollander, and James Merrill; the language poetry of Lyn Hejinian, Bruce Andrews, Clark Coolidge, Ron Silliman, Charles Bernstein, and so on). Knowing that such comparisons are at once alluring and deceptive, I prefer to leave them to the reader. About his own work John Ashbery once said, "I thought that if I could put it all down, that would be one way. And next the thought came to me that to leave all out would be another, and truer, way."[12] The same might be said about my own stages of deliberation on the subject of comparisons.

Spatiality

Perhaps no text is more crucial to our understanding of contemporary poetry than Mallarmé's *Un coup de dés* (A Throw of the Dice). Published in 1897 and rediscovered by the Cubists and André Gide in 1914, it was revolutionary in its use of typographical space. It is the starting point of what today is widely practiced as both concrete and visual poetry. In Mallarmé's extraordinary poem, empty or white space (*blanc* in both senses) is as important as space occupied by the printed word, presence and absence thereby having been placed on equal footing. Type organizes itself on the page ideogrammatically. Lines are differentially measured depending on their role in relation to the poem's overarching theme of shipwreck; the whole poem moves downward on the page to its doom on dry land—"no place but place" itself—and to the conclusion that every thought projects its own throw of the dice, takes its own chance.

When Mallarmé first showed part of his *Coup de dés* to Paul Valéry, his friend is reported to have burst into tears because he understood at once that everything had been changed by this revolutionary event of poetry and art. Jacques Donguy says in his essay "Cyberpoésie" that Mallarmé's epic poem "is the emblematic work of the twentieth century, its portico, and symbolizes the Macluhan-ian 'shipwreck' of the Gutenberg galaxy. For this text is the graph of a shipwreck, written 'from the bottom of a shipwreck,' and ends on the notion of chance, that Cage was later to systematize."[13] In the same essay, Donguy then looks back to Kurt Schwit-

ter's collages, made from findings in the street, and to his *Merz* work (a scrap from the noun *Kommerz,* or commerce); to Tristan Tzara's words cut from a newspaper and jumbled in a hat; to Marcel Duchamp's ready-mades and the Surrealists' collective experiments in creating automatic poetry—all leading to the aleatory experiments of Lionel Ray and other contemporary French poets and to the cut-ups of the Americans Brion Gysin and William Burroughs. The "combine" art of contemporary American artists, especially that of Robert Rauschenberg, who included ordinary objects in his work, is closely related to the found poems and "found objects" (*les objets trouvés*) of the Cubist and Surrealist poets, as well as to Apollinaire's *poèmes-conversation* (conversation poems). What you find in the street or on the Web—all these constitute, inevitably, a sort of reticulated combination poem-painting, a spatialized discourse.

Of course, in France the visual and the verbal were never compartmentalized. Like Cubism in art, contemporaneous poetry similarly involved the idea of looking at one object from several points of view. Although Pierre Reverdy and Max Jacob would have rejected the label Cubist as having nothing essential to say about their compositions, it is in fact a useful reference. Reverdy insisted, in his famous essay on the theory of "the Image," that poetry was to be composed of two different elements from two different realms. The shock of their meeting would give off new creative light, allowing new ways of perceiving. This procedure carried straight over to Surrealism and its concept of the image as a composition of farflung elements. Guillaume Apollinaire, the best known of the Cubist poets, exemplified poetic experimentation in his *Alcools* (1913), drawing on the ancient Latin-Christian tradition of ideogrammatic poetry, in which poems formed pictures—the other side of the concrete poetry so influenced by Stéphane Mallarmé's typographical experiment, already visible in the *idéogrammes* of Paul Claudel. The emphasis on plastic poetry, by way of Max Jacob, Pablo Picasso, and Pierre Reverdy, made way for visual poetics. The juncture of painting and poetry has yielded such enthusiastic exhibitions and publications as *Poésure et peintrie: "D'un art, l'autre"* (Poeting and Paintry) and Yves Peyré's *Peinture et poésie: Le Dialogue par le livre, 1874–2000*) (Painting and Poetry: the Dialogue through the Book.)[14]

Fascination with the spatial has only increased with time. Witness the international excitement of Concrete Poetry: the work of the Swiss poet Eugen Gomringer, who, along with Decio Pignatari, August and Haroldo de Campos, and Mario de Andrade, founded the Noigandres Group; the poetry of the Scot Ian Hamilton Finlay and the American Emmet Williams (and later John Hollander, May Swenson, and many others); and the work of numerous poets in Japan, Argentina, Spain, Italy, and France.

And witness, too, the advent of the Spatialist Poetry of the French poet Henri Chopin and like-minded writers. Manifestos proliferate in the second half of the century, from Spatialism to Scum, from the aesthetic to the political, every movement wanting to proclaim its name and experimental newness.[15]

Later, the stress on the materiality of words and the visuality of the imagination was associated with such movements as L=A=N=G=U=A=G=E poetry in North America. Founded by Bruce Andrews and Charles Bernstein, this movement emphasizes the word itself, as evidenced in the dramatic and eye-catching separation of letters. In its concentration on the very stuff of language, in its consideration of the material of the word as all-important, in its excitement about the process of writing, at least one group in France can be singled out for comparison with the poetry on this side of the Atlantic. The close association of the French poets Emmanuel Hocquard, Olivier Cadiot, Pierre Alféri, Anne-Marie Albiach, and Claude Royet-Journoud can be roughly considered the transatlantic equivalent of the poets of L=A=N=G=U=A=G=E.

John Ashbery asserts that it is not the often warring factions of poetic schools that interest him but individual poets—among them the L=A=N=G=U=A=G=E poet Leslie Scalapino, for instance, and a few others. Experimental poetry and anything liberating, Ashbery says, are what really claim him. Although influenced by the Surrealists, he finds them too "restraining" to be of continuing interest. Similarly, he finds the rules of the L=A=N=G=U=A=G=E poets too constraining. The French poets with whom he feels the most affinity are Pascalle Monnier, Anne Portugal, Michel Deguy, Jacques Dupin, Dominique Fourcade, Emmanuel Hocquard, and Franck André Jamme, all of whom are represented in this volume. His personal reaction is antitraditional, in opposition to the poetry so often taught in the universities—for example, that of Robert Lowell and John Berryman. "I'm always trying to do something I've never done," he says.[16]

Shape

John Berger has entitled a recent collection of essays *The Shape of a Pocket* (2001), a phrase that has led me to think about the nature of poetry. As a heart is shaped by what it loves, and a mind by what it admires, a voice may gain its surest tones by what the speaker or singer reads and hears. (The celebrated singer Patti Smith is fascinated by Blake and Rimbaud, and her verses are recognizably Rimbaldian. She also admires Blaise Cendrars, to whom she dedicated a poem called "Ladies and Gentlemen, Blaise Cendrars Is Not Dead.")

The simplest container of them all, a pocket, is sooner or later shaped

by what is carried in it. Walk poems, perhaps above all others, are modi-
fied by what the speaker carries or picks up along the way. Roger Fry, the
British art critic and painter, never traveled without a small volume of
Mallarmé's poems in his pocket. Kenneth Rexroth and Frank O'Hara
carried small volumes of Reverdy's poems, and William Carlos Williams,
one of René Char's. We remember Williams' credo associated with that
poet of brooding intensity and passion:

> René Char
>   you are a poet who believes
>   in the power of beauty
>   to right all wrongs.
>   I believe it also.
> . . . .
>   let all men believe it,
>   as you have taught me also
>   to believe it.[17]

Jacques Roubaud once walked alongside the Mississippi, carrying in his
pocket Mark Twain's book about the great American river. Roubaud has
written about this experience and the musings it occasioned but has
chosen not to publish these writings for this reason: he has not yet re-
turned to the banks of the Mississippi. It always takes two moments of
seeing the same thing, he says, to really see it, "just as it does two eyes."[18]
In any case, the poet's pocket and the shape of what it bears may well have
replaced what we used to think of as influence. It is not what you emulate
but what you choose to carry with you that matters most.

Overview

With a backward glance at the nineteenth century we can now ap-
preciate the wide range of all that Symbolism is or was: Baudelaire's blend of
romanticism and pre-Symbolism, Mallarmé's extreme far-outness and orig-
inal mysteriousness, Arthur Rimbaud's visuality in *Illuminations* and else-
where, including that shown in his great trip through poetry and the worlds
of adventure called "Le Bateau ivre" (The Drunken Vessel), which conveyed
the poem and its readers into explorations of the twentieth century.

Appropriately, Part 1 of this volume includes the work of two great
Symbolists of the late nineteenth and early twentieth centuries: Saint-Pol
Roux and Paul Claudel. The work of Mallarmé's disciple Paul Valéry
presents the link between Symbolism and post-Symbolism: his poetry is
marked by both classical form and classical references, along with a mod-
ern fascination with epistemology and human consciousness. In Valéry,
Narcissus and Psyche meet contemporary psychological meditation.

The general temper of the French modernist poet is tinged with the kind of visionary exaltation and despair of nineteenth-century romantic revolution against the easy clichés of comfortable bourgeois thought (the "seated," as Arthur Rimbaud called them). Rimbaud's troubled and troubling perception of the split in poetic personality—"*je* est un autre" ("*I* is another"), famously expressed in his letter of May 13, 1871, to Georges Izambard— has never ceased to echo in modern poetry. One of the elements differentiating French and British poetry of the socially concerned sort is an ingrained and seemingly invincible French idealism. As Edward Lucie-Smith and Simon Watson Taylor describe French poetry: "It has a moral force allied with enduring social (and often revolutionary) aspirations which have preserved it both from the narrow parochialism which has been the besetting sin of English poetry since the war, and from the naievety and sentimentality which have often characterized American poetry in its more determinedly experimental moments."[19]

In the minds of many poets of the early twentieth century, poetry and travel seem to have been closely linked. Consider, for example, Apollinaire's celebrated poem "Zone" (1912), which possesses much of the same heightened aura of nostalgia cast by the Symbolists—a feeling that calls to mind those often closed eyes of Redon's faces or the finger on the lips to signal "silence"—but in a joyous combination with the discoveries of an ongoing, open-eyed adventurer-poet. Instead of the silencing of speech, the poet now shouts, reads newspapers aloud, zips about here and there, first across Paris, then across the Continent, the Orient, and the world of myth, celebrating celestial apparitions made modern, like Christ the aviator, and Oceanic figures. When Blaise Cendrars read aloud his unpunctuated and emotionally powerful "Les Pâques à New York" (Easter in New York) at a gathering in Paris, Apollinaire—who was among the listeners— is said to have been inspired to march home and remove the punctuation from his own long poem "Zone." Cendrars' own trans-European travels were set forth in his amazingly forward-looking "La Prose du Transsibérien et de la petite Jeanne de France" (1913). The work was marked "Prose," he said, as a modest equivalent of poetry. The voyage of this "prose" of the Trans-Siberian railway is all the richer for Cendrars' traveling companion, a naïve prostitute named "little Jeanne," who offers this touching refrain as the two travel through distant lands: "Say, Blaise, are we really a long way from Montmartre?" When, finally, the travelers do return to Paris and the Eiffel Tower, the reader may reflect that the poem is indeed a homegrown product of the experimental poetic tornado of Paris (and therefore never a long way from Montmartre after all). The year 1913 was certainly an annus mirabilis in many domains. Proust, Gide, and Valéry were producing the masterpieces we know, and Apollinaire was busy with the publication of *Alcools*.

One of the main sources of poetic excitement in the early part of the century was the cult of the primitive. After the carnage of the First World War, the perceived primitivism of blacks and African art was seen as a challenge to Western "progress" and culture and a repudiation of the colonial enterprise. Before and during the 1920s a wave of negrophilia swept Paris—the influence of black culture abundantly evident in the paintings of Picasso and André Derain, in the poetry of Guillaume Apollinaire, and, slightly later, in the Dada works of the Romanian Tristan Tzara (first performed in 1916 in Zurich in the Cabaret Voltaire). Tzara's magnificent *Vingt-cinq poèmes* are full of sounds imitating "primitive" languages. For example, the poem "Pélamide" begins

a e ou o youyouyou I e ou o
youyouyou
drrrrdrrrrdrrrrgrrrrgrrrr[20]

And the delightful poem "Moi touche-moi touche-moi seulement" (Me touch me just touch me) takes up the same sound:

mécanisme drrrr rrrrr barres écartées

(mechanism drrrr rrrrr bars spread apart)[21]

This explosion of sound is motivated, if not explained, by the narrator's picturing himself as the kind of engine that goes anywhere when it is enamored of something or someone:

je suis tramway quelque-part va-et-vient dans l'amour

(I am a tram somewhere going and coming in love).[22]

Tzara's hatred of the ordinary in language and vision unleashes, in the Dada poems, a frenetic excitement verging on hysteria. If the typographical and sound poetry of this period borrowed from what were giddily considered primitive cultures, the fascination with "the other" continued throughout the early part of the century. Anthropological investigations, such as those in the Swiss journal *Anthropos* gave credibility and backing to poetic experimentation. The distinction drawn by Senghor—"Emotion is black; reason is Hellenic"—was not considered wildly untrue.[23]

The excitement over Dada, mixed with despair over World War I, led in its own noisy way to the more organized collective and manifesto-writing Surrealist movement of the early 1920s. In the early days of Surrealism, André Breton was acknowledged as its Pope, and indeed he comported himself as such. Church doctrine, as decreed by Breton, was heavily based on the belief in "psychic automatism"—freeing the unconscious for verbal and visual experimentation—which included dreams,

trances, and a number of liberating techniques to overthrow the rational reserve that imprisoned the mind and the writing wrist.

A strange coherence is found in these automatic texts. In the neo-Romanticism of Surrealism ("We are the tail of romanticism," Breton used to declare, "but how prehensile"), the enigmatic and the puzzling were perceived as the marvelous—and so, to be saluted as the manifestation of a solution to a problem one didn't know one had.[24] The canonical texts of 1922 (like Breton's "Entry of the Mediums") as well as those of 1924 (the first of Breton's Surrealist manifestos, Aragon's *Vague de rêves*, and his extraordinary *Paysan de Paris* [Paris Peasant]) all salute the power of the image, its ability to bring together what had seemed sadly separate. This is the grand epoch of Surrealism.

These collective games and experiments were carried on amid a circle of vivid characters and brilliant writers that included the novelist Louis Aragon and the poet Paul Éluard, both of whom would later join the Communist Party and remain two of its staunchest adherents. Robert Desnos, perhaps the greatest Surrealist poet, was to die in the Terezin concentration camp, choosing not to testify against other Resistance figures. Just before his death, he turned to a more traditional form of poetry, writing in what could be considered classic verse. Benjamin Péret, Breton's most ardent and faithful disciple, wrote excitedly about automata in his enthusiastic and temperamental way and vilified the political engagement of Aragon and Éluard, believing—as did Breton—that poetry was its own honor and should not fall into any shade of political trap or praise. Antonin Artaud, for a while in charge of the Office of Surrealist Dreams and author of some of the most remarkably passionate texts, including *D'un voyage au pays des Tarahumaras* (A Voyage to the Tarahumaras), lapsed into madness. A few Surrealists were expelled from the group for various reasons, among them making money in order to live or, worse still, indulging in journalistic activities—clear betrayals of Surrealism's antibourgeois ideal. No less sacrilegious was the use of the hallowed name of Lautréamont for a popular nightclub. Isidore Ducasse, better known as the comte de Lautréamont, was a firm believer that "poetry is made by all": in other words, down with the individual poet and the creator (or finder) of the most celebrated Surrealist image, that of the super-erotico-bizarre encounter of a sewing machine and an umbrella on a dissection table. The author of *Maldoror* and forefather of Surrealism was not to be associated with the light, the frivolous, or the horrors of commercial undertakings.

But the Surrealist spirit in poetry, as in life, was to mark successive generations. In World War II, the great poets Char and Reverdy refused to publish during the Occupation. Silence was, they thought, the best

weapon. Breton and several others took refuge in Marseilles at the Bel Air mansion, owned by the American Jane Gold; it was there that Varian Fry ran the Committee for Political Refugees, orchestrating plans for the foremost intellectuals to leave France for the United States. Breton was among the French refugees in New York, which was not to his liking (he preferred the West and Native American culture). In New York, he was briefly associated with Charles Henri Ford's small elegant magazine of art and literature called *View*. Home to the Abstract Expressionists and their expressive personal visions, the magazine occupied an opposite pole from the *Partisan Review* and *The Nation*. With the help of the American artist David Hare, Breton, who learned no English, set up a rival magazine called *VVV*, where the Surrealists could publish, as they often did, in French.

Although Breton managed from his New York headquarters to keep up his and the group's enthusiasm for collective manifestations and the seriously played games of Surrealism, he returned to France as soon as it was safe to do so. But once there, he discovered that conditions were no longer as conducive to the kind of poetry he had championed. In response, he turned toward a more mystical context, still invoking chance and the everyday marvelous, surrounded now by a younger group of adepts.

In the meantime, Surrealism had spread internationally. The Martinican journal *Tropiques* displayed a Surrealism of negritude that was as vivid as anything that had preceded it in Paris. Aimé Césaire, René Ménil, Léon-Gontran Damas, and other Francophone poets held an ongoing belief in the marvelous, that is, the power of surprise, in the Surrealist sense of the word (*le merveilleux*), the overwhelming encounter with a person, an object, or an event that can happen in everyday life to someone in a state of readiness or expectation (*disponibilité*). This openness was to endure beyond the political upheavals of the French presence in Algeria and other tribulations from which poetry often seemed an escape. Martinican Surrealism was a memorial to suffering. Césaire's *Cahier d'un retour au pays natal* (Return of a Manchild to the Promised Land) is a noble record of the poetry of the heart, as are many other postcolonial poems in French. Latter-day manifestations of Surrealism, such as those of Joyce Mansour in her violent texts and the incendiary prose of Annie Le Brun, bear witness to the ongoing force of the Surrealist spirit.

In 1966, the year of Breton's death, it was apparent that the modern poetic spirit was not monolithic: the new experiments differed, ranging from the place-oriented poems of René Char, who had been a Resistance leader, celebrated for his poetic war journal ("Feuillets d'Hypnos") and his lyric evocation of Provence, to *l'objeu* (the object game) of Francis

Ponge, who emphasized the materiality of the poetic process and its product. Ponge placed himself and his work, explicitly based on everyday perception, in a close-up zoom, as he put it in the 1942 title *Le Parti-pris des choses* (On the Side of Things), an attitude congenial to that of the concrete poets.

Also in 1966, Yves Bonnefoy, Jacques Dupin, André du Bouchet, Louis-René des Forêts, and Claude Estéban founded a journal entitled *L'Éphémère,* devoted to the notion of passage and marked by an association between the verbal and the visual (for example, the collaboration between Bonnefoy and Alberto Giacometti). The influence of *L'Éphémère* was to last far beyond its voluntary demise in 1973. The philosophical and poetic writings of Edmond Jabès, an Egyptian Jew whose work was first applauded by Max Jacob and then Jacques Derrida, and the diverse textual representations of the enormously diverse places for poems of the heart and the mind, as well as of the living body, are as representative of the 1970s and 1980s as are the highest flights of French poetry after 1980.

More recently, there have been any number of experimental manifestations that demonstrate new, ever growing and changing ways of looking at poetry, such as Emmanuel Hocquard's *Une journée dans le détroit* (1980), Jacques Roubaud's *Les Troubadours* (1981), Liliane Giraudon's *Je marche ou je m'endors* (1982), Dominique Fourcade's *Le Ciel pas d'angle* (1983), Claude Royet-Journoud's *Les Objets contiennent l'infini* (1983), Anne-Marie Albiach's *Mezza Voce* (1984), and Denis Roché's *La Poésie est inadmissible* (1995).

As is the case with poetry worldwide, there is now a tremendous emphasis on performance, on the oral manifestation essential to the ever more rapidly moving world with which it has to keep pace. Technology and creation walk hand in hand: along with rap, slam, and reggae go all varieties of digital practice and Internet enthusiasm. Just as musical form and an idealism of abstraction were the touchstones that inspired typographical experiments in the late nineteenth century, the technological advances of the late twentieth century have become the model for much of the poetry we experience in the beginning of the twenty-first century. The interactive nature of the contemporary world, psychological and political, local and global, gives poetry a new place. As Edouard Glissant puts it, erstwhile boundaries in this new "tout-monde"—the everyone everywhere world—have become permeable. "Geographically," say the editors of *Zigzag poésie*, "the local becomes fluid and energized."[25] In such a world, poetry has to be a place for increasing exchange.

And it is. As Jacques Derrida notes, translation is generosity. And as Walter Benjamin would have it—and so would we—languages supplement one another. Bilingual anthologies, with all their translation work,

gather innumerable items into innumerable divisions, which any editor, poet, reader, or translator could endlessly alter according to what seems most viable at the moment. John Ashbery gets it right for all of us:

> Yet each knew he saw only aspects,
> That the continuity was fierce beyond all dream of enduring.[26]

The celebrated "death of the author" proclaimed by Roland Barthes, Michel Foucault, and other theorists is taken up later in these essays, along with the additional and perhaps more crucial contemporary worry about the poet, the poem, and their status in view of the constant increase of invasive technology. In my view, all the arguments and debates that arise from these concerns, quite like the seventeenth-century debate over classic and modern forms, known as the "Querelle des Anciens et des Modernes" (The Quarrel of the Ancients and the Moderns), are good for poetry and invigorating for the poetic spirit. Small and large journals and presses remain locked in economic crisis, but at least these heated and attention-getting debates focus on the problem of poetry and the ways poems relate to the world around them, and to us.[27]

Poetry in France remains very much alive. French and the many varieties of flourishing Francophone poetic thought and work, through new experimentation, new forms, new ways of looking, and an increasingly important accent on women's poetry, give us poetic hope for the twenty-first century.

Today

The great nineteenth-century thinker and seer John Ruskin had as his motto just one word: "Today." This anthology is intended to be part of the today in which it has been assembled, meditated upon, and completed. It imagines itself as a generous, loosely linked offering of poetic works in communication with each other, and with us, aimed at a new range of selections and an increased perception of old and new texts. Here I am thinking of Yves Bonnefoy's recent meditation *Sous l'horizon du langage,* in which he expresses the poetic hope that the ongoing quarrel between the sign and the representation does not irreparably undo the mountains and the cleft between them, through which the poet can see— and lets us see—the sky.[28] Today poetry asks as many questions as it always has, about itself and ourselves, and so lets us find, with renewed energy, whatever we might want to become eventually or re-become.

Energy and exchange might well be the watchwords of what we intended to do here. "There ought to be room for more things, for spreading out, like," says John Ashbery.[29] For this big book, the final choice of

poets and poems depended, in many cases, on the individual translators in consultation with the editor. The enduring wish of all those involved in this production is that through their contribution readers may, in their turn, discover something new that may matter even greatly to their future readings.

Notes

1. Epigraph: Jacques Garelli, "Excess of Poetry," in *Anthologie de la poésie française du XXᵉ siècle*, ed. Jean-Baptiste Para (Paris: Gallimard, 2000), p. 393.

2. Terry Eagleton, *Literary Theory: An Introduction* (St. Paul: University of Minnesota Press, 1996), passim.

3. As the poet Maggie Nelson puts it, American women poets seem to be "always constructing some kind of false barrier that we then enjoy crossing and re-crossing" (conversation with the author in fall 2002, upon which much of the material comparing French and American poetry at the present relies). "We are beginning again," she says, burying this tiny large statement in the middle of a prose poem, "Palomas" (from "The Scratch-Scratch Diaries," in Jennifer Barber, Mark Bibbins, and Maggie Nelson, *Take Three*, AGNI New Poets Series, vol. 3 [St. Paul: Graywolf Press, 1998], p. 133). Aren't we all?

4. See Venus Khoury-Ghata, *Here There Was Once a Country*, translated and with an introduction by Marilyn Hacker (Oberlin, Ohio: Oberlin College Press, 2001), p. xviii.

5. Aimé Césaire, "Poésie et connaissance," *Tropiques* (January 1945), p. 166. The information is based on the informative article by Ronnie Scharfman in Denis Hollier, ed., *A New History of French Literature* (Cambridge: Harvard University Press, 1989), pp. 942–48.

6. For information on this period, see Réda Bensmaïa, "The School of Independence," in Hollier, *French Literature*, 1018–22.

7. See Guy Sylvestre, "Canadian Poetry," in *The New Princeton Encyclopedia of Poetry and Poetics*, ed. Alex Preminger and T. V. F. Brogran (Princeton: Princeton University Press, 1993), pp. 165–66.

8. When André Gide was queried as to the greatest poet in France, he is said to have replied, "Victor Hugo, hélas!"

9. See Warren F. Motte, Jr., ed., *Oulipo: A Primer of Potential Literature* (Normal, Ill.: Dalkey Archive Press, 1998).

10. Pierre de Ronsard, in *Les Amours*, ed. Marc Bensimon and James L. Martin (Paris: Garnier/Flammarion, 1981), p. 298. Rough translation: "When you are very old, crouching / By the fire some evening, carding and spinning, you will say, / reciting my poetry and marveling at it / Ronsard sang of me, when I was lovely. / When you won't have a single servant / hearing such a thing, and already / drowsy under her work, who won't / wake straight up at the sound of my name, / blessing your name, with immortal praise. // I will be under the earth and, a ghost without bones, / I'll be resting under the shade of the myrtles; / you'll be crouching at the hearth, old, / regretting my love and your proud disdain, // Live, if you believe me, don't wait for tomorrow; / gather today the roses of life."

11. Claude Berge, "Quand vous serez bien vieille," pp. 117–18, in *Oulipo: A Primer of Potential Literature*, Warren Motte, ed. (Normal, Ill.: Dalkey Archive Press, 1998). For a discussion of combinatory poetry and the Fibonaccian poem, please see Claude Berge, "For a Potential Analysis of Combinatory Literature," pp. 115–25.

12. John Ashbery, "The New Spirit," in *Three Poems* (New York: Viking, 1972), p. 3.

13. *Zigzag poésie: Formes et mouvements: L'Effervescence* (Paris: Zigzag Poésie and Autrement, 2001), p. 174.

14. *Poésure et peintrie: "D'un art, l'autre"* (Paris: Musées nationaux, 1993) and Yves Peyré's *Peinture et poésie: Le Dialogue par le livre, 1874–2000* (Paris: Gallimard, 2001).

15. See Mary Ann Caws, ed., *Manifesto: A Century of Isms* (Lincoln: University of Nebraska Press, 2002), with manifestos such as Spatial Eroticism.

16. John Ashbery, "En France, il y a des châteaux, des fées, des sorcières," *Zigzag poésie,* pp. 232–235.

17. William Carlos Williams, "To a Dog Injured in the Street," in *The William Carlos Williams Reader,* ed. M. L. Rosenthal (New York: New Directions, 1965), p. 64.

18. Jacques Roubaud, conversation with the author, New York, April 2002.

19. Simon Watson Taylor and Edward Lucie-Smith, eds., *French Poetry Today* (New York: Schocken, 1971), p. 33.

20. Tristan Tzara, "Pélamide," in *Tristan Tzara: Œuvres complètes,* ed. Henri Béhar, vol. 1: 1912–1924 (Paris: Flammarion, 1975), p. 102.

21. Tristan Tzara, "Moi touche-moi," *Tristan Tzara,* p. 110.

22. Ibid.

23. For a fascinating account of the involvement of French poets and anthropologists—Leiris in particular—and the primitive pull, see James Clifford, "Negrophilia," in Hollier, *French Literature,* pp. 901–8. For art's engagement with the primitive, see Jack Flam, ed., with Miriam Deutch, *Primitivism and Twentieth-Century Art: A Documentary History* (Berkeley: University of California Press, 2003).

24. In the "First Manifesto of Surrealism," Breton defines the term this way; "SURRÉALISME: Automatisme psychique pur par lequel on se propose d'exprimer, soit verbalement, soit par écrit, soit de toute autre manière, le fonctionnement réel de la pensée. Dictée de la pensée, en l'absence de tout contrôle exercé par la raison, en dehors de toute préoccupation esthétique ou morale" (SURREALISM: Pure psychic automatism, through which we propose to express, in speech, in writing, or any other fashion, the real workings of thought. Dictation of thought, in the absence of any rational control, with no esthetic or moral consideration). And in the same Manifesto: "Le seul mot de liberté est tout ce qui m'exalte" (The word freedom, all by itself, is the only thing that I find exalting). André Breton, *Manifestes du surréalisme* (Paris: Jean-Jacques Pauvert, 1962), pp. 40, 17.

25. *Zigzag poésie,* p. 24.

26. John Ashbery, "Parergon," in *The Double Dream of Spring* (New York: Ecco, 1976), p. 56.

27. Deguy mentions two works: Giorgio Agamben's *La Fin du poème* (Stanford: Meridian, 1999) and Philippe Lacoue-Labarthe's *Poetry as Experience* (Stanford: Meridian, 1999).

28. Yves Bonnefoy, *Sous l'horizon du langage* (Paris: Mercure de France, 2002). See also his *Lieux et destins de l'image: Un cours de poétique au Collège de France, 1981–1993* (Paris: Seuil, 1999).

29. John Ashbery, "For John Clare," in *The Double Dream of Spring* (New York: Ecco, 1976), p. 35.

1

1897–1915:
Symbolism, Post-Symbolism, Cubism, Simultanism

Guillaume Apollinaire, Blaise Cendrars, Paul Claudel, Jean Cocteau, Léon-Paul Fargue, Max Jacob, Pierre-Jean Jouve, Valéry Larbaud, Saint-John Perse, Pablo Picasso, Catherine Pozzi, Pierre Reverdy, Saint-Pol Roux, Victor Segalen, Jules Supervielle, Paul Valéry, Renée Vivien

artyred at the hands of the Nazis, Saint-Pol Roux is the great transitional figure in early twentieth-century French poetry. He and Paul Claudel, seven years his senior, represent the ongoing heritage from the great ur-Symbolist Stéphane Mallarmé—a heritage that continues with Paul Valéry. The latter is best known for his epic poem "Le Cimetière marin," published here in its entirety in a recent translation by the Irish poet Derek Mahon. Just as Valéry's figure of the *rameur,* or rower, strains against the current, so the translator struggles with and against the French rhyme; Mahon places equivalent, if nonrhyming, stresses on his own lines. Valéry's "La Fileuse" remains one of the most difficult and impressive manifestations of how form and visuality work together. Grace Schulman's translation, commissioned for this volume, threads its own understanding through form and vision.

The wide-reaching poems of Saint-John Perse (Alexis Saint-Léger Léger) stretch from his early *Exils* through the classic recall of *Anabase* to the triumph of *Amers,* a title that suggests both the sea (*mer*) and bitter memory (*amer*)—*Seamarks* is Wallace Fowlie's ingenious English title. The poetry of Perse calls to mind Paul Claudel's biblically toned *versets,*

whose length is based on the rhythm of the human breath. Claudel inter-weaves prose and poetry in his longer poems (and in his poetic plays), all of which are unmistakably lofty in style and conception. On the other hand, no one could fail to recognize the powerful simplicity that charac-terizes his prose poetry in *Connaissance de l'Est* (The East I Know). These last brief poems, written when Claudel was the French ambassador to China, remain striking examples of the prose poem: they are unforget-table, inimitable.

Another extraordinary adventurer into China in the early part of the century was Victor Segalen, doctor, essayist, and poet. The hieratic prose poems collected in *Stèles* (Stelae) are a haunting presence, at once exotic and strangely familiar. As one commentator has noted, "Epigraph and carved stone, the stele stands there, body and soul, a complete being . . . this hard composition, this density, this internal equilibrium and these angles. . . . Thence the challenge to whomever would have them say what it is they keep. They scorn to be read. . . . They do not express; they signify; they are."[1] These verbal monuments are not only the records of an eccen-tric and brilliant traveler to the East but a document of the French expan-sion of vision in the twentieth century, to China and beyond. The genre of the stela is unique unto itself, celebrating life, death, and the ongoing construction and duration of poetic monuments.

No twentieth-century French poet is more beloved than the im-mensely appealing Guillaume Apollinaire. As someone once remarked to me, Apollinaire, almost alone among poets, has left a legacy of conge-niality, not only in his time but in ours. Learned "Apollinaire specialists" from around the world collectively celebrate the poet who died of Spanish influenza just as World War I was ending. ("A bas Guillaume," people shouted in the streets; they, of course, meant the emperor, not Apolli-naire.) An elegy to him by Tristan Tzara, founder of the Dada movement, is an unforgettable lament. In Apollinaire's work on the Cubist poets and painters, such as Pablo Picasso, he created an atmosphere conducive to poetic thought and visuality and to the forms of modernism saluted in his epic "Zone," at once nostalgic and forward-looking, combining the cos-mic and the local, the airplane and the newspaper.

Blaise Cendrars—whose adopted name suggests the embers (*la braise*) and ashes (*les cendres*) of inner conflagration, of self-immolation, as only the first step toward re-creation of the self—is a poet of tremendous influence whose contagious enthusiasm endures. Above all else, Cendrars was fascinated with the multiform elements of the modern: "Profound today," the title of one of his essays, might sum up his poetic achievement. His passion for real and imagined travel ("Prose du Transsibérien et de la petite Jeanne de France," this long, superb travel poem called "Prosa,"

after the religious form, as in *Prose pour les morts*) and his hypnotic, emotional power had a decided influence not only on Apollinaire but on English-language poets as well, from the Beats on. The interrelations of prose and poetry are always to be reinvented and rethought. Particularly in the early years of the century, the interrelating of genres provokes a special excitement.

Note

1. Victor Segalen, *Stèles* (Paris: Gallimard, 1973), pp. 21–24. In a letter to Jules de Gaultier of February 3, 1913, Segalen says of these monument poems: "In this Chinese mold, I placed what I had to express" (p. 13). Timothy Billings and Christopher Bush have recently translated and commented upon these poems, at the time of this writing; their work is invaluable.

Guillaume Apollinaire
(Guillaume Apollinaris de Kostrowitzky) 1880–1918
ROME, ITALY

Apollinaire came to the forefront of the modern age through both his poetry and his spirit of invention, serving as a sounding board for many new ideas of his time. He continues to feel among the freshest of contemporary poets. He is credited with publicizing Cubism as a movement, coining the term *surrealism*, which he applied to his play *Les Mamelles de Tirésias*, and inventing the "conversation poem"—for example, a collage of remarks overheard in a bar or a bus. Born in Rome to a Polish mother and Italian father, Apollinaire sometimes claimed he was the Pope's son. He was extremely gregarious and, after moving to Paris at the age of twenty, had friends among painters and writers such as Picasso, André Derain, Marie Laurencin, and Alfred Jarry. Principal works: *Alcools: Poèmes, 1898–1913,* 1913; *Calligrammes: Poèmes de la paix et de la guerre, 1913–1916,* 1918; *Il y a,* 1925; *L'Esprit nouveau et les poètes,* 1946; *Ombre de mon amour (poèmes à Lou),* 1947.

Zone

A la fin tu es las de ce monde ancien

Bergère ô tour Eiffel le troupeau des ponts bêle ce matin

Tu en as assez de vivre dans l'antiquité grecque et romaine

Ici même les automobiles ont l'air d'être anciennes
La religion seule est restée toute neuve la religion
Est restée simple comme les hangars de Port-Aviation

Seul en Europe tu n'es pas antique ô Christianisme
L'Européen le plus moderne c'est vous Pape Pie X
Et toi que les fenêtres observent la honte te retient
D'entrer dans une église et de t'y confesser ce matin
Tu lis les prospectus les catalogues les affiches qui chantent tout haut
Voilà la poésie ce matin et pour la prose il y a les journaux
Il y a les livraisons à 25 centimes pleines d'aventures policières
Portraits des grands hommes et mille titres divers

J'ai vu ce matin une jolie rue dont j'ai oublié le nom
Neuve et propre du soleil elle était le clairon
Les directeurs les ouvriers et les belles sténo-dactylographes
Du lundi matin au samedi soir quatre fois par jour y passent
Le matin par trois fois la sirène y gémit
Une cloche rageuse y aboie vers midi
Les inscriptions des enseignes et des murailles
Les plaques les avis à la façon des perroquets criaillent
J'aime la grâce de cette rue industrielle
Située à Paris entre la rue Aumont-Thiéville et l'avenue
    des Ternes
Voilà la jeune rue et tu n'es encore qu'un petit enfant
Ta mère ne t'habille que de bleu et de blanc
Tu es très pieux et avec le plus ancien de tes camarades René Dalize
Vous n'aimez rien tant que les pompes de l'Église
Il est neuf heures le gaz est baissé tout bleu vous sortez du dortoir
    en cachette
Vous priez toute la nuit dans la chapelle du collège
Tandis qu'éternelle et adorable profondeur améthyste
Tourne à jamais la flamboyante gloire du Christ
C'est le beau lys que tous nous cultivons

6

Zone

You are tired at last of this old world

O shepherd Eiffel Tower the flock of bridges bleats at the morning

You have had enough of life in this Greek and Roman antiquity

Even the automobiles here seem to be ancient
Religion alone has remained entirely fresh religion
Has remained simple like the hangars at the airfield

You alone in all Europe are not antique O Christian faith
The most modern European is you Pope Pius X
And you whom the windows look down at shame prevents you
From entering a church and confessing this morning
You read prospectuses catalogues and posters which shout aloud
Here is poetry this morning and for prose there are the newspapers
There are volumes for 25 centimes full of detective stories
Portraits of famous men and a thousand assorted titles

This morning I saw a pretty street whose name I have forgotten
Shining and clean it was the sun's bugle
Executives and workers and lovely secretaries
From Monday morning to Saturday evening pass here four times a day
In the morning the siren wails three times
A surly bell barks around noon
Lettering on signs and walls
Announcements and billboards shriek like parrots
I love the charm of this industrial street
Located in Paris somewhere between the rue Aumont-Thiéville and the avenue
    des Ternes
Here is the young street and you are once again a little child
Your mother dresses you only in blue and white
You are very pious and with your oldest friend René Dalize
You like nothing so well as the ceremonies of church
It is nine o'clock the gas is down to the blue you come secretly out of the
    dormitory
You pray the whole night in the college chapel
While eternal and adorable an amethyst profundity
The flaming glory of Christ turns for ever
It is the beautiful lily we all cultivate

7

C'est la torche aux cheveux roux que n'éteint pas le vent
C'est le fils pâle et vermeil de la douloureuse mère
C'est l'arbre toujours touffu de toutes les prières
C'est la double potence de l'honneur et de l'éternité
C'est l'étoile à six branches
C'est Dieu qui meurt le vendredi et ressuscite le dimanche
C'est le Christ qui monte au ciel mieux que les aviateurs
Il détient le record du monde pour la hauteur
Pupille Christ de l'œil
Vingtième pupille des siècles il sait y faire
Et changé en oiseau ce siècle comme Jésus monte dans l'air
Les diables dans les abîmes lèvent la tête pour le regarder
Ils disent qu'il imite Simon Mage en Judée
Ils crient s'il sait voler qu'on l'appelle voleur
Les anges voltigent autour du joli voltigeur
Icare Enoch Elie Apollonius de Thyane
Flottent autour du premier aéroplane
Ils s'écartent parfois pour laisser passer ceux que transporte la Sainte-
    Eucharistie
Ces prêtres qui montent éternellement en élevant l'hostie
L'avion se pose enfin sans refermer les ailes
Le ciel s'emplit alors de millions d'hirondelles
A tire-d'aile viennent les corbeaux les faucons les hiboux
D'Afrique arrivent les ibis les flamands les marabouts
L'oiseau Roc célébré par les conteurs et les poètes
Plane tenant dans les serres le crâne d'Adam la première tête
L'aigle fond de l'horizon en poussant un grand cri
Et d'Amérique vient le petit colibri
De Chine sont venus les pihis longs et souples
Qui n'ont qu'une seule aile et qui volent par couples
Puis voici la colombe esprit immaculé
Qu'escortent l'oiseau-lyre et le paon ocellé
Le phénix ce bûcher qui soi-même s'engendre
Un instant voile tout de son ardente cendre
Les sirènes laissant les périlleux détroits
Arrivent en chantant bellement toutes trois
Et tous aigle phénix et pihis de la Chine
Fraternisent avec la volante machine

Maintenant tu marches dans Paris tout seul parmi la foule
Des troupeaux d'autobus mugissants près de toi roulent
L'angoisse de l'amour te serre le gosier

It is the red-headed torch which the wind cannot blow out
It is the pale and ruddy son of a sorrowful mother
It is the tree always thick with prayers
It is the double gallows of honor and of eternity
It is a six-pointed star
It is God who died on Friday and rose again on Sunday
It is Christ who soars in the sky better than any aviator
He breaks the world's altitude record

Christ the pupil of the eye
Twentieth pupil of the centuries he knows how
And turned into a bird this century rises in the air like Jesus
The devils in their abysses lift their heads to look at it
They say it is imitating Simon Magus in Judea
They shout that if it knows how to fly it should be called a flyer
Angels hover about the lovely aerialist
Icarus Enoch Elijah Apollonius of Tyana
Flutter around the original airplane
They separate occasionally to give passage to those whom the Holy Eucharist
    carries up
Those priests who rise eternally in lifting the host
The airplane lands at last without folding its wings
The sky fills up then with millions of swallows
In a flash crows falcons and owls arrive
Ibis flamingoes and marabous arrive from Africa
The great Roc celebrated by story tellers and poets
Glides down holding in its claws Adam's skull the first head
The eagle rushes out of the horizon giving a great cry
From America comes the tiny humming-bird
From China have come long supple pihis
Which only have one wing and fly tandem
Then the dove immaculate spirit
Escorted by the lyre bird and the ocellated peacock
The phoenix that pyre which recreates itself
Veils everything for an instant with its glowing coals
Sirens leaving their perilous straits
Arrive all three of them singing beautifully
And everything eagle phoenix and Chinese pihis
Fraternize with the flying machine

Now you walk through Paris all alone in the crowd
Herds of bellowing busses roll by near you
The agony of love tightens your throat

Comme si tu ne devais jamais plus être aimé
Si tu vivais dans l'ancien temps tu entrerais dans un monastère
Vous avez honte quand vous vous surprenez à dire une prière
Tu te moques de toi et comme le feu de l'Enfer ton rire pétille
Les étincelles de ton rire dorent le fonds de ta vie
C'est un tableau pendu dans un sombre musée
Et quelquefois tu vas le regarder de près

Aujourd'hui tu marches dans Paris les femmes sont ensanglantées
C'était et je voudrais ne pas m'en souvenir c'était au déclin de la beauté

Entourée de flammes ferventes Notre-Dame m'a regardé à Chartres
Le sang de votre Sacré-Cœur m'a inondé à Montmartre
Je suis malade d'ouïr les paroles bienheureuses
L'amour dont je souffre est une maladie honteuse
Et l'image qui te possède te fait survivre dans l'insomnie et dans
    l'angoisse
C'est toujours près de toi cette image qui passe

Maintenant tu es au bord de la Méditerranée
Sous les citronniers qui sont en fleur toute l'année
Avec tes amis tu te promènes en barque
L'un est Nissard il y a un Mentonasque et deux Turbiasques
Nous regardons avec effroi les poulpes des profondeurs
Et parmi les algues nagent les poissons images du Sauveur
Tu es dans le jardin d'une auberge aux environs de Prague
Tu te sens tout heureux une rose est sur la table
Et tu observes au lieu d'écrire ton conte en prose
La cétoine qui dort dans le cœur de la rose

Epouvanté tu te vois dessiné dans les agates de Saint-Vit
Tu étais triste à mourir le jour où tu t'y vis
Tu ressembles au Lazare affolé par le jour
Les aiguilles de l'horloge du quartier juif vont à rebours
Et tu recules aussi dans ta vie lentement
En montant au Hradchin et le soir en écoutant
Dans les tavernes chanter des chansons tchèques

Te voici à Marseille au milieu des pastèques

Te voici à Coblence à l'hôtel du Géant

Te voici à Rome assis sous un néflier du Japon

As if you could never be loved again
If you were living in olden days you would enter a monastery
You are ashamed when you catch yourself saying a prayer
You ridicule yourself and your laughter bursts out like hell fire
The sparks of your laughter gild the depths of your life
It is a picture hung in a somber museum
And sometimes you go to look at it closely

Today you walk through Paris the women are blood-stained
It was and I would prefer not to remember it was during beauty's decline

Surrounded by fervent flames Notre Dame looked at me in Chartres
The blood of your Sacred Heart flooded me in the Montmartre
I am ill from hearing happy words
The love from which I suffer is a shameful sickness
And the image which possesses you makes you survive in sleeplessness and
    anguish
It is always near you this passing image

Now you are on the shore of the Mediterranean
Under the lemon trees which blossom all year
With your friends you take a boat ride
One from Nice one from Menton and two from Turbie
We look down in fear at the octopodes on the bottom
And amid the algae swim fish images of our Saviour
You are in the garden of an inn on the outskirts of Prague
You feel completely happy a rose is on the table
And instead of writing your story in prose you watch
The rosebug which is sleeping in the heart of the rose

Astonished you see yourself outlined in the agates of St. Vitus
You were sad enough to die the day you saw yourself in them
You looked like Lazarus bewildered by the light
The hands of the clock in the Jewish quarter turn backwards
And you go slowly backwards in your life
Climbing up to Hradchin and listening at night
In taverns to the singing of Czech songs

Here you are in Marseilles amid the watermelons

Here you are in Coblenz at the Hotel of the Giant

Here you are in Rome sitting under a Japanese medlar tree

Te voici à Amsterdam avec une jeune fille que tu trouves belle et qui est laide
Elle doit se marier avec un étudiant de Leyde
On y loue des chambres en latin Cubicula locanda
Je m'en souviens j'y ai passé trois jours et autant à Gouda

Tu es à Paris chez le juge d'instruction
Comme un criminel on te met en état d'arrestation
Tu as fait de douloureux et de joyeux voyages
Avant de t'apercevoir du mensonge et de l'âge
Tu as souffert de l'amour à vingt et à trente ans
J'ai vécu comme un fou et j'ai perdu mon temps
Tu n'oses plus regarder tes mains et à tous moments je voudrais
    sangloter
Sur toi sur celle que j'aime sur tout ce qui t'a épouvanté

Tu regardes les yeux pleins de larmes ces pauvres émigrants
Ils croient en Dieu ils prient les femmes allaitent des enfants
Ils emplissent de leur odeur le hall de la gare Saint-Lazare
Ils ont foi dans leur étoile comme les rois-mages
Ils espèrent gagner de l'argent dans l'Argentine
Et revenir dans leur pays après avoir fait fortune
Une famille transporte un édredon rouge comme vous transportez votre cœur
Cet édredon et nos rêves sont aussi irréels
Quelques-uns de ces émigrants restent ici et se logent
Rue des Rosiers ou rue des Écouffes dans des bouges
Je les ai vus souvent le soir ils prennent l'air dans la rue
Et se déplacent rarement comme les pièces aux échecs
Il y a surtout des Juifs leurs femmes portent perruque
Elles restent assises exsangues au fond des boutiques

Tu es debout devant le zinc d'un bar crapuleux
Tu prends un café à deux sous parmi les malheureux

Tu es la nuit dans un grand restaurant

Ces femmes ne sont pas méchantes elles ont des soucis cependant
Toutes même la plus laide a fait souffrir son amant
Elle est la fille d'un sergent de ville de Jersey

Ses mains que je n'avais pas vues sont dures et gercées
J'ai une pitié immense pour les coutures de son ventre

J'humilie maintenant à une pauvre fille au rire horrible ma bouche

Here you are in Amsterdam with a girl you find pretty and who is ugly
She is to marry a student from Leyden
There are rooms for rent in Latin Cubicula locanda
I remember I stayed three days there and as many at Gouda

You are in Paris at the *juge d'instruction*
Like a criminal you are placed under arrest
You have made sorrowful and happy trips
Before noticing that the world lies and grows old
You suffered from love at twenty and thirty
I have lived like a fool and wasted my time
You no longer dare look at your hands and at every moment I want to burst out
  sobbing
For you for her I love for everything that has frightened you

With tear-filled eyes you look at those poor emigrants
They believe in God they pray the women nurse their children
Their odor fills the waiting room of the gare Saint-Lazare
They have faith in their star like the Magi
They hope to make money in Argentina
And come back to their countries having made their fortunes
One family carries a red quilt as one carries one's heart
That quilt and our dream are both unreal
Some of these emigrants stay here and find lodging
In hovels in the rue des Rosiers or the rue des Écouffes
I have often seen them in the evening they take a stroll in the street
And rarely travel far like men on a checker board
They are mostly Jews their wives wear wigs
They sit bloodlessly in the backs of little shops

You are standing at the counter of a dirty bar
You have a cheap coffee with the rest of the riffraff

At night you are in a big restaurant

These women are not wicked still they have their worries
All of them even the ugliest has made her lover suffer
She is the daughter of a policeman on the Isle of Jersey

Her hands which I have not seen are hard and chapped
I have an immense pity for the scars on her belly

I humble my mouth by offering it to a poor slut with a horrible laugh

Tu es seul le matin va venir
Les laitiers font tinter leurs bidons dans les rues

La nuit s'éloigne ainsi qu'une belle Métive
C'est Ferdine la fausse ou Léa l'attentive

Et tu bois cet alcool brûlant comme ta vie
Ta vie que tu bois comme une eau-de-vie
Tu marches vers Auteuil tu veux aller chez toi à pied
Dormir parmi tes fétiches d'Océanie et de Guinée
Ils sont des Christ d'une autre forme et d'une autre croyance
Ce sont les Christ inférieurs des obscures espérances

Adieu Adieu

Soleil cou coupé

L'Adieu

J'ai cueilli ce brin de bruyère
L'automne est morte souviens-t'en
Nous ne nous verrons plus sur terre
Odeur du temps brin de bruyère
Et souviens-toi que je t'attends

Les Fenêtres

Du rouge au vert tout le jaune se meurt
Quand chantent les aras dans les forêts natales
Abatis de pihis
Il y a un poème à faire sur l'oiseau qui n'a qu'une aile
Nous l'enverrons en message téléphonique
Traumatisme géant
Il fait couler les yeux
Voilà une jolie jeune fille parmi les jeunes Turinaises
Le pauvre jeune homme se mouchait dans sa cravate blanche
Tu soulèveras le rideau
Et maintenant voilà que s'ouvre la fenêtre
Araignées quand les mains tissaient la lumière
Beauté pâleur insondables violets

You are alone the morning is almost here
The milkmen rattle their cans in the street

The night departs like a beautiful half-caste
False Ferdine or waiting Leah

And you drink this burning liquor like your life
Your life which you drink like an eau-de-vie
You walk toward Auteuil you want to walk home on foot
To sleep among your fetishes from Oceania and Guinea
They are all Christ in another form and of another faith
They are inferior Christs obscure hopes

Adieu adieu

The sun a severed neck

—ROGER SHATTUCK

The Farewell

I picked this fragile sprig of heather
Autumn has died long since remember
Never again shall we see one another
Odor of time sprig of heather
Remember I await our life together

—ROGER SHATTUCK

Windows

The yellow fades from red to green
When aras sing in their native forest
Pihis giblets
There is a poem to be done on the bird with only one wing
We will send it by telephone
Giant traumatism
It makes one's eyes run
There is one pretty one among all the young girls from Turin
The unfortunate young man blows his nose in his white necktie
You will lift the curtain
And now look at the window opening
Spiders when hands were weaving light
Beauty paleness unfathomable violet tints

Nous tenterons en vain de prendre du repos
On commencera à minuit
Quand on a le temps on a la liberté
Bigorneaux Lotte multiples Soleils et l'Oursin du couchant
Une vielle paire de chaussures jaunes devant la fenêtre
Tours
Les Tours ce sont les rues
Puits
Puits ce sont les places
Puits
Arbres creux qui abritent les Câpresses vagabondes
Les Chabins chantent des airs à mourir
Aux Chabines marronnes
Et l'oie oua-oua trompette au nord
Où les chasseurs de ratons
Raclent les pelleteries
Etincelant diamant
Vancouver
Où le train blanc de neige et de feux nocturnes fuit l'hiver
O Paris
Du rouge au vert tout le jaune se meurt
Paris Vancouver Hyères Maintenon New-York et les Antilles
La fenêtre s'ouvre comme une orange
Le beau fruit de la lumière

Miroir

```
                       DANS
              FLETS        CE
          RE                   MI
         LES                  ROIR
        SONT                   JE
         ME                   SUIS
        COM    Guillaume       EN
        NON                   CLOS
         ET    Apollinaire     VI
        GES                   VANT
          AN                   ET
         LES                  VRAI
          NE                  COM
          GI                   ME
           MA          ON
                   I
```

We shall try in vain to take our ease
They start at midnight
When one has time one has liberty
Periwinkles Turbot multiple Suns and the Sea-urchin of the setting sun
An old pair of yellow shoes in front of the window
Towers
Towers are streets
Wells
Wells are market places
Wells
Hollow trees which shelter vagabond Capresses
The Octoroons sing songs of dying
To their chestnut-colored wives
And the goose honk honk trumpets in the north
When racoon hunters
Scrape their pelts
Gleaming diamond
Vancouver
Where the train white with snow and fires of the night flees the winter
O Paris
The yellow fades from red to green
Paris Vancouver Hyères Maintenon New York and the Antilles
The window opens like an orange
Lovely fruit of light

—ROGER SHATTUCK

Mirror

In this mirror I am enclosed living and true as one imagines angels not as reflections are **Guillaume Apollinaire**

—ROGER SHATTUCK

Toujours

A Madame Faure-Favier

Toujours
Nous irons plus loin sans avancer jamais
Et de planète en planète

De nébuleuse en nébuleuse
Le don Juan des mille et trois comètes
Même sans bouger de la terre
Cherche les forces neuves
Et prend au sérieux les fantômes

Et tant d'univers s'oublient
Quels sont les grands oublieurs
Qui donc saura nous faire oublier telle ou telle partie du monde
Où est le Christophe Colomb à qui l'on devra l'oubli d'un continent
                    Perdre
Mais perdre vraiment
Pour laisser place à la trouvaille
                        Perdre
La vie pour trouver la Victoire

La Petite Auto

Le 31 du mois d'août 1914
Je partis de Deauville un peu avant minuit
Dans la petite auto de Rouveyre

Avec son chauffeur nous étions trois

Nous dîmes adieu à toute une époque
Des géants furieux se dressaient sur l'Europe
Les aigles quittaient leur aire attendant le soleil
Les poissons voraces montaient des abîmes
Les peuples accouraient pour se connaître à fond
Les morts tremblaient de peur dans leurs sombres demeures

Les chiens aboyaient vers là-bas où étaient les frontières
Je m'en allais portant en moi toutes ces armées qui se battaient

Always

To Madame Faure-Favier

> Always
We'll go forward never getting anywhere
And from planet to planet

From nebula to nebula
The Don Juan of a thousand and three comets
Even staying right here
Seeking new strength
Taking all spirits seriously.

And so many worlds lose sight of themselves
Which ones are best at forgetting
Making us forget this or that place
Where is the Columbus to whom we'll owe the loss of a continent
> Losing
But really losing
To leave room for the stroke of luck
> Losing
Life to find Victory

—MARY ANN CAWS AND PATRICIA TERRY

The Little Car

The 31st day of August 1914
I left Deauville a little before midnight
In Rouveyre's little car

With his driver there were three of us

We said goodbye to an entire epoch
Furious giants were rising over Europe
The eagles were leaving their aeries expecting the sun
The voracious fish were rising from the depths
The masses were rushing toward some deeper understanding
The dead were trembling with fear in their dark dwellings

The dogs were barking towards over there where the frontiers are
I went bearing within me all those armies fighting

Je les sentais monter en moi et s'étaler les contrées où elles serpentaient
Avec les forêts les villages heureux de la Belgique
Francorchamps avec l'Eau Rouge et les pouhons
Région par où se font toujours les invasions
Artères ferroviaires où ceux qui s'en allaient mourir
Saluaient encore une fois la vie colorée
Océans profonds où remuaient les monstres
Dans les vieilles carcasses naufragées
Hauteurs inimaginables où l'homme combat
Plus haut que l'aigle ne plane
L'homme y combat contre l'homme
Et descend tout à coup comme une étoile filante
Je sentais en moi des êtres neufs pleins de dextérité
Bâtir et aussi agencer un univers nouveau
Un marchand d'une opulence inouïe et d'une taille prodigieuse
Disposait un étalage extraordinaire
Et des bergers gigantesques menaient
De grands troupeaux muets qui broutaient les paroles
Et contre lesquels aboyaient tous les chiens sur la route

Je n'oublierai jamais ce voyage nocturne où nul de nous ne dit un mot

O			
dé	o		
part	nuit		
sombre	tendre	o	se hât
où mouraient	d'avant	vil	tai le n
nos 3 phares	la guerre	lages où	

MARÉCHAUX-FERRANTS RAPPELÉS

ENTRE MINUIT ET UNE HEURE DU MATIN

        v
    e   r   s   ou bien   v
    LISIEUX   e r s
    la très   aille
     bleu   s d'o
        e   r

et à fois nous nous arrêtâmes pour changer un pneu qui avait éclaté

I felt them rise up in me and spread out over the countries they wound through
With the forests the happy villages of Belgium
Francorchamps with l'Eau Rouge and the mineral springs
Region where the invasions always take place
Railway arteries where those who were going to die
Saluted one last time this colorful life
Deep oceans where monsters were moving
In old shipwrecked hulks
Unimaginable heights where man fights
Higher than the eagle soars
There man fights man
And falls like a shooting star
I felt in myself new and totally capable beings
Build and organize a new universe
A merchant of amazing opulence and astounding size
Was laying out an extraordinary display
And gigantic shepherds were leading
Great silent flocks that were browsing on words
With every dog along the road barking at them
I'll never forget that night when none of us said a single word

O
dark   O
departure   ten
when our   der
three head   pre-   O
lights were   w a r   vil
d y i n g   night   lages   with   the ru
                                                g n i h s

BLACKSMITHS CALLED UP

between midnight and one o'clock in the morning

to   sil
v e r   v e r
y b l u e   or else   v e r
Lisi   s a i l
eux   les
and 3 times we stopped to change a tire that had blown out

Et quand après avoir passé l'après-midi
Par Fontainebleau
Nous arrivâmes à Paris
Au moment où l'on affichait la mobilisation
Nous comprîmes mon camarade et moi
Que la petite auto nous avait conduits dans une époque Nouvelle
Et bien qu'étant déjà tous deux des hommes mûrs
Nous venions cependant de naître

———————————

And when having passed that afternoon
Through Fontainebleau
We arrived in Paris
Just as the mobilization posters were going up
We understood my buddy and I
That the little car had taken us into a New epoch
And although we were both grown men
We had just been born

—RON PADGETT

Blaise Cendrars
(Frederic Louis Sauser) 1887–1961
LA-CHAUX-DES-FONDS, SWITZERLAND

A journalist, merchant seaman, foreign legionnaire, essayist, and art critic, Cendrars also made films with Abel Gance (including *La Roue*) as well as writing seminal texts on cinema and on modernism, collected in *Aujourd'hui*. His extensive travels—real and imagined—furnish the vital matter of his work, both in poetry and in prose. Closely associated with Cubism, he was a leading figure in the twentieth-century literary world. Born to a French father and Swiss mother, he was sent to St. Petersburg in Russia at seventeen to work as a Franco-German correspondent for a Swiss jeweler. After studying briefly in Bern, he settled in Paris in 1910. He served in World War I, losing his right arm in combat. His extensive curiosity about widely differing cultures—particularly black ones—gave him a constantly forward-looking orientation. Principal works: *Les Pâques à New York,* 1912; *La Prose du Transsibérien et de la petite Jeanne de France,* 1913; *Du monde entier,* 1919; *Au coeur du monde,* 1919; *Dix-neuf poèmes élastiques,* 1919; *L'Anthologie nègre,* 1921; *Feuilles de route,* 1924; and the poetic prose of *Le Lotissement du ciel.*

Journal

Christ
Voici plus d'un an que je n'ai plus pensé à Vous
Depuis que j'ai écrit mon avant-dernier poème Pâques
Ma vie a bien changé depuis
Mais je suis toujours le même
J'ai même voulu devenir peintre
Voici les tableaux que j'ai faits et qui ce soir pendent aux murs
Ils m'ouvrent d'étranges vues sur moi-même qui me font penser à Vous.

Christ
La vie
Voilà ce que j'ai fouillé

Mes peintures me font mal
Je suis trop passionné
Tout est orangé.

J'ai passé une triste journée à penser à mes amis
Et à lire le journal
Christ
Vie crucifée dans le journal grand ouvert que je tiens les bras tendus
Envergures
Fusées
Ebullition
Cris.
On dirait un aéroplane qui tombe.
C'est moi.

Passion
Feu
Roman-feuilleton
Journal
On a beau ne pas vouloir parler de soi-même
Il faut parfois crier

Je suis l'autre
Trop sensible

Newspaper

Christ
It's been more than a year now since I stopped thinking about You
Since I wrote my next-to-last poem "Easter"
My life has changed a lot since
But I'm still the same
I've even wanted to become a painter
Here are the pictures I've done and which hang on the walls tonight
For me they open strange views onto myself which make me think of You.

Christ
Life
That's what I've ransacked

My paintings hurt me
I'm too passionate
Everything is oranged up.

I spent a sad day thinking about my friends
And reading the paper
Christ
Life crucified in the wide-open paper I hold at arm's length
Wing-spread
Rockets
Turmoil
Cries.
You'd think an airplane is dropping.
It's me.

Passion
Fire
Serials
Newspaper
It's useless not wanting to talk about yourself
You have to cry out sometimes

I'm the other one
Too sensitive

—RON PADGETT

Ma danse

Platon n'accorde pas droit de cité au poète
Juif errant
Don Juan métaphysique
Les amis, les proches
Tu n'as plus de coûtumes et pas encore d'habitudes
Il faut échapper à la tyrannie des revues
Littérature
Vie pauvre
Orgueil déplacé
Masque
La femme, la danse que Nietzsche a voulu nous apprendre à danser
La femme
Mais l'ironie?

Va-et-vient continuel
Vagabondage spécial
Tous les hommes, tous les pays
C'est ainsi que tu n'es plus à charge
Tu ne te fais plus sentir . . .

Je suis un monsieur qui en des express fabuleux traverse les toujours mêmes
    Europes et regarde découragé par la portière
Le paysage ne m'intéresse plus
Mais la danse du paysage
La danse du paysage
Danse-paysage
Paritatitata
Je tout-tourne

Lettre

Tu m'as dit si tu m'écris
Ne tape pas tout à la machine
Ajoute une ligne de ta main
Un mot un rien oh pas grand'chose
Oui oui oui oui oui oui oui oui

Ma Remington est belle pourtant
Je l'aime beaucoup et travaille bien

My Dance

Plato does not grant city rights to the poet
Wandering Jew
Metaphysical Don Juan
Friends, close ones
You don't have customs anymore and no new habits yet
We must be free of the tyranny of magazines
Literature
Poor life
Misplaced pride
Mask
Woman, the dance Nietzsche wanted to teach us to dance
Woman
But irony?

Continual coming and going
Procuring in the street
All men, all countries
And so you are no longer a burden
It's like you're not there anymore . . .

I am a gentleman who in fabulous express trains crosses the same old Europe
    and gazes disheartened from the doorway
The landscape doesn't interest me anymore
But the dance of the landscape
The dance of the landscape
Dance-landscape
Paritatitata
I all-turn

—RON PADGETT

Letter

You said to me if you write me
Don't just use the typewriter
Add a line in your own hand
A word a nothing oh a little something
Yes yes yes yes yes yes yes yes

But my Remington is beautiful
I really love it and the work goes well

Mon écriture est nette et claire
On voit très bien que c'est moi qui l'ai tapée

Il y a des blancs que je suis seul à savoir faire
Vois donc l'œil qu'a ma page
Pourtant pour te faire plaisir j'ajoute à l'encre
Deux trois mots
Et une grosse tache d'encre
Pour que tu ne puisses pas les lire

Prose du Transsibérien et de la petite Jeanne de France (extraits)

Dédiée aux musiciens

En ce temps-là j'étais en mon adolescence
J'avais à peine seize ans et je ne me souvenais déjà plus de mon enfance
J'étais à 16.000 lieues du lieu de ma naissance
J'étais à Moscou, dans la ville des mille et trois clochers et des sept
    gares
Et je n'avais pas assez des sept gares et des mille et trois tours
Car mon adolescence était alors si ardente et si folle
Que mon cœur, tour à tour, brûlait comme le temple d'Ephèse ou comme la
    Place Rouge de Moscou
Quand le soleil se couche
Et mes yeux éclairaient des voies anciennes.
Et j'étais déjà si mauvais poète
Que je ne savais pas aller jusqu'au bout.

Le Kremlin était comme un immense gâteau tartare
Croustillé d'or
Avec les grandes amandes des cathédrales toutes blanches
Et l'or mielleux des cloches . . .
Un vieux moine me lisait la légende de Novgorode
J'avais soif
Et je déchiffrais des caractères cunéiformes
Puis, tout à coup, les pigeons du Saint-Esprit s'envolaient sur la place
Et mes mains s'envolaient aussi avec des bruissements d'albatros
Et ceci, c'était les dernières réminiscences du dernier jour
Du tout dernier voyage
Et de la mer.

My writing is sharp and clear
It's very easy to see that I did the typing

There are white spaces only I know how to make
See how my page looks
Still to please you I add in ink
Two or three words
And a big blot of ink
So you can't read them

—RON PADGETT

The Prose of the Trans-Siberian and of Little Jeanne of France

Dedicated to the musicians

Back then I was still young
I was barely sixteen but my childhood memories were gone
I was 48,000 miles away from where I was born
I was in Moscow, city of a thousand and three bell towers and seven train
    stations
And the thousand and three towers and seven stations weren't enough for me
Because I was such a hot and crazy teenager
That my heart was burning like the Temple of Ephesus or like Red Square in
    Moscow
At sunset
And my eyes were shining down those old roads
And I was already such a bad poet
That I didn't know how to take it all the way.

The Kremlin was like an immense Tartar cake
Iced with gold
With big blanched-almond cathedrals
And the honey gold of the bells . . .
An old monk was reading me the legend of Novgorod
I was thirsty
And I was deciphering cuneiform characters
Then all at once the pigeons of the Holy Ghost flew up over the square
And my hands flew up too, sounding like an albatross taking off
And, well, that's the last I remember of the last day
Of the very last trip
And of the sea.

Pourtant, j'étais fort mauvais poète.

Je ne savais pas aller jusqu'au bout.

J'avais faim

Et tous les jours et toutes les femmes dans les cafés et tous les verres

J'aurais voulu les boire et les casser

Et toute les vitrines et toutes les rues

Et toutes les maisons et toutes les vies

Et toutes les roues des fiacres qui tournaient en tourbillon sur les mauvais pavés

J'aurais voulu les plonger dans une fournaise de glaives

Et j'aurais voulu broyer tous les os

Et arracher toutes les langues

Et liquéfier tous ces grands corps étranges et nus sous les vêtements qui
     m'affolent . . .

Je pressentais la venue du grand Christ rouge de la révolution russe . . .

Et le soleil était une mauvaise plaie

Qui s'ouvrait comme un brasier.

En ce temps-là j'étais en mon adolescence

J'avais à peine seize ans et je ne me souvenais déjà plus de ma naissance

J'étais à Moscou, où je voulais me nourrir de flammes

Et je n'avais pas assez des tours et des gares que constellaient mes yeux

En Sibérie tonnait le canon, c'était la guerre

La faim le froid la peste le choléra

Et les eaux limoneuses de l'Amour charriaient des millions de charognes

Dans toutes les gares je voyais partir tous les derniers trains

Personne ne pouvait plus partir car on ne délivrait plus de billets

Et les soldats qui s'en allaient auraient bien voulu rester . . .

Un vieux moine me chantait la légende de Novgorode.

Moi, le mauvais poète qui ne voulais aller nulle part, je pouvais aller partout

.   .   .

«Dis, Blaise, sommes-nous bien loin de Montmartre?»

Oui, nous le sommes, nous le sommes

Tous les boucs émissaires ont crevé dans ce désert

Entends les clochettes de ce troupeau galeux

Tomsk Tchéliabinsk Kainsk Obi Taïchet Verkné-Oudinsk Kourgane Samara
     Pensa-Touloune

La mort en Mandchourie

Est notre débarcadère est notre dernier repaire

Ce voyage est terrible

30

Still, I was a really bad poet.
I didn't know how to take it all the way.
I was hungry
And all those days and all those women in all those cafés and all those glasses
I wanted to drink them down and break them
And all those windows and all those streets
And all those houses and all those lives
And all those carriage wheels raising swirls from the broken pavement
I would have liked to have rammed them into a roaring furnace
And I would have liked to have ground up all their bones
And ripped out all those tongues
And liquefied all those big bodies naked and strange under clothes that drive me
    mad . . .
I foresaw the coming of the big red Christ of the Russian Revolution . . .
And the sun was an ugly sore
Splitting apart like a red-hot coal.

Back then I was still quite young
I was barely sixteen but I'd already forgotten about where I was born
I was in Moscow wanting to wolf down flames
And there weren't enough of those towers and stations sparkling in my eyes
In Siberia the artillery rumbled—it was war
Hunger cold plague cholera
And the muddy waters of the Amur carrying along millions of corpses
In every station I watched the last trains leave
That's all: they weren't selling any more tickets
And the soldiers would far rather have stayed . . .
An old monk was singing me the legend of Novgorod.

Me, the bad poet who wanted to go nowhere, I could go anywhere

.   .   .

"Say, Blaise, are we really a long way from Montmartre?"

Yes, we are, we are
All the scapegoats have swollen up and collapsed in this desert
Listen to the cowbells of this mangy troop
Tomsk Chelyabinsk Kansk Ob' Tayshet Verkne-Udinsk Kurgan Samara Penza-
    Tulun
Death in Manchuria
Is where we get off is our last stop
This trip is terrible

Hier matin
Ivan Oulitch avait les cheveux blancs
Et Kolia Nicolaï Ivanovitch se ronge les doigts depuis quinze jours . . .
Fais comme elles la Mort la Famine fais ton métier
Ça coûte cent sous, en transsibérien, ça coûte cent roubles
Enfièvre les banquettes et rougoie sous la table
Le diable est au piano
Ses doigts noueux excitent toutes les femmes
La Nature
Les Gouges
Fais ton métier
Jusqu'à Kharbine . . .

«Dis, Blaise, sommes-nous bien loin de Montmartre?»

Non mais . . . fiche-moi la paix . . . laisse-moi tranquille
Tu as les hanches angulaires
Ton ventre est aigre et tu as la chaude-pisse
C'est tout ce que Paris a mis dans ton giron
C'est aussi un peu d'âme . . . car tu es malheureuse
J'ai pitié j'ai pitié viens vers moi sur mon cœur
Les roues sont les moulins à vent du pays de Cocagne
Et les moulins à vent sont les béquilles qu'un mendiant fait tournoyer
Nous sommes les culs-de-jatte de l'espace
Nous roulons sur nos quatre plaies
On nous a rogné les ailes
Les ailes de nos sept péchés
Et tous les trains sont les bilboquets du diable
Basse-cour
Le monde moderne
La vitesse n'y peut mais
Le monde moderne
Les lointains sont par trop loin
Et au bout du voyage c'est terrible d'être un homme avec une femme . . .

«Blaise, dis, sommes-nous bien loin de Montmartre?»

J'ai pitié j'ai pitié viens vers moi je vais te conter une histoire
Viens dans mon lit
Viens sur mon cœur
Je vais te conter une histoire . . .

. . .

Yesterday morning
Ivan Ulitch's hair turned white
And Kolia Nikolai Ivanovitch has been biting his fingers for two weeks . . .
Do what Death and Famine do, do your job
It costs one hundred sous—in Trans-Siberian that's one hundred rubles
Fire up the seats and blush under the table
The devil is at the keyboard
His knotty fingers thrill all the women
Instinct
OK gals
Do your job
Until we get to Harbin . . .

"Say, Blaise, are we really a long way from Montmartre?"

No, hey . . . Stop bothering me . . . Leave me alone
Your pelvis sticks out
Your belly's sour and you have the clap
The only thing Paris laid in your lap
And there's a little soul . . . because you're unhappy
I feel sorry for you come here to my heart
The wheels are windmills in the land of Cockaigne
And the windmills are crutches a beggar whirls over his head
We are the amputees of space
We move on our four wounds
Our wings have been clipped
The wings of our seven sins
And the trains are all the devil's toys
Chicken coop
The modern world
Speed is of no use
The modern world
The distances are too far away
And at the end of a trip it's horrible to be a man with a woman . . .

"Blaise, say, are we really a long way from Montmartre?"

I feel so sorry for you come here I'm going to tell you a story
Come get in my bed
Put your head on my shoulder
I'm going to tell you a story . . .

.   .   .

Autant d'images-associations que je ne peux pas développer dans mes vers
Car je suis encore fort mauvais poète
Car l'univers me déborde
Car j'ai négligé de m'assurer contre les accidents de chemin de fer
Car je ne sais pas aller jusqu'au bout
Et j'ai peur.

J'ai peur
Je ne sais pas aller jusqu'au bout

Comme mon ami Chagall je pourrais faire une série de tableaux déments
Mais je n'ai pas pris de notes en voyage
«Pardonnez-moi mon ignorance
«Pardonnez-moi de ne plus connaître l'ancien jeu des vers»
Comme dit Guillaume Apollinaire
Tout ce qui concerne la guerre on peut le lire dans les *Mémoires de Kouropatkine*
Ou dans les journaux japonais qui sont aussi cruellement illustrés
A quoi bon me documenter
Je m'abandonne
Aux sursauts de ma mémoire . . .

.   .   .

O Paris
Grand foyer chaleureux avec les tisons entre-croisés de tes rues et tes vieilles
    maisons qui se penchent au-dessus et se réchauffent
Comme des aïeules
Et voici des affiches, du rouge du vert multicolores comme mon passé bref du
    jaune
Jaune la fière couleur des romans de la France à l'étranger.
J'aime me frotter dans les grandes villes aux autobus en marche
Ceux de la ligne Saint-Germain-Montmartre m'emportent à l'assaut de la Butte
Les moteurs beuglent comme les taureaux d'or
Les vaches du crépuscule broutent le Sacré-Cœur
O Paris
Gare centrale débarcadère des volontés carrefour des inquiétudes
Seuls les marchands de couleur ont encore un peu de lumière sur leur porte
La Compagnie Internationale des Wagons-Lits et des Grands Express Européens
    m'a envoyé son prospectus
C'est la plus belle église du monde
J'ai des amis qui m'entourent comme des garde-fous
Ils ont peur quand je pars que je ne revienne plus
Toutes les femmes que j'ai rencontrées se dressent aux horizons

So many associations images I can't get into my poem
Because I'm still such a really bad poet
Because the universe rushes over me
And I didn't bother to insure myself against train wreck
Because I don't know how to take it all the way
And I'm scared.

I'm scared
I don't know how to take it all the way.

Like my friend Chagall I could do a series of irrational paintings
But I didn't take notes
"Forgive my ignorance
Pardon my forgetting how to play the ancient game of Verse"
As Guillaume Apollinaire says
If you want to know anything about the war read Kuropotkin's *Memoirs*
Or the Japanese newspapers with their ghastly illustrations
But why compile a bibliography
I give up
Bounce back into my leaping memory . . .

.   .   .

O Paris
Great warm hearth with the intersecting embers of your streets and your old
    houses leaning over them for warmth
Like grandmothers
And here are posters in red in green all colors like my past in a word yellow
Yellow the proud color of the novels of France
In big cities I like to rub elbows with the buses as they go by
Those of the Saint-Germain—Montmartre line that carry me to the assault of
    the Butte
The motors bellow like golden bulls
The cows of dusk graze on Sacré-Coeur
O Paris
Main station where desires arrive at the crossroads of restlessness
Now only the paint store has a little light on its door
The International Pullman and Great European Express Company has sent me
    its brochure
It's the most beautiful church in the world
I have friends who surround me like guardrails
They're afraid that when I leave I'll never come back
All the women I've ever known appear around me on the horizon

Avec les gestes piteux et les regards tristes des sémaphores sous la pluie
Bella, Agnès, Catherine et la mère de mon fils en Italie
Et celle, la mère de mon amour en Amérique

Il y a des cris de sirène qui me déchirent l'âme
Là-bas en Mandchourie un ventre tressaille encore comme dans un
    accouchement
Je voudrais
Je voudrais n'avoir jamais fait mes voyages
Ce soir un grand amour me tourmente
Et malgré moi je pense à la petite Jehanne de France.
C'est par un soir de tristesse que j'ai écrit ce poème en son honneur
Jeanne
La petite prostituée
Je suis triste je suis triste
J'irai au *Lapin agile* me ressouvenir de ma jeunesse perdue
Et boire des petits verres
Puis je rentrerai seul

Paris

Ville de la Tour unique du grand Gibet et de la Roue

———————————

Holding out their arms and looking like sad lighthouses in the rain
Bella, Agnès, Catherine, and the mother of my son in Italy
And she who is the mother of my love in America

Sometimes the cry of a whistle tears me apart
Over in Manchuria a belly is still heaving, as if giving
   birth
I wish
I wish I'd never started traveling
Tonight a great love is driving me out of my mind
And I can't help thinking about little Jeanne of France.
It's through a sad night that I've written this poem in her honor
Jeanne
the little prostitute
I'm sad so sad
I'm going to the Lapin Agile to remember my lost youth again
Have a few drinks
And come back home alone

Paris

City of the incomparable Tower the great Gibbet and the Wheel

—RON PADGETT

Paul Claudel 1868–1955
VILLENEUVE-SUR-FÈRE, FRANCE

A poet, essayist, and dramatist, Claudel was influenced early on by the Symbolists. Although his Catholic upbringing snuffed out his faith, he reconverted dramatically to Catholicism on Christmas Day of 1886 after a religious revelation. From 1893 to 1955 he served in diplomatic posts across America, Europe, and China. His travels in the Orient provided him with material for the prose poems entitled *Connaissance de l'Est* (1900). He also served as

Octobre

C'est en vain que je vois les arbres toujours verts.

Qu'une funèbre brume l'ensevelisse, ou que la longue sérénité du ciel l'efface, l'an n'est pas d'un jour moins près du fatal solstice. Ni ce soleil ne me déçoit, ni l'opulence au loin de la contrée; voici je ne sais quoi de trop calme, un repos tel que le réveil est exclu. Le grillon à peine a commencé son cri qu'il s'arrête; de peur d'excéder parmi la plénitude qui est seul manque du droit de parler, et l'on dirait que seulement dans la solennelle sécurité de ces campagnes d'or il soit licite de pénétrer d'un pied nu. Non, ceci qui est derrière moi sur l'immense moisson ne jette plus la même lumière, et selon que le chemin m'emmène par la paille, soit qu'ici je tourne le coin d'une mare, soit que je découvre un village, m'éloignant du soleil, je tourne mon visage vers cette lune large et pâle qu'on voit pendant le jour.

Ce fut au moment de sortir des graves oliviers, où je vis s'ouvrir devant moi la plaine radieuse jusqu'aux barrières de la montagne, que le mot d'introduction me fut communiqué. O derniers fruits d'une saison condamnée! dans cet achève-ment du jour, maturité suprême de l'année irrévocable. *C'en est fait.*

Les mains impatientes de l'hiver ne viendront point dépouiller la terre avec barbarie. Point de vents qui arrachent, point de coupantes gelées, point d'eaux qui noient. Mais plus tendrement qu'en mai, ou lorsque l'insatiable juin adhère à la source de la vie dans la possession de la douzième heure, le Ciel sourit à la Terre avec un ineffable amour. Voici, comme un cœur qui cède à un conseil continuel, le consentement; le grain se sépare de l'épi, le fruit quitte l'arbre, la Terre fait petit à petit délaissement à l'invincible, solliciteur de tout, la mort desserre une main trop pleine! Cette parole qu'elle entend maintenant est plus sainte que celle du jour de ses noces, plus profonde, plus tendre, plus riche: *C'en est fait!* L'oiseau dort, l'arbre s'endort dans l'ombre qui l'atteint, le soleil au niveau du sol le couvre d'un rayon égal, le jour est fini, l'année est consommée. A la céleste interrogation cette réponse amoureusement *C'en est fait* est répondue.

French ambassador to Tokyo, Washington, and Brussels, becoming a famous target of the Surrealists because of his diplomatic roles and religious beliefs. He later became one of the leading figures in French-Catholic literature, concentrating on biblical exegesis, especially of the Old Testament. Principal works: *Cinq grandes odes*, 1910; *La Cantate à trois voix*, 1912; *L'Oiseau noir dans le soleil levant*, 1927; *Cent phrases pour éventails*, 1927.

October

In vain do I see that the trees are still green.

Whether the year is shrouded in a funereal haze or hidden under a long calm sky, we are not one day less close to its fatal solstice. The sun does not disappoint me, or the vast opulence of the landscape, but there is something too calm, a rest from which there is no awakening. The cricket has no sooner begun to chirp than it stops for fear of being superfluous in the midst of this plenty that alone takes away our right to speak; and it seems as though one can only go barefooted into the solemn fastnesses of these golden fields. No, the sky behind me no longer casts the same light over the huge harvest; and as the road leads me by the stacks, whether I go around a pool or come upon a village as I walk away from the sun, I turn towards the large pale moon you see by day.

It was just as I came out of the dark olive-trees and caught sight of the radiant plain open before me as far as the mountain barriers, that the initiatory word was given to me. Oh, the last fruit of a condemned season! At day's end, the supreme ripeness of the irrevocable year. *It is all over.*

Winter's impatient hands will not come and brutally strip the earth. No winds tear at her, no frosts cut her, no waters drown her. But more tenderly than May, or when a thirsty vine clings to the source of life in the thrall of noon, the sky smiles on the earth with an ineffable love. Here now, like a heart that yields to constant prompting, is the time of consent: the grain leaves the ear, the fruit leaves the tree, the earth little by little surrenders to the invincible claimant of all things, death unclenches a hand too full! The words she hears are holier now than those of her wedding day—deeper, richer, more bountiful: *It is all over.* The birds are sleeping; the tree falls to sleep in the lengthening shade; the sun grazes the earth, covering it with an even ray. The day is done, the year is at an end. A loving response is made to heaven's question: *It is all over.*

—JAMES LAWLER

Tristesse de l'eau

Il est une conception dans la joie, je le veux, il est une vision dans le rire. Mais ce mélange de béatitude et d'amertume que comporte l'acte de la création, pour que tu le comprennes, ami, à cette heure où s'ouvre une sombre saison, je t'expliquerai la tristesse de l'eau.

Du ciel choit ou de la paupière déborde une larme identique.

Ne pense point de ta mélancolie accuser la nuée, ni ce voile de l'averse obscure. Ferme les yeux, écoute! la pluie tombe.

Ni la monotonie de ce bruit assidu ne suffit à l'explication.

C'est l'ennui d'un deuil qui porte en lui-même sa cause, c'est l'embesognement de l'amour, c'est la peine dans le travail. Les cieux pleurent sur la terre qu'ils fécondent. Et ce n'est point surtout l'automne et la chute future du fruit dont elles nourrissent la graine qui tire ces larmes de la nue hivernale. La douleur est l'été et dans la fleur de la vie l'épanouissement de la mort.

Au moment que s'achève cette heure qui précède Midi, comme je descends dans ce vallon qu'emplit la rumeur de fontaines diverses, je m'arrête ravi par le chagrin. Que ces eaux sont copieuses! et si les larmes comme le sang ont en nous une source perpétuelle, l'oreille à ce chœur liquide de voix abondantes ou grêles, qu'il est rafraîchissant d'y assortir toutes les nuances de sa peine! Il n'est passion qui ne puisse vous emprunter ses larmes, fontaines! et bien qu'à la mienne suffise l'éclat de cette goutte unique qui de très haut dans la vasque s'abat sur l'image de la lune, je n'aurai pas en vain pour maints après-midi appris à connaître ta retraite, val chagrin.

Me voici dans la plaine. Au seuil de cette cabane où, dans l'obscurité intérieure, luit le cierge allumé pour quelque fête rustique, un homme assis tient dans sa main une cymbale poussiéreuse. Il pleut immensément; et j'entends seul, au milieu de la solitude mouillée, un cri d'oie.

———————————

The Sadness of Water

There is a source of invention in joy, I agree, of vision in laughter. But, so that you understand the mixture of blessedness and bitterness in the act of creation, I will explain to you, my friend, at a time when the sombre season begins, the sadness of water.

From the sky and the eyelid wells up an identical tear.

Do not think of imputing your melancholy to the clouds or to this veil of the dark shower. Shut your eyes, listen! The rain is falling.

And it is not the monotony of this unvarying noise that is sufficient to explain it.

It is the weariness of a grief whose cause is in itself, the travail of love, the hard toil of work. The skies weep over the earth they make fertile. And it is not, above all, autumn and the approaching fall of fruit whose seed they nourish that draws these tears from the wintry clouds. The pain is in summer itself, and death's bloom on the flower of life.

Just when the hour before noon is coming to an end, as I go down into the valley full of the murmur of various fountains, I pause, enchanted by the chagrin. How plentiful are these waters! And if tears, like blood, are a constant well-spring within us, how fresh it is to listen to this liquid choir of voices rich and frail, and to match them with all the shades of our grief! There is no passion that can fail to lend you its tears, O fountains! And although I am content with the impact of a single drop falling into the basin from high above on the image of the moon, I will not in vain have learnt to know your haven over many afternoons, vale of sorrow.

Now, once more, I am in the plain. On the threshold of this hut where a candle is lit in the inner darkness for some rustic feast, a man is sitting with a dusty cymbal in his hand. The rain is pouring down; and alone, in the midst of the wet solitude, I hear the squawk of a goose.

—JAMES LAWLER

Jeune fille endormie

Rendez-vous derrière l'arbre à songes;
Encore faut-il savoir auquel aller.
Souvent on embrouille les anges,
Victimes du mancenillier.

Nous qui savons ce que ce geste attire:
Quitter le bal et les buveurs de vin,
A bonne distance des tirs
Nous ne dormirons pas en vain.

Dormons sous un prétexte quelconque
Par exemple: voler en rêve;
Et mettons-nous en forme de quinconce
Pour surprendre les rendez-vous.

Jean Cocteau 1889–1963
MAISONS-LAFITTE (FRANCE)

Cocteau was an accomplished artist in many fields; his poetry, fiction, film, ballet, opera, and painting have entertained international audiences for decades. He prized poetry above all other art forms and used it across media to explore the origin of artistic inspiration, to navigate between reality and dreams, and to juxtapose symbolic images with narrative form. He was known as the "Frivolous Prince," after his novel of the same title, because of his provocative wardrobe. Cocteau was born to a wealthy family. His father committed suicide when he was nine, an event that would later profoundly influence him. He counted among his friends Picasso, Erik Satie, Marcel Proust, and Sergey Diaghilev and was for years closely associated with the actor Jean Marais, who starred in many of his creations. Principal works: *Plain chant,* 1923; *Les Enfants terribles,* 1929; *Le Sang d'un poète,* 1930; *Les Parents terribles,* 1938; *La Belle et la bête,* 1946; *Poèmes,* 1948; *La Partie d'échecs,* 1961; *Faire part,* 1968.

Young Girl Sleeping

Beneath the Tree of Vision's where we'll meet.
Make sure, though, that you locate the right one.
We often mix our angels up and then get stuck
With casualties done in by a manchineel.

Oh, we know already what will be said:
Ducking out early from the ball, the revel,
Beyond the range of people's wine-soaked barbs,
Not for nothing shall we have gone to bed.

Best cook up some excuse for toddling off—
Like, say, *We've booked the night flight on Air Dream.*
That, or, *We're going to change into a Persian
Garden, so we can spy on lovers' trysts.*

C'est le sommeil qui fait ta poésie
Jeune fille avec un seul bras paresseux;
Déjà le rêve à grand spectacle t'a saisie
Et plus rien d'autre ne t'intéresse.

———————————

Une odeur nocturne . . .

Une odeur nocturne, indéfinissable et qui m'apporte un doute obscur, exquis et tendre, entre par la fenêtre ouverte dans la chambre où je travaille.

Mon chat guette la nuit, tout droit, comme une cruche . . . Un trésor au regard subtil me surveille par ses yeux verts . . .

La lampe fait son chant léger, doux comme on l'entend dans les coquillages. Elle étend ses mains qui apaisent. J'entends les litanies, les chœurs et les répons des mouches dans son auréole. Elle éclaire les fleurs au bord de la terrasse. Les plus proches s'avancent timidement pour me voir, comme une troupe de nains qui découvre un ogre . . .

Sleep's the sum total of your poetry,
Young Ms., you with your lazy, dangling arm.
Dreamland's big set piece has taken you hostage.
And other options? Yawn, you couldn't care less.

—ALFRED CORN

Léon-Paul Fargue 1876–1947
PARIS, FRANCE

A poet, anecdotalist, and literary journalist, Fargue was initially very much influenced by the Symbolists, particularly Stéphane Mallarmé, whose "Tuesdays" he attended. He quickly moved to adopt a unique style, however, recording his own conversations. His vivid descriptions of Parisian streets, bars, and train stations by day and night led him to call himself the "Paris stroller." He was a fellow student with Alfred Jarry and a close friend of André Gide, Erik Satie, and Paul Valéry. In 1923 Fargue founded the review *Commerce* with Valéry and Philippe Larbaud. Principal works: *Nocturnes,* 1905; *Pour la musique,* 1912; *Banalité,* 1928; *Espaces,* 1929; *Sous la lampe,* 1929; *Les Ludions,* 1930.

A Fragrance of Night . . .

A fragrance of night, not to be defined, that brings on an obscure doubt, exquisite, tender, comes by the open window into the room where I am at work . . .

My cat watches the darkness, as rigid as a jug. A fortune of subtle seeing looks at me through its green eyes . . .

The lamp sings its slight song quietly, subdued as the song one hears in a shell. The lamp reaches out its placating hands. In its aureole, I hear the litanies, the choruses and the responses of flies. It lights up the flowers at the edge of the terrace. The nearest ones come forward timidly to see me, like a troop of dwarfs that discover an ogre . . .

Le petit violon d'un moustique s'obstine. On croirait qu'un soliste joue dans une maison très lointaine . . . Des insectes tombent d'une chute oblique et vibrent doucement, sur la table. Un papillon blond comme un fétu de paille se traine dans la petite vallée de mon livre . . .

Une horloge pleure. Des souvenirs dansent une ronde enfantine . . .

Le chat se fend à fond. Son nez dessine en l'air quelque vol invisible . . . Une mouche a posé ses ciseaux dans la lampe . . .

Des bruits de cuisine s'entassent dans une arrière-cour. Des voix contradictoires jouent à pigeon-vole. Une voiture démarre. Un train crie dans la gare prochaine. Une plainte lointaine et longue s'élève . . .

Et je pense à quelqu'un que j'aime, et qui est si petit d'être si loin, peut-être, par-delà des pays noirs, par-delà des eaux profondes. Et à son regard qui m'est invisible . . .

The minute violin of a mosquito goes on and on. One could believe that a person was playing alone in a house at a remote distance . . . Insects fall with a sidewise fall and writhe gently on the table. A butterfly yellow as a wisp of straw drags itself along the little yellow valley that is my book . . .

A big clock outdoors intones drearily. Memories take motion like children dancing in a ring . . .

The cat stretches itself to the uttermost. Its nose traces in the air an imperceptible evolution. A fly fastens its scissors in the lamp . . .

Kitchen clatter mounts in a back-yard. Argumentative voices play at pigeon-vole. A carriage starts up and away. A train chugs at the next station. A long whistle rises far-off . . .

I think of someone whom I love, who is so little to be so separated, perhaps beyond the lands covered by the night, beyond the profundities of water. I am able to engage her glance . . .

—WALLACE STEVENS

Max Jacob 1876–1944
QUIMPER, FRANCE

Jacob was a painter and poet, a writer and critic, and a leading figure in Cubism and in the literary group surrounding Apollinaire. His dream-inspired work forged a link between Symbolism and Surrealism. Born to a middle-class Jewish family in the Breton town of Quimper, he worked at a variety of jobs before devoting himself to writing, which led to friendships with Picasso, Cocteau, and other creative giants of the period. In 1909 he purportedly saw a vision of Christ and six years later converted to Catholicism, choosing Picasso as his godfather. His conversion, however, did not prevent him from being arrested by the Gestapo in 1944 while attending mass at Saint-Benoît-sur-Loire, the abbey to which he had definitively retired. Jacob died of pneumonia at Drancy shortly after being detained. Principal works: *La Côte: Chants bretons,* 1911; *Les Oeuvres burlesques et mystiques de Frère Matorel,* 1912; *Le Cornet à dés,* 1917; *La Défense de*

La Rue Ravignan

«On ne se baigne pas deux fois dans le même fleuve», disait le philosophe Héraclite. Pourtant, ce sont toujours les mêmes qui remontent! Aux mêmes heures, ils passent gais ou tristes. Vous tous, passants de la rue Ravignan, je vous ai donné les noms des défunts de l'Histoire! Voici Agamemnon! voici Mme Hanska! Ulysse est un laitier! Patrocle est au bas de la rue qu'un Pharaon est près de moi. Castor et Pollux sont les dames du cinquième. Mais toi, vieux chiffonnier, toi, qui, au féerique matin, viens enlever les débris encore vivants quand j'éteins ma bonne grosse lampe, toi que je ne connais pas, mystérieux et pauvre chiffonnier, toi, chiffonnier, je t'ai nommé d'un nom célèbre et noble, je t'ai nommé Dostoïevsky.

La Révélation

Je suis revenu de la Bibliothèque Nationale; j'ai déposé ma serviette; j'ai cherché mes pantoufles et quand j'ai relevé la tête, il y avait quelqu'un sur le mur! il y avait quelqu'un! il y avait quelqu'un sur la tapisserie rouge. Ma chair est tombée par terre! j'ai été déshabillé par la foudre! Oh! impérissable seconde! oh! vérité! vérité! larmes de la vérité! joie de la vérité! inoubliable vérité. Le Corps Céleste est sur le mur de la pauvre chambre! Pourquoi, Seigneur? Oh! pardonnez-moi! Il est dans un paysage, un paysage que j'ai dessiné jadis, mais Lui! quelle beauté! élégance et douceur! Ses épaules, sa démarche! Il a une robe de soie jaune et des parements bleus. Il se retourne et je vois cette face paisible et rayonnante. Six moines alors emportent dans la chambre un cadavre. Une femme, qui a des serpents autour des bras et des cheveux, est près de moi.

L'ANGE

Tu as vu Dieu, innocent! tu ne comprends pas ton bonheur.

MOI

Pleurer! pleurer! je suis une pauvre bête humaine.

L'ANGE

Le démon est parti! il reviendra.

MOI

Le démon! oui!

L'ANGE

Intelligence.

Tartufe, 1919; *Le Laboratoire central*, 1921; *Visions infernales*, 1924; *Les Penitents en maillots roses*, 1925; *Fond de peau*, 1927; *Sacrifice impérial*, 1929; *Rivage*, 1931; *Conseils à un jeune poète*, 1945; *Le Cornet à dés II*, 1955; *L'Homme de cristal*, 1967.

The Rue Ravignan

"One does not bathe twice in the same stream," said the philosopher Heraclitus. Yet it is always the same ones who mount the street! Always at the same time of day they pass by, happy or sad. All of you, passers-by of the Rue Ravignan, I have named you after the illustrious dead. There is Agamemnon! There is Madame Hanska! Ulysses is a milkman! When Patroclus appears at the end of the street a Pharaoh is beside me! Castor and Pollux are the ladies of the fifth floor. But thou, old ragpicker, who come in the enchanted morning to take away the still living rubbish as I am putting out my good big lamp, thou whom I know not, mysterious and impoverished ragpicker, I have given thee a celebrated and noble name, I have named thee Dostoievsky.

—JOHN ASHBERY

The Revelation

I came back from the National Library; I put down my briefcase; I hunted around for my slippers and when I looked up, there was someone on the wall; there was someone there! There was someone on the red wallpaper. My flesh fell away! I was stripped naked by a lightning-bolt! Imperishable moment! Truth, oh, truth! Truth with its tears and its joy! Never-to-be-forgotten truth! The Divine Body is on the wall of a shabby room. Why, Lord? Forgive me! He's in a landscape, a landscape I drew a long time ago, but how beautiful *He* is! How graceful and gentle! The way He bears himself, the way He walks! He wears a yellow silk robe and blue facings. He turns around and I can see that peaceful, radiant countenance. Six monks now come into the room carrying a dead body. Near me is a woman with snakes around her arms and hair.

THE ANGEL: Innocent fool! You have seen God! You do not realize how fortunate you are.

ME: Let me weep; oh, let me weep! I am just a poor human creature.

THE ANGEL: The Evil Spirit has gone. He will be back.

ME: The Evil Spirit! Yes, I see!

THE ANGEL: Understanding.

MOI

Tu ne sais pas le bien que tu me fais.

L'ANGE

Nous t'aimons, paysan. Consulte-toi!

MOI

Ravissement! Seigneur! Je comprends, ah! je comprends.

Visitation

Ma chambre est au fond d'une cour et derrière des boutiques, le n° 7 de la rue Ravignan! tu resteras la chapelle de mon souvenir éternel. J'ai pensé, étendu sur le sommier que quatre briques supportent; et le propriétaire a percé le toit de zinc pour augmenter la lumière. Qui frappe si matin?— Ouvrez! ouvrez la porte! ne vous habillez pas! — Seigneur! — La croix est lourde : je veux la déposer.— Comment entrera-t-elle? la porte est bien étroite. — Elle entrera par la fenêtre. — Mon Seigneur! chauffez-vous! il fait si froid. — Regarde la croix! — Oh! Seigneur! toute ma vie.

Mauvais caractère

J'aime trop l'univers pour vivre avec un seul être.

Comment m'entendre avec un humain sans l'offenser au nom de tous? Démon, je ne puis m'entendre avec Dieu; ange, avec le démon. Comment m'entendre avec toi si je ne m'entends pas avec moi-même? Où fuir si le ciel et l'enfer me sont aussi fermés que la terre?

Réunion

Danse solitaire sur les méandres du tapis rouge : on peut arriver à danser en marchant. Braque essaie de m'inviter et me paraît un écolier : à genoux devant le divan, j'explique : «Tu auras beau être riche tu ne pourras pas faire repriser convenablement tes chaussettes et tu essaieras toujours par manie, c'est une des difficultés de la vie. Une ouvrière reprise le linge et non les chaussettes, si elle les reprise, elle ne va jamais jusqu'au bout ou avec une laine d'une autre couleur.» Je conclus pour les enfants : «Il y a un bœuf dans la chambre, dans votre chambre.»

ME: You don't know what a comfort it is to have you near me.
THE ANGEL: We love you, man of no account. Think upon it.
ME: Oh, rapture! I understand, Lord; oh, yes, I understand!

—MOISHE BLACK AND MARIA GREEN

Visitation

My room is at the far end of a courtyard and behind some shops, at number 7 Ravignan Street. Room, house, you will always be the chapel of my undying remembrance! I lay there thinking, stretched out on the box-spring held up by four bricks; and the landlord made an opening in the zinc roof to let in more light. Who's knocking at my door so early in the morning?—Open up! Open the door! Don't get dressed!—It's you, Lord!—The cross is heavy: I want to set it down.—The door is very narrow; how will it get in?—It can come in through the window.—Warm yourself in here, Lord! It's so cold out!—Look at the cross!—My whole life long, Lord!

—MOISHE BLACK AND MARIA GREEN

Shady Soul

I am too fond of the universe to live with just one being.

How could I get along with a human and not offend him in the name of everyone? A demon, I can't get along with God; an angel, with the demon. How could I get along with you if I don't get along with myself? Where to escape, if the sky and hell are as closed to me as the earth?

—MARY ANN CAWS

Meeting

A solitary dance on the windings of the red carpet: you can manage to dance while walking. Braque tries to invite me, and looks to me like a schoolboy: kneeling in front of the sofa, I explain: "You may be rich but you won't ever have your socks mended correctly and you will always be crazy enough to try to, that's one of life's difficulties. A seamstress mends undergarments and not socks, if she mends them, she never finishes, or does it with a thread of another color." I wind up, for the children: "There's an ox in the bedroom, in your bedroom."

—MARY ANN CAWS

Un œuf

Le hasard fit casser un œuf dans le Paradis terrestre.
Adam depuis ce jour essayait de briser les cailloux qui ressemblaient à un œuf.

*   *   *

Ce n'est pas une pomme que tendit Ève à Adam. C'est une clé. Cette clé, je l'ai retrouvée : elle était bien rouillée, la pauvre.

*   *   *

J'ai vu les trois Parques comme on verrait ses fautes. Elles étaient dans les stalles de mon église : l'une assise à ma place et les autres debout. Elles sont vêtues de crêpe noir, l'une manie de grands ciseaux de tailleur, une autre des instruments, je crois, de boulanger (?). La troisième lançait en l'air des perles qu'un très grand chien jaune griffon essayait d'attraper au vol. Et moi qui souhaitais la mort hier, me voici transi de peur à l'idée des ciseaux et du fil de mes jours.

An Egg

Chance had an egg break in earthly Paradise.
From that day on, Adam kept trying to break apart the pebbles that looked like an egg.

* * *

It wasn't an apple that Eve held out to Adam. It was a key. I came across this key: it was quite rusty, poor thing.

* * *

I saw the three Fates the way you would see one's faults. They were in the stalls of my church: one seated in my place and the others standing. They were clothed in black crepe, one was handling large tailor's scissors, another some equipment—a baker's, I think (?). The third was tossing up into the air some pearls that a very large yellow terrier was trying to catch. And I who was hoping for death yesterday, here I am frozen with fear at the idea of the scissors and the thread of my days.

—MARY ANN CAWS

Pierre-Jean Jouve 1887–1976
ARRAS, FRANCE

Although Jouve would eventually become known as a novelist, his first passion was music. It was not until he met Mallarmé that he turned his talents toward literature. He was a believer in Unanism and its spirit of universal participation, which led him to volunteer at a military hospital during World War I. In 1924, Jouve suffered a psychological breakdown. With the benefit of psychoanalysis and the strength of his newfound faith in Christianity, he recovered. The latter enabled him to surmount his dark pessimism; the former led him to explore and write under what he called "the impulse of eros and death, knotted together." Principal works: *Artificiel*, 1909; *Les Aéroplanes*, 1911; *Présences*, 1912;

Lamentations au cerf

Sanglant comme la nuit, admirable en effroi, et sensible
        Sans bruit, tu meurs à notre approche.
Apparais sur le douloureux et le douteux
Si rapide impuissant de sperme et de sueur
Qu'ait été le chasseur; si coupable son
        Ombre et si faible l'amour
Qu'il avait! Apparais dans un corps
Pelage vrai et
        Chaud, toi qui passes la mort.
Oui toi dont les blessures
        Marquent les trous de notre vrai amour
A force de nos coups, apparais et reviens
Malgré l'amour, malgré que
        Crache la blessure.

De plus en plus femme

Oui féminine et grasse et vermeille
Je me suis vu sur le sommier écartelé
Pour recevoir l'hôte de pierre
Lèvres! celui que je suis et que je hais

J'étais cave et j'étais mouillée
De bonheurs montant plus laves que le lait
Que retiennent les étoiles de ma gorge
Et j'arrivais disais-je à cette mort exquise

Je me relevais fécondé.

Parler, 1913; *Vous êtes des hommes,* 1915; *Huit poèmes de la solitude,* 1918; *Heures, livre de la grâce,* 1920; *Tragiques,* 1923; *Prière,* 1924; *Les Mystérieuses Noces,* 1925; *Nouvelles noces,* 1926; *Le Paradis perdu,* 1929; *Noces,* 1931; *Sueur de sang,* 1933; *Ode au peuple,* 1939; *Gloire,* 1940; *Le Bois des pauvres,* 1943; *Lyrique,* 1956; *Inventions,* 1958; *Ténèbre,* 1965.

Lament for the Stag

Bloody like night, splendid in terror, highstrung,
          Whimperless you die at our approach.
Come forth now above pain and perplexity.
However hasty, made impotent by sperm and sweat the
Hunter may have been, however culpable his
          Shadow and feeble the love
He held! Come forth corporeal
Fur genuine and
          Warm, crossing your death.
You whose wounds
          Mark the craters of our true love's
Demolition— return, come forth again
In spite of love, despite how your wound
          Spits.

—KEITH WALDROP

More and More Woman

Yes feminine and fat and scarlet
I saw myself spread on the mattress
To receive the stone guest
Lips! The one I am and hate

I was hollow and I was wet
With rising joy more lava than milk
Retaining the stars of my breast
And I reached I said this exquisite death

Fecund I stood up once more.

—MARY ANN CAWS

Après le déluge

La lune diminue, divin septembre.
Les montagnes sont apaisées dans leur lumière,
L'ombre plus tôt fait ombre et l'or se repose
Subtilement dans le vert. Toute chaleur
Est morte hier comme une muraille était noire
Que dissipa la nuit avec étoiles claires,
Avec vent et silence déjà, pensée de la mort.

———————————

After the Deluge

The moon is waning, September sublime.
The mountains lie stilled in their light
Shadows are quicker to darken and subtle golds
Repose within the green. Yesterday
The final warmth died out as a wall of darkness
That night dispelled with the clarity of stars,
With winds and ready silence, a presentiment of death.

—LEE FAHNESTOCK

Valery Larbaud 1881–1957

VICHY, FRANCE

A poet, essayist, novelist, translator, and world traveler—thanks to his personal fortune—Larbaud aspired to be a man of letters from an early age. He spoke six languages and was responsible for introducing many previously unknown foreign works to the French public. Larbaud's first written work was a translation of Coleridge's *The Rime of the Ancient Mariner.* He went on to do first translations of works by Joseph Conrad, Thomas Hardy, Samuel Butler, and Walt Whitman. He also translated James Joyce's *Ulysses.* His own work often took Europe as its subject, and he was most noted for his creation of the character A. O. Barnabooth, to whom several of his works were attributed. He helped found Sylvia Beach's bookstore, Shakespeare and Company, and in 1952 was awarded the Prix National des Lettres. Principal works: *Les Portiques,* 1896; *Poèmes par un riche amateur, ou œuvres françaises de M. Barnabooth,* 1908; reprinted in *A. O. Barnabooth, ses œuvres complètes,* 1913.

Ode

Prête-moi ton grand bruit, ta grande allure si douce,
Ton glissement nocturne à travers l'Europe illuminée,
Ô train de luxe ! et l'angoissante musique
Qui bruit le long de tes couloirs de cuir doré,
Tandis que derrière les portes laquées, aux loquets de cuivre lourd,
Dorment les millionnaires.
Je parcours en chantonnant tes couloirs
Et je suis ta course vers Vienne et Budapesth,
Mêlant ma voix à tes cent mille voix,
Ô Harmonika-Zug !

J'ai senti pour la première fois toute la douceur de vivre,
Dans une cabine du Nord-Express, entre Wirballen et Pskow.
On glissait à travers des prairies où des bergers,
Au pied de groupes de grands arbres pareils à des collines,
Étaient vêtus de peaux de moutons crues et sales . . .
(Huit heures du matin en automne, et la belle cantatrice
Aux yeux violets chantait dans la cabine à côté.)
Et vous, grandes places à travers lesquelles j'ai vu passer la Sibérie et les monts
    du Samnium,
La Castille âpre et sans fleurs, et la mer de Marmara sous une pluie tiède !

Prêtez-moi, ô Orient-Express, Sud-Brenner-Bahn, prêtez-moi
Vos miraculeux bruits sourds et
Vos vibrantes voix de chanterelle ;
Prêtez-moi la respiration légère et facile
Des locomotives hautes et minces, aux mouvements
Si aisés, les locomotives des rapides,
Précédant sans effort quatre wagons jaunes à lettres d'or
Dans les solitudes montagnardes de la Serbie,
Et, plus loin, à travers la Bulgarie pleine de roses . . .

Ah ! il faut que ces bruits et que ce mouvement
Entrent dans mes poèmes et disent
Pour moi ma vie indicible, ma vie
D'enfant qui ne veut rien savoir, sinon
Espérer éternellement des choses vagues.

Ode

Lend me your great sound, your fine smooth speed,
Slipping at night through all the lights of Europe,
O elegant train! and the heartrending music
Resounding the length of your gilt leather corridors,
While behind the laquered doors with their latches of brass,
The millionaires are asleep.
I move through your corridors humming,
With you on your race toward Vienna and Budapest,
My voice mingling with your hundred thousand voices,
O Harmonika-Zug!

For the first time I felt the sweetness of living,
In a compartment of the North-Express between Wirballen and Pskow,
Slipping through meadows where shepherds,
At the foot of tall trees in clusters, like hills,
Were dressed in sheepskins rough and gray . . .
(A fall morning at eight, and a lovely singer
with violet eyes, sang in the next compartment.)
And you, great squares through which I saw Siberia passing and the Samnium
    heights,
Harsh unflowering Castille and the sea of Marmara under a warm rain!

Lend me, O Orient Express, Sud-Brenner-Bahn, lend me
Your miraculous muffled sounds and
Your vibrant chanterelle voices;
Lend me the light free breathing
Of the high, slim locomotives, their easy
Motions, the effortless locomotives
Drawing four yellow cars with golden letters
Through Serbian mountain solitudes,
And, further, across Bulgaria full of roses . . .

Ah! these sounds and this movement
Must enter my poems and speak
My unsayable life, my life of a child
Who wants to know nothing, just
Hopes eternally for vague things.

—MARY ANN CAWS AND PATRICIA TERRY

Le Don de soi-même

Je m'offre à chacun comme sa récompense ;
Je vous la donne même avant que vous l'ayez méritée.

Il y a quelque chose en moi,
Au fond de moi, au centre de moi,
Quelque chose d'infiniment aride
Comme le sommet des plus hautes montagnes ;
Quelque chose de comparable au point mort de la rétine,
Et sans écho,
Et qui pourtant voit et entend ;
Un être ayant une vie propre, et qui, cependant,
Vit toute ma vie, et écoute, impassible,
Tous les bavardages de ma conscience.

Un être fait de néant, si c'est possible,
Insensible à mes souffrances physiques,
Qui ne pleure pas quand je pleure,
Qui ne rit pas quand je ris,
Qui ne rougit pas quand je commets une action honteuse,
Et qui ne gémit pas quand mon cœur est blessé ;
Qui se tient immobile et ne donne pas de conseils,
Mais semble dire éternellement :
« Je suis là, indifférent à tout. »

C'est peut-être du vide comme est le vide,
Mais si grand que le Bien et le Mal ensemble
Ne le remplissent pas.
La haine y meurt d'asphyxie,
Et le plus grand amour n'y pénètre jamais.

Prenez donc tout de moi : le sens de ces poèmes,
Non ce qu'on lit, mais ce qui paraît au travers malgré moi :
Prenez, prenez, vous n'avez rien.
Et où que j'aille, dans l'univers entier,
Je rencontre toujours,
Hors de moi comme en moi,
L'irremplissable Vide,
L'inconquérable Rien.

The Gift of Oneself

I offer myself to everyone as a reward,
Even before you've deserved it.

There is something in me,
In the depths, in the center of me,
Something infinitely arid
Like the top of the highest mountains,
Something like the eye's blind spot,
And without echo,
But which sees and hears;
A being with its own life, who yet
Lives all my life, and listens, impassive,
To the chattering of my conscience.

A being made of nothing, if that can be,
Insensitive to the body's pain,
Not weeping when I weep,
Not laughing when I laugh,
Not blushing when I act in shame,
Not moaning when my heart is stricken;
Unmoving, not giving advice,
Seeming endlessly to say,
"Here I am, caring for nothing."

It's perhaps empty, as is emptiness,
But so vast that good and bad together
Don't fill it up.
In it hatred dies for lack of air,
And the greatest love cannot come in.

So take everything I am: the meaning of these poems,
Not what you read, but what shows through despite me;
Don't refuse, you have nothing
And wherever I go, in the whole universe,
I always meet,
Outside myself as in myself,
Emptiness that can't be filled,
Nothingness that can't be won.

—MARY ANN CAWS AND PATRICIA TERRY

Chanson

Il naissait un poulain sous les feuilles de bronze. Un homme mit des baies amères dans nos mains. Étranger. Qui passait. Et voici qu'il est bruit d'autres provinces à mon gré . . . «Je vous salue, ma fille, sous le plus grand des arbres de l'année.»

*   *   *

Car le Soleil entre au Lion et l'Étranger a mis son doigt dans la bouche des morts. Étranger. Qui riait. Et nous parle d'une herbe. Ah! tant de souffles aux provinces! Qu'il est d'aisance dans nos voies! que la trompette m'est délice et la plume savante au scandale de l'aile! . . . «Mon âme, grande fille, vous aviez vos façons qui ne sont pas les nôtres.»

*   *   *

Il naquit un poulain sous les feuilles de bronze. Un homme mit ces baies amères dans nos mains. Étranger. Qui passait. Et voici d'un grand bruit dans un arbre de bronze. Bitume et roses, don du chant! Tonnerre et flûtes dans les chambres! Ah! tant d'aisance dans nos voies, ah! tant d'histoires à l'année, et

Saint-John Perse

(Alexis Saint-Léger Léger) 1887–1975

GUADELOUPE

Both a poet and a politician, Perse used the pseudonym Saint-John Perse
to keep his careers separate. Recognized by his literary peers for a small
but respected body of published work, he eventually won the Nobel
Prize in Literature (1960). It has been suggested that his interest in the symbolic
and the personal had its origin in his Caribbean upbringing. Perse did not begin
to write poetry until the sudden death of his father in 1907. After five years in
China as a diplomat, he became secretary general at the quai d'Orsay. When
France was invaded, he refused to act as a collaborator in his post as foreign
secretary and in 1940 settled in the United States, where he served at the Library
of Congress as a consultant in French poetry. Principal works: *Éloges,* 1911; *Amitié
du prince,* 1924; *Exil,* 1942; *Neiges,* 1944; *Pluies,* 1944; *Vents,* 1946; *Amers,* 1957;
Chroniques, 1960; *Oiseaux,* 1962; *Chant pour un équinoxe,* 1975.

Song

Under the bronze leaves a colt was foaled. Came such an one who laid bitter
bay in our hands. Stranger. Who passed. Here comes news of other provinces
to my liking.—"Hail, daughter! under the most considerable of the trees of
the year."

*   *   *

For the Sun enters the sign of the Lion and the Stranger has laid his finger on
the mouth of the Dead. Stranger. Who laughed. And tells us of an herb. O from
the provinces blow many winds. What ease to our ways, and how the trumpet
rejoices my heart and the feather adept of the scandal of the wing! "My Soul,
great girl, you had your ways which are not ours."

*   *   *

Under the bronze leaves a colt had been foaled. Came such an one who laid
this bitter bay in our hands. Stranger. Who passed. Out of the bronze tree comes
a great bruit of voices. Roses and bitumen, gift of song, thunder and fluting in the
rooms. O what ease in our ways, how many gestes to the year, and by the roads of

l'Étranger à ses façons par les chemins de toute la terre! . . . «Je vous salue, ma fille, sous la plus belle robe de l'année.»

Chanson

Mon cheval arrêté sous l'arbre plein de tourterelles, je siffle un sifflement si pur, qu'il n'est promesses à leurs rives que tiennent tous ces fleuves. (Feuilles vivantes au matin sont à l'image de la gloire) . . .

*   *   *

Et ce n'est point qu'un homme ne soit triste, mais se levant avant le jour et se tenant avec prudence dans le commerce d'un vieil arbre, appuyé du menton à la dernière étoile, il voit au fond du ciel à jeun de grandes choses pures qui tournent au plaisir . . .

*   *   *

Mon cheval arrêté sous l'arbre qui roucoule, je siffle un sifflement plus pur . . . Et paix à ceux, s'ils vont mourir, qui n'ont point vu ce jour. Mais de mon frère le poète on a eu des nouvelles. Il a écrit encore une chose très douce. Et quelques-uns en eurent connaissance . . .

Nocturne

Les voici mûrs, ces fruits d'un ombrageux destin. De notre songe issus, de notre sang nourris, et qui hantaient la pourpre de nos nuits, ils sont les fruits du long souci, ils sont les fruits du long désir, ils furent nos plus secrets complices et, souvent proches de l'aveu, nous tiraient à leurs fins hors de l'abîme de nos nuits . . . Au feu du jour toute faveur! les voici mûrs et sous la pourpre, ces fruits d'un impérieux destin. Nous n'y trouvons point notre gré.

Soleil de l'être, trahison! Où fut la fraude, où fut l'offense? où fut la faute et fut la tare, et l'erreur quelle est-elle? Reprendrons-nous le thème à sa naissance? revivrons-nous la fièvre et le tourment? . . . Majesté de la rose, nous ne sommes point de tes fervents: à plus amer va notre sang, à plus sévère vont nos soins, nos routes sont peu sûres, et la nuit est profonde où s'arrachent nos dieux. Roses canines et ronces noires peuplent pour nous les rives du naufrage.

Les voici mûrissants, ces fruits d'une autre rive. «Soleil de l'être, couvre-moi!»—parole du transfuge. Et ceux qui l'auront vu passer diront: qui fut cet

all the earth the Stranger to his ways . . . "Hail, daughter! robed in the loveliest robe of the year."

—T. S. ELIOT

Song

I have halted my horse by the tree of the doves, I whistle a note so sweet, shall the rivers break faith with their banks? (Living leaves in the morning fashioned in glory) . . .

* * *

And not that a man be not sad, but arising before day and biding circumspectly in the communion of an old tree, leaning his chin on the last fading star, he beholds at the end of the fasting sky great things and pure that unfold to delight. . . .

* * *

I have halted my horse by the dove-moaning tree, I whistle a note more sweet. . . . Peace to the dying who have not seen this day! But tidings there are of my brother the poet: once more he has written a song of great sweetness. And some there are who have knowledge thereof. . . .

—T. S. ELIOT

Nocturne

Now! they are ripe, these fruits of a jealous fate. From our dream grown, on our blood fed, and haunting the purple of our nights, they are the fruits of long concern, they are the fruits of long desire, they were our most secret accomplices and, often verging upon avowal, drew us to their ends out of the abyss of our nights. . . . Praise to the first dawn, now they are ripe and beneath the purple, these fruits of an imperious fate.—We do not find our liking here.

Sun of being, betrayal! Where was the fraud, where was the offense? where was the fault and where the flaw, and the error, which is the error? Shall we trace the theme back to its birth? shall we relive the fever and the torment? . . . Majesty of the rose, we are not among your adepts: our blood goes to what is bitterer, our care to what is more severe, our roads are uncertain, and deep is the night out of which our gods are torn. Dog roses and black briars populate for us the shores of shipwreck.

Now they are ripening, these fruits of another shore. "Sun of being, shield me!"—turncoat's words. And those who have seen him pass will say: who was

homme, et quelle, sa demeure? Allait-il seul au feu du jour montrer la pourpre de ses nuits? . . . Soleil de l'être, Prince et Maître! nos œuvres sont éparses, nos tâches sans honneur et nos blés sans moisson: la lieuse de gerbes attend au bas du soir.— Les voici teints de notre sang, ces fruits d'un orageux destin.

À son pas de lieuse de gerbes s'en va la vie sans haine ni rançon.

Ses grosses cuisses

Ses grosses cuisses
Ses seins
Ses hanches
Ses fesses
Ses bras

that man, and which his home? Did he go alone at dawn to show the purple of his nights? . . . Sun of being, Prince and Master! our works are scattered, our tasks without honor and our grain without harvest: the binder of sheaves awaits, at the evening's ebb.—Behold, they are dyed with our blood, these fruits of a stormy fate.

At the gait of a binder of sheaves life goes, without hatred or ransom.
—RICHARD HOWARD

Pablo Picasso 1881–1973

MÁLAGA, SPAIN

A cofounder of Cubism, along with Braque, Picasso was one of the great geniuses of the twentieth century, experimenting and excelling in virtually every artistic mode. A child prodigy, he was ably abetted in his early work by his father, an art teacher himself. Picasso frequented cafés in Barcelona before moving to Paris, where he was influenced by the work of Manet, Courbet, Toulouse-Lautrec, and, most profoundly, Matisse. For each of his many lovers, famously including Dora Maar and Françoise Gilot, he modified his painting style in order to best express his love. Under the impulse of his friendship with André Breton, he wrote reams of "automatic poems" and Surrealist plays, among which the most famous is *Le Désir attrapé par la queue*. Among his most renowned paintings are *Les Demoiselles d'Avignon* (1907) and *Guernica* (1937).

Her Great Thighs

Her great thighs
Her breasts
Her hips
Her buttocks
Her arms

Ses mollets
Ses mains
Ses yeux
Ses joues
Ses cheveux
Son nez
Sa gorge
Ses larmes

les planètes les larges rideaux tirés et le ciel transparent caché derrière le
    grillage—
les lampes à l'huile et les grelots des canaris sucre entre les figues—
le bol de lait des plumes arrachés à chaque rire déshabillant le nu du poids des
    armes
enlevées aux fleurs du potager

tant de jeux morts pendus aux branches du préau de l'école irisées des chansons
lac leurre de sang et d'orties
roses trémières jouées aux dés
aiguilles d'ombre liquide et bouquets d'algues de cristal
ouvertes aux pas de danse des mouvantes couleurs
agités aux fond du verre versé
au mas que lilas vêtue de pluie

Her calves
Her hands
Her eyes
Her cheeks
Her hair
Her nose
Her throat
Her tears

the planets the wide curtain drawn and the transparent sky hidden behind the
    grill—
the oil lamp and the little bells of the canaries sweet between the figs—
the bowl of milk of feathers snatched from each laugh undressing
the nude removing the weight of the weapons taken from the garden flowers

so many games deadmen hanging from the branches of the schoolyard haloed
    with songs
lake the lure of blood and thistles
hollyhocks played in the dice
needles of liquid shadow and bouquet of crystal algae
open to the dance step of the moving colours
shaken in the bottom of the glass poured out
on the lilac mask dressed with rain

—MARY ANN CAWS

Catherine Pozzi 1882–1934
PARIS, FRANCE

Pozzi wrote metaphysical and love poems. Inspired by sixteenth-century Italian poets, she often expressed a desire to return to a period in which thought and feeling were melded, before the intervention of the seventeenth century and what T. S. Eliot called the "dissociation of sensibility." She is often remembered more for her affair with the poet Paul Valéry than for her own

Nyx

À Louise aussi de Lyon et d'Italie

Ô vous mes nuits, ô noires attendues
Ô pays fier, ô secrets obstinés
Ô longs regards, ô foudroyantes nues
Ô vol permis outre les cieux fermés.

Ô grand désir, ô surprise épandue
Ô beau parcours de l'esprit enchanté
Ô pire mal, ô grâce descendue
Ô porte ouverte où nul n'avait passé

Je ne sais pas pourquoi je meurs et noie
Avant d'entrer à l'éternel séjour.
Je ne sais pas de qui je suis la proie.
Je ne sais pas de qui je suis l'amour.

—————

work. Born to a wealthy Parisian family, Pozzi frequented the salons of the time. When she learned in 1910 that she had contracted tuberculosis, she threw herself into the study of philosophy, religion, math, and science, receiving her bachelor's degree in 1918. In 1920 Pozzi and Valéry broke off their relationship. As a result, she lost many of her former friends and contacts, which marked the beginning of a slow decline in her health. Principal works: *Agnès*, 1927; *Mesures*, 1935; *Oeuvres poétiques*, 1988.

Nyx

For Louise also from Lyon and Italy

Oh you my nights, oh dark awaited
Oh country proud, oh secrets lasting
Oh long gazing, oh thundering clouds
Oh flight allowed beyond closed skies.

Oh great desire, oh wide surprise
Oh lovely traverse of the enchanted mind
Oh worst of worst, oh grace descended
Oh opened door none had passed through

I don't know why I die and drown
Before I enter that eternal sojourn.
I don't know of what I am the prey.
I don't know of whom I am the love.

—MARY ANN CAWS

Dans les champs ou sur la colline

Non
                    Le personnage historique
Et là le soleil s'arrêtait
C'était un homme qui passait
                    Le cheval si maigre
                        Qu'aucune ombre ne poursuivait

La neige serait étonnante
                    Tout était blanc à quelques pas

Sur tous les animaux qui moururent de froid
                    Entre les arbres et la mer
L'eau clapotante
                        Le ciel amer
            Resté seul entre les paysans et la lune

Pierre Reverdy 1889–1960
NARBONNE, FRANCE

Reverdy, considered a Cubist poet, along with Apollinaire and Max Jacob, inspired the Surrealist movement and its leaders, in particular through his theory of the image as constituted by two elements from widely differing fields, forming a vitalizing explosion upon their meeting. He moved from his native Narbonne to Paris in 1910. In 1917 he founded the journal *Nord-Sud,* which attracted such contributors as Apollinaire, Jacob, Aragon, Breton, Soupault, and Tzara. Reverdy also wrote for the literary reviews *Littéra-ture* and *Sic.* In 1926 he moved with his wife to the abbey at Solesmes but frequently returned to Paris. His prose poems have had an extraordinary influence on poets from his time to ours. Principal works: *Poèmes en prose,* 1915; *La Lucarne ovale,* 1916; *Les Ardoises du toit,* 1918; *Les Jockeys camouflés,* 1918; *La Guitare endormie,* 1919; *Étoiles peintes,* 1921; *Les Épaves du ciel,* 1924; *Grande nature,* 1925; *La Balle au bond,* 1928; *Flaques de verre,* 1929; *Sources du vent,* 1929; *Pierres blanches,* 1930; *Ferraille,* 1937; *Plein verre,* 1940; *Le Chant des morts,* 1948; *Au soleil du plafond,* 1955; *La Liberté des mers,* 1959; *Sable mouvant,* 1966.

In the Fields or on the Hill

    No
        Historical figure
And there the sun was coming to a stop
It was a man passing by
        His horse so thin
        Not the slightest shadow followed

The snow would be enormous
        A few steps away and everything was white

Over all the animals who died of cold
    Between the trees and the sea
Quick lapping water
            The bitter sky
  Left alone between the peasants and the moon

Le soir qui descendait devait venir de loin
Lentement la chanson dépassait nos mémoires
                   Fallait-il sourire ou y croire
       On attendait
               On regardait
C'est à tout ce qui se passait ailleurs que l'on pensait

La Trame

    Une main, d'un mouvement rythmique
et sans pensée, jetait ses cinq doigts vers
le plafond où dansaient des ombres fantastiques.
    Une main détachée du bras, une main
libre, éclairée par la lueur du foyer qui
venait de plus bas—et cette tête innocente
et vide qui souriait à l'araignée activant
dans la nuit son chef-d'œuvre inutile.

Souffle

    Il neige sur mon toit et sur les arbres. Le mur et le jardin sont blancs, le sentier
noir et la maison s'est écroulée sans bruit. Il neige.

La Tête pleine de beauté

    Dans l'abîme doré, rouge, glacé, doré, l'abîme où gîte la douleur, les tour-
billons roulants entraînent les bouillons de mon sang dans les vases, dans les
retours de flammes de mon tronc. La tristesse moirée s'engloutit dans les cre-
vasses tendres du cœur. Il y a des accidents obscurs et compliqués, impossibles à
dire. Et il y a pourtant l'esprit de l'ordre, l'esprit régulier, l'esprit commun à tous
les désespoirs qui interroge. Ô toi qui traînes sur la vie, entre les buissons fleuris
et pleins d'épines de la vie, parmi les feuilles mortes, les reliefs de triomphes, les
appels sans secours, les balayures mordorées, la poudre sèche des espoirs, les
braises noircies de la gloire, et les coups de révolte, toi, qui ne voudrais plus
désormais aboutir nulle part. Toi, source intarissable de sang. Toi, désastre in-
tense de lueurs qu'aucun jet de source, qu'aucun glacier rafraîchissant ne tentera
jamais d'éteindre de sa sève. Toi, lumière. Toi, sinuosité de l'amour enseveli qui se
dérobe. Toi, parure des ciels cloués sur les poutres de l'infini. Plafond des idées
contradictoires. Vertigineuse pesée des forces ennemies. Chemins mêlés dans le
fracas des chevelures. Toi, douceur et haine—horizon ébréché, ligne pure de

The evening was coming down and from far away
Slowly the song was leaving our memories behind
     Were we supposed to smile or believe it
  We were waiting
      And watching
Everything happening elsewhere was in our minds.

            —PATRICIA TERRY

The Web

 A hand, with a rhythmic and thoughtless motion,
was throwing its five fingers up towards the ceiling
where fantastic shadows were dancing.
 A hand detached from its arm, a free hand,
illumined from below by the glow of the hearth—
and that innocent empty head smiling at the spider
setting forth in the night its useless masterpiece.

      —MARY ANN CAWS AND PATRICIA TERRY

Breath

 It is snowing on my roof and on the trees. The wall and the garden are white,
the path black, and the house has given way without a sound. It is snowing.

      —MARY ANN CAWS AND PATRICIA TERRY

The Head Filled with Beauty

 In the gilded abyss, crimson, frozen, gilded, the abyss where sorrow shelters, the twisting whirlwinds entice my boiling blood into the slime, into the tortuous flames of my trunk. Sadness in moiré pattern is swallowed up in the heart's tender crevasses. Obscure and complicated accidents take place, impossible to describe. And nevertheless the spirit of order, the even spirit, the spirit common to all despairs is questioning. Oh, as you walk through life, between the flowering and thorn-filled shrubs of life, among the dead leaves, the outlines of triumph, the helpless appeals, the bronze dust sweepings, the dry powder of hopes, the blackened embers of fame, and the revolt, you would never desire an end any-where, ever again. You, unquenchable source of blood. You, disaster intense with gleams which no surging spring, no cooling glacier will ever try to extinguish with its sap. You, light. You, sinuosity of buried love, hiding. You, ornament of heavens nailed upon the pilings of the infinite. Ceiling of contradictory ideas. Vertiginous balance of enemy forces. Paths confused in the fray of hair. You, gentleness and hatred—horizon chipped away, pure line of indifference and

l'indifférence et de l'oubli. Toi, ce matin, tout seul dans l'ordre, le calme et la révolution universelle. Toi, clou de diamant. Toi, pureté, pivot éblouissant du flux et du reflux de ma pensée dans les lignes du monde.

Plus lourd

On attendait que l'homme étendu en travers du chemin se réveillât. La courbe de la nuit s'arrêtait à la chaumière encore éclairée, au bord du pré, devant la forêt qui fermait ses portes. Toute la fraîcheur audedans. Les animaux n'étaient là que pour animer le paysage pendant que tout le reste marchait.

Car tout marchait, sauf les animaux, le paysage et moi, qui étais, avec cette statue, plus immobile que l'autre, là-haut, sur le piédestal des nuages.

Ça

Les quelques raies qui raccourcissent le mur sont des indications pour la police. Les arbres sont des têtes, ou les têtes des arbres, en tout cas les têtes des arbres me menacent.

Elles courent tout le long du mur et j'ai peur d'arriver à l'endroit où l'on ouvre la grille. Sur la route mon ombre me suit, oblique, et me dit que je cours trop vite. C'est moi qui ai l'air d'un voleur. Enfin, près du petit bois d'où sort le pavillon, je vais crier, je crie mais des pas tranquilles me rassurent. Et quelqu'un vient m'ouvrir. Par la porte j'aperçois des amis qui sont en train de rire.

Peut-être est-il question de moi?

. . . S'entre-bâille

Du triangle des trottoirs de la place partent tous les fils et la faux de l'arc-en-ciel, brisée derrière les nuages.

Au milieu celui qui attend, rouge, ne sachant où se mettre.

Tout le monde regarde et c'est au même endroit que le mur découvre sa blessure.

La main qui ferme le volet s'en va, la tête que coupe le rayon ne tombe pas—et il reste cette illusion qui attirait, au même instant, tous les regards vers ce drame qui se jouait, face au couchant, sur la fenêtre.

oblivion. You, this morning, totally alone in order, calm, and universal revolution. You, diamond nail. You, purity, dazzling swivel of the ebb and flow of my thought in the lines of the world.

—MARY ANN CAWS

Heavier

They waited for the man stretched out across the road to wake up. The curve of the night stopped at the thatched cottage which was still lit up, at the edge of the meadow, in front of the forest which was closing its gates. All the freshness inside. The animals were there only to enliven the landscape while all the rest walked.

For everything was walking, except the animals, the landscape and me, who with that statue, more immobile than the other one, was up there, on the pedestal of clouds.

—JOHN ASHBERY

That

The few stripes that foreshorten the wall are indications for the police. The trees are heads, or the heads trees, in any case the heads of the trees threaten me.

They run the whole length of the wall and I'm afraid of arriving at the place where the grating is opened. On the highway my shadow follows me, oblique, and tells me I'm running too fast. It's I who look like a thief. Finally, near the little wood from which the villa emerges, I'm going to yell, I do yell, but calm footsteps reassure me. And someone comes to let me in. Through the doorway I notice friends who are laughing.

Perhaps about me?

—JOHN ASHBERY

. . . Is Ajar

From the triangle of the sidewalks of the square all the wires start, and the scythe of the rainbow, broken behind the clouds.

In the center the one who waits, blushes, not knowing where to stand.

Everyone is looking and in that same place the wall reveals its wound.

The hand that closes the shutter disappears, the head cut by the ray doesn't fall—and there remains that illusion which at the same moment drew everyone's eyes toward the drama that was being enacted, opposite the sunset, against the window.

—JOHN ASHBERY

La Volière

Aigles ou roitelets, dispersés en étincelles ou rassemblés en candélabres, ces oiseaux dessinent leur vol précieux sur le velours du firmament.

Il semble qu'ils se sont allumés chacun, pour voir comme un œil.

Étoiles, ils battent de l'aile, planètes ils planent, virant tout autour d'un oblique perchoir sur quoi nul ne se pose, hormis la fauvette qui fait le pommeau fixement.

Étoiles ou planètes, les unes vont, les autres viennent à la manière d'un rondeau, toutes les rimes en bijoux.

On les croirait mécaniques parfois, un oiselier tournant la manivelle. Déjà faisan doré, la plus belle est partie — on la dit du berger — partie on ne sait où garder quelque troupeau de songes.

Par ci par là, ces poules médiocres picorent les perles tombées du tamis de la Lune, si nombreuses que çà finit par faire un chemin blanc.

Jamais le moindre heurt, chaque rythme à sa place toujours.

S'il advient un léger frottement, c'est comme pour une allumette folle, le

Saint-Pol Roux (Pierre-Paul Roux) 1861–1940
PROVENCE, FRANCE

D ubbed "the magnificent," "the divine one," and "the crucified one" by his fellow Symbolist poets, Roux preceded the Surrealists. His mysticism and his prolific and surprising images and metaphors became legendary. In 1886 he founded the journal *La Pléiade*. Seeking a life of solitude, at the end of the century he moved to the peninsula of Roscanvel, in Brittany, where his daughter, Divine, was born. There the so-called "Magus of Camaret" built a manor on the hill of Camaret, where he meditated on his grand project, *La Répoétique*. In 1925, the Surrealists held a banquet in his honor in Paris, which he fled in panic. In 1940, under the Occupation, the Nazis looted his home, destroying most of his manuscripts and badly injuring Roux and his daughter. He died four months later at his daughter's bedside. Principal works: *Les Reposoirs de la procession (La Rose et les épines du chemin; De la colombe au corbeau par le paon; Les Féeries intérieures)*, 1893; *La Dame à la faulx*, 1895; *Anciennetés*, 1903; *Le Tragique dans l'homme*, 1983, 1984.

The Aviary

Whether eagles or wrens, scattered in sparks or perched like candelabra, each species sketches on the firmament's velvet its unique flight.

It looks as if each single one has been lit up to see like an eye.

Stars flapping a wing, planets planing along, they hover over an angled perch without ever alighting.

No sooner has one star or planet vanished than in the manner of a round the next jewelled rhyme arrives.

It's almost mechanical, as if there were a birdseller about flicking switches. Already the prettiest golden pheasant has gone, gone like a shepherd to guard her dream flock.

Here and there a few paltry chickens are pecking away among the moon's debris of fallen pearls, pearls in such quantities that it eventually forms a white path.

Never any jerkiness, each rhythm always in place.

A bit of a flicker, like a crazed match, and phosphorescence in the guise

phosphore tombe en vol d'hirondelle parmi l'infini jusqu'à ce qu'il rencontre le vœu d'une vierge qui monte.

Vous ne voyez donc pas l'étoile de la crèche?

Elle est en vous, pardi!

Mais voici la belle, de nouveau sur le velours, en train de se passer une chemise d'aube.

Soudain le simple coq du voisinage lance un grand cri de clef rouillée dans la serrure.

Vénus n'a que le temps de se blottir dans un rosier, et comme, du bout du pauvre monde à l'autre bout, les moindres coqs agitent les charnières, la Volière s'ouvre finalement, en immense paupière, toute vide . . .

Plus de velours ni de bijoux, plus d'hirondelles ni de vœux, plus d'oiseaux rares ni de poules, plus de perchoir, plus de fauvettes en guise de pommeau, plus de chemin ni de rosier, plus de chemise ni de belle, plus rien — plus rien que dans sa gloire de saphir le haut Paon de la Vie qui fait la roue avec nos yeux!

Lever de soleil

À Eugène Pierre

La Joue splendide émerge des mousselines d'aubépine.

— Ô charitable épanoui, manifesté par uniment ceci de rose, te serai-je, au cours de ta ronde quotidienne, te serai-je par mon faire indigne ou par mon faire sage, te serai-je une caresse ou te serai-je le soufflet, soleil, et t'attarderas-tu devant mon signe ami de Josué charmant ou bien, Judas farouche, acculerai-je ta pudeur derrière les immeuses nénuphars du ciel jusqu'à l'heure de saigner sur les coquilles exileuses de la mer?

La Joue splendide émerge des mousselines d'aubépine.

---

of a swallow hurtles through the infinite only to encounter a virgin's rising vow.

You can't miss the manger star.

It's of course within you.

But here back on the velvet is beauty all involved with putting on her dawn blouse.

Suddenly the neighbourhood rooster lets forth with a great crow of a rusted key in a lock.

Venus has just slipped behind a rose bush when from one end of this wretched world to the other the roosters are all flinging open the shutters. Now at last the Aviary opens up, a vast utterly blank eyelid.

No more velvet or jewels, no more swallows or vows, no more rare birds or chickens, no perch, no white path or rose bush, no blouse or beauty, nothing at all—nothing but the great Peacock of Life in all his sapphire glory making a wheel out of our eyes.

—ROBIN MAGOWAN

Sunrise

To Eugène Pierre

The splendid Cheek emerges from the hawthorn muslins.

—Oh charitable full-blown, manifest so smoothly in this rosiness, shall I be to you, during your daily round, shall I be to you by my unworthy deeds or my wise ones, shall I be to you a caress or shall I be to you the bellows, sun, and will you linger before my sign as charming Joshua's friend or then, savage Judas, shall I drive back your modesty behind the immense waterlilies of the sky until it's time to bleed on the banished seashells?

The splendid Cheek emerges from the hawthorn muslins.

—MARY ANN CAWS

詔卜皇陵

Édit funéraire

Décider du tombeau impérial.

Moi l'Empereur ordonne ma sépulture : cette montagne hospitalière, le champ qu'elle entoure est heureux. Le vent et l'eau dans les veines de la terre et les plaines du vent sont propices ici. Ce tombeau agréable sera le mien.

* * *

Barrez donc la vallée entière d'une arche quintuple : tout ce qui passe est ennobli.

Étendez la longue allée honorifique : — des bêtes ; des monstres ; des hommes.

Levez là-bas le haut fort crénelé. Percez le trou solide au plein du mont.

Victor Segalen 1878–1919
BREST, FRANCE

Segalen was a traveler, poet, essayist, and novelist whose work has attracted increasing attention to this day. He attended medical school in Brest and went on to become a naval doctor; this led to a post in Tahiti, where he spent two years. Segalen arrived just three months after Gauguin's death and collected the painter's last works, using them for inspiration as he wrote his novel *Les Immémoriaux* (1907). During his time in French Polynesia he wrote on the influence of French missionaries and colonialism; he was one of the first in the West to take the viewpoint of the colonized. His curiosity also took him to China, which provided him with material for his poems. Segalen wrote essays on Rimbaud and Gauguin, and provided libretti for his friend Claude Debussy. Principal works: *Stèles*, 1912; *Peintures*, 1916; *Odes*, 1926; *Équipée*, 1929; *Thibet*, 1963; *Briques et tuiles*, 1967.

Funerary Edict

Testament divining the imperial tomb.

I, the Emperor, will have my burial place as I desire: this hospitable mountain, fortunate is the field that it surrounds. Here the wind and the water in the veins of the earth and the plains of the wind are propitious. This pleasant tomb shall be mine.

*   *   *

With a five-tiered arch close off the entire valley: ennobled will be whatever passes.

Extend the long ceremonial way: — animals, monsters, men.

There you shall place the lofty crenelated fortress. Carve in the depths of the mountain a hole without weakness.

Ma demeure est forte. J'y pénètre. M'y voici. Et refermez la porte, et maçonnez l'espace devant elle. Murez le chemin aux vivants.

* * *

Je suis sans désir de retour, sans regrets, sans hâte et sans haleine. Je n'étouffe pas. Je ne gémis point. Je règne avec douceur et mon palais noir est plaisant.

Certes la mort est plaisante et noble et douce. La mort est fort habitable. J'habite dans la mort et m'y complais.

* * *

Cependant, laissez vivre, là, ce petit village paysan. Je veux humer la fumée qu'ils allument dans le soir.

Et j'écouterai des paroles.

Par respect

Caractères omis par respect.

Par respect de l'indicible, nul ne devra plus divulguer le mot GLOIRE ni commettre le caractère BONHEUR.

Même qu'on les oublie de toutes les mémoires : tels sont les signes que le Prince a choisis pour dénommer son règne,

Qu'ils n'existent plus désormais.

* * *

Silence, le plus digne hommage! Quel tumulte d'amour emplit jamais le très profond silence?

Quel éclat de pinceau oserait donc le geste qu'elle ingénument dessine?

* * *

Non! que son règne en moi soit secret. Que jamais il ne m'advienne. Même que j'oublie : que jamais plus au plus profond de moi n'éclose désormais son nom,

Par respect.

My dwelling is strong. I make my way inside. Behold me there. And now close the door, and wall up the space before it. Bar the road to all the living.

* * *

I am without any wish to return, without regrets, without haste and without breath. I am not suffocating. I do not lament. I rule with gentleness and my dark palace is pleasing.

Indeed death is agreeable and noble and sweet. A place one can dwell in. I dwell in death and I am content there.

* * *

But let that little peasant village over there survive. I wish to savor the smoke from their evening fires.

And I shall listen to words.

—MARY ANN CAWS AND PATRICIA TERRY

Out of Respect

Characters omitted out of respect.

Out of respect for what cannot be said, no one is ever again to reveal the word GLORY or commit the character HAPPINESS.

Let them even be effaced from all memory: by these signs the Prince has chosen to identify his reign.

Let them no longer exist.

* * *

Silence, the worthiest homage! What fury of love ever filled the depths of silence?

What dazzling brushstroke would dare the gesture that she, in her innocence, imagines.

* * *

No! let her reign in me be secret. Let it never come to pass. Let it even be forgotten: let her name never flower within my deepest self,

Out of respect.

—MARY ANN CAWS AND PATRICIA TERRY

Éloge du Jade

C'est pourquoi le sage l'estimait.

Si le Sage, faisant peu de cas de l'albâtre, vénère le pur Jade onctueux, ce n'est point que l'albâtre soit commun et l'autre rare : Sachez plutôt que le Jade est bon,

Parce qu'il est doux au toucher—mais inflexible. Qu'il est prudent : ses veines sont fines, compactes et solides.

Qu'il est juste puisqu'il a des angles et ne blesse pas. Qu'il est plein d'urbanité quand, pendu de la ceinture, il se penche et touche terre.

Qu'il est musical : sa voix s'élève, prolongée jusqu'à la chute brève. Qu'il est sincère, car son éclat n'est pas voilé par ses défauts ni ses défauts par son éclat.

Comme la vertu, dans le Sage, n'a besoin d'aucune parure, le Jade seul peut décemment se présenter seul.

Son éloge est donc l'éloge même de la vertu.

Trahison fidèle

En quête d'un écho amical.

Tu as écrit : « Me voici, fidèle à l'écho de ta voix, taciturne, inexprimé. » Je sais ton âme tendue juste au gré des soies chantantes de mon luth :

C'est pour toi seul que je joue.

In Praise of Jade

guì   gù
zhī   jūn

For these reasons, wise men have esteemed it.   yě   zǐ

If the Sage, making light of alabaster, venerates the pure and unctuous Jade, it is not because alabaster is common and the other rare: Rather, know that Jade is good

Because it is smooth to the touch—but unyielding. And prudent: its veins are fine, compact, and solid.

And just, since it has angles but does not cut. And full of urbanity when, hung from a belt, it bends low and touches earth.

And musical, raising its voice, sustained until the sudden fall. And sincere, for its luster is not veiled by its faults nor its faults by its luster.

As virtue, in the Sage, needs no fine ornament, Jade alone can decently present itself alone.

To praise it is thus to praise virtue itself.

—TIMOTHY BILLINGS AND CHRISTOPHER BUSH

qíu

Faithful Betrayal

yǒu

In search of a friendly echo.   shēng

You wrote: "I am here, faithful to the echo of your voice: silent, unexpressed." I know your soul tuned just to accord with the singing silks of my lute:

It's only for you that I play.

Écoute en abandon et le son et l'ombre du son dans la conque de la mer où tout plonge. Ne dis pas qu'il se pourrait qu'un jour tu entendisses moins délicatement!

Ne le dis pas. Car j'affirme alors, détourné de toi, chercher ailleurs qu'en toi-même le répons révélé par toi. Et j'irai, criant aux quatre espaces :

Tu m'as entendu, tu m'as connu, je ne puis pas vivre dans le silence. Même auprès de cet autre que voici, c'est encore,

C'est pour toi seul que je joue.

Listen with abandon not just to the sound but the shadow of sound in the whorls of the sea where all things plunge. Don't say that one day you may hear less discerningly!

Don't say it. For I avow that, turned away from you, I seek somewhere beyond you the response revealed by you. And I will go, crying out to the four spaces:

You have heard me, you have known me, I cannot live in silence. Even in the company of this other beside me here, it's still,

It's only for you that I play.

—TIMOTHY BILLINGS AND CHRISTOPHER BUSH

Jules Supervielle 1884–1960
MONTEVIDEO, URUGUAY

A poet, playwright, and novelist, Supervielle did not claim a preference for either side in the battle between tradition and the quick-changing invention of his time; instead he remained part of both, a human example of *l'entre-deux,* or betweenness. He was born in Uruguay to French parents, but both disappeared after the family returned to France when he was just six months old. From an early age Supervielle used poetry to explore his sense of emptiness and loss, though he later turned to themes of coexistence and exchange in his poems, which are convincing and easily grasped. He counted Rainier Maria Rilke, André Gide, Henri Michaux, and Paul Valéry among his friends. Principal works: *Brumes du passé,* 1900; *Comme des voiliers,* 1910; *Paysages,* 1919; *Les Poèmes de l'humeur triste,* 1919; *Voyage en soi,* 1919; *Débarcadères,* 1922; *Gravitations,* 1925; *Saisir,* 1929; *Les Amis inconnus,* 1934; *La Fable du monde,* 1939; *Poèmes de la France malheureuse,* 1941; *Oublieuse mémoire,* 1949; *Le Corps tragique,* 1959.

Un poète

Je ne vais pas toujours seul au fond de moi-même
Et j'entraîne avec moi plus d'un être vivant.
Ceux qui seront entrés dans mes froides cavernes
Sont-ils sûrs d'en sortir, même pour un moment?
J'entasse dans ma nuit, comme un vaisseau qui sombre,
Pêle-mêle, les passagers et les marins,
Et j'éteins la lumière aux yeux, dans les cabines,
Je me fais des amis des grandes profondeurs.

Le Regret de la terre

Un jour, quand nous dirons: «C'était le temps du soleil,
Vous souvenez-vous, il éclairait la moindre ramille,
Et aussi bien la femme âgée que la jeune fille étonnée,
Il savait donner leur couleur aux objets dès qu'il se posait,
Il suivait le cheval coureur et s'arrêtait avec lui,
C'était le temps inoubliable où nous étions sur la Terre,
Où cela faisait du bruit de faire tomber quelque chose,
Nous regardions alentour avec nos yeux connaisseurs,
Nos oreilles comprenaient toutes les nuances de l'air
Et lorsque le pas de l'ami s'avançait nous le savions,
Nous ramassions aussi bien une fleur qu'un caillou poli,
Le temps où nous ne pouvions attraper la fumée,
Ah! c'est tout ce que nos mains sauraient saisir maintenant.»

A Poet

I don't always go alone to the bottom of my self;
Quite often living captives keep me company.
Those who have stepped inside my cold caverns,
Are they sure that they can ever leave again?
Like a sinking ship I pile up in my night
Pell-mell all the passengers and sailors,
Then I turn off every cabin's light;
The great depths will soon become my friends.

—PATRICIA TERRY

Regretting the Earth

Some day we will be saying, "That was the time of the sun,
Do you remember its light fell on the slightest twig,
The elderly woman or young astonished girl,
As soon as it touched it gave their color to things,
Kept pace with the galloping horse and stopped when he did,
That unforgettable time when we were still on Earth
Where if we dropped something it made a noise,
We would look around us with our knowing eyes,
And our ears would catch the slightest nuance in the air,
When the footsteps of a friend approached, we knew,
We used to gather flowers or smooth pebbles,
At that time we never could take hold of smoke,
Ah! What else can our hands do for us now?"

—PATRICIA TERRY

La Fileuse

Lilia . . . , neque nent

Assise, la fileuse au bleu de la croisée
Où le jardin mélodieux se dodeline;
Le rouet ancien qui ronfle l'a grisée.

Lasse, ayant bu l'azur, de filer la câline
Chevelure, à ses doigts si faibles évasive,
Elle songe, et sa tête petite s'incline.

Un arbuste et l'air pur font une source vive
Qui, suspendue au jour, délicieuse arrose
De ses pertes de fleurs le jardin de l'oisive.

Paul Valéry 1871–1945

SÈTE, FRANCE

Valéry was a poet and essayist—a master of irony—who valued lucidity and precision of thought above all. His work is defined by his conviction that poetry was primarily a mental process. He was educated in the French Mediterranean. After a night of moral and intellectual anguish in October 1892, he renounced poetry for mathematics and the study of mental processes, returning to poetry writing just before World War I. In 1894 he moved to Paris and concentrated solely on notebooks that he wrote in the morning before going to work at the French War Ministry. He was Mallarmé's favorite disciple and served as best man at Breton's wedding. Considered an unofficial poet laureate, he took Anatole France's vacated seat in the Académie française in 1925 and was named professor of poetics at the Collège de France in 1937. His poems are among the masterpieces of the twentieth century. Principal works: *La Jeune Parque*, 1917; *Le Cimetière marin*, 1920; *Charmes ou poèmes*, 1922; *Poésies*, 1929; *Amphion, Sémiramis*, 1931, 1934; *Paraboles*, 1935; *Cantate du Narcisse*, 1939.

The Spinner

The spinner, seated near the window sash
that opens where a melodious garden sways,
drowses by an old snoring wheel.

Tired, drunk on azure blue, on guiding
Wheedling hairs that dodge her feeble hands,
She dreams. And now her tiny head is nodding.

A living spring, formed by leaves and air,
Rising in sunlight, sprinkles fresh water
Over her garden as she slumbers there.

Une tige, où le vent vagabond se repose,
Courbe le salut vain de sa grâce étoilée,
Dédiant magnifique, au vieux rouet, sa rose.

Mais la dormeuse file une laine isolée;
Mystérieusement l'ombre frêle se tresse
Au fil de ses doigts longs et qui dorment, filée.

Le songe se dévide avec une paresse
Angélique, et sans cesse, au doux fuseau crédule,
La chevelure ondule au gré de la caresse . . .

Derrière tant de fleurs, l'azur se dissimule,
Fileuse de feuillage et de lumière ceinte :
Tout le ciel vert se meurt. Le dernier arbre brûle.

Ta sœur, la grande rose où sourit une sainte,
Parfume ton front vague au vent de son haleine
Innocente, et tu crois languir . . . Tu es éteinte

Au bleu de la croisée où tu filais la laine.

Le Rameur

à André Lebey

Penché contre un grand fleuve, infiniment mes rames
M'arrachent à regret aux riants environs;
Ame aux pesantes mains, pleines des avirons,
Il faut que le ciel cède au glas des lentes lames.

Le cœur dur, l'œil distrait des beautés que je bats,
Laissant autour de moi mûrir des cercles d'onde,
Je veux à larges coups rompre l'illustre monde
De feuilles et de feu que je chante tout bas.

Arbres sur qui je passe, ample et naïve moire,
Eau de ramages peinte, et paix de l'accompli,
Déchire-les, ma barque, impose-leur un pli
Qui coure du grand calme abolir la mémoire.

A stalk in wind that wanders and is still
Bows with a proud salute of starry grace,
Promising its rose to the ancient wheel.

And still the sleeper spins a single thread,
For a mysterious shadow, braided with the yarn
Of her long sleeping fingers, is spun.

Her dream unwinds, as on a gentle spindle
That caresses as it rolls around
Unendingly, and with the ease of angels.

The deep blue pales beyond so many blossoms.
Beyond the spinner's belt of leaves and light,
The sky, now green, darkens. The last tree flames.

The saint, your sister, smiles in the rose-window,
Perfumes your dazed forehead with her innocent breath,
And you wither, growing faint in the twilight,

Near the casement, where you sat spinning.

—GRACE SCHULMAN

The Oarsman

to André Lebey

Leaning against a strong river, my infinite stroke
Pulls me reluctant from the pleasant shores,
My hands heavy, weighed down by the oars.
The sky must yield to the slow tolling of blades.

My heart is hardened to the beauty I cleave,
The circles of waves blossoming around me,
I will my wide strokes to break the bright world
Of leaves and of fire, and sing them in quiet.

I pass over trees and full-patterned
Water painted with foliage, finally peace,
And tear them apart, imprint on them a pleat,
Hasten to end the memory of that calm.

Jamais, charmes du jour, jamais vos grâces n'ont
Tant souffert d'un rebelle essayant sa défense :
Mais, comme les soleils m'ont tiré de l'enfance,
Je remonte à la source où cesse même un nom.

En vain, toute la nymphe énorme et continue
Empêche de bras purs mes membres harassés;
Je romprai lentement mille liens glacés
Et les barbes d'argent de sa puissance nue.

Ce bruit secret des eaux, ce fleuve étrangement
Place mes jours dorés sous un bandeau de soie;
Rien plus aveuglément n'use l'antique joie
Qu'un bruit de fuite égale et de nul changement.

Sous les ponts annelés, l'eau profonde me porte,
Voûtes pleines de vent, de murmure et de nuit,
Ils courent sur un front qu'ils écrasent d'ennui,
Mais dont l'os orgueilleux est plus dur que leur porte.

Leur nuit passe longtemps. L'âme baisse sous eux
Ses sensibles soleils et ses promptes paupières,
Quand, par le mouvement qui me revêt de pierres,
Je m'enfonce au mépris de tant d'azur oiseux.

Le Cimetière marin

> Μή, φίλα ψυχά, βίον ἀθάνατον
> σπεῦδε, τάν δ'ἔμπρακτον ἄντλει
> μαχανάν.
> PINDARE, *Pythiques, III*

Ce toit tranquille, où marchent des colombes,
Entre les pins palpite, entre les tombes;
Midi le juste y compose de feux
La mer, la mer, toujours recommencée!
Ô récompense après une pensée
Qu'un long regard sur le calme des dieux!

Never, charm of daylight, has your grace
So suffered from self-defense,
Yet, since the suns drew me from childhood,
I'll return to the source where names cease to be.

The pure endless arms of the goddess
Vainly oppose me, harassing my strength.
But a thousand icy bonds gradually give way
And the silver shards of her naked majesty.

This secret sound of water, this river strangely
Places my sunlit days beneath a band of silk;
Nothing more blindly wears down the age-old joy
Than a sound of smooth and monotone flight.

The deep current carries me under bridges,
Arches full of wind, of murmuring dark,
They rush over me, their tedium crushing
My proud skull stronger than their doors.

Their night passes slowly. Under such weight,
My very soul almost yields up its light
Until in a gesture that clothes me in stone,
I sweep onward to the scorn of such idle sky.

—MARY ANN CAWS AND PATRICIA TERRY

The Seaside Cemetery

*My soul, do not seek immortal life,
but exhaust the realm
of the possible.*
Pindar, Pythian Odes

A tranquil surface where a spinnaker moves
flickers among the pines, among the graves;
objective noon films with its fiery glaze
a shifting sea, drifters like pecking doves,
and my reward for thought is a long gaze
down the blue silence of celestial groves.

Quel pur travail de fins éclairs consume
Maint diamant d'imperceptible écume,
Et quelle paix semble se concevoir!
Quand sur l'abîme un soleil se repose,
Ouvrages purs d'une éternelle cause,
Le Temps scintille et le Songe est savoir.

Stable trésor, temple simple à Minerve,
Masse de calme, et visible réserve,
Eau sourcilleuse, Œil qui gardes en toi
Tant de sommeil sous un voile de flamme,
Ô mon silence!... Édifice dans l'âme
Mais comble d'or aux mille tuiles, Toit!

Temple du Temps, qu'un seul soupir résume,
À ce point pur je monte et m'accoutume,
Tout entouré de mon regard marin;
Et comme aux dieux mon offrande suprême,
La scintillation sereine sème
Sur l'altitude un dédain souverain.

Comme le fruit se fond en jouissance,
Comme en délice il change son absence
Dans une bouche où sa forme se meurt,
Je hume ici ma future fumée,
Et le ciel chante à l'âme consumée
Le changement des rives en rumeur.

Beau ciel, vrai ciel, regarde-moi qui change!
Après tant d'orgueil, après tant d'étrange
Oisiveté, mais pleine de pouvoir,
Je m'abandonne à ce brillant espace,
Sur les maisons des morts mon ombre passe
Qui m'apprivoise à son frêle mouvoir.

L'âme exposée aux torches du solstice,
Je te soutiens, admirable justice
De la lumière aux armes sans pitié!
Je te rends pure à ta place première :
Regarde-toi!... Mais rendre la lumière
Suppose d'ombre une morne moitié.

When, as now, light freezes above the gulf,
a gem revolving in its radiant gleam
such many-faceted and glittering foam
that a great peace seems to extend itself,
those clear-cut artefacts of the continuum,
time and knowledge, take the shape of a dream.

Wide-open vault and chaste shrine to Athene,
deep reservoir of calmly shining money,
like an eye the supercilious water-structure
lies somnolent beneath its burning veils;
and my soul-silence too is architecture,
a golden hoard roofed with a thousand tiles.

Temple of time I breathe when I breathe in,
to this high point I climb and feel at home
ordering all things with a seaward stare
of circumspection; and, as my supreme
offering to the gods, the serene glare
sows on the depths an imperious disdain.

But even as fruit consumes itself in taste,
even as it translates its own demise
deliciously in the mouth where its form dies,
I sniff already my own future smoke
while light sings to the ashen soul the quick
change starting now on the murmuring coast.

Under this clear sky it is I who change—
after so much conceit, after such strange
lassitude, but bursting with new power,
I give myself up to these brilliant spaces;
on the mansions of the dead my shadow passes
reminding me of its own ephemeral hour.

A soul-exposure to the solar torches
I can endure, and the condign tortures
of the midsummer's pitiless bronze light;
and though submission show a midnight face
invisible in daytime, to that bright
presence I concede the superior place.

Ô pour moi seul, à moi seul, en moi-même,
Auprès d'un cœur, aux sources du poème,
Entre le vide et l'événement pur,
J'attends l'écho de ma grandeur interne,
Amère, sombre et sonore citerne,
Sonnant dans l'âme un creux toujours futur !

Sais-tu, fausse captive des feuillages,
Golfe mangeur de ces maigres grillages,
Sur mes yeux clos, secrets éblouissants,
Quel corps me traîne à sa fin paresseuse,
Quel front l'attire à cette terre osseuse ?
Une étincelle y pense à mes absents.

Fermé, sacré, plein d'un feu sans matière,
Fragment terrestre offert à la lumière,
Ce lieu me plaît, dominé de flambeaux,
Composé d'or, de pierre et d'arbres sombres,
Où tant de marbre est tremblant sur tant d'ombres ;
La mer fidèle y dort sur mes tombeaux !

Chienne splendide, écarte l'idolâtre !
Quand solitaire au sourire de pâtre,
Je pais longtemps, moutons mystérieux,
Le blanc troupeau de mes tranquilles tombes,
Éloignes-en les prudentes colombes,
Les songes vains, les anges curieux !

Ici venu, l'avenir est paresse.
L'insecte net gratte la sécheresse ;
Tout est brûlé, défait, reçu dans l'air
A je ne sais quelle sévère essence . . .
La vie est vaste, étant ivre d'absence,
Et l'amertume est douce, et l'esprit clair.

Les morts cachés sont bien dans cette terre
Qui les réchauffe et sèche leur mystère.
Midi là-haut, Midi sans mouvement
En soi se pense et convient à soi-même . . .
Tête complète et parfait diadème,
Je suis en toi le secret changement.

Stopped at a cistern with a pumping heart
between the vacuum and the creative act
whispering to my preliminary tact,
I await the echo of an interior force,
that bitter, dark and sonorous water-source
ringing in depths beyond the reach of art.

Caged though you seem behind a mesh of branches,
great gulf, consumer of these meagre fences,
a blinding secret on the lids, reveal
what body draws me to its indolences,
what face invites me to this bony soil.
A faint spark ponders these inheritances.

Composed of sombre trees, of light and stone,
an earthly splinter held up to the sun,
sacred, enclosed in immaterial fire,
I like this place with its dark poplar flames,
the marble glimmering in the shadows here
where a faithful sea snores on the table-tombs.

And if, sole shepherd, with a pastoral eye
I gaze too long on these mysterious flocks,
on these white souls, each in its tranquil box,
may the sea's growl dispel the idolatrous things,
frightening off the prudent doves, the coy
illusions and the angels' curious wings.

The future, here already, scarcely moves.
A quick insect scratches the dry leaves;
everything is exhausted, scorched by the air
into I don't know what rigorous form.
Dazed with diversity, the enormous swarm
of life is bitter-sweet and the mind clear.

The hidden dead lie easy in this soil
which holds them tight and seasons their mystique;
high up the southern noon, completely still,
reflects upon itself where none may look.
Absolute monarch, firmament of blue,
I am the secret difference now in you.

Tu n'as que moi pour contenir tes craintes!
Mes repentirs, mes doutes, mes contraintes
Sont le défaut de ton grand diamant . . .
Mais dans leur nuit toute lourde de marbres,
Un peuple vague aux racines des arbres
A pris déjà ton parti lentement.

Ils ont fondu dans une absence épaisse,
L'argile rouge a bu la blanche espèce,
Le don de vivre a passé dans les fleurs!
Où sont des morts les phrases familières,
L'art personnel, les âmes singulières?
La larve file où se formaient des pleurs.

Les cris aigus des filles chatouillées,
Les yeux, les dents, les paupières mouillées,
Le sein charmant qui joue avec le feu,
Le sang qui brille aux lèvres qui se rendent,
Les derniers dons, les doigts qui les défendent,
Tout va sous terre et rentre dans le jeu!

Et vous, grande âme, espérez-vous un songe
Qui n'aura plus ces couleurs de mensonge
Qu'aux yeux de chair l'onde et l'or font ici?
Chanterez-vous quand serez vaporeuse?
Allez! Tout fuit! Ma présence est poreuse,
La sainte impatience meurt aussi!

Maigre immortalité noire et dorée,
Consolatrice affreusement laurée,
Qui de la mort fais un sein maternel,
Le beau mensonge et la pieuse ruse!
Qui ne connaît, et qui ne les refuse,
Ce crâne vide et ce rire éternel!

Pères profonds, têtes inhabitées,
Qui sous le poids de tant de pelletées,
Êtes la terre et confondez nos pas,
Le vrai rongeur, le ver irréfutable
N'est point pour vous qui dormez sous la table,
Il vit de vie, il ne me quitte pas!

I am the one your worst fears validate—
my cowardice, my bad thoughts, my contrition
make up the one flaw in your precious opal;
and meanwhile, in a dense marmoreal night
among the roots, a vague oceanic people
have long ago arrived at your conclusion.

Mixed in a thick solution underground
the white clay is drunk by the crimson kind;
its vigour circulates in the veined flowers.
Where now are the colloquial turns of phrase,
the individual gifts and singular souls?
Where once a tear gathered the grub crawls.

The ticklish virgins with their twittering cries,
the teeth, the eyelids and the gentle eyes,
enchanted breasts heaving in provocation,
glistening lips shiny with invitation,
the last delights, the fingers that resist,
all join the circle and return to dust.

And you, great soul, dare you hypostasize
a world untarnished by the luminous lies
the sun and sea suggest to mortal eyes?
Will you still sing when you've become a ghost?
Nonsense, everything flows, ourselves the most;
the hunger for eternity also dies.

Gaunt immortality, gold inscribed on black,
cold consolation crowned with a laurel wreath
that makes a maternal bosom of grim death,
a gorgeous fiction and a lugubrious joke—
who doesn't know, and who would not decline
the empty skull with its eternal grin?

Archaic progenitors, your derelict heads
returned to pasture by so many spades,
no longer knowing the familiar tread—
the real ravager, the irrefutable worm
is not for you, at rest now in the tomb;
it lives on life and never leaves my side.

Amour, peut-être, ou de moi-même haine?
Sa dent secrète est de moi si prochaîne
Que tous les noms lui peuvent convenir!
Qu'importe! Il voit, il veut, il songe, il touche!
Ma chair lui plaît, et jusque sur ma couche,
À ce vivant je vis d'appartenir!

Zénon! Cruel Zénon! Zénon d'Élée!
M'as-tu percé de cette flèche ailée
Qui vibre, vole, et qui ne vole pas!
Le son m'enfante et la flèche me tue!
Ah! le soleil . . . Quelle ombre de tortue
Pour l'âme, Achille immobile à grands pas!

Non, non! . . . Debout! Dans l'ère successive!
Brisez, mon corps, cette forme pensive!
Buvez, mon sein, la naissance du vent!
Une fraîcheur, de la mer exhalée,
Me rend mon âme . . . Ô puissance salée!
Courons à l'onde en rejaillir vivant!

Oui! Grande mer de délires douée,
Peau de panthère et chlamyde trouée
De mille et mille idoles du soleil,
Hydre absolue, ivre de ta chair bleue,
Qui te remords l'étincelante queue
Dans un tumulte au silence pareil,

Le vent se lève! . . . Il faut tenter de vivre!
L'air immense ouvre et referme mon livre,
La vague en poudre ose jaillir des rocs!
Envolez-vous, pages tout éblouies!
Rompez, vagues! Rompez d'eaux réjouies
Ce toit tranquille où picoraient des focs!

Self-love, self-hatred, what's the difference?
Its secret mordancy is so intense
the silent gnawing goes by many names.
Watching, desiring, nibbling, considering,
it likes the flesh and, even, in my dreams,
I live on sufferance of this ravenous thing.

Zeno, harsh theorist of conceptual zero,
have you transfixed me with your winged arrow
which quivers, flies, yet doesn't fly at all?
Does the twang wake me and the arrow kill?
Sunlight, is it merely a tortoise-shade,
the mighty hero frozen in mid-stride?

No, no; get up; go on to the next phase—
body, shake off this meditative pose
and, chest, inhale the first flap of the air.
A palpable new freshness off the sea,
an ozone rush, restores my soul to me
and draws me down to the reviving shore.

Great sea endowed with frenzy and sensation,
slick panther-hide and heaving vegetation
sown with a million images of the sun;
unchained monster drunk on your blue skin,
chewing for ever your own glistening tail
in a perpetual, silent-seeming turmoil—

the wind rises; it's time to start. A stiff breeze
opens and shuts the notebook on my knees
and powdery waves explode among the rocks
flashing; fly off, then, my sun-dazzled pages
and break, waves, break up with ecstatic surges
this shifting surface where the spinnaker flocks!

—DEREK MAHON

La Rançon

Viens, nous pénétrerons le secret du flot clair,
Et je t'adorerai, comme un noyé la mer.

Les crabes dont la faim se repaît de chair morte
Nous feront avec joie une amicale escorte.

Reine, je t'élevai ce palais qui reluit,
Du débris d'un vaisseau naufragé dans la nuit . . .

Les jardins de coraux, d'algues et d'anémones,
N'y défleurissent point au souffle des automnes.

Burlesquement, avec des rires d'arlequins,
Nous irons à cheval sur le dos des requins.

Renée Vivien (Pauline Tarn) 1877–1909
LONDON, ENGLAND

Vivien was a prolific poet, one of the last to claim allegiance to the Symbolist movement. She gained as much notoriety for her lifestyle as for her writing, participating in the weekly Friday salon of Nathalie Barney, her lover; eating almost nothing; and keeping mysterious assignations (never elucidated to this day) that greatly provoked Barney. The two were leading proponents of the "lesbian-chic" movement in Paris in the 1890s. Barney's salon drew such guests as Auguste Rodin, Rainier Maria Rilke, James Joyce, Gertrude Stein, Alice B. Toklas, Max Jacob, André Gide, Sylvia Beach, and Mary McCarthy. Although English was her native language, Vivien wrote exclusively in French. Only the work *Chansons* (1907) bears her given name; she used the masculine form of her pseudonym, "René," to sign her first works of poetry. Principal works: *Brumes de fjords*, 1902; *Cendres et poussières*, 1902; *Du vert au violet*, 1903; *Évocations*, 1903; *Sappho*, 1903; *La Vénus des aveugles*, 1903; *A l'heure des mains jointes*, 1906; *Chansons pour mon ombre*, 1907; *Sillages*, 1907; *Flambeaux éteints*, 1908; *Haillons*, 1910.

The Ransom

Come, let's find the secret of the clear waters;
I'll adore you, as a drowned person does the sea.

Those crabs whose hunger is sated on dead flesh
Will be our friendly escorts, in joy.

Queen, I raised to you this shining palace,
From the remains of a vessel shipwrecked at night . . .

The gardens of corals, anemones, and algae
Lose nothing from the autumn's breath.

Laughing like harlequins in a burlesque,
We'll mount astride the backs of sharks.

Tes yeux ressembleront aux torches de phosphore
A travers la pénombre où ne rit point l'aurore.

Je suis l'être qu'hier ton sein nu vint charmer,
Qui ne sut point assez te haïr ni t'aimer,

Que tu mangeas, ainsi que mange ton escorte,
Les crabes dont la faim se repaît de chair morte . . .

Viens, je t'entraînerai vers l'océan amer
Et j'aimerai ta mort dans la nuit de la mer.

———————————

Your eyes will gleam like phosphor
Through the dusk where no dawn laughs.

I am the being your bare breast once charmed,
Unable to hate or love you enough,

Whom you devoured as does your own escort,
Those crabs whose hunger is sated on dead flesh . . .

Come, I'll draw you the bitter water,
To love your death there in the sea's night.

—MARY ANN CAWS

———————————————

2

1916–1930:
Dada and the Heroic Period of
Surrealism

Louis Aragon, Antonin Artaud, Georges Bataille, Samuel Beckett, André Breton, Claude Cahun, Malcolm de Chazal, Robert Desnos, Paul Éluard, Jean Follain, Greta Knutson, Michel Leiris, Henri Michaux, Benjamin Péret, Francis Ponge, Jacques Prévert, Raymond Queneau, Léopold Sédar Senghor, Philippe Soupault, Jean Tardieu, Tristan Tzara, Marguerite Yourcenar

Dada had a striking and lasting impact on American poetry, from the Beats through the New York School—witness John Cage's mesostics, Frank O'Hara's "Second Avenue," Kenneth Koch's "When the Sun Tries to Go On," and much of John Ashbery's work. Now the current generation of young American poets seems to have discovered Dada for itself, finding its "chatty abstractions" as usefully subversive and ironically charming as Dada once did. The excitement of Dada—its performative violence coincident with World War I—was born anew after World War II, when the Abstract Expressionist Robert Motherwell published his celebrated *The Dada Painters and Poets.*[1] When the poet Allen Ginsberg first met Motherwell, as the painter told it, he rushed up, embraced him, and shouted his delight in Motherwell's formative anthology. Many other poets and readers have since echoed Ginsberg's sentiment. Tristan Tzara ("Papa-Dada"), who died in 1963, became something of a cult hero in the 1960s, when many, both young and not-so-young, wore NADADA buttons. During the early years of the Vietnam era, Tzara's early plays began to enjoy revivals in art galleries. On one such occasion, in the former Cordier-Ekstrom Gallery, Andy Warhol played the role of Nose in *La*

Deuxième Aventure céleste de M. Antipyrine (The Second Celestial Adventure of Mr. Aspirin) by simply standing behind the actor reciting the lines. Standing behind, Warhol seemed to be saying, can be as important as standing for.

Between 1916 and the early 1930s, French writers and intellectuals developed an intense fascination with African cultures and the notion of an exciting and novel primitive mentality: affective, wild, illogical, mystical—what Marcel Mauss, lecturing at the École pratique des hautes études, termed negrophilia. African art had a powerful influence on the painters and poets Pablo Picasso, André Derain, and Guillaume Apollinaire. At that time, almost everyone involved in the arts was exploring things African. The *Anthologie nègre* assembled by the Cubist poet Blaise Cendrars was immensely influential.

Part of the novelty of the Dadaist experiments in language was Tzara's imitation of primitive languages that had a distinctly African resonance. In 1916, he and Hugo Ball invented Negro chants. The conclusion of Tzara's early poem "Le Géant Blanc Lépreux du paysage" (White Giant Leper of the Countryside) finishes with a deliberate insult to the reader, likely to be seduced into Dada thereby, all the while flaunting its un-French, un-Cartesian language:

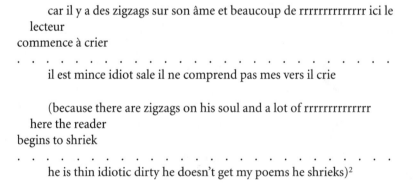

> car il y a des zigzags sur son âme et beaucoup de rrrrrrrrrrrrrr ici le
> lecteur
> commence à crier
>
> ·
>
> il est mince idiot sale il ne comprend pas mes vers il crie
>
> (because there are zigzags on his soul and a lot of rrrrrrrrrrrrrr
> here the reader
> begins to shriek
>
> ·
>
> he is thin idiotic dirty he doesn't get my poems he shrieks)[2]

With time, the eccentricities of Dada gave way to the more organized Surrealist movement; this momentous new poetic energy lasted a number of years—in both its behavior in accord with "lyric values," as Breton put it, and its powerful poetry of the everyday marvelous.[3] The Surrealists, believing, as did the philosophers Gaston Bachelard and Ludwig Wittgenstein, that the limits of our universe are determined by those of our language, expanded the powers of writing and speech beyond the rational and the ordinary—with a positive purpose. Eventually, the heroic epoch of the movement came to an end, owing to the excommunication of many of the Surrealists poets from the "chapel" run by Breton, the desertion of Louis Aragon and Paul Éluard to the Communist Party, and the

exile of many Surrealist painters and poets, including Breton, André Masson, Matta, and Kurt Seligmann, to New York during World War I.

In New York, the Abstract Expressionist painters, through the Chilean Surrealist painter Matta and his American friend Robert Motherwell, adopted what was best about the spontaneous inspiration or the "psychic automatism" of Surrealism. In drawing or painting, the initial subliminal line that Motherwell termed the doodle—which the poet Robert Desnos had used in his early Surrealist drawings—was the visual equivalent of the unthinking and uncensored speech that was thought to unleash the powers of the subconscious. American painters, and then poets, tapped into this spontaneity and energy, but in the reverse order of the movement in France, where the poets had led the way.

Nor had places like Haiti, Martinique, Guadeloupe, and Senegal remained untouched by Surrealism, for Breton had multiple contacts with poets beyond the six sides of the Hexagon that is France. Stopping in Martinique on his way to New York, Breton was moved to write the eulogistic tract *Martinique charmeuse de serpents* (Martinique Charmer of Snakes). Aimé Césaire, Léopold Sédar Senghor, Léon-Gontran Damas, and other poets reveled in the new possibilities of experimental techniques and the revitalization of language, vision, and optimism.

Francis Ponge's experimental work investigates not only the world of things but the language used to describe them. In his *Le Parti pris des choses* (Taking the Side of Things) he celebrates the dailiness of objects and their mundane but important presence. As Michel Deguy put it, "*Homo faber* has never done anything that can equal what he receives, be it cauliflower or sun—that's what Ponge did."[4]

The mystical side of poetry came to the fore with René Daumal's *Le Grand Jeu* (The Great Game), Breton's notion of *le point sublime* (in which all contraries meet), and some American experimental poetics. Even Breton, after his exile in New York and his encounter with the Native Americans of the Southwest (particularly the Hopis in Arizona), developed a strongly mystical streak. By the time he returned to France, Surrealism—and the epoch that had nourished it—had changed, but its legacies remain undeniable. In Canada, Surrealist painters and poets flourish; in South America, Magical Realism, a cousin to Surrealism, has taken on the brightest of colors; and in the United States, its influence is ubiquitous.

Notes

1. Robert Motherwell, *The Dada Painters and Poets: An Anthology* (New York: Wittenborn, 1951).

2. Tristan Tzara, *Oeuvres complètes*, ed. Henri Béhar, vol. 1, 1912–1924 (Paris: Flammarion, 1975), pp. 87–88. *Tristan Tzara, Approximate Man and Other Writings*, ed. and trans. Mary Ann Caws (Detroit: Wayne State University Press, 1973), p. 159.

3. André Breton, *Second Manifeste du surréalisme*, in *Manifestes du surréalisme* (Paris: Jean-Jacques Pauvert, 1962), p. 195.

4. Michel Deguy, *Po&sie* 92 (2003): 13.

Louis Aragon 1897–1982
PARIS, FRANCE

Aragon was a noted poet, novelist, and essayist whose work has exercised an enormous influence on literary theory and encompasses most of the primary literary trends and ideas of the twentieth century—from Surrealism through Social Realism. He was born in the fashionable sixteenth arrondissement, where his family ran a pension. He met André Breton while studying military medicine and serving in a psychiatric center for soldiers. Together with Philippe Soupault, the three began the review *Littérature*, funded by Soupault's private fortune. During this period Aragon wrote his first automatic texts and Dadaist invectives against bourgeois values. His early novels, the boldly innovative *Anicet ou le panorama* (1921), *Le Paysan de Paris* (1926), and his ironic *Traité du style* (1928), are easily counted among the masterpieces of early Surrealism. Like many other Surrealists of the time, he believed revolution could occur only through a change in the predominant social structure. Deciding this was best done through politics, he broke with Breton in 1933 and, with his Russian wife, the novelist Elsa Triolet, joined the Communist Party. Aragon became one of the leading figures of the Resistance. Principal works: *Feu de joie*, 1920; *Le Mouvement perpétuel*, 1925; *Persécuté persécuteur*, 1931; *En étrange pays dans mon pays lui-même*, 1945; *Le Voyage de Hollande*, 1964.

Pièce à grand spectacle

L'ami sans cœur ou théâtre
Adieu
      Celui qui est trop gai
c'est-à-dire trop rouge
pour vivre loin du feu des rampes
De la salle
         ficelles pendantes
Des coulisses
          on ne voit qu'un nuage doré
               machine-volante
Le Régisseur croyait à l'amour d'André
Les   trois   coups
   L'oiseau   s'envole
On avait oublié de planter le décor
Tintamarre
        Le pantin verse des larmes de bois
        Pour Prendre Congé

Parti pris

Je danse au milieu des miracles
Mille soleils peints sur le sol
Mille amis Mille yeux ou monocles
m'illuminent de leurs regards
Pleurs du pétrole sur la route
Sang perdu depuis les hangars

Je saute ainsi d'un jour à l'autre
rond polychrome et plus joli
qu'un paillasson de tir ou l'âtre
quand la flamme est couleur du vent
Vie ô paisible automobile
et le joyeux péril de courir au devant

Je brûlerai du feu des phares

Big Spectacular Play

The friend with no heart or theater
Farewell
      The one who is too gay
that is to say too lit up
to live far from the stage lights
From the room
        threads dangling
From the corridors
        you see just a golden cloud
              flying machine
The Director believed in André's love
Curtain   rises
    The bird   flies off
We had forgotten to plant the sets
Hullabaloo
        The puppet sheds wood tears
        To Take Leave

—MARY ANN CAWS

Partial

I dance amid the miracles
A thousand suns painted on the ground
A thousand friends A thousand eyes or monocles
illuminate me with their gazes
Tears of petrol on the road
Blood spilled up to the hangars

Thus I leap from one day to the next
multicolored round and lovelier
than a shooting mat or the hearth
when the flame is wind-colored
Life oh peaceful car
and the joyous danger of dashing forward

I shall burn with the headlights' glare

—MARY ANN CAWS

L'Étreinte

L'an 1905 Pablo
        Picasso quel âge
A-t-il vingt-trois vingt
            quatre on était au printemps
Ou qui sait à l'automne Il suffit qu'ici règne
La lumière d'être jeune Une chambre pour
Les amants liés n'a besoin de rien que d'un
Lit

Il y
    avait de cela douze ans quand je vins
Boulevard Saint-Germain 202 chez Guillaume
Apollinaire On entendait au loin tousser
La Bertha

Toute chose prenait couleur de bouche close
Les étages tournaient sur moi dans l'escalier
Cela ressemblait à l'arbre de Robinson
Un œil
      brille dans l'espion de la porte
                  Et comme

Un gros oiseau vêtu d'horizon le poète
M'ouvre les pieds déchaussés là-haut dans son nid
Voilà donc l'Enchanteur Où sont les Sept Epées

Blessé à la tête trépané sous le chloroforme

Je n'ai de rien souvenir d'aucune parole
Rien que de ce cœur enfant en moi qui tremblait
J'avais une petite moustache pâle et
Mes vingt ans qui mettaient sur tout leur doux bruit d'ailes
La patte du soleil au piège des volets
En moi le chat des vers obscurément ronronne

Je me disais Guillaume il est temps que tu viennes

Il me disait Que disait-il Et m'a conduit
En s'excusant Les Picassos sont à la cave

The Embrace

AD 1905 Pablo
         Picasso how old
Was he then twenty-three twenty-
               four it was spring
Or perhaps autumn What matters is that here there reigns
The light of youth A room for
Entwined lovers needs nothing but a
Bed

It was
     twelve years later that I arrived
Boulevard Saint-Germain 202 to visit Guillaume
Apollinaire From the distance came the coughing of
Big Bertha

Everything took on a tight-lipped air
The storeys spiralled about me on the staircase
It was like Robinson Crusoe's tree
An eye
     glittered in the spyhole of the door
                      And like

A plump bird clothed in the horizon the poet
In his socks welcomed me there in his nest
So here's the Enchanter Where are the Seven Swords

Wounded in the head trepanned under chloroform

I don't remember anything not a single word
Nothing but that childish heart within me trembling
I had a little pale moustache and
My twenty years which brushed everything with their soft sound of wings
The sun's paw in the shutters' trap
And within me the cat of verse obscurely purring

I said to myself Guillaume it is time you came

He said to me What did he say And showed me round
With excuses The Picassos are in the cellar

Excepté
>> La main montre le mur où se fait

L'amour dans la pièce
>> à côté

Tout le reste ô baiser baiser perpétuel
Nuit et jour jour et nuit ce long arrêt d'horloge
Et la lèvre à la lèvre et le souffle accouplé
Et la vie au-dessous Réel le lit pourtant
Bien moins réel que l'instant fixé sur la toile
N'est qu'un pléonasme à l'étreinte à la durée

La vaste vie un peu toujours le cinéma
D'alors où le piano d'un petit air pardonne
Les mots qu'on tait

De tous ses yeux la salle écoute la rengaine
Et ce bouquet des doigts pour dire Elle est jolie

Ne sommes-nous pas encore au temps du muet
Un demi-siècle après c'est la même musique
Même silence dans les squares sur les bancs

Au coin des rues
>> Au ventre sombre des maisons
Seuls rien qu'eux seuls jamais lassés d'être enlacés
Tressaillants et pressés dans leurs bras dans leurs jambes
>> Les amants de 1905

>> Dont soit le plaisir éternel

Except
        His hand indicates the wall where love

Is being made in the room
                next door

All the rest o kiss perpetual kiss
Night and day day and night this long halt of the clock
And lip upon lip and the linked breathing
And the life beneath Real the bed yet
Much less real than the moment fixed upon the canvas
The bed is only a pleonasm to the embrace to time's continuance

Life's hugeness always a little like the cinema
Of those days where the piano with a little tune forgives
The words which are not said

The hall listens with all its eyes to the refrain
And this bouquet of fingers to say It is beautiful

Are we not still in the age of silent films
Half a century later it's still the same music
Same silence in the public gardens on the benches

At the corners of the streets
                In the dark bellies of the houses
Alone nothing but them alone never weary of their embrace
Trembling held in each other's arms and legs
        The lovers of 1905

        May their pleasure be eternal
                                —EDWARD LUCIE-SMITH

———————————

Le Pèse-nerfs (extraits)

Un acteur on le voit comme à travers des cristaux.
L'inspiration à paliers.
Il ne faut pas trop laisser passer la littérature.

.   .   .

En sommeil, nerfs tendus tout le long des jambes.
Le sommeil venait d'un déplacement de croyance, l'étreinte se relâchait, l'ab-
surde me marchait sur les pieds.

.   .   .

Antonin Artaud 1896–1948

MARSEILLES, FRANCE

An actor turned poet and essayist, Artaud was identified for a short while with Surrealism and was briefly in charge of its experimental Dream Center. In 1929 he was expelled from the group, along with Desnos. In an early essay, he developed the concept of the "theater of cruelty," in which participants would not rely on any artificial conventions of society and would instead use only gesture, movement, and other prelanguage tools. His work, violent and directed against civilization, was often censured, just as the writer himself was kept out of society's view. First confined to a sanitarium in Marseilles at the age of eighteen, he also spent nine years at the end of his life in an asylum at Rodez, undergoing repeated shock therapy. Upon his release, he was remarkably prolific and wrote extensively against psychiatrists and society; anguished and exulting in the torment of his mind, he perceived himself and his language as living examples of the divine. He was much revered by Parisian writers and artists and in 1947 lectured at the Vieux colombier to André Breton, Henri Michaux, André Gide, and Albert Camus, among others; the lecture ended in disaster as the poet scattered his papers in confusion. Principal works: *L'Ombilic des limbes*, 1925; *Le Pèse-nerfs*, 1925; *Le Théâtre et son double*, 1938; *Van Gogh et le suicidé de la société*, 1947; *Pour en finir avec le jugement de Dieu*, 1948.

The Nerve Meter

You see an actor as if through crystal.
Inspiration with its stairs.
Literature must not too readily pass.

· · ·

In sleep, the nerves extend along the legs. Sleep came from a displacement of belief, the embrace loosened, the absurd having stepped on my toes.

· · ·

Se retrouver dans un état d'extrême secousse, éclaircie d'irréalité, avec dans un coin de soi-même des morceaux du monde réel.

. . .

Une espèce de déperdition constante du niveau normal de la réalité.

. . .

Un impouvoir à cristalliser inconsciemment, le point rompu de l'automatisme à quelque degré que ce soit.

. . .

Savez-vous ce que c'est que la sensibilité suspendue, cette espèce de vitalité terrifique et scindée en deux, ce point de cohésion nécessaire auquel l'être ne se hausse plus, ce lieu menaçant, ce lieu terrassant.

. . .

En voilà un dans l'esprit duquel aucune place ne devient dure, et qui ne sent pas tout à coup son âme à gauche, du côté du cœur. En voilà un pour qui la vie est un point, et pour qui l'âme n'a pas de tranches, ni l'esprit de commencements.

. . .

Si l'on pouvait seulement goûter son néant, si l'on pouvait se bien reposer dans son néant, et que ce néant ne soit pas une certaine sorte d'être mais ne soit pas la mort tout à fait.

Il est si dur de ne plus exister, de ne plus être dans quelque chose. La vraie douleur est de sentir en soi se déplacer sa pensée. Mais la pensée comme un point n'est certainement pas une souffrance.

J'en suis au point où je ne touche plus à la vie, mais avec en moi tous les appétits et la titillation insistante de l'être. Je n'ai plus qu'une occupation, me refaire.

L'Amour sans trêve

Ce triangle d'eau qui a soif
cette route sans écriture
Madame, et le signe de vos mâtures
sur cette mer où je me noie

Les messages de vos cheveux
le coup de fusil de vos lèvres
cet orage qui m'enlève
dans le sillage de vos yeux.

To find oneself jolted to an extreme, lit by the unreal, with, in a corner of oneself, fragments of the real world.

. . .

A kind of constant displacement of the normal level of reality.

. . .

The unconscious has no power to crystallize, to any degree whatsoever, the fixed unbroken point of automatism.

. . .

Are you acquainted with that sensitivity hanging in mid-air, that kind of vitality terrifying and split in two, that indispensable point of cohesion to which being no longer rises, that place of menace, that place that hurls you to the ground?

. . .

Here's someone with no place hardening in his mind, who doesn't all of a sudden find his soul on his left, on the side of the heart. Here's someone for whom life is not a fixed point, for whom the soul has no sections, nor the mind beginnings.

. . .

If only you could taste your nothingness, if you could find repose in your nothingness, and if this nothingness would not be a kind of being and not really death either.

It's so hard not to exist any more, not to be something any more. Real suffering is to feel the movement of thought within oneself. But when thought is a fixed point, it is certainly not a suffering.

I am at the point where I no longer touch life, but with all the appetites still within me, and the insistent titillation of being. I have nothing to do now but make myself over.

—MARY ANN CAWS AND PATRICIA TERRY

Love with No Letup

This triangle of water athirst
this unwritten road
Madam, and the sight of your masts
upon this sea I drown in

The messages of your hair
the gunshot of your lips
this storm that seizes me
in the wake of your eyes.

Cette ombre enfin, sur le rivage
où la vie fait trêve, et le vent,
et l'horrible piétinement
de la foule sur mon passage.

Quand je lève les yeux vers vous
on dirait que le monde tremble,
et les feux de l'amour ressemblent
aux caresses de votre époux.

At last, this shadow on the bank
where life lets up and the wind
and the horrid trampling
of the crowd as I pass by.

When I raise my eyes toward you
you'd think the world trembling
and the fires of love
resembling your beloved's.

—MARY ANN CAWS

Georges Bataille 1897–1962
BILLON, FRANCE

A Surrealist poet, novelist, and anthropologist who associated eroticism with death, Bataille held that through sexual intercourse two normally discrete subjects merge to lose their rational selves, that all activity of the will should be bent toward this kind of annihilation of the rational subject. Bataille suffered a troubled childhood; the paralysis, blindness, and early death of his father and repeated suicide attempts of his mother deeply marked his views. In 1929–1930, in the pages of his dissident Surrealist journal *Documents,* he actively studied ethnographic undertakings, linking the avant-garde, the academic, and the literary. Breton excommunicated him from the Surrealists because of his divisive presence in the group, though the two later resolved their differences for a time and cofounded Contre-Attaque, a group committed to fighting fascism. For years he was a librarian in Provence and in Paris. In 1938, he founded the Collège de sociologie with Michel Leiris and Roger Caillois. Bataille was the first to publish the work of Roland Barthes, Maurice Blanchot, Jacques Derrida, and Michel Foucault in his review *Critique,* which appeared in 1946. Principal works: *Histoire de l'oeil,* 1928; *L'Expérience intérieure,* 1943; *Le Bleu du ciel,* 1945; *L'Érotisme,* 1957.

La Nuit est ma nudité

La nuit est ma nudité
les étoiles sont mes dents
je me jette chez les morts
habillé de blanc soleil.

La mort habite mon cœur
comme une petite veuve
elle sanglote elle est lâche
j'ai peur je pourrai vomir
la veuve rit jusqu'au ciel
et déchire les oiseaux.

J'imagine
dans la profondeur infinie
l'étendue déserte
différente du ciel que je vois
ne contenant plus ces points de lumière qui vacillent
mais des torrents de flammes
plus grands qu le ciel
plus aveuglants que l'aube
abstraction informe
zébrée de cassures
amoncellement
d'inanités d'oublis
d'un côté le sujet je
et de l'autre l'objet
l'univers
charpie de notions mortes
où JE jette en pleurant les détritus
les impuissances
les hoquets
les discordants cris de coq des idées
ô néant fabriqué
dans l'usine de la vanité infinie
comme une caisse de dents fausses
JE penche sur la caisse
JE ai
mon envie de vomir en vie
ô ma faillite
extase qui me dort

Night Is My Nudity

Night is my nudity
the stars my teeth
I hurl myself among the dead
dressed in white sun

Death dwells within my heart
like a little widow
she weeps, the coward,
I'm afraid I might vomit
the widow's laughter soars to the sky
and rips the birds asunder

I imagine
in the infinite depths
the deserted expanses
different from the sky that I see
no longer containing those wavering points of light
but torrents of flames
higher than heaven
more blinding than dawn
shapeless abstraction
striped with splits
accumulation
of forgotten inanities
on one side the subject I
on the other the object
the universe
rags of dead notions
where I hurl the detritus, weeping,
the powerlessness
the hiccoughs
the discordant crowing of the cock of ideas
o void fabricated
in the factory of infinite vanity
like a chest of false teeth
I leaning over the chest
I have
my desire to vomit my ire
o my ruin
ecstasy sleeping me

quand je crie
toi que est qui seras
quand je ne serai plus
X sourd
maillet géant
brisant ma tête de nuit.

Je rêvais de toucher

Je rêvais de toucher la tristesse du monde
au bord désenchanté d'un étrange marais
je rêvais d'une eau lourde où je retrouverais
les chemins égarés de ta bouche profonde

j'ai senti dans mes mains un animal immonde
échappé à la nuit d'une affreuse forêt
et je vis que c'était le mal dont tu mourais
que j'appelle en riant la tristesse du monde

une lumière folle un éclat de tonnerre
un rire libérant ta longue nudité
une immense splendeur enfin m'illuminèrent

et je vis ta douleur comme une charité
rayonnant dans la nuit la longue forme claire
et le cri de tombeau de ton infinité.

when I cry
You who are and will be
when I am no more
X the deaf
the giant mallet
breaking my head of night.

—ROSEMARY LLOYD

I Dreamed of Touching

I dreamed of touching the world's grief
on the disenchanted edge of a strange fen
I dreamed of heavy water where I would find again
the paths that had drifted from your mouth so deep

I felt in my hands a disgusting beast
fled from the hideous forest's black stain
and I saw that this was your mortal bane
that I laughingly call the world's grief

a wild light, the thunder's roar
a laugh liberating your long nudity
an immense splendor at last I saw

and I saw your grief as a charity
glowing in the night in the long bright form
and the graveyard cry of your infinity.

—ROSEMARY LLOYD

Musique de l'indifférence

musique de l'indifférence
coeur temps air feu sable
du silence éboulement d'amours
couvre leurs voix et que
je ne m'entende plus
me taire

Dieppe

encore le dernier reflux
le galet mort
le demi-tour puis les pas
vers les vieilles lumières

Samuel Beckett 1906–1989

DUBLIN, IRELAND

Beckett was one of the greatest poets, dramatists, and novelists of the twentieth century. A protégé of James Joyce, he took dictation for what would become *Finnegans Wake*. One of the first absurdists to gain international recognition, Beckett used only the most minimal of gestures and words to portray the reality of human drama. His work consistently examined failed communication between individuals—and the meaninglessness and suffering that result. In 1937 he moved to Paris, which remained his center after several years of traveling throughout Europe. During the Resistance, he was in Roussillon. He wrote most of his works in French, his adopted language; he possessed a perfect ear for both English and French and was a well-known translator. In 1961 he won the Prix International des Éditeurs and in 1969 the Nobel Prize. Principal works: *Whoroscope*, 1930; *More Pricks Than Kicks*, 1934; *Murphy*, 1938; *Malone meurt*, 1951; *Molloy*, 1951; *En attendant Godot*, 1952; *L'Innommable*, 1953; *Watt*, 1953; *Textes pour rien*, 1958; *All that Fall*, 1959; *Embers*, 1959; *Krapp's Last Tape*, 1959; *Comme c'est*, 1961; *Collected Poems in English and French*, 1977.

Music of Indifference

music of indifference
heart time air fire sand
from the silence loves' collapse
covers their voices and
let me no longer hear
myself keeping still

—MARY ANN CAWS

Dieppe

again the last ebb
the dead shingle
the turning then the steps
towards the lights of old

—SAMUEL BECKETT

Je suis

je suis ce cours de sable qui glisse
entre le galet et la dune
la pluie d'été pleut sur ma vie
sur moi ma vie qui me fuit me poursuit
et finira le jour de son commencement

cher instant je te vois
dans ce rideau de brume qui recule
où je n'aurai plus à fouler ces longs seuils mouvants
et vivrai le temps d'une porte
qui s'ouvre et se referme

Que ferais-je

que ferais-je sans ce monde sans visage sans questions
où être ne dure qu'un instant où chaque instant
verse dans le vide dans l'oubli d'avoir été
sans cette onde où à la fin
corps et ombre ensemble s'engloutissent
que ferais-je sans ce silence gouffre des murmures
haletant furieux vers le secours vers l'amour
sans ce ciel qui s'élève
sur la poussière de ses lests

que ferais-je je ferais comme hier comme aujourd'hui
regardant par mon hublot si je ne suis pas seul
à errer et à virer loin de toute vie
dans un espace pantin
sans voix parmi les voix
enfermées avec moi

———————————

My Way

my way is in the sand flowing
between the shingle and the dune
the summer rain rains on my life
on me my life harrying fleeing
to its beginning to its end

my peace is there in the receding mist
when I may cease from treading these long shifting
                                      thresholds
and live the space of a door
that opens and shuts

—SAMUEL BECKETT

What Would I Do

what would I do without this world faceless incurious
where to be lasts but an instant where every instant
spills in the void the ignorance of having been
without this wave where in the end
body and shadow together are engulfed
what would I do without this silence where the murmurs die
the pantings the frenzies towards succour towards love
without this sky that soars
above its ballast dust

what would I do what I did yesterday and the day before
peering out of my deadlight looking for another
wandering like me eddying far from all the living
in a convulsive space
among the voices voiceless
that throng my hiddenness

—SAMUEL BECKETT

Le Corset Mystère

Mes belles lectrices,

à force d'en voir **de toutes les couleurs**
Cartes splendides, *à effets de lumière,* Venise

André Breton 1896–1966
TINCHEBRAY, FRANCE

Published in 1924, Breton's "Manifesto of Surrealism" initiated the Surrealist movement and situated him as its undisputed leader. Despite many arguments that would divide and change the movement over the years, Breton remained, until his death, in the vanguard of the most talented and gifted writers of his time. Long after Surrealist thought had been eclipsed by the rising popularity of Jean-Paul Sartre and existentialism in the 1940s, Breton remained true to the original conception of the tenets of the movement, frequently citing Rimbaud and Marx, who espoused the notion of changing humankind and the world by freeing the human spirit from the bounds of reason. Born in northern France, Breton studied medicine and worked in psychiatric hospitals during World War I. Through his studies he discovered Freud. He was attracted initially to the Dadaists; Surrealism, however, enabled him to approach more directly human desire and the unconscious. His work, philosophic, poetic, and deeply allusive, approached the "marvelous" first through the automatic process and subsequently through a mystical orientation. With his wife, Jacqueline Lamba, and their daughter, Aube, he went into exile in New York during World War II, returning after the war to a greatly changed Paris and the accusation of the irrelevance of Surrealist thinking and writing in the new climate. He nonetheless continued to assemble around him in Paris and in the Lot, at Saint-Cirq-la Popie, a group of enthusiastic followers. Principal works: *Mont de piété*, 1919; *Champs magnétiques* (automatic prose, with Philippe Soupault), 1920; *Clair de terre*, 1923; *Poisson soluble*, 1924; *Nadja*, 1928; *L'Union libre*, 1931; *Le Revolver à cheveux blancs*, 1932; *L'Air de l'eau*, 1934; *Constellations*, 1959.

The Mystery Corset

My lovely readers,

by seeing **in all colors**
Splendid postcards, *with lighting effects*, Venice

Autrefois les meubles de ma chambre étaient fixés solidement aux murs et je me
faisais attacher pour écrire :
J'ai le pied marin

nous adhérons à une sorte de **Touring Club** sentimental

UN CHATEAU A LA PLACE DE LA TÊTE
c'est aussi le **Bazar de la Charité**

Jeux très amusants pour tous âges ;

Jeux poétiques, etc.

Je tiens Paris comme — pour vous dévoiler l'avenir — votre main ouverte
la taille bien prise.

Vigilance

A Paris la tour Saint-Jacques chancelante
Pareille à un tournesol
Du front vient quelquefois heurter la Seine et son ombre
    glisse imperceptiblement parmi les remorqueurs
A ce moment sur la pointe des pieds dans mon sommeil
Je me dirige vers la chambre où je suis étendu
Et j'y mets le feu
Pour que rien ne subsiste de ce consentement qu'on m'a arraché
Les meubles font alors place à des animaux de même taille
    qui me regardent fraternellement
Lions dans les crinières desquels achèvent de se consumer les chaises
Squales dont le ventre blanc s'incorpore le dernier frisson des
    draps
A l'heure de l'amour et des paupières bleues
Je me vois brûler à mon tour je vois cette cachette solennelle
    de riens
Qui fut mon corps
Fouillée par les becs patients des ibis du feu
Lorsque tout est fini j'entre invisible dans l'arche
Sans prendre garde aux passants de la vie qui font sonner
    très loin leurs pas traînants
Je vois les arêtes du soleil
A travers l'aubépine de la pluie
J'entends se déchirer le linge humain comme une grande
    feuille

It used to be that my room's furnishings were solidly
fixed to the walls and I had to be strapped down to write:
I'm a good sailor

we belong to a sort of sentimental **Touring Club**

A CHATEAU INSTEAD OF A HEAD
that's the **Charity Bazaar** *too*

Delightful games for all ages;
Poetic games, etc.

I hold Paris like — to unveil the future for you — your open hand
with a waist tightly bound.

—MARY ANN CAWS

Vigilance

In Paris, the Tour Saint-Jacques
Swaying like a sunflower
Sometimes against the Seine its shadow moves among the
    tugboats
Just then on tiptoe in my sleep
I move towards the room where I am lying
And set it afire
Nothing remains of the consent I had to give
The furniture makes way for beasts looking at me like
    brothers
Lions whose manes consume the chairs
Sharks' white bellies absorb the sheets' last
    quiver
At the hour of love and blue eyelids
I see myself burning now I see that solemn hiding place of
    nothings
Which was once my body
Probed by the patient beaks of firebirds
When all is finished I enter the ark unseen
Taking no need of life's passersby whose shuffling steps are heard
    far off
I see the ridges of the sun
Through the hawthorn of the rain
I hear human linen tearing like a great
    leaf

Sous l'ongle de l'absence et de la présence qui sont de
    connivence
Tous les métiers se fanent il ne reste d'eux qu'une dentelle
    parfumée
Une coquille de dentelle qui a la forme parfaite d'un sein
Je ne touche plus que le coeur des choses je tiens le fil

Toujours pour la première fois

Toujours pour la première fois
C'est à peine si je te connais de vue
Tu rentres à telle heure de la nuit dans une maison
    oblique à ma fenêtre
Maison tout imaginaire
C'est là que d'une seconde à l'autre
Dans le noir intact
Je m'attends à ce que se produise une fois de plus la
    déchirure fascinante
La déchirure unique
De la façade et de mon cœur
Plus je m'approche de toi
En réalité
Plus la clé chante à la porte de la chambre inconnue
Où tu m'apparais seule
Tu es d'abord tout entière fondue dans le brillant
L'angle fugitif d'un rideau
C'est un champ de jasmin que j'ai contemplé à l'aube
    sur une route des environs de Grasse
Avec ses cueilleuses en diagonale
Derrière elles l'aile sombre tombante des plantes
    dégarnies
Devant elles l'équerre de l'éblouissant
Le rideau invisiblement soulevé
Rentrent en tumulte toutes les fleurs
C'est toi aux prises avec cette heure trop longue jamais
    assez trouble jusqu'au sommeil
Toi comme si tu pouvais être
La même à cela près que je ne te rencontrerai peut-être
    jamais
Tu fais semblant de ne pas savoir que je t'observe
Merveilleusement je ne suis plus sûr que tu le sais

Under the fingernails of absence and presence in
    collusion
All the looms are withering just a bit of perfumed
    lace
A shell of lace remains in a perfect breast shape
Now I touch nothing but the heart of things I hold the thread

—MARY ANN CAWS

Always for the First Time

Always for the first time
I scarcely know you when I see you
You return sometime in the night
    to a house at an angle to my window
A wholly imaginary house
From one second to the next
There in the complete darkness
I wait for the strange rift to recur the
    unique rift
In the façade and in my heart
The nearer I come to you
In reality
The louder the key sings in the door of the unknown room
Where you appear alone before me
First you merge with the brightness
The fleeting angle of a curtain
A jasmine field I gazed on at dawn on a road
    near Grasse
The jasmine-pickers bending over on a slant
Behind them the dark profile of plants
    stripped bare
Before them the dazzling light
The curtain invisibly raised
In a frenzy all the flowers swarm back
You facing this long hour never dim enough
    until sleep
You as if you could be
The same except I may never
    meet you
You pretend not to know I'm watching you
Marvellously I'm no longer sure you know it

Ton désœuvrement m'emplit les yeux de larmes
Une nuée d'interprétations entoure chacun de tes
  gestes
C'est une chasse à la miellée
Il y a des rocking-chairs sur un pont il y a des bran-
  chages qui risquent de t'égratigner dans la forêt
Il y a dans une vitrine rue Notre-Dame-de-Lorette
Deux belles jambes croisées prises dans de hauts bas
Qui s'évasent au centre d'un grand trèfle blanc
Il y a une échelle de soie déroulée sur le lierre
Il y a
Qu'à me pencher sur le précipice
De la fusion sans espoir de ta présence et de ton absence
J'ai trouvé le secret
De t'aimer
Toujours pour la première fois

On me dit que là-bas

On me dit que là-bas les plages sont noires
De la lave allée à la mer
Et se déroulent au pied d'un immense pic fumant de neige
Sous un second soleil de serins sauvages
Quel est donc ce pays lointain
Qui semble tirer toute sa lumière de ta vie
Il tremble bien réel à la pointe de tes cils
Doux à ta carnation comme un linge immatériel
Frais sorti de la malle entr'ouverte des âges
Derrière toi
Lançant ses derniers feux sombres entre tes jambes
Le sol du paradis perdu
Glace de ténèbres miroir d'amour
Et plus bas vers tes bras qui s'ouvrent
A la preuve par le printemps
D'APRÈS
De l'inexistence du mal
Tout le pommier en fleur de la mer

Your idleness fills my eyes with tears
A nimbus of meanings surrounds each of
   your gestures
Like a honeydew hunt
There are rocking-chairs on a bridge there are branches that might scratch you
   in the forest
In a window on the rue Notre-Dame-de-Lorette
Two lovely crossed legs are caught in long stockings
Flaring out in the centre of a great white clover
There is a silk ladder unrolled across the ivy
There is
That leaning over the precipice
Of the hopeless fusion of your presence and absence
I have found the secret
Of loving you
Always for the first time

—MARY ANN CAWS

They Tell Me That Over There

They tell me that over there the beaches are black
From the lava running to the sea
Stretched out at the foot of a great peak smoking with snow
Under a second sun of wild canaries
So what is this far-off land
Seeming to take its light from your life
It trembles very real at the tip of your lashes
Sweet to your carnation like an intangible linen
Freshly pulled from the half-open trunk of the ages
Behind you
Casting its last sombre fires between your legs
The earth of the lost paradise
Glass of shadows mirror of love
And lower towards your arms opening
On the proof by springtime
of AFTERWARDS
Of evil's not existing
All the flowering appletree of the sea

—MARY ANN CAWS

L'Union libre

Ma femme à la chevelure de feu de bois
Aux pensées d'éclairs de chaleur
À la taille de sablier
Ma femme à la taille de loutre entre les dents du tigre
Ma femme à la bouche de cocarde et de bouquet d'étoiles de dernière grandeur
Aux dents d'empreintes de souris blanche sur la terre blanche
À la langue d'ambre et de verre frottés
Ma femme à la langue d'hostie poignardée
À la langue de poupée qui ouvre et ferme les yeux
À la langue de pierre incroyable
Ma femme aux cils de bâtons d'écriture d'enfant
Aux sourcils de bord de nid d'hirondelle
Ma femme aux tempes d'ardoise de toit de serre
Et de buée aux vitres
Ma femme aux épaules de champagne
Et de fontaine à têtes de dauphins sous la glace
Ma femme aux poignets d'allumettes
Ma femme aux doigts de hasard et d'as de cœur
Aux doigts de foin coupé
Ma femme aux aisselles de martre et de fênes
De nuit de la Saint-Jean
De troène et de nid de scalares
Aux bras d'écume de mer et d'écluse
Et de mélange du blé et du moulin
Ma femme aux jambes de fusée
Aux mouvements d'horlogerie et de désespoir
Ma femme aux mollets de moelle de sureau
Ma femme aux pieds d'initiales
Aux pieds de trousseaux de clés aux pieds de calfats qui boivent
Ma femme au cou d'orge imperlé
Ma femme à la gorge de Val d'or
De rendez-vous dans le lit même du torrent
Aux seins de nuit
Ma femme aux seins de taupinière marine
Ma femme aux seins de creuset du rubis
Aux seins de spectre de la rose sous la rosée
Ma femme au ventre de dépliement d'éventail des jours
Au ventre de griffe géante
Ma femme au dos d'oiseau qui fuit vertical
Au dos de vif-argent

Free Union

My love whose hair is woodfire
Her thoughts heat lightning
Her waist an hourglass
My love an otter in the tiger's jaws
Her mouth a rosette bouquet of stars of the highest magnitude
Her teeth footprints of white mice on white earth
Her tongue of rubbed amber and glass
My love her tongue a sacred host stabbed through
Her tongue a doll whose eyes close and open
Her tongue an incredible stone
Each eyelash traced by a child's hand
Her eyebrows the edge of a swallow's nest
My love her temples slates on a greenhouse roof
And their misted panes
My love whose shoulders are champagne
And dolphin heads of a fountain under ice
My love her wrists thin as matchsticks
Whose fingers are chance and the ace of hearts
Whose fingers are mowed hay
My love with marten and beechnut between her arms
Of Midsummer night
Of privet and the nests of angel fish
Whose arms are sea foam and river locks
And the mingling of wheat and mill
My love whose legs are fireworks
Moving like clockwork and despair
My love her calves of elder tree marrow
My love whose feet are initials
Are key rings and sparrows drinking
My love her neck pearled with barley
My love her throat of a golden valley
Rendez-vous in the torrent's very bed
Her breasts of night
My love her breasts molehills beneath the sea
Crucibles of rubies
Spectre of the dew-sparkled rose
My love whose belly unfurls the fan of every day
Its giant claws
Whose back is a bird's vertical flight
Whose back is quicksilver

Au dos de lumière
À la nuque de pierre roulée et de craie mouillée
Et de chute d'un verre dans lequel on vient de boire
Ma femme aux hanches de nacelle
Aux hanches de lustre et de pennes de flèche
Et de tiges de plumes de paon blanc
De balance insensible
Ma femme aux fesses de grès et d'amiante
Ma femme aux fesses de dos de cygne
Ma femme aux fesses de printemps
Au sexe de glaïeul
Ma femme au sexe de placer et d'ornithorynque
Ma femme au sexe d'algue et de bonbons anciens
Ma femme au sexe de miroir
Ma femme aux yeux pleins de larmes
Aux yeux de panoplie violette et d'aiguille aimantée
Ma femme aux yeux de savane
Ma femme aux yeux d'eau pour boire en prison
Ma femme aux yeux de bois toujours sous la hache
Aux yeux de niveau d'eau de niveau d'air de terre et de feu

Sur la route de San Romano

La poésie se fait dans un lit comme l'amour
Ses draps défaits sont l'aurore des choses
La poésie se fait dans les bois

Elle a l'espace qu'il lui faut
Pas celui-ci mais l'autre que conditionnent

     L'œil du milan
     La rosée sur une prèle
     Le souvenir d'une bouteille de Traminer embuée sur un plateau
       d'argent
     Une haute verge de tourmaline sur la mer
     Et la route de l'aventure mentale
     Qui monte à pic
     Une halte elle s'embroussaille aussitôt

Cela ne se crie pas sur les toits
Il est inconvenant de laisser la porte ouverte
Ou d'appeler des témoins

Whose back is light
The nape of her neck is crushed stone and damp chalk
And the fall of a glass where we just drank
My love whose hips are wherries
Whose hips are chandeliers and arrow feathers
And the stems of white peacock plumes
Imperceptible in their sway
My love whose buttocks are of sandstone
Of swan's back and amianthus
And of springtime
My love whose sex is gladiolus
Is placer and platypus
Algae and sweets of yore
Is mirror
My love her eyes full of tears
Of violet panoply and magnetic needle
My love of savannah eyes
My love her eyes of water to drink in prison
My love her eyes of wood always to be chopped
Eyes of water level earth and air and fire

—MARY ANN CAWS AND PATRICIA TERRY

On the Road to San Romano

Poetry is made in a bed like love
Its rumpled sheets are the dawn of things
Poetry is made in the woods

It has the space it needs
Not this one but the other shaped by

> The hawk's eye
> The dew on a horsetail
> The memory of a bottle frosted over on a
>   silver tray
> A tall rod of tourmaline on the sea
> And the road of the mental adventure
> That climbs abruptly
> One stop and bushes cover it instantly

That isn't to be shouted on the rooftops
It's improper to leave the door open
Or to summon witnesses

> Les bancs de poissons les haies de mésanges
> Les rails à l'entrée d'une grande gare
> Les reflets des deux rives
> Les sillons dans le pain
> Les bulles du ruisseau
> Les jours du calendrier
> Le millepertuis

L'acte d'amour et l'acte de poésie
Sont incompatibles
Avec la lecture du journal à haute voix

> Le sens du rayon de soleil
> La lueur bleue qui relie les coups de hache du bûcheron
> Le fil du cerf-volant en forme de cœur ou de nasse
> Le battement en mesure de la queue des castors
> La diligence de l'éclair
> Le jet de dragées du haut des vieilles marches
> L'avalanche

La chambre aux prestiges
Non messieurs ce n'est pas la huitième Chambre
Ni les vapeurs de la chambrée un dimanche soir

> Les figures de danse exécutées en transparence au-dessus des mares
> La délimitation contre un mur d'un corps de femme au lancer de
>   poignards
> Les volutes claires de la fumée
> Les boucles de tes cheveux
> La courbe de l'éponge des Philippines
> Les lacés du serpent corail
> L'entrée du lierre dans les ruines
> *Elle a tout le temps devant elle*

L'étreinte poétique comme l'étreinte de chair
Tant qu'elle dure
Défend toute échappée sur la misère du monde

The shoals of fish the hedges of titmice
The rails at the entrance of a great station
The reflections of both riverbanks
The crevices in the bread
The bubbles of the stream
The days of the calendar
The St John's wort

The acts of love and poetry
Are incompatible
With reading the newspaper aloud

The course of a sunbeam
The blue light linking the woodcutter's axe blows
The kite string shaped like a heart or a hoop net
The beavers' tails beating in time
The diligence of a flash
The casting of candy from the old stairs
The avalanche

The room of marvels
No gentleman is not a courtroom
Nor the haze in a roomful of soldiers one Sunday evening

Dance figures transparent above ponds
The outline on the wall of a woman's body at daggerthrow
The bright spirals of smoke
The curls of your hair
The curve of the Philippine sponge
The twists of a coral snake
The ivy creeping into the ruins
It has all the time it needs

The embrace of poetry like that of the flesh
As long as it lasts
Shuts out all the woes of the world

—MARY ANN CAWS

La Sadique Judith

Qui était Judith

Elle s'était fait en haut de sa maison une chambre secrète où elle demeurait enfermée . . .

Et, ayant un cilice sur les reins, elle jeûnait tous les jours de sa vie, hors les jours de sabbat . . .

Discours de Judith au Peuple

Je ne veux point que vous vous mettiez en peine de savoir ce que j'ai dessein de faire . . .

Mais ceux . . . qui ont témoigné leur impatience . . . ont été exterminés par l'ange exterminateur, et ont péri par les morsures des serpents.

Claude Cahun (Lucy Schwob) 1894–1954
NANTES, FRANCE

C ahun was a versatile artist, poet, essayist, literary critic, political activist, and photographer. Subversive, provocative, and in many ways ahead of its time, her work was exhibited with that of the Surrealists in Paris. Her self-portraits depict a fluid cast of characters and identities; she flaunted, for example, the crossover between genders, appearing in suit and monocle as well as in an elegant evening gown. Born in Nantes, she moved to Paris in 1922 and remained there until 1938. During the Paris years, she and her lover, Suzanne Malherbe (known as Moore), participated in all the literary gatherings of the time. Later, they moved to the island of Jersey, where they tried to inspire German troops to mutiny by pinning butterflies on their tanks. Cahun and Malherbe were arrested by the Gestapo in 1944 and sentenced to death. Eventually released, Cahun was unable to rejoin the Surrealists in Paris because of illness and instead returned to Jersey, where many of her photographs and archives had been destroyed by the Nazis. Principal works: *Héroïnes*, 1925; *Aveux non avenus*, 1930; *Les Paris sont ouverts*, 1934.

Sadistic Judith

Who Was Judith

She had made atop her house a secret room where she remained closed in . . .
And with a hair shirt over her body, she fasted every day of her life, except for the Sabbath . . .

Judith's Speech to the People

I don't want you to try to know what I mean to do . . .
But those . . . who showed their impatience . . . were exterminated by the exterminating angel, and perished from the bites of serpents.

*C'est pourquoi ne témoignons point
d'impatience . . .
Mais considérons que ces supplices
sont encore beaucoup moindres que nos
péchés . . .*

Discours de Judith à Holopherne

*Tout le monde publie que vous êtes le
seul dont la puissance . . .
Et votre discipline militaire est louée
dans tous les pays.
(Livre de Judith — VIII et IX)*

À Erich von Stroheim

« Il faut croire qu'il méprise les femmes, et ne s'en cache point (car lui-même laisse dire); qu'il est grossier, tel que seul un guerrier peut l'être. Après qu'il a baisé son esclave il s'essuie furtivement la lèvre. Il n'ôte point ses vêtements de peur de souiller de son corps plus qu'il n'est indispensable. Les nuits d'amour, la pourpre dans laquelle il se vautre, symboliquement teinte du venin rouge des victimes, ses bottes la maculent, du haut en bas y traînent, selon la saison, la poussière ou la boue des chemins, ou pire. Mais dès le chant du coq, il prend un bain, met la fille à la porte — et fait changer les draps (la soie, le sang figé des draps).

« On dit aussi qu'il est le plus laid des hommes; et ceux qui craignent qu'il ne séduise leurs servantes assurent qu'il ressemble à un porc.

Mais je l'ai vu, tandis que son armée victorieuse défilait devant nos portes closes, car (ayant silencieusement égorgé mon chien dont l'agitation me gênait) j'ai pu regarder par le trou de la serrure :

« Que me plaît ce front fuyant, ces yeux morts, si lents — des yeux petits, étroits, aux paupières énormes; ce menton charnu mais point trop saillant; cette bouche bestiale aux lèvres sensuelles, mais de la même peau, semble-t-il, que le reste du visage — bouche dont la fente, la gueule seule est admirablement dessinée, expressive, et dès qu'elle s'ouvre en demi-couronne, sombre, met en valeur les canines taillées en pointe comme les ongles de Judith!

« Ah! surtout, que me plaisent ces oreilles en éventail, cette nuque au poil court — et la superbe verticale du crâne au cou, s'il penche la tête en arrière, brisée par des plis de reptile! Je les aime parce que j'y reconnais les caractères distinctifs, odieux, de la race ennemie.

« Une femme est en marche. — Vers le camp du vainqueur! . . .

So let's not show any impatience . . .
But let's consider that these tortures
are still less than our sins . . .

Judith's Speech to Holofernes

Everyone says that you are the only
one who has power . . .
And your military discipline is
praised in all countries.
(Book of Judith VIII and IX)

To Erich von Stroheim

"We have to believe that he despises women, and doesn't hide it (for he himself lets it be known); that he is vulgar, as only a warrior can be. After making love to his slave he furtively wipes his lips. He doesn't take off his clothes for fear of soiling his body more than necessary. On the nights of love, his boots spot the purple in which he wallows, symbolically dyed with the red venom of his poisons, and from top to bottom, the dust or the mud of the paths or worse trail across it, depending on the season. But at cockcry, he takes a bath, sends the girl away — and has the sheets changed (the silk, the blood coagulated on them).

"They also say that he is the ugliest of men; and those who fear he will seduce their servants swear he looks like a pig.

But I have seen him, while his victorious army was parading before our closed doors, for (having silently slit the throat of my dog, whose excitement bothered me), I could see through the keyhole:

"How pleasing I find this receding forehead, these dead eyes, so slow — little eyes, narrow ones, with enormous eyelids; this fleshy chin not too prominent; this animal mouth with its sensual lips, of the same skin, it seems, as the rest of his face — his mouth whose split, whose muzzle is admirably drawn, expressive, and as soon as it half-opens, so darkly, it shows the canines filed to a point like Judith's nails!

"Ah, above all, how I love those ears fanning out, this nape of the neck with its short hair — and the superb vertical line from the skull to the neck, when he leans his head backwards, broken with reptilian pleats! I love them because I recognize in them the distinctive, odious traits of the enemy race.

"A woman is walking. — Towards the victor's camp! . . .

«Un oiseau sans ailes, un tout petit tombé du nid est à mes pieds. Je m'age-nouille (il est vivant!), je le tiens dans ma main : "Il est un duvet plus tendre, cher cœur affolé, douceur, douceur sans défense, plus tendre que le ventre de ta mère, que les brins de mousse rousse et de soies réunis par ses soins . . ." Le voilà presque rassuré, plus chaud que mon aisselle fiévreuse. Je le tiens sous mon bras serré — ô caresse de ses plumes naissantes! . . . — En route! . . . et je serre un peu davantage — pour qu'il ne tombe pas, pour le sentir contre ma chair brûler, se refroidir, pour un spasme — et qu'il meure! . . .

« *C'est d'un mauvais présage.* — Dégoût! . . . Pourquoi dégoût? La vie serait donc si propre, plus propre que la mort? Au moins c'est un cadavre qui n'est pas encombrant.

«Serai-je de force à le porter tout entier — l'autre — ou faudra-t-il dépecer, choisir les meilleurs morceaux? . . .

« —Oh! je me suis fait peur! Rien n'est accompli pourtant; je pensais cela . . . pour plaisanter.

« . . . Suis-je vraiment condamnée, criminelle depuis l'enfance, à détruire tout ce que j'aime? Non : il empêchera le sacrifice infâme. N'est-il pas mon élu parce qu'il est le plus fort? — Barbare! asservis-moi; ne me livre d'abord que le plus vulgaire de ton corps, ce que j'ai le moins appris à chérir. Prends bien garde à cette bouche, à cette nuque, à ces oreilles — à tout ce qui peut se mordre, se déchirer, se sucer jusqu'à l'épuisement de ton sang étranger — délicieux.

«C'est ta faute! Pourquoi ne m'as-tu pas devinée? Pourquoi ne m'as-tu pas livrée aux bourreaux? Je t'aimerais encore, je fusse morte heureuse. Je te voulais vainqueur et tu t'es laissé vaincre! . . .

«À quoi bon ces reproches? Il ne m'écoute pas, il ne peut pas m'écouter . . .

«À moi seule : Pourquoi l'avoir vaincu? (Ai-je donc voulu cesser de t'aimer, Holopherne?) — Puérile, ô puérile! . . . Pourquoi manger? La question ne se pose qu'alors qu'on n'a plus faim . . .

«Et voici mes frères! Ceux-là n'ont rien à craindre, car ils me font horreur. Patrie, prison de l'âme! Enfermée, moi du moins j'ai su voir les barreaux, et même entre les barreaux . . .»

Le Peuple d'Israël acclame Judith.

Mais elle, d'abord plus étonnée qu'un enfant qu'on maltraite, se laisse porter en triomphe — comme endormie. Bientôt elle se réveille, ivre de rire et d'inso-lence, et dressée sur le socle de chair humaine elle s'écrie :

«Peuple! *qu'y a-t-il ae commun entre toi et moi?* Qui t'a permis de pénétrer ma vie privée? de juger mes actes et de les trouver beaux? de me charger (moi si faible et si lasse, leur éternelle proie) de ta gloire abominable?»

"A wingless bird, a tiny little one fallen from his nest is at my feet. I kneel down (he is living!), I hold him in my hand: 'There is a comforter softer, dear panicked heart, sweetness, defenseless sweetness, softer than your mother's stomach, than the bits of reddish moss and silks she gathered . . .' Now he's almost reassured, warmer than my feverish armpit. I hold him under my arm clasped to my side — oh caress of his nascent feathers! . . . Let's start off! . . . and I hold him a little more tightly — so he won't fall, so I'll feel him burning against my flesh, growing cold, for a final spasm — and dying!—

"*That's a bad omen.* — Disgust! . . . Why disgust? So life is that clean, cleaner than death? At least this corpse doesn't take up much space.

"Shall I have the strength to carry him whole — the other one — or will it be better to cut him into pieces, to choose the best bits? . . .

"Oh! I frightened myself! Nothing has been accomplished; I was thinking that . . . as a joke.

". . . Have I really been a criminal from childhood, condemned to destroy everything I love? No: he will prevent the infamous sacrifice. Isn't he my chosen one because he is the strongest? — Barbarian! enslave me; deliver to me first just the most vulgar part of your body, the one I've learned to cherish the least. Watch out for this mouth, this nape, these ears — for everything that can be bitten, torn, sucked until your foreign blood is exhausted — delicious.

"It's your fault! Why didn't you find me out? Why didn't you turn me over to the executioners? I would still love you, I would have perished happy. I want you to be the victor and you left yourself be conquered! . . .

"What's the point of all this reproach? He isn't listening to me, he can't listen to me . . .

"For myself alone: Why did I vanquish him? (Have I then stopped loving you, Holofernes?) — Childish, oh childish! . . . Why do we eat? We only ask the question when we aren't hungry any longer . . .

"And now my brothers! Those have nothing to fear, for they strike me with horror. Countryland, prison of the soul! Imprisoned, at least I knew how to see the bars, and even between the bars . . ."

The People of Israel acclaim Judith.

But she, at first more astonished than a mistreated child, lets herself be carried in triumph — as if she were asleep. Soon she wakes, drunk with laughter and insolence, and standing on the stump of human flesh she cries:

"People! *what is there in common between you and me?* Who allowed you to penetrate my private life! to judge my acts and find them beautiful? to load me down (me so feeble and so tired, their eternal prey) with your abominable glory?"

Mais ses paroles ne furent point comprises, ni même entendues. La joie d'une foule a mille bouches — et pas d'oreilles.

————————————

Sens plastique (1947)
(extraits)

L'idiot bêle du regard.

Les épices font fox-trotter la langue et valser le palais.

. . .

Le gris est le cendrier du soleil.

L'éclat, c'est les hanches de la lumière ; et les scintillements, les seins.

. . .

But her words were not understood, or even heard. The joy of a crowd has a thousand mouths — and no ears.

—MARY ANN CAWS

Malcolm de Chazal 1902–1981
VACOAS, MAURITIUS

O riginally hailed as a Surrealist by André Breton, de Chazal was later disowned because of his interest in the occult. His work went far beyond the wordplay, metaphor, and free associations of Surrealism to a sensuous examination of the possible connections between elements in nature, humans and nature, mind and body. De Chazal was schooled in engineering and wrote in French rather than English, though his writing remained true to the exotic land of his youth. In the 1960s the president of Senegal, Léopold Sédar Senghor, a poet himself, nominated him for the Nobel Prize in Literature for his essentially African poetry. Principal works: *Pensées et sens plastique,* 1945; *Sens plastique II,* 1945; *Sens magique,* 1956; *Le Sens unique,* 1986.

Plastic Sense

The idiot bleats with his gaze.

Spices set the tongue fox-trotting and the palate waltzing.

. . .

Grey is the ashtray of the sun.

Flashing are the hips of the sun; and gleaming are its breasts.

. . .

157

La pluie est une épingle d'eau, et une aiguille de lumière, dans le dé du vent.

Le rose, c'est les dents de lait du soleil.

La voix humaine est le midi des sons.

Sens plastique (1948) (extraits)

La volupté est la plus puissante sensation que nous ayons de la vitesse.

Le nez est tout dos : le nez a toujours l'air de regarder *dans* la face. Le nez n'assume un visage en propre que lorsque l'homme rit.

Le regard humain est un phare qui navigue.

L'homme en crachant, crache sa salive. L'eau en crachant, crache sa bouche.

Les contre-courants créent des visages dans l'eau, mais visages dont les traits se succèdent à la queu leu leu, comme dans les faces «liquides» des gens bêtes.

L'hypocrisie met le regard en patte d'oie.

Si l'on pouvait tapoter la voix humaine, comme un diaphragme qu'on agite, on obtiendrait la voix de l'eau.

Le regard est le plus long râteau.

L'absolu du neuf, c'est le nu total.

Le brouillard arrondit les sons. Toutes les voix dans le brouillard prennent un ton gai.

L'espace est la plus grosse de toutes les bouches.

La mort est une «perte de souffle» étagée. La volupté est une « perte de souffle » en rond.

Le bleu est le summum du propre. Après une longue contemplation d'un ciel d'azur, nous avons l'œil lavé et bouchonné. Après son bain, l'homme a des regards bleus.

The rain is a pin of water, and a needle of light, in the dice of the wind

Rose-color, the milk teeth of the sun.

The human voice is the noon of sounds.

—MARY ANN CAWS

Plastic Sense

Sensuality is the most powerful feeling of speed we can have.

The nose is all back: the nose always seems to be looking *into* the face. The nose only takes on a real face when someone is laughing.

The human gaze is a lighthouse sailing around.

When a man's spitting, he's spitting out his saliva. Water when it's spitting, is spitting out its mouth.

Countercurrents create faces in the water, but faces whose traits come one after the other any which way, as in the "fluid" faces of stupid people.

Hypocrisy gives crow's-feet to the gaze.

If you could drum on the human voice, like a diaphragm you shake, you'd get the voice of water.

The gaze is the longest rake.

The absolute new is the total nude.

Fog gives a round shape to every noise. Every voice in the fog takes on a cheerful tone.

Space is the widest of all mouths.

Death is a "loss of breath" in steps. Voluptuousness is a "loss of breath" in a circle.

Blue is the essence of the neat. After a long look at a blue sky, we have our eyes washed and stopped up. After his bath, man has a blue gaze.

Le sein est une pomme dans une poire, où pointe un grain de raisin. Le sein est le maximum du fondu ; tous les fruits en un.

La volupté nous « involue », comme un gant qu'on retourne, nous faisant faire du narcissisme à rebours, comme l'épiderme voyant le corps du dedans. Dans la volupté l'homme s'auto-voit, comme l'enfant venu au monde, avant de jeter son premier cri, ou tel le mort soudainement jailli dans le monde spirituel en naissance brusque, avant d'avoir pris conscience de son nouveau corps, le cherche en lui-même pour un temps.

La Logique

La logique
Ne s'est
Jamais
Raisonnée.

L'œuf
Est
Tout
En mentons.

L'homme qui n'accolerait
À une image
Aucune idée
Connaîtrait
L'esprit pur.

The breast is an apple in a pear, with a grape seed just showing through. The breast is melting at its maximum; all fruits in one.

Sensuality "involutes" us like a glove you turn inside out, making us create narcissism backwards, like the skin seeing the body from the inside. In voluptuousness, man sees himself, like the child come into the world before uttering his first cry, or like the dead man suddenly sprang into the spiritual world in a brusque birth, before having become aware of his new body, looks into himself for a while.

—MARY ANN CAWS

Logic

Logic
Never
Thought
Itself out.

The egg
Is
Just
Chins.

The man who'd not tie
To an image
Any idea
Would know
Pure mind.

—MARY ANN CAWS

Notre paire

Notre paire quiète, ô yeux!
que votre «non» soit sang (t'y fier?)
que votre araignée rie,
que votre vol honteux soit fête (au fait)
sur la terre (commotion).

Donnez-nous, aux joues réduites,
notre pain quotidien.
Part, donnez-nous, de nos oeufs foncés
comme nous part donnons
à ceux qui nous ont offensés.
Nounou laissez-nous succomber à la tentation
et d'aile ivrez-nous du mal.

Robert Desnos 1900–1945
PARIS, FRANCE

One of the original participants in Surrealism, the Parisian Desnos was a master of several of the techniques that have led some to consider the early 1920s Surrealism's greatest moment. Desnos had a remarkable ability to write and speak in a trancelike state during the era of the "hypnotic sleeps." He practiced, as did all the Surrealists, automatic writing and drawing under the dictates of the newly freed consciousness: for example, in the drawings and writings called "le cadavre exquis" (the exquisite corpse), the first player puts down the face or the first word, the second player follows, without cognizance of the original contribution, and so on. Desnos also wrote as Rrose Sélavy ("eros is life"), a personage created by Marcel Duchamp as his alter ego. Her/his word play, untranslatable, is one of the summits of this "laboratory" phase of Surrealism. Breton once commended Desnos for best exemplifying the truth of Surrealism—before excommunicating him for his radio and publicity work. Desnos was arrested by the Gestapo and died of typhus just after the liberation of the Nazi camp Terezin, where he was incarcerated. Principal works: *Deuil pour deuil*, 1924; *A la mystérieuse*, 1926; *La Liberté ou l'amour!* 1927; *Les Ténèbres*, 1927; *Contrée*, 1944.

Hour Farther

Hour farther witch art in Heaven
Hallowed bee, thine aim
Thy king done come!
Thy will be done in
ersatz is in Heaven.

Kippers this day-hour, Delhi bread.
And four kippers, sour trace, pa says,
As we four give them that trace paths against us.
And our leader's not in to tempt Asians;
Butter liver (as from Eve) fill our men.

—MARTIN SORRELL

Comme

Come, dit l'Anglais à l'Anglais, et l'Anglais vient.

Côme, dit le chef de gare, et le voyageur qui vient dans cette ville descend du
    train sa valise à la main.

Come, dit l'autre, et il mange.

Comme, je dis comme et tout se métamorphose, le marbre en eau, le ciel en
    orange, le vin en plaine, le fil en six, le coeur en peine, la peur en seine.

Mais si l'Anglais dit as, c'est à son tour de voir le monde changer de forme à sa
    convenance

Et moi je ne vois plus qu'un signe unique sur une carte

L'as de coeur si c'est en février,

L'as de carreau et l'as de trèfle, misère en Flandre,

L'as de pique aux mains des aventuriers.

Et si cela me plaît à moi de vous dire machin,

Pot à eau, mousseline et potiron.

Que l'Anglais dise machin,

Que machin dise le chef de gare,

Machin dise l'autre,

Et moi aussi.

Machin.

Et même machin chose.

Il est vrai que vous vous en foutez

Que vous ne comprenez pas la raison de ce poème.

Moi non plus d'ailleurs.

Poème, je vous demande un peu?

Poème? je vous demande un peu de confiture,

Encore un peu de gigot,

Encore un petit verre de vin

Pour nous mettre en train . . .

Non l'amour n'est pas mort

Non, l'amour n'est pas mort en ce cœur et ces yeux et cette bouche qui
proclamait ses funérailles commencées.

Écoutez, j'en ai assez du pittoresque et des couleurs et du charme.

J'aime l'amour, sa tendresse et sa cruauté.

Mon amour n'a qu'un seul nom, qu'une seule forme.

Tout passe. Des bouches se collent à cette bouche.

Mon amour n'a qu'un nom, qu'une forme.

Like

Laïque, says the Frenchman to the Frenchman, and the Frenchman is civil.
Lake? says the pleasure-boat captain, and the tripper trips up the gangplank.
Leica, explains the tourist snap-happily.
Like, I say like and everything is metamorphosed, marble into water, the sky
    into orange ribbons, wine into new bottles, three into two, the heart into little
    pieces, one's back into it, laughter into tears.
But when the Englishman says as, it's his turn to see the world change shape to
    his liking.
As for me, I only see a single aspect, one sign on a playing-card,
The ace of hearts if it's astringent February,
The ace of diamonds and the ace of clubs, penury in Asturias.
The ace of spades ready for the assault.
What if it pleases me to say "whatsit" to you,
Pitcher, mashed potato, pumpkin.
Let the English say whatsit,
Whatsit the stationmaster,
Whatsit what's his name,
And me as well.
Whatsit.
Even whatsit thingummy.
It's true you don't give a toss
Whether you get the point of this poem.
Me neither for that matter.
Poem, I've one or two favours to ask you.
Poem, could you give me a little more jam,
A little more lamb,
Another little glass of wine
To get us going properly . . .

—MARTIN SORRELL

No, Love Is Not Dead

    No, love is not dead in this heart and these eyes and this mouth which announced the beginning of its burial.
    Listen, I have had enough of the picturesque and the colourful and the charming.
    I love love, its tenderness and cruelty.
    My love has but one name, but one form.
    All passes. Mouths press against this mouth.
    My love has but one name, but one form.

Et si quelque jour tu t'en souviens

O toi, forme et nom de mon amour,

Un jour sur la mer entre l'Amérique et l'Europe,

A l'heure où le rayon final du soleil se réverbère sur la surface ondulée des vagues, ou bien une nuit d'orage sous un arbre dans la campagne ou dans une rapide automobile,

Un matin de printemps boulevard Malesherbes,

Un jour de pluie,

A l'aube avant de te coucher,

Dis-toi, je l'ordonne à ton fantôme familier, que je fus seul à t'aimer davantage et qu'il est dommage que tu ne l'aies pas connu.

Dis-toi qu'il ne faut pas regretter les choses : Ronsard avant moi et Baudelaire ont chanté le regret des vieilles et des mortes qui méprisèrent le plus pur amour.

Toi quand tu seras morte

Tu seras belle et toujours désirable.

Je serai mort déjà, enclos tout entier en ton corps immortel, en ton image étonnante présente à jamais parmi les merveilles perpétuelles de la vie et de l'éternité, mais si je vis

Ta voix et son accent, ton regard et ses rayons,

L'odeur de toi et celle de tes cheveux et beaucoup d'autres choses encore vivront en moi,

En moi qui ne suis ni Ronsard ni Baudelaire,

Moi qui suis Robert Desnos et qui pour t'avoir connue et aimée,

Les vaux bien.

Moi qui suis Robert Desnos, pour t'aimer

Et qui ne veux pas attacher d'autre réputation à ma mémoire sur la terre méprisable.

Si tu savais

Loin de moi et semblable aux étoiles, à la mer et à tous les accessoires de la mythologie poétique,

Loin de moi et cependant présente à ton insu,

Loin de moi et plus silencieuse encore parce que je t'imagine sans cesse,

Loin de moi, mon joli mirage et mon rêve éternel, tu ne peux pas savoir.

Si tu savais.

Loin de moi et peut-être davantage encore de m'ignorer et m'ignorer encore.

Loin de moi parce que tu ne m'aimes pas sans doute ou ce qui revient au même, que j'en doute.

Loin de moi parce que tu ignores sciemment mes désirs passionnés.

Loin de moi parce que tu es cruelle.

Si tu savais.

And if some day you remember
O form and name of my love,
One day on the ocean between America and Europe,
At the hour when the last sunbeam reverberates on the undulating surface of waves, or else a stormy night beneath a tree in the countryside or in a speeding car,
A spring morning on the boulevard Malesherbes,
A rainy day,
At dawn before sleeping,
Tell yourself, I command your familiar spirit, that I alone loved you more and that it is sad you should not have known it.
Tell yourself one must not regret things: Ronsard before me and Baudelaire have sung the regrets of ladies old or dead who despised the purest love.
When you are dead
You will be beautiful and always desirable
I will already be dead, enclosed forever complete within your immortal body, in your astonishing image present forever among the constant marvels of life and of eternity, but if I live
Your voice and its tone, your look and its radiance,
Your fragrance, the scent of your hair and many other things besides will still live in me,
Who am neither Ronsard nor Baudelaire,
I who am Robert Desnos and who for having known and loved you,
Am easily their equal.
I who am Robert Desnos, to love you
Wanting nothing else to be remembered by on the despicable earth.

—MARY ANN CAWS

If You Knew

Far from me and like the stars, the sea, and all the props of poetic legend,
Far from me and present all the same, yet unaware,
Far from me and still more silent in my endless imagining,
Far from me, my lovely mirage and my eternal dream, you cannot know.
If you knew.
Far from me and perhaps still farther being unaware of me and still unaware.
Far from me for you doubtless do not love me or, not so different, I doubt your love.
Far from me for you cleverly ignore my passionate desires.
Far from me for you are cruel.
If you knew.

Loin de moi, ô joyeuse comme la fleur qui danse dans la rivière au bout de sa tige aquatique, ô triste comme sept heures du soir dans les champignonnières.

Loin de moi silencieuse encore ainsi qu'en ma présence et joyeuse encore comme l'heure en forme de cigogne qui tombe de haut.

Loin de moi à l'instant où chantent les alambics, à l'instant où la mer silencieuse et bruyante se replie sur les oreillers blancs.

Si tu savais.

Loin de moi, ô mon présent présent tourment, loin de moi au bruit magnifique des coquilles d'huîtres qui se brisent sous le pas du noctambule, au petit jour, quand il passe devant la porte des restaurants.

Si tu savais.

Loin de moi, volontaire et matériel mirage.

Loin de moi c'est une île qui se détourne au passage des navires.

Loin de moi un calme troupeau de bœufs se trompe de chemin, s'arrête obstinément au bord d'un profond précipice, loin de moi, ô cruelle.

Loin de moi, une étoile filante choit dans la bouteille nocturne du poète. Il met vivement le bouchon et dès lors il guette l'étoile enclose dans le verre, il guette les constellations qui naissent sur les parois, loin de moi, tu es loin de moi.

Si tu savais.

Loin de moi une maison achève d'être construite.

Un maçon en blouse blanche au sommet de l'échafaudage chante une petite chanson très triste et, soudain, dans le récipient empli de mortier apparaît le futur de la maison : les baisers des amants et les suicides à deux et la nudité dans les chambres des belles inconnues et leurs rêves à minuit, et les secrets voluptueux surpris par les lames de parquet.

Loin de moi,

Si tu savais.

Si tu savais comme je t'aime et, bien que tu ne m'aimes pas, comme je suis joyeux, comme je suis robuste et fier de sortir avec ton image en tête, de sortir de l'univers.

Comme je suis joyeux à en mourir.

Si tu savais comme le monde m'est soumis.

Et toi, belle insoumise aussi, comme tu es ma prisonnière.

O toi, loin-de-moi à qui je suis soumis.

Si tu savais.

Jamais d'autre que toi

Jamais d'autre que toi en dépit des étoiles et des solitudes
En dépit des mutilations d'arbre à la tombée de la nuit
Jamais d'autre que toi ne poursuivra son chemin qui est le mien
Plus tu t'éloignes et plus ton ombre s'agrandit

Far from me, oh joyous as the flower dancing in the river on its watery stem, oh sad as seven in the evening in the mushroom fields.

Far from me still silent as in my presence and still joyous as the stork-shaped hour falling from on high.

Far from me at the moment when the alembics sing, when the silent and noisy sea curls up on the white pillows.

If you knew.

Far from me, oh my present present torment, far from me with the splendid sound of oyster shells crunched under the nightwalker's step, at dawn, when he passes by the door of restaurants.

If you knew.

Far from me, willed and material mirage.

Far from me an island turns aside at the passing of ships.

Far from me a calm herd of cattle mistakes the path, stops stubbornly at the brink of a steep precipice, far from me, oh cruel one.

Far from me, a falling star falls in the night bottle of the poet. He corks it instantly to watch the star enclosed within the glass, the constellations come to life against the sides, far from me, you are far from me.

If you knew.

Far from me a house is built just now.

A white-clothed worker atop the structure sings a sad brief song and suddenly, in the hod of mortar there appears the future of the house: lovers' kisses and double suicides and nakedness in the rooms of lovely unknown girls and their midnight dreams, and the voluptuous secrets surprised by the parquet floors.

Far from me.

If you knew.

If you knew how I love you and though you do not love me, how I am happy, how I am strong and proud, with your image in my mind, to leave the universe.

How I am happy enough to perish from it.

If you knew how the world submits to me.

And you, oh beautiful unsubmissive one, how you are also my prisoner.

Oh far-from-me to whom I submit.

If you knew.

—MARY ANN CAWS

Never Anyone but You

Never anyone but you in spite of stars and solitudes
In spite of mutilated trees at nightfall
Never anyone but you will take a path which is mine also
The farther you go away the greater your shadow grows

Jamais d'autre que toi ne saluera la mer à l'aube quand fatigué d'errer moi sorti
   des forêts ténébreuses et des buissons d'orties je marcherai vers l'écume
Jamais d'autre que toi ne posera sa main sur mon front et mes yeux
Jamais d'autre que toi et je nie le mensonge et l'infidélité
Ce navire à l'ancre tu peux couper sa corde
Jamais d'autre que toi
L'aigle prisonnier dans une cage ronge lentement les barreaux de cuivre vert-de-
   grisés
Quelle évasion!
C'est le dimanche marqué par le chant des rossignols dans les bois d'un vert
   tendre l'ennui des petites filles en présence d'une cage où s'agite un serin
   tandis que dans la rue solitaire le soleil lentement déplace sa ligne mince sur
   le trottoir chaud
Nous passerons d'autres lignes
Jamais jamais d'autre que toi
Et moi seul seul seul comme le lierre fané des jardins de banlieue seul comme le
   verre
Et toi jamais d'autre que toi.

J'ai tant rêvé de toi

J'ai tant rêvé de toi que tu perds ta réalité.

Est-il encore temps d'atteindre ce corps vivant et de baiser sur cette bouche la naissance de la voix qui m'est chère?

J'ai tant rêvé de toi que mes bras habitués en étreignant ton ombre à se croiser sur ma poitrine ne se plieraient pas au contour de ton corps, peut-être.

Et que, devant l'apparence réelle de ce qui me hante at me gouverne depuis des jours et des années, je deviendrais une ombre sans doute.

O balances sentimentales.

J'ai tant rêvé de toi qu'il n'est plus temps sans doute que je m'éveille. Je dors debout, le corps exposé à toutes les apparences de la vie et de l'amour et toi, la seule qui compte aujourd'hui pour moi, je pourrais moins toucher ton front et tes lèvres que les premières lèvres et le premier front venu.

J'ai tant rêvé de toi, tant marché, parlé, couché avec ton fantôme qu'il ne me reste plus peut-être, et pourtant, qu'à être fantôme parmi les fantômes et plus ombre cent fois que l'ombre qui se promène et se promènera allégrement sur le cadran solaire de ta vie.

Never anyone but you will salute the sea at dawn when tired of wandering
    having left the dark-shadowed forests and thistle bushes I shall walk toward
    the foam
Never anyone but you will place her hand on my forehead and my eyes
Never anyone but you and I deny falsehood and infidelity
This anchored boat you may cut its rope
Never anyone but you
The eagle prisoner in a cage pecks slowly at the copper bars turned green
What an escape!
It's Sunday marked by the song of nightingales in the woods of a tender green
    the tedium felt by little girls before a cage where a canary flies about while in
    the solitary street the sun slowly moves its narrow line across the heated
    sidewalk
We shall pass other lines
Never never anyone but you
And I alone like the faded ivy of suburban gardens alone like glass
And you never anyone but you.

—MARY ANN CAWS

I've Dreamt of You So Often

I've dreamt of you so often that you become unreal.

Is there still time to reach this living body and to kiss on its mouth the birth of the voice so dear to me?

I've dreamt of you so often that my arms used to embracing your shadow and only crossing on my own chest might no longer meet your body's shape.

And before the real appearance of what has haunted and ruled me for days and years I would doubtless become a shadow.

Oh the shifts of feeling.

I've dreamt of you so often that it is doubtless no longer time for me to wake. I sleep standing, my body exposed to all the appearances of life and love and you, who only count today for me, I could touch your forehead and your lips less easily than any other lips and forehead.

I've dreamt of you so often, walked, spoken, slept so often with your phantom that perhaps all that yet remains for me is to be a phantom among the phantoms and a hundred times more shadow than the shadow which saunters and will saunter so gladly over the sundial of your life.

—MARY ANN CAWS

L'Amoureuse

Elle est debout sur mes paupières
Et ses cheveux sont dans les miens,
Elle a la forme de mes mains,
Elle a la couleur de mes yeux,
Elle s'engloutit dans mon ombre
Comme une pierre sur le ciel.

Paul Éluard (Eugène Grindel) 1895–1952
SAINT-DENIS, FRANCE

É luard is celebrated as the author of some of the best Surrealist poetry. In his verse, the play of dualities is always evident. He was also associated with the French Dadaists, such as Breton, Aragon, and Soupault, before Surrealism had been codified. Éluard broke with Surrealism in 1938 after a disagreement with Breton; like many Surrealists, he was a member of the Communist Party. Like Aragon and unlike Breton, he remained with the party faithful. He met his first love, Gala (Elena Dimitrievna Diakonova)—who had been associated with Max Ernst and was to leave Éluard for Salvador Dalí—and wrote his first lines of poetry while recuperating from tuberculosis in a Swiss sanitarium. The singer-actress Maria Benz, known as Nusch Éluard after their marriage, would serve as muse for three of his poetry collections. Like Soupault, he was especially drawn to popular poetry and sayings, aphorisms and maxims. During the German Occupation, Éluard took part in the Resistance through his energetic and militant writings, produced clandestinely at the risk of arrest. Principal works: *Le Devoir et l'inquiétude*, 1917; *Poèmes pour la paix*, 1918; *Les Animaux et leurs hommes, les hommes et leurs animaux*, 1920; *Pour vivre ici*, 1920; *Les Nécessités de la vie et les conséquences des rêves*, 1921; *Les Malheurs des immortels*, 1922; *Répétitions*, 1922; *Mourir de ne pas mourir*, 1924; *Capitale de la douleur*, 1926; *Le Temps déborde*, 1927; *L'Amour la poésie*, 1929; *Ralentir travaux* (with Breton and Char), 1930; *La Vie immédiate*, 1932; *Les Yeux fertiles*, 1936; *Cours naturel*, 1938; *Le Livre ouvert*, 1938–1944; *Donner à voir*, 1939; *Le Dur Désir de durer*, 1946; *Pouvoir tout dire*, 1951.

Loving

She is standing on my eyelids
And her hair is in my hair,
She has the shape of my hands,
The color of my eyes,
She is absorbed in my shadow
Like a stone within the sky.

Elle a toujours les yeux ouverts
Et ne me laisse pas dormir.
Ses rêves en pleine lumière
Font s'évaporer les soleils,
Me font rire, pleurer et rire,
Parler sans avoir rien à dire.

Je te l'ai dit

Je te l'ai dit pour les nuages
Je te l'ai dit pour l'arbre de la mer
Pour chaque vague pour les oiseaux dans les feuilles
Pour les cailloux du bruit
Pour les mains familières
Pour l'œil qui devient visage ou paysage
Et le sommeil lui rend le ciel de sa couleur
Pour toute la nuit bue
Pour la grille des routes
Pour la fenêtre ouverte pour un front découvert
Je te l'ai dit pour tes pensées pour tes paroles
Toute caresse toute confiance se survivent.

Le Diamant qu'il ne t'a pas donné

Le diamant qu'il ne t'a pas donné c'est parce qu'il l'a eu à la fin de sa vie, il n'en connaissait plus la musique, il ne pouvait plus le lancer en l'air, il avait perdu l'illusion du soleil, il ne voyait plus la pierre de ta nudité, chaton de cette bague tournée vers toi.

De l'arabesque qui fermait les lieux d'ivresse, la ronce douce, squelette de ton pouce et tous ces signes précurseurs de l'incendie animal qui dévorera en un clin de retour de flamme ta grâce de la Sainte-Claire.

Dans les lieux d'ivresse, la bourrasque de palmes et de vin noir fait rage. Les figures dentelées du jugement d'hier conservent aux journées leurs heures entrouvertes. Es-tu sûre, héroïne aux sens de phare, d'avoir vaincu la miséricorde et l'ombre, ces deux sœurs lavandières, prenons-les à la gorge, elles ne sont pas jolies et pour ce que nous voulons en faire, le monde se détachera bien assez vite de leur crinière peignant l'encens sur le bord des fontaines.

Her eyes she keeps always open
And doesn't let me sleep.
Her dreams in broad daylight
Make the suns evaporate,
Make me laugh, weep and laugh,
And speak, with nothing to say.

—MARY ANN CAWS

I've Told You

I've told you for the clouds
Told you for the ocean's tree
For each wave for birds in the leaves
For the small stones of sound
For the familiar hands
For the eye changing to face or landscape
And sleep restores color to the sky
For all the night drunk deep
For the grillwork of the roads
For the window opened for a forehead laid bare
I've told you for your thoughts your words
Every caress every confidence survives.

—MARY ANN CAWS

The Diamond He Didn't Give You

The diamond he didn't give you, because he only had it as his life was ending, he didn't know its music any longer, he couldn't toss it into the air, he had lost the illusion of the sun, he no longer saw the stone of your nakedness, the jewel of this ring turned towards you.

From the arabesque closing the places of drunkenness, the sweet thorn, the skeleton of your thumb and all these foreseeing signs of the animal fire that will swallow in one returning wink of flame your Santa Clara grace.

In the places of drunkenness, the shudder of palms and black wine rages. The figures in jagged relief of yesterday's judgment keep for the days their half-open hours. Are you sure, oh heroine with lighthouse senses, of having vanquished all mercy and shadow, these two washerwoman sisters? Let's seize them by the throat, they are without loveliness and for what we want to do with them, the world will detach itself rather quickly from their mane, painting incense along the edge of the fountains.

—MARY ANN CAWS

Elle est

Elle est — mais elle n'est qu'à minuit quand tous les oiseaux blancs ont refermé leurs ailes sur l'ignorance des ténèbres, quand la sœur des myriades de perles a caché ses deux mains dans sa chevelure morte, quand le triomphateur se plaît à sangloter, las de ses dévotions à la curiosité, mâle et brillante armure de luxure. Elle est si douce qu'elle a transformé mon cœur. J'avais peur des grandes ombres qui tissent les tapis du jeu et les toilettes, j'avais peur des contorsions du soleil le soir, des incassables branches qui purifient les fenêtres de tous les confessionnaux où des femmes endormies nous attendent.

O buste de mémoire, erreur de forme, lignes absentes, flamme éteinte dans mes yeux clos, je suis devant ta grâce comme un enfant dans l'eau, comme un bouquet dans un grand bois. Nocturne, l'univers se meut dans ta chaleur et les villes d'hiver ont des gestes de rue plus délicats que l'aubépine, plus saisissants que l'heure. La terre au loin se brise en sourires immobiles, le ciel enveloppe la vie : un nouvel astre de l'amour se lève de partout — fini, il n'y a plus de preuves de la nuit.

La Terre est bleue comme une orange

La terre est bleue comme une orange
Jamais une erreur les mots ne mentent pas
Ils ne vous donnent plus à chanter
Au tour des baisers de s'entendre
Les fous et les amours
Elle sa bouche d'alliance
Tous les secrets tous les sourires
Et quels vêtements d'indulgence
À la croire toute nue.

Les guêpes fleurissent vert
L'aube se passe autour du cou
Un collier de fenêtres
Des ailes couvrent les feuilles
Tu as toutes les joies solaires
Tout le soleil sur la terre
Sur les chemins de ta beauté.

She Exists

She exists, but only at midnight, when the wings of the white birds have folded on the ignorance of darkness, when their sister, whose pearls cannot be counted, has hidden her hands in her lifeless hair, when the victor delights in his own tears, weary of worshiping the not-yet-known, the virile and gleaming armor of sensuality. So kind is she that my heart has been transformed. No longer do I fear the great shadows weaving the fabric of play and finery. No longer do I fear the twists and turns of the evening sun, the unbreakable branches, cleansing the windows of all the confessionals where sleeping women await us.

O torso of memory, mistaken form, absent lines, flame extinguished behind my closed eyes. In the presence of your grace I am as a child in water, a bouquet in a forest. Nocturnal, the universe moves in your warmth, and in the streets of the cities of yesterday gestures appear, more delicate than the hawthorn, more gripping than the hour. Far off, the land is streaked with motionless smiles. The sky encloses life. A new star of love rises in all directions—finished, there are no further proofs of the night.

—MARY ANN CAWS

The Earth Is Blue like an Orange

The earth is blue like an orange
Never an error words do not lie
They no longer supply what to sing with
It's up to kisses to get along
Mad ones and lovers
She her wedding mouth
All secrets all smiles
And what indulgent clothing
She looks quite naked.

The wasps are flowering green
Dawn is placing around its neck
A necklace of windows
Wings cover up the leaves
You have all the solar joys
All sunshine on the earth
On the paths of your loveliness.

—MARY ANN CAWS

Nuits partagées (extraits)

Je m'obstine à mêler des fictions aux redoutables réalités. Maisons inhabitées, je vous ai peuplées de femmes exceptionnelles, ni grasses, ni maigres, ni blondes, ni brunes, ni folles, ni sages, peu importe, de femmes plus séduisantes que possibles par un détail. Objets inutiles, même la sottise qui procéda à votre fabrication me fut une source d'enchantements. Etres indifférents, je vous ai souvent écoutés, comme on écoute le bruit des vagues et le bruit des machines d'un bateau, en attendant délicieusement le mal de mer. J'ai pris l'habitude des images les plus inhabituelles. Je les ai vues où elles n'étaient pas. Je les ai mécanisées comme mes levers et mes couchers. Les places, comme des bulles de savon, ont été soumises au gonflement de mes joues, les rues à mes pieds l'un devant l'autre et l'autre passe devant l'un, devant deux et fait le total, les femmes ne se déplaçaient plus que couchées, leur corsage ouvert représentant le soleil. La raison, la tête haute, son carcan d'indifférence, lanterne à tête de fourmi, la raison, pauvre mât de fortune pour un homme affolé, le mât de fortune du bateau . . . voir plus haut.

Pour me trouver des raisons de vivre, j'ai tenté de détruire mes raisons de t'aimer. Pour me trouver des raisons de t'aimer, j'ai mal vécu.

D'un et de deux, de tous

Je suis le spectateur et l'acteur et l'auteur,
Je suis la femme et son mari et leur enfant,
Et le premier amour et le dernier amour,
Et le passant furtif et l'amour confondu.

Et de nouveau la femme et son lit et sa robe,
Et ses bras partagés et le travail de l'homme,
Et son plaisir en flèche et la houle femelle.
Simple et double, ma chair n'est jamais en exil.

Car, où commence un corps, je prends forme et conscience.
Et, même quand un corps se défait dans la mort,
Je gis en son creuset, j'épouse son tourment,
Son infamie honore et mon cœur et la vie.

Shared Nights

I persist in mingling fictions with the most fearful realities. Deserted houses, I have peopled you with exceptional women, neither fat nor thin, neither blond nor dark, neither mad nor wise, it doesn't matter, women as seductive as possible, through some detail. Useless objects, even the silliness that made you was a delight to me. Indifferent beings, I have often listened to you, as you listen to the sound of waves and the noise of the engines of the boat, deliciously waiting to be seasick. I've picked up the habit of the least ordinary images. I've seen them where they weren't. I've made them ordinary like getting up and going to bed. City squares, like soap bubbles, have been subject to the rounding of my cheeks, and the streets to my feet one before the other and the other before the first, before them both and adding up, the women no longer moved except lying down, their blouses open to represent the sun. Reason, her head high, her burden of indifference, that lantern with an ant's head, reason, poor jury-rudder for a man gone mad, the rudder for the boat . . . see above.

To find my reasons for living, I've tried to undo my reasons for loving you. To find my reasons for loving you, I've not lived well.

—MARY ANN CAWS

Of One and Two, of All

I am spectator actor and author
I am the woman her husband and their child
And the first love and the last love
And the furtive passerby and the love abashed.

And again the woman and her bed and gown
And her arms shared and the man's work
And his love darting forth and the woman's increase,
Simple and double, my flesh is never in exile.

For where a body begins I take form and conscience
And even when a body is undone in death
I lie down in its crucible, I wed its torment
Its infamy honors my heart and life.

—MARY ANN CAWS

Églogue

Dans la maison refermée
il fixe un objet dans le soir
et joue à ce jeu d'exister
un fruit tremble
au fond d'un verger
des débris de modes pompeuses
où pendent les dentelles
des morts
flottent en épouvantail à l'arbre
que le vent fait gémir
mais sur un chêne foudroyé
l'oiseau n'a pas peur de chanter
un vieillard a posé sa main
à l'endroit d'un jeune coeur
voué à l'obéissance.

Jean Follain 1903–1971

CANISY, FRANCE

Through his poetry and prose, Follain explored the menace of time—the pressure of history upon the moment and the pressure of mortality upon the individual. He was particularly known for his celebration of the everyday object, in poems generally brief. Follain studied law in Caen and then moved to Paris to work as a lawyer. There he formed close friendships with Max Jacob and André Salmon. In 1928 his poetry began appearing in reviews and winning prizes, including the Grand Prix de Poésie de l'Académie Française. He died in a car accident in Paris. Principal works: *La Main chaude*, 1933; *Le Gant rouge*, 1936; *Chants terrestres*, 1937; *L'Épicerie d'enfance*, 1938; *Inventaire*, 1942; *Exister*, 1947; *Territoires*, 1953; *Objets*, 1955; *Tout instant*, 1957; *Des heures*, 1960; *Pour exister encore*, 1972; *Falloir vivre*, 1976; *Le Pain et la boulange*, 1977; *Présent jour*, 1978.

Eclogue

In the closed house
he fixes on an object in the evening
and plays at that game of existing
a fruit trembles
at the end of the orchard
ruins of pompous fashions
hung with the lacework
of the dead
float a scarecrow in the tree
that groans in the wind
but on a blasted oak
the bird is not afraid to sing
an old man has put his hand
on a young heart
pledged to obedience.

—STEPHEN ROMER

Félicité

La moindre fêlure
d'une vitre ou d'un bol
peut ramener la félicité d'un grand souvenir
les objets nus
montrant leur fine arête
étincellent d'un coup
au soleil
mais perdus dans la nuit
se gorgent aussi bien d'heures
longues
ou brèves.

La Pomme rouge

Le Tintoret peignit sa fille morte
il passait des voitures au loin
le peintre est mort à son tour
de longs rails aujourd'hui
corsettent la terre
et la cisèlent
la Renaissance résiste
dans le clair-obscur des musées
les voix se muent
souvent même le silence
est comme épuisé
mais la pomme rouge demeure.

Quincaillerie

Dans une quincaillerie de détail en province
des hommes vont choisir
des vis et des écrous
et leurs cheveux sont gris et leurs cheveux sont roux
ou roidis ou rebelles.
La large boutique s'emplit d'un air bleuté ;
dans son odeur de fer
de jeunes femmes laissent fuir
leur parfum corporel.

Bliss

The slightest crack
in a pane or a bowl
can restore the bliss of some great memory
bare objects
showing their delicate edge
flash for an instant
in the sun
but left in the night
feed just as well on hours
long
or short.

—STEPHEN ROMER

The Red Apple

Tintoretto painted his dead daughter
carriages were passing in the distance
the painter died in his turn
long rails today
corset the earth
and chisel it
the Renaissance resists
in the chiaroscuro of museums
voices change
often even silence
is almost exhausted
but the red apple remains.

—SERGE GAVRONSKY

Hardware Store

In a provincial retail hardware store
men come to choose
nuts and screws
and their hair is grizzled or their hair is red
slicked down or wild.
The vast shop fills up with blue-tinted air;
into its ferrous odor
young women let their
bodily fragrance flee.

Il suffit de toucher verrous et croix de grilles
qu'on vend là virginales
pour sentir le poids du monde inéluctable.

Ainsi la quincaillerie vogue vers l'éternel
et vend à satiété
les grands clous qui fulgurent.

———————————————

Pêche lunaire

Celui qui est assis penché en avant sur le banc n'est pas toi.

La main posée sur un genou étranger n'est pas la tienne, ton visage n'est pas le tien.

À chaque pulsation de ton cœur devait suivre une autre : la certitude vivait encore, l'herbe ne craignait encore rien. Bientôt tu allais m'appeler, mes pas allaient rencontrer les tiens dans le sable vivant.

It's enough to touch the bolts and wrought-iron crosses
sold there in their virginity
to feel the world's inevitable weight.

So the hardware store floats toward eternity
and sells, till everyone has got enough,
great nails, in flames.

—MARILYN HACKER

Greta Knutson 1899–1983
SWEDEN

The painter and poet Greta Knutson married Tristan Tzara in Stockholm in 1925. The celebrated architect Adolph Loos built them a house at 15 avenue Junot in Montmartre, which became a gathering spot for the Surrealists. In 1935, Tzara broke definitively with the Surrealists, and Knutson left him a year later. She was then associated with the Provençal poet René Char, whose portrait she painted several times. Her poetry is imbued with the transformative power of a Surrealist nocturnal vision. Clouds white and dark dissolve daytime reality, as images float about unhindered and "break apart, drift away, flow into sight and sink under the waves." Nothing is fixed, so everything is newly possible. Principal work: *Lunaires*, 1985.

Moon Fishing

The one seated on the bench leaning forward isn't you.
The hand resting on a stranger's knee isn't yours, nor is your face.
After each of your heartbeats, another was to follow: certainty was still alive, the grass didn't fear anything yet. Soon you were going to summon me, my steps were going to join yours in the living sand.

Les chansons devaient venir et passer sans traces. Chaque objet nous regardait avec des yeux d'enfant, avant la naissance de la peur.

Maintenant les montagnes brûlent et je suis un pays dévasté.

———————————

Songs were to come and go, leaving no traces. Each object looked at us with a child's eyes, before the birth of fear.

Now the mountains are burning, and I am a country laid waste.

—MARY ANN CAWS

Michel Leiris 1901–1990
PARIS, FRANCE

L eiris was a poet who, on the side of the Surrealists, sought to change the world via humanism and, on the side of the existentialists, sought to found a morality based on authenticity. He broke with Surrealism in 1929. In 1931 he joined the ethnologist Marcel Griaule and a group of linguists and ethnologists in the Mission Dakar-Djibouti. Together the team explored sub-Saharan Africa and its cultures, bringing back to Paris more than three thousand objects destined for the Musée d'ethnographie du Trocadéro, a witness to the negrophilia omnipresent in that period. During the two-year expedition he wrote his first book, *L'Afrique fantôme,* discovering through the process his dual passion for ethnography and autobiography. He continued to study the various facets of subjectivity in his prolific autobiographical writings. In 1938 he founded the Collège de sociologie with Georges Bataille and Roger Caillois. When he died, he left a great deal of his work unpublished. Principal works: *Le Point cardinal,* 1927; *Tauromachies,* 1937; *L'Age d'homme,* 1939; *Glossaire, j'y serre mes gloses,* 1940; *Haut mal,* 1943; *Nuits sans nuit,* 1945; *Aurora,* 1946; *La Règle du jeu: Biffures,* 1948; *Fourbis,* 1955; *Grande fuite de neige,* 1964; *Fibrilles,* 1966; *Autres Lancers,* 1969.

Vertical

Sur nos têtes
l'espace finement zébré
et parfois le labour des courants d'air violents

Charge de nuages vivants
horizon des épaules

A la ceinture
l'échevèlement des routes
les souches ensoleillées du cœur

Herbe
soif du sol laminé
vers la roche des genoux

Sous nos pieds
morceau de ciel noirci
l'ombre que nous découpons

Avare

M'alléger
me dépouiller

réduire mon bagage à l'essentiel

Abandonnant ma longue traîne de plumes
de plumages
de plumetis et de plumets

devenir oiseau avare
ivre du seul vol de ses ailes

Maldonne

Les dés
éphémèrement unis
sur la table sont séparés

Vertical

On our heads
the finely striped space
and sometimes the work of swift gusts of air

Charge of living clouds
the shoulders' horizon

At the waist
the tousled routes
the sunny stumps of the heart

Grass
thirst of the threadbare earth
toward the rock of knee

Beneath our feet
piece of blackened sky
the shadow we cut

—COLE SWENSEN

Miserly

Lighten me
unfeather me

strip my baggage down to bare

Abandoning my long-plumed train
of plumage
of needlepoint and feather spray

to become miser-bird
lyre of the lone flight of its wings

—COLE SWENSEN

Misdeal

Dice
momentarily together
fly apart on the table

Amour
lourde figure à jouer

Dames Rois et Valets
de rouge et de noir rehaussés
s'ébattent sur un air ancien

————————————

Love
facecard troublesome to play

Queens Kings and Jacks
set off in red and black
frolic to an old air

—KEITH WALDROP

Henri Michaux 1899–1984
NAMUR, BELGIUM

A painter, essayist, and poet, the reclusive Michaux ("Belgian, from Paris") became one of France's foremost writers. André Gide, in his article "Discovering Henri Michaux" (1941), played a large part in publicizing his work as did Jean Paulhan. Michaux moved to Paris in 1923 and soon afterward began to paint and contribute to avant-garde reviews. He traveled widely throughout North and South America, Asia, and Africa, documenting his trips in *Ecuador* (1929) and *Un Barbare en Asie* (1933). He also experimented with mescaline; his writings, and the drawings that accompany them, explored exaltation and agony as states induced by the drug. In 1965 he refused to accept the Grand Prix National des Lettres in protest against the practice of awarding such prizes. Principal works: *Un certain plume*, 1930; *La Nuit remue*, 1935; *Lointain intérieur*, 1938; *Peintures*, 1939; *Épreuves, exorcismes*, 1940–1944; *Apparitions*, 1946; *La Vie dans les plis*, 1949; *Passages*, 1950; *Mouvements*, 1952; *Misérable Miracle*, 1956; *Paix dans les brisements*, 1959; *Émergences-resurgences*, 1972; *En rêvant à partir de peintures énigmatiques*, 1972; *Affrontements*, 1986.

Avenir

Siècles à venir
Mon véritable présent, toujours présent,
obsessionnellement présent . . .

Moi qui suis né à cette époque où l'on hésitait encore à aller de Paris à Péking,
    quand l'après-midi était avancée, parce qu'on craignait de ne pouvoir rentrer
    pour la nuit.
Oh ! siècles à venir, comme je vous vois.

Un petit siècle épatant, éclatant, le 1400e siècle après J.-C., c'est moi qui vous
    le dis.
Le problème était de faire aspirer la lune hors du système solaire. Un joli
    problème. C'était à l'automne de l'an 134957 qui fut si chaud, quand la lune
    commença a bouger à une vitesse qui éclaira la nuit comme vingt soleils d'été,
    et elle partit suivant le calcul.
Siècles infiniment éloignés,
Siècles des homoncules vivant de 45 à 200 jours, grands comme un parapluie
    fermé, et possédant leur sagesse comme il convient,
Siècles des 138 espèces d'hommes artificiels, tous ou presque tous, croyant en
    Dieu — naturellement ! — et pourquoi non ? volant sans dommage pour leur
    corps soit dans la stratosphère, soit à travers 20 écrans de gaz de guerre.

Je vous vois,

Mais non je ne vous vois pas.
Jeunes filles de l'an douze mille, qui dès l'âge où l'on se regarde dans un
    miroir, aurez appris à vous moquer de nos lourds efforts de mal dételés de
    la terre.
Que vous me faites mal déjà.
Un jour pour être parmi vous et je donnerais toute ma vie tout de suite.
Pas un diable hélas pour me l'offrir.

Les petites histoires d'avions (on en était encore au pétrole, vous savez les
    moteurs à explosion), les profondes imbécillités d'expériences sociales encore
    enfantines ne nous intéressaient plus, je vous assure.

On commençait à détecter l'écho radioélectrique en direction du Sagittaire situé
    à 2 250 000 kilomètres qui revient après 15 secondes et un autre tellement plus
    effacé, situé à des millions d'années-lumière ; on ne savait encore qu'en faire.

Future

Centuries to come
My absolute present, always present,
obsessionally present . . .

Born as I was when it didn't seem all that easy to go from Paris to Peking, when
   it was so late in the afternoon we were afraid of not getting home before dark.
Oh! Centuries to come, I see you so clearly.

A great little century, all bright and shiny, the fourteen-thousandth century CE,
   believe me!
The project was to get the moon aspirated out of the solar system. A nice
   problem. It was in that terribly hot autumn of the year 134957 when the moon
   began to move so fast that it lit up the night like twenty summer suns, and left
   as planned.
Centuries infinitely far off.
Centuries when the homunculi, the size of a closed umbrella, lived from 45 to
   200 days, in possession of the appropriate wisdom.
Centuries of 138 species of artificial men, all, or almost all, of them true
   believers—of course!—and why not? flying undamaged, whether in the
   stratosphere or through twenty layers of poisoned gas.

I see you,

No I don't.
Girls of the year twelve thousand who, as soon as people start looking into
   mirrors, will know how to make fun of our clumsy efforts, so close to the
   ground.
You're hurting me already.
If I could be with you for just one day I'd give up my life right away.
Pity there's no one to offer me that chance.

All that fooling around with airplanes (we were still using gasoline, you know,
   jet-propelled), the profound imbecilities of still childish social experiments
   bored us to hell, believe me.

They were beginning to detect the radioelectric echo coming from the direction
   of Sagittarius, 2,250,000 kilometers away, recurring every fifteen seconds, and
   another, so much fainter, millions of light years away; they had no idea what
   to do with them.

Vous qui connaîtrez les ultra-déterminants de la pensée et du caractère de
l'homme, et sa surhygiène
qui connaîtrez le système nerveux des grandes nébuleuses
qui serez entrés en communication avec des êtres plus spirituels que l'homme,
s'ils existent
qui vivrez, qui voyagerez dans les espaces interplanétaires,
Jamais, Jamais, non JAMAIS, vous aurez beau faire, jamais ne saurez quelle
misérable banlieue c'était que la Terre. Comme nous étions misérables et
affamés de plus Grand.
Nous sentions la prison partout, je vous le jure.
Ne croyez pas nos écrits (les professionnels, vous savez . . .)
On se mystifiait comme on pouvait, ce n'était pas drôle en 1937, quoiqu'il ne s'y
pássât rien, rien que la misère et la guerre.

On se sentait là, cloué dans ce siècle,
Et qui irait jusqu'au bout ? Pas beaucoup. Pas moi . . .

On sentait la délivrance poindre, au loin, au loin, pour vous.
On pleurait en songeant à vous,
Nous étions quelques-uns.
Dans les larmes nous voyions l'immense escalier des siècles et vous au bout,
nous en bas,
Et on vous enviait, oh ! Comme on vous enviait et on vous haïssait, il ne
faudrait pas croire, on vous haïssait aussi, on vous haïssait . . .

Mes statues

J'ai mes statues. Les siècles me les ont léguées : les siècles de mon attente, les
siècles de mes découragements, les siècles de mon indéfinie, de mon inétouffable
espérance les ont faites. Et maintenant elles sont là.

Comme d'antiques débris, point ne sais-je toujours le sens de leur représenta-
tion.

Leur origine m'est inconnue et se perd dans la nuit de ma vie, où seules leurs
formes ont été préservées de l'inexorable balaiement.

Mais elles sont là, et durcit leur marbre chaque année davantage, blanchissant
sur le fond obscur des masses oubliées.

You who will understand the finest structures of the thought and character of
   man, and his superhygiene,
who will have explored the nervous system of the great nebulae,
who will have begun to communicate with beings wittier than man, if any,
who will live, who will travel through interplanetary space,
Never, Never, no NEVER, however hard you try, you'll never know what a
   miserable suburb the Earth was. How wretched we were and starved for
   Higher Things.
Everywhere felt like a prison, I swear!
Don't believe what you read (professionals, you know . . .)
We deluded ourselves as best we could, 1937 wasn't funny, though nothing was
   happening except starvation and war . . .

There we were, nailed to that century,
And who would go all the way? Not many. Not me.

We sensed the dawning of freedom, in the far distance, for you.
We wept, thinking of you.
There were a few of us.
Through our tears we saw the immense stairway of the centuries, with you at its
   end,
we at the bottom,
And we were filled with envy, Oh! How we envied you, and hated you too, don't
   think we didn't, we hated you . . .

—MARY ANN CAWS AND PATRICIA TERRY

My Statues

I have my statues. The ages have bequeathed them to me: the ages of my
waiting, the ages of my discouragements, the ages of my undefined, of my un-
quenchable hope have created them. And now, they are there.

Like the shards of ancient ruins, I do not always know their meaning.

Their origin is unknown to me, lost in the night of my life, where their forms
alone have survived the inexorable sweep of time.

But there they are, and their marble hardens every year, growing whiter
against the dark background of the many forgotten ones.

—MARY ANN CAWS AND PATRICIA TERRY

Tranches de savoir (extraits)

Si votre enfant a une trompe sur le nez, ne soyez pas effrayé par les éléphants.

* * *

Là l'homme ennuyé s'enkyste. Toujours quelques années de gagnées . . .

* * *

Il lui tranche la tête avec un sabre d'eau, puis plaide non coupable et le crime disparaît avec l'arme qui s'écoule.

* * *

Il n'est pas rare qu'un fils de Directeur de Zoo naisse les pieds palmés. C'est néanmoins, comme tout malheur, une surprise.

Cependant que l'enfant est évacué vers l'Extrême Nord où l'on espère qu'il se confondra avec la présentation d'une nature plus appropriée, la famille, de secrète qu'elle était, devient extrêmement, infiniment secrète. Qui peut se vanter d'avoir connu à fond la famille d'un directeur de Zoo ?

* * *

Quand un borgne arrive à la gare des boiteux, il y a rassemblement. Et si c'est un paralytique qui arrive, il y a rassemblement, il y a mécontentement, il y a malveillance dans les expressions et aisance du diable et salut à la terre. Mais il est refoulé de la gare et des abords de la gare, qui n'est pas la sienne, avec mépris et commandement qu'il s'en aille puisqu'aussi bien il a trouvé quelqu'un dans le filet de la pitié pour se faire traîner partout il lui plaît. Qu'il parte, profitant de sa veine exorbitante. La gare des boiteux est suffisamment encombrée.

* * *

L'éléphant avec une fracture du bassin voudrait être petit, tout petit, petit comme une araignée jeunette que le vent emporte, enroule, enlève dans les cieux de la facilité, des prolongements, de la perpétuation, loin, loin, loin, au-delà des plumes, des peluches, des spérules, sans un os du poids d'un cil, sans un seul os, sans en avoir besoin, dans la vie, dans la vie en l'air, dans la vie repartie.

* * *

Je fus le vivant qui dit « Je veux d'abord hiverner. »

* * *

Quand le son devient aigu, jetez la girafe à la mer.

* * *

Slices of Knowledge

If your child has a trunk on its nose, be not afraid of elephants.

*   *   *

There he who is bored grows encased in a cyst. At least that's a few years won . . .

*   *   *

He cuts off her head with a saber of water then pleads not guilty and the crime disappears with the weapon that flows away.

*   *   *

It is not rare for the son of a Zoo Director to be born with palmate feet. It is nevertheless, like all misfortunes, a surprise.

While the child is evacuated towards the Far North where it is hoped he will blend in with the presentation of a more appropriate nature, the family, once secretive, becomes extremely, infinitely secretive. Who can boast of having intimate knowledge of a Zoo Director's family?

*   *   *

When a one-eyed man arrives at the station of the lame, there is a gathering. And if it's a paralytic who arrives, there is a gathering, there is discontent, there is ill will in the expressions and contentment in the devil and salvation on earth. But he is driven out of the station and the station surrounds, for it is not his station, with scorn and commands that he go elsewhere because what is more he has found someone in the net of pity who will drag him about wherever he wishes to go. Let him leave, profiting from his exorbitant good luck. The station of the lame is sufficiently crowded.

*   *   *

The elephant with a fractured pelvis wishes he were small, very small, small as a very young spider whom the wind whisks away, whirls away, raises up in the heavens of ease, of prolongations, of perpetuation, far, far, far beyond the plumes and plushes and spherules, without a bone weighing more than an eyelash, without any bones, without needing any bones, into life, into life in the air, into life born again.

*   *   *

I was the mortal who said: "First I want to hibernate."

*   *   *

When the sound becomes acute, throw the giraffe into the sea.

*   *   *

Ne pas laisser condamner à défaire les chignons de bronze.

*   *   *

Nous leur lançâmes des obus de safran. Au point où nous en étions . . .

*   *   *

C'était à l'époque où la barque se retire dans l'obélisque.

*   *   *

Nous passions nos journées, enfants à Prétoria, à voir grossir un gros, gros hippopotame, atteint de dégénérescence gazeuse qui grossissait, qui grossissait, et nous avec l'appréhension au cœur de l'éclatement et lui qui grossissait, chaque jour qui grossissait toujours. Qu'est-ce qu'il a pu devenir depuis vingt ans ?

*   *   *

Comme on détesterait moins les hommes s'ils ne portaient pas tous figure.

*   *   *

Qu'importe de voler le tympan d'un sourd ? Mais ainsi commence la malhonnêteté. De la malhonnêteté, l'envie du gain suit, le goût du commerce, de là le goût du calcul, puis de la mesure, enfin de l'analyse, et de fil en aiguille, au sourd, on ne lui laisse que les os.

Do not allow anyone to be condemned to undo bronze chignons.

* * *

We bombed them with saffron shells. Given the state we'd reached . . .

* * *

It was at the stage where the little boat withdraws into the obelisk.

* * *

As children in Pretoria we spent our days watching a fat, fat hippopotamus grow fatter, a hippopotamus suffering from a gassy degeneration that grew fatter and fatter, and our hearts were full of fear he would burst and he grew fatter, each day grew fatter forever. I wonder what's become of him over the last twenty years?

* * *

How one would hate men less if they didn't all have faces.

* * *

Why should it matter if you steal the eardrum of a deaf man? But that is how dishonesty begins. After dishonesty comes the desire for gain, the taste for commerce, and that gives rise to the taste for calculations, then measure, and at last analysis, and one thing leads to another so you end up leaving the deaf man nothing but his bones.

—ROSEMARY LLOYD

Benjamin Péret 1899–1959
REZÉ, FRANCE

A member of the Surrealist movement from its inception, the irreverent and imaginative Péret was André Breton's most faithful companion and remained active in the group until his death. His first poems were printed in *Littérature,* and his *Au 125 du boulevard Saint-Germain* (1923) is often considered the first Surrealist work of fiction. He cofounded and directed the

Allo

Mon avion en flammes mon château inondé de vin du Rhin
mon ghetto d'iris noir mon oreille de cristal
mon rocher dévalant la falaise pour écraser le garde champêtre
mon escargot d'opale mon moustique d'air
mon édredon de paradisiers ma chevelure d'écume noire
mon tombeau éclaté ma pluie de sauterelles rouges
mon île volante mon raisin de turquoise
ma collision d'autos folles et prudentes ma plate-bande sauvage
mon pistil de pissenlit projeté dans mon œil
mon oignon de tulipe dans le cerveau
ma gazelle égarée dans un cinéma des boulevards
ma cassette de soleil mon fruit de volcan
mon rire d'étang caché où vont se noyer les prophètes distraits
mon inondation de cassis mon papillon de morille
ma cascade bleue comme une lame de fond qui fait le printemps
mon revolver de corail dont la bouche m'attire comme l'œil d'un puits
    scintillant
glacé comme le miroir où tu contemples la fuite des oiseaux-mouches de ton
    regard
perdu dans une exposition de blanc encadrée de momies
je t'aime

review *La Révolution surréaliste* with Pierre Navaille. So opposed was he to the merging of politics and poetry that he wrote "Le Déshonneur des poètes," a rebuttal to the collective volume *L'Honneur des poètes*, extolling, by example, the glories of Resistance poetry. In his absolute view, no pragmatic use should be made of the poetic. Péret joined the Communist Party in 1926 and went to Brazil to work as a party organizer in 1931. He was arrested by the Gestapo in 1940 for subversive activities but succeeded in escaping to Mexico, where he married the Surrealist painter Remedios Varo. His poetic inventions are numerous and increasingly appreciated by young and emerging poets; his sense of humor is contagious, and his political-poetic positions vigorous. Principal works: *Le Passager du transatlantique*, 1921; *Immortelle maladie*, 1924; *Dormir dormir dans les pierres*, 1927; *Le Grand Jeu*, 1928; *La Pêche en eau trouble*, 1928; *De derrière les fagots*, 1934; *Je ne mange pas de ce pain-là*, 1936; *Jeu sublime*, 1936; *Dernier malheur dernière chance*, 1945; *Feu central*, 1947; *Air mexicain*, 1949.

Hello

My airplane in flames my castle flooded with Rhenish wine
my black iris ghetto my crystal ear
my rock hurtling down the cliff to smash the country policeman
my opal snail my air mosquito
my quilt of birds of paradise my hair of black foam
my tomb burst open my red grasshopper rain
my flying island my turquoise grape
my wreck of cars mad and careful my wild flowerbed
my pistil of dandelion projected in my eye
my tulip onion in the brain
my gazelle wandering off in some moviehouse
my casket of sun my volcano fruit
my laugh like a hidden pool where distraught prophets drown
my flood of blackcurrant my nightshade butterfly
my blue waterfall like a tidal wave making springtime
my coral revolver's mouth drawing me like the gleaming well
glassy as the mirror where you watch the hummingbirds of your gaze
    escaping
lost in a linen show framed with mummies
I love you

—MARY ANN CAWS

Clin d'œil

Des vols de perroquets traversent ma tête quand je te vois de profil
et le ciel de graisse se strie d'éclairs bleus
qui tracent ton nom dans tous les sens
Rosa coiffée d'une tribu nègre étagée sur un escalier
où les seins aigus des femmes regardent par les yeux des hommes
Aujourd'hui je regarde par tes cheveux
Rosa d'opale du matin
et je m'éveille par tes yeux
Rosa d'armure
et je pense par tes seins d'explosion
Rosa d'étang verdi par les grenouilles
et je dors dans ton nombril de mer Caspienne
Rosa d'églantine pendant la grève générale
et je m'égare entre tes épaules de voie lactée fécondée par des comètes
Rosa de jasmin dans la nuit de lessive
Rosa de maison hantée
Rosa de forêt noire inondée de timbres-poste bleus et verts
Rosa de cerf-volant au-dessus d'un terrain vague où se battent des enfants
Rosa de fumée de cigare
Rosa d'écume de mer faite cristal
Rosa

Où es-tu

Je voudrais te parler cristal fêlé hurlant comme un chien dans une nuit de draps
    battants
comme un bateau démâté que la mousse de mer commence d'envahir
où le chat miaule parce que tous les rats sont partis
Je voudrais te parler comme un arbre renversé par la tempête
qui a tellement secoué les fils télégraphiques
qu'on dirait une brosse pour les montagnes pareilles à la mâchoire inférieure
    d'un tigre
qui me déchire lentement avec un affreux bruit de porte enfoncée
Je voudrais te parler comme une rame de métro en panne à l'entrée
d'une station où je pénètre avec une écharde dans un orteil pareil à un oiseau
    dans une vigne
qui ne donnera pas plus de vin qu'une rue barrée
où j'erre comme une perruque dans une cheminée
qui n'a plus rien chauffé depuis si longtemps

Wink

Parakeets fly through my head when I see you in profile
and the greasy sky streaks with blue flashes
tracing your name in all directions
Rosa coiffed with a black tribe standing in rows on the stairs
where women's pointed breasts look out through men's eyes
Today I look out through your hair
Rosa of morning opal
and I wake through your sight
Rosa of armour
I think through your exploding breasts
Rosa of a pool the frogs turn green
and I sleep in your navel of Caspian sea
Rosa of honeysuckle in the general strike
and I'm lost in your milky way shoulders the comets made fecund
Rosa of jasmine in the night of washing
Rosa of haunted house
Rosa of black forest filled with blue and green stamps
Rose of kite over a vacant lot where children are fighting
Rose of cigar smoke
Rose of seafoam made crystal
Rosa

—MARY ANN CAWS

Where Are You

I would speak to you cracked crystal howling like a dog on a night of flailing
   sheets
like a dismasted boat the foam begins to invade
where the cat meows because all the rats have left
I would speak to you like a tree uprooted by the storm
which so shook the telegraph wires
they seem a brush for mountains resembling a tiger's lower jaw
tearing me apart slowly noisily like a battered-in door
I would speak to you like a metro train broken down at the entrance
of a station I enter with a splinter in my toe like a bird in a vineyard
which will yield no more wine than a barricaded street
where I wander like a wig in a fireplace
which hasn't heated anything so long

qu'elle se croit le comptoir d'un café
où les cercles laissés par les verres dessinent une chaîne
Je te dirais simplement
que je t'aime comme le grain de blé aime le soleil se levant en haut de sa tête
    de merle

Source

Il est Rosa moins Rosa
dit la giboulée qui se réjouit de rafraîchir le vin blanc
en attendant de défoncer les églises un quelconque jour de Pâques
Il est Rosa moins Rosa
et quand le taureau furieux de la grande cataracte m'envahit
sous ses ailes de corbeaux chassés de mille tours en ruines
quel temps fait-il
Il fait un temps Rosa avec un vrai soleil de Rosa
et je vais boire Rosa en mangeant Rosa
jusqu'à ce que je m'endorme d'un sommeil de Rosa
vêtu de rêves Rosa
et l'aube Rosa me réveillera comme un champignon Rosa
où se verra l'image de Rosa entourée d'un halo Rosa

it thinks itself a cafe counter
where the circles left by the glasses trace a chain
I would only say to you
I love you like the grain of wheat loves the sun rising above its blackbird
    head

—RACHEL STELLA

Fountain

He is Rosa without Rosa
says the frost glad to chill the white wine
about to crash in the churches some Easter day
He is Rosa without Rosa
and when the mad bull of the great cataract invades me
under his raven wings chased from a thousand towers in ruin
what's the weather like
It's Rosa weather with a real Rosa sun
and I'm about to drink Rosa while eating Rosa
until I drowse off in a Rosa sleep
dressed in Rosa dreams
and Rosa dawn will wake me like a Rosa mushroom
with the image of Rosa surrounded by a Rosa halo

—MARY ANN CAWS

Francis Ponge 1899–1988
MONTPELLIER, FRANCE

Ponge, a prose poet, journalist, and editor, was interested in producing a "cosmogony," not in writing poetry. His work described natural objects and attempted to explain the existence of both things and humans in the cosmos. In an article written in the 1940s, Sartre identified him as an existentialist poet, doing much to publicize his work. Ponge's combinations of genres and ideas have endured, inimitably: his *proèmes* join prose and poetry, and his

Les Plaisirs de la porte

Les rois ne touchent pas aux portes.

Ils ne connaissent pas ce bonheur : pousser devant soi avec douceur ou rudesse l'un de ces grands panneaux familiers, se retourner vers lui pour le remettre en place, — tenir dans ses bras une porte.

. . . Le bonheur d'empoigner au ventre par son nœud de porcelaine l'un de ces hauts obstacles d'une pièce ; ce corps à corps rapide par lequel un instant la marche retenue, l'œil s'ouvre et le corps tout entier s'accommode à son nouvel appartement.

D'une main amicale il la retient encore, avant de la repousser décidément et s'enclore, — ce dont le déclie du ressort puissant mais bien huilé agréablement l'assure.

Les Mûres

Aux buissons typographiques constitués par le poème sur une route qui ne mène hors des choses ni à l'esprit, certains fruits sont formés d'une agglomération de sphères qu'une goutte d'encre remplit.

Noirs, roses et kakis ensemble sur la grappe, ils offrent plutôt le spectacle d'une famille rogue à ses âges divers, qu'une tentation très vive à la cueillette.

Vue la disproportion des pépins à la pulpe les oiseaux les apprécient peu, si peu de chose au fond leur reste quand du bec à l'anus ils en sont traversés.

objeu merges object and game. Taking "the side of things," he enlarges both their scope and their substance. In 1937 he joined the Communist Party and was active in the Resistance. In 1947, however, he broke with communism. From 1952 until 1965 he taught in Paris at the Alliance française and in 1976 won the Neustadt International Prize for Literature. Principal works: *Douze petits écrits,* 1926; *Le Parti-pris des choses,* 1942; *Le Peintre à l'étude,* 1948; *Proèmes,* 1948; *La Seine,* 1950; *La Rage de l'expression,* 1952; *Le Grand recueil,* 1961; *Le Savon,* 1967; *La Fabrique du pré,* 1971; *Abrégé de l'aventure organique,* 1976; *L'Atelier contemporain,* 1977; *Comment une "Figue" de paroles et pourquoi,* 1977.

The Pleasures of a Door

Kings never touch a door.

It is a joy unknown to them: pushing open whether rudely or kindly one of those great familiar panels, turning to put it back in place—holding a door in one's embrace.

. . . The joy of grasping one of those tall barriers to a room by the porcelain knob in its middle; the quick contact in which, with forward motion briefly arrested, the eye opens wide, and the whole body adjusts to its new surroundings.

With a friendly hand it is stayed a moment longer before giving it a decided shove and closing oneself in, a condition pleasantly confirmed by the click of the strong but well-oiled lock.

—LEE FAHNESTOCK

Blackberries

On typographical bushes constituted by the poem along a road which leads neither beyond things nor to the spirit, certain fruits are formed by an agglomeration of spheres filled by a drop of ink.

Blacks, pinks, khakis, all on a cluster, they look more like members of an arrogant family of varying ages than a very lively temptation to pick them off.

Given the disproportion of the seeds to the pulp, birds find little to appreciate, so little in the end remains by the time it has traveled from the beak to the anus.

Mais le poète au cours de sa promenade professionnelle, en prend de la graine à raison: «Ainsi donc, se dit-il, réussissent en grand nombre les efforts patients d'une fleur très fragile quoique par un rébarbatif enchevêtrement de ronces défendue. Sans beaucoup d'autres qualités,—*mûres,* parfaitement elles sont mûres—comme aussi ce poème est fait.»

L'Huître

L'huître, de la grosseur d'un galet moyen, est d'une apparence plus rugueuse, d'une couleur moins unie, brillamment blanchâtre. C'est un monde opiniâtrement clos. Pourtant on peut l'ouvrir: il faut alors la tenir au creux d'un torchon, se servir d'un couteau ébréché et peu franc, s'y reprendre à plusieurs fois. Les doigts curieux s'y coupent, s'y cassent les ongles: c'est un travail grossier. Les coups qu'on lui porte marquent son enveloppe de ronds blancs, d'une sorte de halos.

A l'intérieur l'on trouve tout un monde, à boire et à manger: sous un *firmament* (à proprement parler) de nacre, les cieux d'en-dessus s'affaissent sur les cieux d'en-dessous, pour ne plus former qu'une mare, un sachet visqueux et verdâtre, qui flue et reflue à l'odeur et à la vue, frangé d'une dentelle noirâtre sur les bords.

Parfois très rare une formule perle à leur gosier de nacre, d'où l'on trouve aussitôt à s'orner.

Les Arbres se défont à l'intérieur d'une sphère de brouillard

Dans le brouillard qui entoure les arbres, les feuilles leur sont dérobées; qui déjà, décontenancées par une lente oxydation, et mortifiées par le retrait de la sève au profit des fleurs et fruits, depuis les grosses chaleurs d'août tenaient moins à eux.

Dans l'écorce des rigoles verticales se creusent par où l'humidité jusqu'au sol est conduite à se désintéresser des parties vives du trone.

Les fleurs sont dispersées, les fruits sont déposés. Depuis le plus jeune âge, la résignation de leurs qualités vives et de parties de leur corps est devenue pour les arbres un exercice familier.

L'Ardoise

L'ardoise — à y bien réfléchir c'est-à-dire peu, car elle a une gamme de reflets très réduite et un peu comme l'aile du bouvreuil passant vite, excepté sous l'effet des précipitations critiques, du ciel gris bleuâtre au ciel noir — s'il y a un livre en

But the poet on his professional walk mulls this over in his mind: "Clearly," he says to himself, "the patient efforts of a very delicate flower succeed to a large extent although protected by a forbidding tangle of brambles. Lacking many other qualities—*blackberries* are perfectly ripe—the way this poem is ready."

—SERGE GAVRONSKY

The Oyster

The oyster, the size of an average pebble, looks tougher, its color is less uniform, brilliantly whitish. It is a stubbornly closed world. And yet, it can be opened: one must then hold it in the hollow of a dish towel, use a jagged and rather tricky knife, repeat this many times. Curious fingers cut themselves on it, nails break on it: it's tough going. Hitting it that way leaves white circles, like halos, on its envelope.

Inside, one finds a whole world to drink and eat: under a nacreous *firmament* (strictly speaking), the heavens above recline on the heavens below and form a single pool, a viscous and greenish bag, that flows in and out when you smell it or look at it, fringed with blackish lace along the edges.

Sometimes, a very rare formula pearls in their nacreous throat, and right away you have an ornament.

—SERGE GAVRONSKY

Trees That Come Undone within a Sphere of Fog

Within a fog that enfolds the trees, their leaves are spirited away. They—those leaves—already taken aback by slow oxidation, and mortified by the withdrawal of sap for the greater good of flower and fruit, have been loosening their ties since the sweltering heat of August.

Vertical channels open within the bark, and through them moisture is drawn down to the ground, drawn to lose interest in vital portions of the trunk.

The flowers are scattered, the fruit is dropped. From a tender age, the relinquishing of their living attributes and bodily parts has been a familiar exercise for trees.

—LEE FAHNESTOCK

Slate

If one reflects well on slate—in other words, not very much, since its range of reflections is very limited and not unlike the wing of a bullfinch in full flight, except under the effect of critical precipitations, of skies changing from blue-grey

elle, il n'est que de prose: une pile sèche; une batterie déchargée; une pile de quotidiens au cours des siècles, quoique illustrés par endroits des plus anciens fossiles connus, soumis à des pressions monstrueuses et soudés entre eux; mais enfin le produit d'un métamorphisme incomplet.

Il lui manque d'avoir été touchée à l'épaule par le doigt du feu. Contrairement aux filles de Carrare, elle ne s'enveloppera donc ni ne développera jamais de lumière.

Ces demoiselles sont de la fin du secondaire tandis qu'elle appartient aux établissements du primaire, notre institutrice de vieille roche, montrant un visage triste, abattu: un teint évoquant moins la nuit que l'ennuyeuse pénombre des temps.

Délitée, puis sciée en quernons, sa tranche atteinte au vif, compacte, mate, n'est que préparée au poli, poncée: jamais rien de plus, rien de moins, si la pluie quelquefois, sur le versant nord, y fait luire comme les bourguignottes d'une compagnie de gardes, immobile.

Pourtant, il y a une idée de crédit dans l'ardoise.

Humble support pour une humble science, elle est moins faite pour ce qui doit demeurer en mémoire que pour des formulations précaires, crayeuses, pour ce qui doit passer d'une mémoire à l'autre, rapidement, à plusieurs reprises, et pouvoir être facilement effacée.

De même, aux offenses du ciel elle s'oppose en formation oblique, une aile refusée.

Quel plaisir d'y passer l'éponge.

Il y a moins de plaisir à écrire sur l'ardoise qu'à tout y effacer d'un seul geste, comme le météore négateur qui s'y appuie à peine et qui la rend au noir.

Mais un nouveau virage s'accomplit vite; d'humide à humble elle perd ses voyelles, sèche bientôt:

«Laissez-moi sans souci détendre ma glabelle et l'offrir au moindre écolier, qui du moindre chiffon l'essuie.»

L'ardoise n'est enfin qu'une sorte de pierre d'attente, terne et dure.

Songeons-y.

to black—one may come to the conclusion that any book it may contain will consist entirely of prose: a dry cell; a drained battery; a pile of newspapers reaching back through the centuries, illustrated in places by some of the oldest known fossils which, though submitted to monstrous pressures, and now welded into the pile, are still the product of an incomplete metamorphosis.

It suffers from having never been touched on the shoulder by the finger of fire. Unlike the daughters of Carrara, therefore, it will never swathe itself in light nor radiate light.

These damsels come from the end of the secondary, whereas slate belongs to the establishments of the primary, and is our old-time governess, stony-hearted, showing a sad, dejected face: a complexion less evocative of night than of the dull penumbra of the ages.

Cut along the line of stratification, then sawn into square blocks, slate's compact, dull-hued cross-section, once the quick has been reached, is simply prepared for polishing, pumiced: never anything more or anything less, except perhaps when the rain sometimes makes it shine, on the northern slope, like the vizorless helmets of a company of royal guards at attention.

Nevertheless, a great deal of credit attaches to slate, is put on the slate.

A humble prop for a humble science, it is designed less for what must be retained by the memory than for precarious, chalky formulations, for what must be transmitted from one memory to another, rapidly, repeatedly, for what can easily be obliterated.

In the same way, it resists the sky's transgressions deviously, at an angle, keeping one wing hidden.

Let's say no more about it. Clean slate!

There is less pleasure to be gained in writing on a slate, on the subject of slate, than in obliterating one's words, one's thoughts, with a single gesture, like that corrective weather phenomenon the sudden squall which has only to brush up against it for a moment to turn it black, painting a gloomy picture of it in an instant.

But it quickly changes colour again, loses its vowels between moistness and modesty, soon dries:

"Let me unknit my brow and offer its smooth surface to the humblest schoolboy, who may wipe it with the humblest rag."

A slate is really nothing but a kind of temporary stone, lustreless and hard.

Worth contemplating.

—SIMON WATSON TAYLOR

Barbara

Rappelle-toi Barbara
Il pleuvait sans cesse sur Brest ce jour-là
Et tu marchais souriante
Epanouie ravie ruisselante
Sous la pluie
Rappelle-toi Barbara
Il pleuvait sans cesse sur Brest
Et je t'ai croisée rue de Siam
Tu souriais
Et moi je souriais de même
Rappelle-toi Barbara
Toi que je ne connaissais pas
Toi qui ne me connaissais pas
Rappelle-toi
Rappelle-toi quand même ce jour-là
N'oublie pas
Un homme sous un porche s'abritait
Et il a crié ton nom

Jacques Prévert 1900–1977
NEUILLY-SUR-SEINE, FRANCE

P révert was immortalized with his first collection of poems, *Paroles,*
which has been translated many times since its publication. His decep-
tively simple style and lyric treatment of universal themes, along with
the joyous innocence and spontaneous expression of his spirit, quickly won him
many admirers. Although Prévert actively supported left-wing French politics,
he did not allow potentially alienating views to creep into his work. His child-
hood was spent in Paris. After serving in World War I, he returned to the city and
joined the Surrealist movement, which was already well under way. He first
gained recognition as a filmmaker in the 1930s and 1940s, writing scripts for Jean
Renoir *(Le Crime de Monsieur Lange)* and Marcel Carné *(Drôle de drame, Quai
des brumes, Le Jour se lève, Les Visiteurs du soir, Les Enfants du paradis).* Principal
works: *Paroles,* 1945; *Histoires,* 1946; *Spectacle,* 1951; *La Pluie et le beau temps,* 1955;
Arbres, 1976.

Barbara

Barbara remember
The rain was falling all that day on Brest
And you were walking smiling
Radiant full of joy streaming wet
In the rain
Barbara remember
All day the rain fell on Brest
I ran into you in the rue de Siam
You were smiling
And I was smiling too
Barbara remember
I didn't know you
You didn't know me
Remember
You should remember that day all the same
Don't forget
A man was sheltering in a porch
And he called out your name

Barbara
Et tu as couru vers lui sous la pluie
Ruisselante ravie épanouie
Et tu t'es jetée dans ses bras
Rappelle-toi cela Barbara
Et ne m'en veux pas si je te tutoie
Je dis tu à tous ceux que j'aime
Même si je ne les ai vus qu'une seule fois
Je dis tu à tous ceux qui s'aiment
Même si je ne les connais pas
Rappelle-toi Barbara
N'oublie pas
Cette pluie sage et heureuse
Sur ton visage heureux
Sur cette ville heureuse
Cette pluie sur la mer
Sur l'arsenal
Sur le bateau d'Ouessant
Oh Barbara
Quelle connerie la guerre
Qu'es-tu devenue maintenant
Sous cette pluie de fer
De feu d'acier de sang
Et celui qui te serrait dans ses bras
Amoureusement
Est-il mort disparu ou bien encore vivant
Oh Barbara
Il pleut sans cesse sur Brest
Comme il pleuvait avant
Mais ce n'est plus pareil et tout est abîmé
C'est une pluie de deuil terrible et désolée
Ce n'est même plus l'orage
De fer d'acier de sang
Tout simplement des nuages
Qui crèvent comme des chiens
Des chiens qui disparaissent
Au fil de l'eau sur Brest
Et vont pourrir au loin
Au loin très loin de Brest
Dont il ne reste rien.

Barbara
And you ran towards him in the rain
Steaming wet full of joy radiant
And you threw yourself into his arms
Barbara remember that
Don't be cross if I'm direct
I can't be bothered with niceties
When I love someone
Even if I've seen them only once
I'm never formal with people in love
Even if I've not met them before
Barbara remember
Don't forget
That wet wise happy rain
On your happy face
On that happy town
That rain on the sea
On the munitions dump
On the Ushant boat
Oh Barbara
What a bloody waste war is
Where the hell are you now
Under this downpour of iron
Of fire of steel of blood
And the man who hugged you in his arms
Full of love
Did he die disappear or is he still alive
Oh Barbara
It rains and rains on Brest
As it rained before
But it's not the same any more and all is ruined
It's the desolate terrible rain of bereavement
No longer even the same thunder
Of iron of steel of blood
Just simply clouds going under
Like dead dogs disappearing
Floating downstream out of Brest
To rot far far away from Brest
Of which there's left
Nothing.

—MARTIN SORRELL

Renfort
[1]

Je vous dis adieu monsieur mon sergent
qui vous en allez à la guerre
vous en aurez pour votre argent
moi je reste avec les mémères
et les vieux de la der des der
qui furent nommés adjudants
et qui au jour de maintenant
sont absolument en retraite
je vous dis adieu monsieur mon sergent
je ne connais que la défaite

Raymond Queneau 1903–1976
LE HAVRE, FRANCE

A poet, novelist, publisher, and mathematician, Queneau saw language itself as his subject; inventive wordplay, neologisms, scientific language, and use of slang mark his work, which is, in turn, funny, moving, and highly experimental. A member of the Surrealist group for a short time, Queneau broke with Breton in 1929 and later served as a link between the original group and the growing number of existentialist and absurdist artists; he was closely associated with the OULIPO (Ouvroir de Littérature Potentielle). Queneau collaborated with Georges Bataille on his review *Documents* and directed, appropriately enough, the *Encyclopédie de la Pléiade,* reflecting his truly encyclopedic spirit. He did his military service in North Africa; while there the conversations between his fellow soldiers sparked his interest in language. He also collaborated with several film directors; his best-known novel, *Zazie dans le métro,* was made into a successful film in 1960, directed by Louis Malle. Principal works: *Chêne et chien,* 1937; *Les Ziaux,* 1943; *L'Instant fatal,* 1946; *Bucoliques,* 1947; *Exercises de style,* 1947; *Petite cosmogonie portative,* 1950; *Si tu t'imagines,* 1952; *Le Chien à la mandoline,* 1958; *Zazie dans le métro,* 1959; *Battre la campagne,* 1968; *Fendre les flots,* 1969; *Morale élémentaire,* 1975.

Reinforcements
[I]

Good-bye now sergeant sir
since you're heading off to war
where you'll get your money's worth
me I'll stay here with the women
and survivors of the one-to-end-'em-all
who commanded say a platoon
and ever since from that day on
retire into complete retreat
good-bye now Sergeant sir
all my dreams are of defeat

Renfort
[2]

Je suis vieux et je suis lourd
mon âge compte on le soupèse
et l'on me dit que vieux et lourd
j'attendrai que la mort me baise
dans un coin — comme un vieux et comme un lourd

Je crains pas ça tellment

Je crains pas ça tellment la mort de mes entrailles
et la mort de mon nez et celle de mes os
Je crains pas ça tellment moi cette moustiquaille
qu'on baptisa Raymond d'un père dit Queneau

Je crains pas ça tellment où va la bouquinaille
les quais les cabinets la poussière et l'ennui
Je crains pas ça tellment moi qui tant écrivaille
et distille la mort en quelques poésies

Je crains pas ça tellment La nuit se coule douce
entre les bords teigneux des paupières des morts
Elle est douce la nuit caresse d'une rousse
le miel des méridiens des pôles sud et nord

Je crains pas cette nuit Je crains pas le sommeil
absolu Ça doit être aussi lourd que le plomb
aussi sec que la lave aussi noir que le ciel
aussi sourd qu'un mendiant bêlant au coin d'un pont

Je crains bien le malheur le deuil et la souffrance
et l'angoisse et la guigne et l'excès de l'absence
Je crains l'abîme obèse où gît la maladie
et le temps et l'espace et les torts de l'esprit

Mais je crains pas tellment ce lugubre imbécile
qui viendra me cueillir au bout de son curdent
lorsque vaincu j'aurai d'un œil vague et placide
cédé tout mon courage aux rongeurs du présent

Reinforcements
[II]

I am old and I am heavy
my age counts up adds pounds to me
and they tell me that old and heavy
I've just to wait for death to screw me
in a corner—like somebody old somebody heavy

—KEITH WALDROP

That Don't Scare Me

That don't scare me so much death of my guts
death of my bones death of my nose
That don't scare me so much me a skeeter sort
baptized Raymond from a line of Queneaus

That don't scare me so much where my books get stacked
in book stalls in johns in dust and doldrums
That don't scare me so much me who scribble a pack
and boil down death into some poems

That don't scare me so much Soft night flows
between ringwormy eyelids over dead eyeballs
Night is soft a redhead's kiss
honey of meridians at north and south poles

I'm not scared of that night not scared of absolute
sleep It must be heavy as lead
dry as lava dark as the sky
deaf as a beggar bellowing on a bridge

I'm scared stiff of unhappiness crying pain
and dread and rotten luck and parting too long
I'm scared of the lardbellied abyss that holds sickness
and time and space and the mind gone wrong

But I'm not so scared of that lugubrious imbecile
Who'll come and spit me on his toothpick point
when I'm down and with eyes vague and placid I'll
have lost my cool to the collecting rats

Un jour je chanterai Ulysse ou bien Achille
Enée ou bien Didon Quichotte ou bien Pansa
Un jour je chanterai le bonheur des tranquilles
les plaisirs de la pêche ou la paix des villas

Aujourd'hui bien lassé par l'heure qui s'enroule
tournant comme un bourin tout autour du cadran
permettez mille excuz à ce crâne — une boule —
de susurrer plaintif la chanson du néant

Pour nourrir les petits oiseaux

« Le plantain est une espèce de
plante fort commune dont
la semence sert à la nourriture des
           petits oiseaux »
      plantain   fort   de
      plante   sert   dont
           petits oiseaux   des

le plantain est un végétal
fort banal
qui peut servir à l'occasion de thème
à un poème

un jour à travers champs marchait un sacristain
pour ses petits oiseaux il cherchait du plantain

« au sein des Gamopétales
supérovariées bicarpellées
la petite famille des Plantaginacées
est bien difficile à placer »

le Larousse et la Pléiade
ont fourni ces deux tirades
l'amour des petits oiseaux
n'empêche point celui des mots

Someday I'll sing Ulysses or maybe Achilles
Aeneas or maybe Dido Quixote maybe Sancho
Someday I'll sing pleasures the idle know
the fun of fishing or the peace of villas

All fagged out today by the hours as they wind out
trudging like an old nag around the dial
a thousand pardons from this skull—a ball—
for doling out plaintively this song of the void

—KEITH WALDROP

The Nourishment of Little Birds

"The plantain is
a species of very common
plant whose seed serves as
nourishment for
            little birds"

    plantain   seed   is
    plant   serves   as
       little birds   us

the plantain is vegetal
and rather banal
and for poets is capable of serving them
as occasion for a po-em

one day across the fields walked a sacristan
for his little birds he searched for plantain

"in the house of Gamopetallate
superovaried, bicarpellate
the little family of Plantaginacae
is very difficult to place"

We find both these tirade(s)
in Larousse and Pléiade
The love of little birds
doesn't halt the love of words

—TEO SAVORY

Prière aux masques

Masques! O Masques!
Masque noir masque rouge, vous masques blanc-et-noir
Masques aux quatre points d'où souffle l'Esprit
Je vous salue dans le silence!
Et pas toi le dernier, Ancêtre à tête de lion.
Vous gardez ce lion forclos à tout rire de femme, à tout sourire qui se fane
Vous distillez cet air d'éternité où je respire l'air de mes Pères.
Masques aux visages sans masque, dépouillés de toute fossette comme de toute ride
Qui avez composé ce portrait, ce visage mien penché sur l'autel de papier blanc
A votre image, écoutez-moi!
Voici que meurt l'Afrique des empires — c'est l'agonie d'une princesse pitoyable

Léopold Sédar Senghor 1906–2001

JOAL, SENEGAL

S enghor was renowned as a poet, teacher, and head of state. He received a scholarship to study at the Lycée Louis-le-Grand, where he met Aimé Césaire and Léon-Gontran Damas. He was the chief architect of *négritude,* an intellectual movement the three would develop and popularize together. Négritude sought to restore pride to the colonized and to raise a cry for their independence. At the Sorbonne, Senghor studied Harlem Renaissance poetry and was the first black African to attain the highest rank for teachers in the country as an *agrégé.* His poetry is marked by strong rhythm and evocative patterns, much of it recalling African dance. Until the onset of World War II he taught high school in Paris. After the war he was elected to the French Parliament and helped convince Charles de Gaulle to free Senegal from French rule. In 1960 he was elected president of the Republic of Senegal; in 1980 he became the first African president to step down voluntarily from office. Senghor returned to France to pursue cultural interests and in 1990 was elected to the Académie française. Principal works: *Chants d'ombre,* 1945; *Hosties noires,* 1948; *Chant pour Naett,* 1949; *Éthiopiques,* 1956; *Nocturnes,* 1961; *Élégie des alizés,* 1969; *Lettres d'hivernage,* 1973; *Paroles,* 1975; *Élégies majeures,* 1979.

Prayer to the Masks

Masks! O Masks!
Black mask, red mask, masks black-and-white,
Masks from all four points where Spirit blows,
I greet you in silence!
And lion-headed Ancestor, you among the first.
You guard this place from laughing women and sagging smiles,
You exude the eternal air where I breathe my Fathers' air.
Masks with unmasked faces, stripped of every dimple and every crease,
Who shaped this portrait in your image, this face of mine
Bent over the altar of an empty page,
Listen to me!
A pitiful princess is dying, the Africa of empires,

Et aussi l'Europe à qui nous sommes liés par le nombril.
Fixez vos yeux immuables sur vos enfants que l'on commande
Qui donnent leur vie comme le pauvre son dernier vêtement.
Que nous repondions présents à la renaissance du Monde
Ainsi le levain qui est nécessaire à la farine blanche.
Car qui apprendrait le rythme au monde défunt des machines et des canons?
Qui pousserait le cri de joie pour réveiller morts et orphelins à l'aurore?
Dites, qui rendrait la mémoire de vie à l'homme aux espoirs éventrés?
Ils nous disent les hommes du coton du café de l'huile
Ils nous disent les hommes de la mort.
Nous sommes les hommes de la danse, dont les pieds reprennent vigueur en
 frappant le sol dur.

Le Salut du jeune soleil

Le salut du jeune soleil
Sur mon lit, la lumière de ta lettre
Tous les bruits qui fusent du matin
Les cris métalliques des merles, les clochettes des gonoleks
Ton sourire sur le gazon, sur la rosée splendide.

Dans la lumière innocente, des milliers de libellules
Des frisselants, comme de grandes abeilles d'or ailes noires
Et comme des hélicoptères aux virages de grâce et de douceur
Sur la plage limpide, or et noir les Tramiae basilares
Je dis la danse des princesses du Mali.

Me voici à ta quête, sur le sentier des chats-tigres.
Ton parfum toujours ton parfum, de la brousse bourdonnante des buissons
Plus exaltant que l'odeur du lys dans sa surrection.
Me guide ta gorge odorante, ton parfum levé par l'Afrique
Quand sous mes pieds de berger, je foule les menthes sauvages.
Au bout de l'épreuve et de la saison, au fond du gouffre
Dieu! que je te retrouve, retrouve ta voix, ta fragrance de lumière vibrante.

And our navel is tied to a Europe in death throes too.
Fix your changeless eyes on your marshaled children
Who are giving up their lives like a pauper his last clothes.
Let us answer "present" at the World's rebirth
As the leaven that makes white flour into bread.
Tell me, who else could teach rhythm to a grave of guns and machines?
Or raise dawn's joyous cry to wake the orphans and the dead?
Or spark life's memory again in a man of gutted hopes?
They call us men of cotton, of coffee, of oil.
They call us men of death.
But we are men of dance,
Whose feet grow strong by pounding the hard earth.

—HOYT ROGERS

The Young Sun's Greeting

The young sun's greeting
On my bed, your letter's glow
All the sounds that burst from morning
Blackbirds' brassy calls, jingle of gonoleks
Your smile on the grass, on the radiant dew.

In the innocent light, thousands of dragonflies
Quivering, like large black-winged golden bees
And like helicopters turning with gentle grace
On the limpid beach, gold and black the Tramiae basilares
I say the dance of Mali's princesses.

You are the one I seek, on the path of the tiger-cats.
Your scent always yours, from the buzzing brambles of the bush
Headier than a growing lily's perfume.
Your redolent throat leads me on, your scent wafted by Africa
When with my shepherd's feet I trample tufts of wild mint.
The season done, my trials overcome, in the depths of the abyss
God! may I find you again, find your voice, your fragrance of vibrant light.

—HOYT ROGERS

Georgia

Je ne dors pas Georgia
je lance des flèches dans la nuit Georgia
j'attends Georgia
je pense Georgia

Philippe Soupault 1897–1990
CHAVAILLE, FRANCE

S oupault provided the first example of automatic writing in his *Les Champs magnétiques* (1920), composed with André Breton in ten days just before the summer of 1919. Guillaume Apollinaire introduced the two after seeing Soupault's first poem, "Départ," which was written in a military hospital and which the author claimed was dictated to him by his unconscious. Breton, Soupault, and Aragon quickly united to begin the Surrealist revolution, its advent marked by the publication of the review *Littérature,* which the writers, often called "les trois mousquetaires," cofounded in 1919; by September 1922 Soupault was the director of the journal. Between 1917 and 1919 he composed a series of "cinematographic poems" and "animated snapshots," both of which express his visual approach to writing. He traveled widely beyond Paris, as indicated by his celebrated title *Westwego:* he was in the United States in 1929 and 1931, in Russia in 1930, and in Germany and Scandinavia between 1932 and 1935. After leaving Surrealism and its tight inner circles, he worked as a journalist but was arrested in 1942 for his antifascist activities. Upon his release he was charged with reorganizing Agence France-Presse in Latin America and worked for both radio and UNESCO. His novel *Les Dernières Nuits de Paris* was translated into English by William Carlos Williams in 1929. Principal works: *Aquarium,* 1917; *Rose des Vents,* 1919; *Les Champs magnétiques* (with André Breton), 1920; *L'Invitation au suicide,* 1921; *Westwego,* 1922; *Georgia,* 1926; *Les Dernières Nuits de Paris,* 1928; *Il y un océan,* 1936; *Ode à Londres bombardé,* 1944; *Odes,* 1946; *L'Ame secrète,* 1946; *Message de l'île déserte,* 1947; *Chansons,* 1949; *Sans phrases,* 1953; *Arc en ciel,* 1979; *Poèmes retrouvés,* 1982.

Georgia

I'm not sleeping Georgia
I'm shooting arrows into the night Georgia
I'm awaiting Georgia
I'm thinking Georgia

Le feu est comme la neige Georgia
La nuit est ma voisine Georgia
j'écoute les bruits tous sans exception Georgia
je vois la fumée qui monte et qui fuit Georgia
je marche à pas de loups dans l'ombre Georgia
je cours voici la rue les faubourgs Georgia
Voici une ville qui est la même
et que je connais pas Georgia
je me hâte voici le vent Georgia
et le froid silence et la peur Georgia
je fuis Georgia
je cours Georgia
les nuages sont bas ils vont tomber Georgia
j'étends les bras Georgia
je ne ferme pas les yeux Georgia
j'appelle Georgia
je crie Georgia
j'appelle Georgia
je t'appelle Georgia
Est-ce que tu viendras Georgia
bientôt Georgia
Georgia Georgia Georgia
Georgia
je ne dors pas Georgia
je t'attends
Georgia

Horizon

à Tristan Tzara

Toute la ville est entrée dans ma chambre
les arbres disparaissaient
et le soir s'attache à mes doigts
Les maisons deviennent des transatlantiques
le bruit de la mer est monté jusqu'à moi
Nous arriverons dans deux jours au Congo
j'ai franchi l'Équateur et le Tropique du Capricorne
je sais qu'il y a des collines innombrables
Notre-Dame cache le Gaurisankar et les aurores boréales

The fire is like the snow Georgia
The night is my neighbour Georgia
I'm listening to every single sound Georgia
I see the smoke rising and flying off Georgia
I'm walking like a wolf in the shadow Georgia
I'm running here are the streets the suburbs Georgia
Here's a town which is the same
and that I don't know Georgia
I'm rushing here's the wind Georgia
and the cold and the silence and the fear Georgia
I'm fleeing Georgia
I'm running Georgia
the clouds are low they're about to fall Georgia
I stretch out my arms Georgia
I don't close my eyes Georgia
I call Georgia
I cry Georgia
I call Georgia
I call you Georgia
Will you come Georgia
soon Georgia
Georgia Georgia Georgia
Georgia
I'm not sleeping Georgia
I'm waiting for you
Georgia

—MARY ANN CAWS AND PATRICIA TERRY

Horizon

for Tristan Tzara

The whole town came into my room
the trees were disappearing
and the evening sticks to my fingers
The houses are becoming steamships
the sound of the sea has reached me
In two days we'll be in the Congo
I have crossed the Equator and the Tropic of Capricorn
I know there are innumerable hills
Notre Dame is hiding Gaurisankar and the Aurora Borealis

la nuit tombe goutte à goutte
j'attends les heures

Donnez-moi cette citronnade et la dernière cigarette
je reviendrai à Paris

Cinéma-palace

à Blaise Cendrars

Le vent caresse les affiches
Rien
la caissière est en porcelaine

l'Écran

le chef d'orchestre automatique dirige le pianola
il y a des coups de revolver
applaudissements
l'auto volée disparaît dans les nuages
et l'amoureux transi s'est acheté un faux col

Mais bientôt les portes claquent
Aujourd'hui très élégant
Il a mis son chapeau claque
Et n'a pas oublié ses gants

Tous les vendredis changement de programme

Chanson pour des fantômes et pour celles qui ont disparu

Aujourd'hui ce sont des mains que j'aime
Hier c'était une nuque
Demain ce seront des lèvres
et le soir un sourire
Dans trois jours un visage
Enfin chaque jour de la semaine
je m'émerveillerai de vivre encore
je me souviendrai peut-être lundi de votre démarche

night is falling drop by drop
I've been waiting for hours

Give me that lemonade and the last cigarette
I'll come back to Paris

—MARY ANN CAWS AND PATRICIA TERRY

Movie-house

for Blaise Cendrars

The wind strokes the posters
Blank
the cashier is made of china

        Screen

the robot conductor directs the player piano
shots are heard
          applause
the stolen car disappears into the clouds
and the frozen lover has purchased a celluloid collar

   But soon doors slam
   Very elegant today
   He has put on his top hat
   His gloves too

The program changes every Friday

—MARY ANN CAWS

Song for Ghosts and for Those Now Gone

Today there are hands I love,
Yesterday it was a nape
Tomorrow it will be lips
and this evening a smile
In three days a face
So each day in the week
I marvel at still living
Monday I may recall the way you walk

et mardi sans doute des cheveux
Il faudra aussi écouter la voix
celle des fantômes
celle qui hésite celle qui persuade
que la vie n'est pas si atroce
que je voulais le croire tout à l'heure
mercredi tout oublier
Mais jeudi c'est un parfum
qu'on ne peut oublier
le parfum de l'arc-en-ciel
Les autres jours
Tous les autres jours
j'ai promis
de ne rien dire qu'à moi-même

---

and Tuesday perhaps your hair
I'll also have to hear the voice
that of the ghosts
one hesitating one persuading
that life is not so terrible
as I thought it just now
Wednesday forget everything
But Thursday it's a perfume
you can't forget
the perfume of the rainbow
The other days
All the other days
I've promised not
to say a thing except to me

—MARY ANN CAWS

Jean Tardieu 1903–1995
SAINT-GERMAIN-DE-JOUX, AIN, FRANCE

A poet, playwright, and critic of music and the visual arts, Tardieu attempted to introduce new images and sounds during an era already highly inventive. Although he resisted identification with any particular group, he was most closely associated with the Theater of the Absurd. He translated metaphysical anguish with extreme concision in his theatrical works and with great subtlety in his poetry and prose. He was appointed head of the drama department of French radio and began the radio station that would become France-musique. Principal works: *Le Fleuve caché*, 1933; *Accents*, 1939; *Le Témoin invisible*, 1943; *Les Dieux étouffés*, 1946; *Jours pétrifiés*, 1947; *Poèmes à jouer*, 1950; *Monsieur Monsieur*, 1951; *Un mot pour un autre*, 1951; *La Première Personne du singulier*, 1952; *Une voix sans personne*, 1954; *Histoires obscures*, 1961; *Les Portes de toile*, 1969; *Formeries*, 1976; *Comme ceci, comme cela*, 1979; *Poèmes à voir*, 1990; *Le Miroir ébloui*, 1993; *Da Capo*, 1995.

La Mouche et l'océan

Une mouche se balançait
Au-dessus d'un océan.
Tout à coup elle se sentit
Prise dans du froid.

Moralité

Il faut toujours faire attention.

Les Jours

Dans une ville noire entraînée par le temps
(toute maison d'avance au fil des jours s'écroule)
je rentrais, je sortais avec toutes mes ombres.
Mille soleils montaient comme du fond d'un fleuve,
mille autres descendaient, colorant les hauts murs;
je poursuivais des mains sur le bord des balcons;
des formes pâlissaient (la lumière est sur elles)
ou tombaient dans l'oubli (les rayons ont tourné).
Les jours, les jours . . . Qui donc soupire et qui m'appelle,
pour quelle fête ou quel supplice ou quel pardon?

La Seine de Paris

De ceux qui préférant à leurs regrets les fleuves
et à leurs souvenirs les profonds monuments
aiment l'eau qui descend au partage des villes,
la Seine de Paris me sait le plus fidèle
à ses quais adoucis de livres. Pas un souffle
qui ne vienne vaincu par les mains des remous
sans me trouver prêt à le prendre et à relire
dans ses cheveux le chant des montagnes, pas un
silence dans les nuits d'été où je ne glisse
comme une feuille entre l'air et le flot, pas une aile
blanche d'oiseau remontant de la mer
ne longe le soleil sans m'arracher d'un cri
strident à ma pesanteur monotone! Les piliers
sont lourds après le pas inutile et je plonge

The Fly and the Ocean

A fly swayed
Above an ocean.
Suddenly it felt
Caught up in the cold.

Moral:

Always pay attention.

—DAVID KELLEY

Days

In a city of darkness caught up in time
(each building crumbles in time before its time)
with all my shadows I went in and went out.
Suns in their thousands rose as from a river bed,
a thousand sunsets coloured the towering walls;
I followed hands on the balconies' edge;
forms faded (bearing the brunt of light)
or fell into oblivion (with the turning rays).
Days and days . . . Who then sighs and who calls,
and to what feast what torture or what pardon?

—DAVID KELLEY

The Seine in Paris

Since I prefer rivers to regrets
the grave profundity of monuments to memories,
love the water's flow dividing cities,
the Seine in Paris knows me deeply faithful
to its gentle book-lined quays. Not a breath
arrives defeated by the eddying waters
but that I am ready to take it and to read again
in its hair the mountain song, not a
summer night-time silence but that I glide
like a leaf between air and water, not a white
gull's wing returned from the sea pursuing the sun
but that I am wrenched from the weight of my monotony
by a strident cry! The pillars weigh heavy
after the unnecessary step and I plunge

par eux jusqu'à la terre et quand
je remonte et ruisselle et m'ébroue,
j'invoque un dieu qui regarde aux fenêtres
et brille de plaisir dans les vitres caché.
Protégé par ses feux je lutte de vitesse
en moi-même avec l'eau qui ne veut pas attendre
et du fardeau des bruits de pas et de voitures
et de marteaux sur des tringles et de voix
tant de rapidité me délivre . . . Les quais
et les tours sont déjà loin lorsque soudain
je les retrouve, recouvrant comme les siècles,
avec autant d'amour et de terreur, vague après vague,
méandres de l'esprit la courbe de mon fleuve.

Cézanne

Comme au-dessus du ciel il y a le ciel et après la vie la vie, — au-delà du regard il y a le regard.

Apre, violent, obstiné, le regard qui jaillit comme l'étincelle entre deux pierres, — et sa joie confine à la panique et son élan si loin l'engage qu'il menace à la fois le secret de l'esprit et celui des choses.

Lieu caché au fond du plein jour, domaine du feu primitif et des surprises de la condensation, second regard! C'est là qu'au milieu du strident silence des cigales, un Enchanteur seul, fumant de colère et de volonté, fait effort pour rapprocher peu à peu l'une de l'autre les rebelles et rivales évidences du monde sensible et de la pensée impalpable.

Tandis que d'autres cherchent la lumière (cette abstraction), il écarte d'un geste le poudroiement des rayons et, possédé par les fureurs de la découverte, il touche à la nature des choses: la Couleur.

Une parure? — Non! Un masque? — Non! l'Être même! Vérité venue du centre des objets, puisée à leur substance, lentement repoussée sur leurs bords par le travail des intimes échanges, purifiée par son ascension, hissée enfin à son comble: l'air libre, — plus elle s'évapore, plus elle se renouvelle et plus elle reste fraîche aux lèvres des yeux altérés.

Oui. Fraîche. Acide. Verte. Minérale. Absolue. Couleur, pierre de la construction du monde, degré d'intensité des formes (qu'elle étire et modèle à son gré), limite et lien des éléments, inséparable de la Création, comme elle inépuisable . . .

Telle dans sa splendeur elle est donc aussi le secret, le carrefour magique et mouvant où se rencontrent l'âme qui voit et les présences qui sont vues. Sans quitter les plans qu'elle a construits, elle se plaît aux métamorphoses, s'altère

by them to earth, and when I climb up again
streaming and shake myself,
I invoke a god who looks through windows
and gleams with pleasure in the panes.
Protected by his rays I conduct an inner race
with water which will not wait
and from the burden of footsteps and motorcar noises
the beating of hammers on bars and voices
that rapid flow frees me . . . Quaysides
and towers are already far away when
suddenly I rediscover them, covering like the centuries,
with equal love and equal terror, wave upon wave,
meanderings of the mind and the bend of my river.

—DAVID KELLEY

Cézanne

Just as beyond the sky is the sky, beyond life, life,—beyond seeing is seeing.

Harsh, violent, stubborn, that moment of seeing which flashes like a spark between two flints—and the joy it induces touches on panic, and its irruption involves it so far that it threatens the secret of the mind and the secret of things.

A private space hidden in the full light of day, realm of primitive fire and the surprises of condensation, second act of seeing! There, in the strident silence of grasshoppers, a solitary Enchanter, fuming with rage and with will power, struggles gradually to bring together the rebellious and rival affirmations of the sensible world and impalpable thought.

Where others seek light (that abstraction), he brushes aside at a stroke the shimmering of rays, and, possessed by the fury of discovery, touches on the nature of things: Colour.

A raiment?—No! A mask?—No! Being itself! Truth deriving from the core of objects, drawn from the well of their substance, slowly displaced towards their edges by the working of intimate exchanges, purified by its ascension, finally drawn up to its pinnacle: free air,—the more it evaporates, the more it is renewed, the more it retains its coolness on the lips of quenched eyes.

Yes. Cool. Sharp. Green. Mineral. Absolute. Colour, the world's keystone, point of intensity of forms (which it draws out and models at its will), limit and link of the elements, inseparable from Creation, and like Creation, inexhaustible . . .

Such in its splendour is it also the secret, the magic and moving intersection of the seeing soul and seen presences. Without leaving the planes it has constructed, it takes pleasure in metamorphoses, changes as volumes turn, as specta-

quand tournent les volumes, quand les spectacles s'éloignent. Elle se meut dans son propre mystère et fait bouger plus loin qu'elles-mêmes, dans le sillage des planètes, ailleurs, là-bas où nous ne sommes pas encore, les éclatantes et souveraines masses d'une pomme, d'une chaise, d'un rideau d'arbres ou des joueurs de cartes soudain figés dans leur mouvement personnel par l'élan de la bourrasque invisible qui les entraîne.

Désormais sûre d'elle-même, cette puissance enfin peut se permettre les plus délicats des jeux: sur la feuille transparente de l'étendue, parfois quelques touches légères, une poignée d'allusions suffisent à bâtir une montagne.

Alors, entre les teintes espacées, il n'y a plus que des lacunes sans visage, il n'y a plus que le vide. Pourtant on voit que la montagne tient toujours.

C'est comme si (je tremble de le dire), comme si peu à peu la réalité se mélangeait à une sorte d'absence toute-puissante . . .

Et tout à coup notre cœur s'arrête. L'Enchanteur a trouvé: terre, mer et ciel, le monde vient de basculer dans l'esprit.

---

cles recede. Its movement takes place within its own mystery, and gives movement elsewhere, in regions we have not yet attained, in the wake of the planets, beyond themselves, to the shattering sovereign masses of an apple, a chair, a curtain of trees or a group of card-players, suddenly frozen in their own movement by the surge of the invisible squall which carries them on.

Confident now, this force can finally allow itself the most exquisite form of play: on the transparent leaf of the stretched surface, a few light touches, a handful of hints, sometimes suffice to build a mountain.

Then, in the spaces between the touches of colour, there are no more than faceless gaps, no more than the void. And yet, manifestly, the mountain still stands.

As though (I tremble to say it), as though gradually reality were mingling with a kind of omnipotent absence . . .

And suddenly our heart misses its beat: the Enchanter has won his trick: earth, sea and sky, the world has been thrown off its axis in the mind.

—DAVID KELLEY

Tristan Tzara (Sami Rosenstock) 1896–1963
ROMANIA

The founder of the Dada movement, first in Zurich (1916), then in Paris (1919–1920), Tzara became known as "Papa-Dada." Dadaism, which predated Surrealism, mounted a nihilistic attack on the values of bourgeois society; Tzara issued the group's first manifesto in 1918. In 1919, he moved to Paris, where Breton had been eagerly expecting him. Aragon and Breton participated in the revolutionary activities of the Dadaists until founding the Surrealist movement. For a time, however, the writers would continue to be linked by their sympathy for communism. Although Tzara's poetic masterpiece, the epic *L'Homme approximatif*—as important for French poetry as T. S. Eliot's *Waste Land* was for Anglophone poetry—has strongly Surrealist overtones, his later poems, after 1939 especially, are of a clarity and simplicity appropriate to his political adhesion. Like the poems of Aragon and Éluard after their departure

Le Géant Blanc Lépreux du paysage

le sel se groupe en constellation d'oiseaux sur la tumeur de ouate

dans ses poumons les astéries et les punaises se balancent
les microbes se cristallisent en palmiers de muscles balançoires
bonjour sans cigarette tzantzantza ganga
bouzdouc zdouc nfoùnfa mbaah mbaah nfoùnfa
macrocystis perifera embrasser les bateaux chirurgien des bateaux cicatrice
    humide propre
paresse des lumières éclatantes
les bateaux nfoùnfa nfoùnfa nfoùnfa
je lui enfonce les cierges dans les oreilles gangànfah hélicon et boxeur sur le
    balcon le violon de l'hôtel en baobabs de flammes
les flammes se développent en formation d'éponges

les flammes sont des éponges ngànga et frappez
les échelles montent comme le sang gangà
les fougères vers les steppes de laine mon hazard vers les cascades
les flammes éponges de verre les paillasses blessures paillasses
les paillasses tombent wancanca aha bzdouc les papillons
les ciseaux les ciseaux les ciseaux et les ombres
les ciseaux et les nuages les ciseaux les navires
le thermomètre regarde l'ultra-rouge gmbabàba
berthe mon éducation ma queue est froide et monochromatique nfoua loua la
les champignons oranges et la famille des sons au delà du tribord
à l'origine à l'origine le triangle et l'arbre des voyageurs à l'origine
mes cerveaux s'en vont vers l'hyperbole

240

from Surrealism to the Communist Party, Tzara's are straightforward in imagery and tone, eschewing the kind of lofty and often hermetic lyricism of Surrealist poetry and prose and its experimental wordplay. Principal works: *La Première Aventure céleste de Monsieur Antipyrine*, 1916; *Vingt-cinq poèmes*, 1918; *Cinéma calendrier du coeur abstrait, Maisons*, 1920; *De nos oiseaux*, 1923; *Indicateur des chemins du coeur*, 1928; *L'Arbre des voyageurs*, 1930; *L'Homme approximatif*, 1931; *Où boivent les loups*, 1932; *L'Antitête*, 1933; *Grains et issues*, 1935; *Sur le champ*, 1935; *Midis gagnés*, 1939; *Le Coeur à gaz*, 1946; *Le Signe de vie*, 1946; *Terre sur terre*, 1946; *Parler seul*, 1950; *De mémoire d'homme*, 1950; *La Face intérieure*, 1952; *Miennes*, 1955; *Le Fruit permis*, 1956; *Juste Présent*, 1961.

White Giant Leper of the Countryside

salt groups itself in a constellation of birds on the cotton tumor

in its lungs starfish and bedbugs swing
the microbes crystallize in palms of muscles swings
goodmorning without cigarette tzantzantza ganga
bouzdouc zdouc nfounfa mbaah mbaah nfounfa
macrocystis perifera to kiss the boats boat surgeon scar
     clean damp
laziness of brilliant lights
boats nfounfa nfounfa nfounfa
I stick candles in his ears ganganfah helicon and boxer on the balcony the hotel's
     violin in baobabs of flames
the flames develop in spongelike formation

the flames are sponges nganga and strike
the ladders climb like blood ganga
the ferns toward the woolen steppes my chance toward the waterfalls
the flames glass sponges mattresses wounds mattresses
the mattresses fall wancanca aha bzdouc the butterflies
scissors scissors scissors and shadows
scissors and clouds scissors ships
the thermometer looks at the ultrared gmbababa
bertha my education my tail is cold and monochromatic nfoua loua la
mushrooms oranges and the family of sounds beyond starboard
at the origin at the origin the triangle and the travelers' tree at the origin
my brains go off toward hyperbole

le caolin fourmille dans sa boîte crânienne
dalibouli obok et tombo et tombo son ventre est une grosse caisse
ici intervient le tambour major et la cliquette
car il y a des zigzags sur son âme et beaucoup de rrrrrrrrrrrrrr ici le lecteur
    commence à crier
il commence à crier commence à crier puis dans ce cri il y a des flûtes qui se
    multiplient des corails
le lecteur veut mourir peut-être ou danser et commence à crier
il est mince idiot sale il ne comprend pas mes vers il crie
il est borgne
il y a des zigzags sur son âme et beaucoup de rrrrrrr
nbaze baze baze regardez la tiare sousmarine qui se dénoue en algues d'or
hozondrac trac
nfoùnda nbabàba nfoùnda tata
nbabàba

Le Dompteur de lions se souvient

regarde-moi et sois couleur
plus tard
ton rire mange soleil pour lièvres pour caméléons
serre mon corps entre deux lignes larges que la famine soit lumière
dors dors vois-tu nous sommes lourds antilope bleue sur glacier oreille dans les
    pierres belles frontières — entends la pierre
vieux pêcheur froid grand sur lettre nouvelle apprendre les filles en fil de fer et
    sucre tournent longtemps les flacons sont grands comme les parasols blancs
    entends roule roule rouge
aux colonies
souvenir senteur de propre pharmacie vieille servante
cheval vert et céréales
corne crie
flûte
bagages ménageries obscures
mords scie veux-tu
horizontale voir

the kaolin swarms in its brain-pan

dalibouli obok and tombo and tombo its stomach is a big chest here the drum-
  major intervenes and castanets

for there are zigzags on his soul and lots of rrrrrrrrrrrrrr here the reader begins
  to yell

he begins to yell begins to yell then in that yell there are flutes that multiply and
  corals

the reader wants to die perhaps or dance and begins to yell

he is thin stupid dirty he doesn't understand my verses he yells

he is one-eyed

there are zigzags on his soul and lots of rrrrrrr

nbaze baze baze look at the submarine tiara which unravels in golden seaweed

hozondrac trac

nfounda nbababa nfounda tata

nbababa

—MARY ANN CAWS

The Lion Tamer Remembers

look at me and be color
later
your laugh eats sun for hares for chameleons
squeeze my body between two thick lines let famine be light
sleep sleep do you see we are heavy blue antelope on a glacier ear in the stones
  lovely frontiers—hear the stone
old fisherman cold tall on new letter learn the girls in iron wire and sugar turn a
  long time the bottles are tall like white parasols listen roll roll red
in the colonies
memory odor of a clean pharmacy old servant
green horse and cereals
horn cry
flute
baggage obscure menageries
bite saw do you want
horizontal to see

—MARY ANN CAWS

Réalités cosmiques vanille tabac éveils

I

écoute je ferai un poème mais ne ris pas
quatre rues nous entourent et nous leur disons lumière
SUR LES POTEAUX DE PRIÈRE ET TU PARLAIS AUX
éléphants au cirque comme la lumière
je ne veux plus que tu sois malade sais-tu
mais pourquoi pourquoi ce matin tu veux siffler
téléphone
je ne veux pas je ne veux pas et il me serre TROP
TROP FORT

II

ce matin
de cuivre ta voix grelottait sur le fil
le jaune s'enfermait dans le pavillon comme le sang
la femme couverte de vert-de-gris de vert-de-gris
se dissipa comme la brume dans les clochettes
pleure — rose des vents — pleure blanc
voici une lumière qui pourrait être noire
fleur

III

sur des lys d'acier et de sel dis-moi encore une fois que ta mère fut bonne

IV

je suis ligne qui se dilate et je veux croître dans un tube de fer d'étain
je dis cela pour t'amuser

V

non pas parce que j'aurais pu être archange de cire
ou pluie du soir et catalogue d'automobiles

VI

dans les fosses la vie rouge bout
pour silence je veux compter mes joies

Cosmic Realities Vanilla Tobacco Wakings

I

listen I'll write a poem but don't laugh
four streets surround us and we tell them light
ON THE PRAYER POSTS AND YOU WERE TALKING TO
elephants luminous in the circus
I don't want you to be sick any more you know
but why why do you want to whistle this morning
telephone
I don't want to I don't want to and he is squeezing me TOO
TOO HARD

II

this morning
of copper your voice shivered on the wire
the yellow closed itself in the mouthpiece like blood
the woman covered with verdigris with ver-di-gris
dissolved like fog in the bell flowers
weep—rose of the winds—weep white
here is a light which could be black
flower

III

on steel salt lilies tell me again that your mother was good

IV

I am a line dilating and I want to grow in a tube of tin
I say that just to amuse you

V

not because I could have been a wax archangel
or evening rain and car catalog

VI

in the pits life boils crimson
to have some silence I want to count my joys

tu m'as dit que j'aie pitié de toi
et je n'ai pas pleuré lorsque tu m'as vu, mais j'aurais voulu pleurer dans le
    tramway
tu me dis je veux partir
les perles de la tour de mon gosier étaient froides tambour major pour les cœurs
    et glisse
les insectes dans la pensée ne me mordent pas,

ah $\left\{ \begin{array}{l} \text{fleur des doigts} \\ \text{l'eau aboie} \end{array} \right.$

et si tu veux je rirai comme une cascade et comme une incendie

VII

dis : vide pensée
vite tu sais
je serai
violoncelle

VIII

je te tiens le manteau lorsque tu pars comme si tu n'étais pas ma sœur

IX

en acier de gel
sonne
dors-tu lorsqu'il pleut?

X

les serviteurs de la ferme lavent les chiens de chasse
et le roi se promène suivi par les juges qui ressemblent aux colombes
j'ai vu aussi au bord de la mer la tour bandagée avec son triste
PRISONNIER
dans les fosses ouvrez l'électricité
par conséquent
seigneur seigneur $\left. \begin{array}{l} \\ \\ \\ \end{array} \right\}$ de glace
pardonnez-moi

XI

GRANDES LARMES glissent le long des draperies
tête de chevaux sur le basalte comme

you told me that I pity you
and I didn't cry when you saw me, but I would have liked to cry in
   the tram
you tell me I want to leave
the pearls of my throat's tower were cold drum major for hearts
   and slide
insects in the thought don't bite me,

         ah $\left\{\begin{array}{l}\text{finger flower}\\\text{the water barks}\end{array}\right.$

and if you like I'll laugh like a waterfall and like a conflagration

VII

    say: empty thought
    quickly you know
    I'll be a
    cello

VIII

I hold your coat when you leave as if you weren't my sister

IX

    in frosted steel
    ring the bell
    do you sleep when it's raining?

X

the farm helpers wash the hunting dogs
and the king takes a walk followed by the judges who look like doves
at the sea side I also saw the bandaged tower with its sad
PRISONER
in the pits turn on the light
consequently
lord lord $\left.\begin{array}{l}\\\\\\\end{array}\right\}$ of ice
forgive me

XI

BIG TEARS slide along the draperies
horses' heads on the basalt like

des jouets de verre cassent entre les étoiles avec les chaînes pour les
    animaux
et dans les glaciers j'aimerais suivre
avec racine
avec ma maladie
avec le sable qui fourmille dans mon cerveau
car je suis très intelligent
et avec l'obscurité

XII

                    EN PORCELAINE la chanson pensée
                      je suis fatigué — la chanson des reines
l'arbre crève de la nourriture comme une lampe
JE PLEURE vouloir se lever plus haut que le jet-d'eau serpente au ciel car il
    n'existe plus la gravité terrestre à l'école et dans le cerveau
ma main est froide et sèche mais elle a caressé le jaillissement de l'eau
et j'ai vu encore quelque chose (au ciel) comme l'eau visse les fruits et
    la gomme

XIII

mais je suis sérieux en pensant à ce qui m'est arrivé
lila
LILA

ton frère crie
tu lui dis
entre les feuillets du livre la main humide
avec la chaux peins ma croyance
brûle sans lumière en fil de fer
LILA

glass toys shatter among the stars with chains
for animals
and in the glaciers I'd like to come along
with root
with my sickness
with the sand swarming in my brain
for I'm very smart
and with darkness

XII

IN PORCELAIN the song imagined
I'm tired—the queens' song
the tree bursts with food like a lamp
I WEEP longing to rise above the fountain twists to the sky because there is no
    more terrestrial gravity in school and in the brain
my hand is cold and dry but it has stroked the surging forth of water
and I've also seen something (in the sky) like water screwing down the fruits
    and the eraser

XIII

but I think serious thoughts about what's happened to me
lila
LILA

LILA
LILA
LILA

your brother is yelling
tell him
between the leaves of the book the humid
hand
paint my belief with lime
burn dark in the wire
LILA

XIV

ton œil est grand
seigneur dans les draperies
ton œil court derrière moi
ton œil est grand comme un vaisseau pardonne-moi
envoie des médicaments
la pierre

XIV BIS

cœur de l'amant ouvert dans le ruisseau et l'électricité
regardons le point
toujours le même
des cheveux poussent autour de lui
il commence à sautiller
s'agrandir
monter vers les éclats définitifs
encercler glisse
vite
vite
roulant
nocturne
virages

XV

parmi les douleurs il y a des organismes et la pluie
tes doigts VIRAGES

XVI

golfe
ton cœur volera faisant choses si hautes
en escaliers de frissons serrés comme l'arbre
entre les rougeurs des éclats
tu t'en vas
les chemins
les branches
lèchent la neige des hanches

XIV

your eye is large
lord in the draperies
your eye pursues me
your eye is a ship's size excuse me
send medicines
stone

XIV encore

lover's heart open in the stream and electricity
let's look at the point
it's always the same
hairs grown around it
it begins to skip
to get larger
to rise toward the final flashes
surrounding it slides
quickly
quickly
rolling
nocturnal
turnings

XV

among the pains there are organisms and rain
your fingers TURNINGS

XVI

gulf
your heart will soar doing such lofty things
on the shiver stairs huddled together like the tree
between the reddish flashes
you go away
roads
branches
lick the snowy hips

XVII

où l'on voit les ponts qui relient les respirations dans la nuit
l'obscurité se partage et se groupe dans des pavillons
tendus par les chemins et les vents vers ta caresse
la plaie

XVIII

le cheval mange des serpents de couleur
tais-toi

XIX

la pierre
danse danse seigneur
la fièvre pense une fleur
danse danse sur la pierre
chaude tresse
recommence en dissonance pour l'obscurité ma sœur, ma sœur?

La Mort de Guillaume Apollinaire

nous ne savons rien
nous ne savions rien de la douleur
la saison amère du froid
creuse de longues traces dans nos muscles
il aurait plutôt aimé la joie de la victoire
sages sous les tristesses calmes   en cage
ne pouvoir rien faire
si la neige tombait en haut
si le soleil montait chez nous pendant la nuit
pour nous chauffer
et les arbres pendaient avec leur couronne
— unique pleur —
si les oiseaux étaient parmi nous pour se mirer
dans le lac tranquille au-dessus de nos têtes
ON POURRAIT COMPRENDRE
la mort serait un beau long voyage
et les vacances illimitées de la chair des structures et des os

XVII

where you see the bridges linking night breathing
darkness splits and clusters in pavilions
stretched down roads and winds toward your caress
the wound

XVIII

the horse devours colored snakes
be quiet

XIX

the stone
dance dance lord
the fever thinks a flower
dance dance on the stone
hot braid
starts again in dissonance on the way to darkness my sister, my sister?

—MARY ANN CAWS

The Death of Guillaume Apollinaire

we know nothing
we knew nothing of grief
the bitter season of cold

digs long furrows in our muscles
he would have preferred the joy of victory

wise under calm sorrows   caged
unable to do anything at all
if snow fell upward
if the sun rose to meet us during the night

to warm us
and trees hung with their crown upside down

—unique teardrop—
if birds were here with us to contemplate themselves
in the tranquil lake above our heads

WE COULD UNDERSTAND
death would be a beautiful long voyage
and an unlimited vacation from the flesh of structures and of bones

—MARY ANN CAWS

Le Cheval

C'est vrai que je croyais en la ferveur immense de vivre. Chaque pas amplifiait en moi de vieilles mais toujours mouvantes adorations. Ce pouvait être un arbre, la nuit, c'étaient des forêts de routes, ou le ciel et sa vie tourmentée, à coup sûr le soleil.

Un jour je vis la solitude. Au faîte d'un monticule, un cheval, un seul, immobile, était planté dans un univers arrêté. Ainsi mon amour, suspendu dans le temps, ramassait en un moment sur lui-même sa mémoire pétrifiée. La vie et la mort se complétaient, toutes portes ouvertes aux prolongements possibles. Pour une fois, sans partager le sens des choses, j'ai vu. J'ai isolé ma vision, l'élargissant jusqu'à l'infinie pénétration de ses frontières. Je laissais à plus tard le soin de voir ce qu'on allait voir. Mais qui saurait affirmer que les promesses ont été tenues ?

———————————

The Horse

It is true that I believed in the immense privilege of living. Each step amplified in me old but always mobile adorations. It was a tree, the night, whole forests of roads, or the sky and its troubled life, certainly the sun.

One day I saw solitude. At the top of hill, a horse, alone, immobile, was planted in an arrested universe. So my love, suspended in time, gathered to itself in one instant its petrified memory. Life and death completed each other, all doors open to possible prolongations. For once, without sharing in the meaning of things, I saw. I isolated my vision, enlarging its borders infinitely. I left for later the concern of seeing what one was to see. But who could maintain that the promises had been kept?

—MARY ANN CAWS

Marguerite Yourcenar
(Marguerite Antoinette Jeanne Marie Ghislaine
Cleenwerke de Crayencour) 1903–1987
BRUSSELS, BELGIUM

A poet, historian, and novelist, Yourcenar explored in her writings the possibility of an idealized humanity that might correct wrongs, both societal and ecological. Her mother died shortly after giving birth to her; her French father, who was a friend, confidant, and teacher, helped arrange the publication of her first work, written at the age of sixteen. When he died, he left her independently wealthy, in addition to bequeathing the legacy of culture and nonconformist beliefs to which he had exposed her. At the onset of World War II, she moved to the United States to teach at Sarah Lawrence College and Georgetown University. In 1980 she became the first woman elected to the Académie française. She lived for many years in Maine in an outspoken and greatly respected lesbian lifestyle. Principal works: *Mémoires d'Hadrien*, 1951; *L'Oeuvre au noir*, 1968; *Feux*, 1974; *Les Charités d'Alcippe*, 1984.

Épitaphe, temps de guerre

Le ciel de fer s'est abattu
Sur cette tendre statue.

Journaux quotidiens

Le strontium descend des hauteurs du ciel bleu.
Donnez-nous aujourd'hui notre pain quotidien, mon Dieu!

Poème pour une poupée achetée dans un bazar russe

Moi
Je suis
Bleu de roi
Et noir de suie.

Je suis le grand Maure
(Rival de Petrouchka).
La nuit me sert de troïka;
J'ai le soleil pour ballon d'or.

Presque aussi vaste que les ténèbres,
Mais tout aussi fragile qu'un vivant,
Le moindre souffle émeut mon corps sans vertèbres.

Je suis très résigné, car je suis très savant :
Ne raillez pas mon teint noir, ni mes lèvres béantes,
Je suis, comme vous, un pantin entre des mains géantes.

———————————

Epitaph in Time of War

A steel sky's smashed to smithereens
This lovely tender figurine.

—MARTIN SORRELL

Daily Papers

Out of a blue heaven, a shower of strontium-90.
Give us this day our daily bread, Lord God Almighty!

—MARTIN SORRELL

Poem for a Doll Bought in a Russian Bazaar

Me
I am
Royal blue,
Black with soot.

I am the great Moor
(Petrushka's rival).
I use night as my troïka;
The sun is my golden balloon.

Almost as vast as the shadowlands
But as fragile as a living person,
The least puff moves my invertebrate body.

Very knowledgeable, I am very resigned:
Don't mock my skin's darkness nor my gaping lips,
I am, as you are, no more than a puppet held in giant hands.

—MARTIN SORRELL

———

3

1931–1945:
Prewar and War Poetry

Claude de Burine, Aimé Césaire, René Char, Andrée Chédid, Léon-
Gontran Damas, René Daumal, Michel Deguy, René Depestre,
Mohammed Dib, Louis-René des Forêts, André Frénaud, Jean
Grosjean, Eugène Guillevic, Anne Hébert, Radovan Ivsic, Edmond
Jabès, Pierre-Albert Jourdan, Gherasim Luca, Dora Maar, Joyce
Mansour, Meret Oppenheim, Valentine Penrose, Gisèle Prassinos,
Boris Vian

Even as the dark years of World War II approached, Surreal-
ism continued, in a more established, less revolutionary
mode. It was during this time, that is, after its initial phase,
that women were increasingly included in its ranks. The young poet
Gisèle Prassinos, well known for her "automatic writing," was a favorite of
the Surrealists when she was only fourteen. Her stories have a particular
twist, as do her poems, one of which is included here. Another poet, Dora
Maar, was known only as a photographer and painter, particularly for
some of her photographs, such as the very Surrealist *Father Ubu* (a mon-
strous animal with tiny paws, presumably an armadillo fetus) and *Rue
d'Astorg* (a strange statue of a small-headed woman seated on a tiny bench
before a background of doors and warped arches). These photographs of
1933–1934 were used as postcards by the Surrealists. During this period,
Maar was linked with Georges Bataille and then, from 1936 to 1942, was
the companion of Pablo Picasso, whose great painting *Guernica* she pho-
tographed in its many stages of composition. Valentine Penrose, through
her husband, Roland Penrose, was associated with members of the inner
circle of Surrealists and was closely connected with Alice Rahon, later the
wife of the painter Wolfgang Paalen: bisexual relations had a certain

fascination for several in the Surrealist group. Joyce Mansour was part of the group until Breton's death.

Surrealist poetry, marked by images and grammatical structures in unlikely confrontations, often has an unforgettable intensity: among its greatest practitioners were some extraordinary love poets, perhaps the greatest being Robert Desnos—known for his facility in sleep-trance experiments and remembered for his tragic death, in his early forties, in the concentration camp of Terezin. Paul Éluard, the great lyric poet, André Breton, the founder of Surrealism, Philippe Soupault, Michel Leiris, Louis Aragon, and Benjamin Péret all wrote poetry in verse and prose of unmistakable emotional strength—recognizably Surrealist in feeling.

The youngest of them, the Provençal poet René Char, was introduced to the Surrealist group by Éluard. Through his startling prose poem "Artine," he gained entry into their ranks. Char participated in the demonstrations of the Surrealists until deciding to go his own way, free of any group or movement. Much contemporary poetry in France and Francophone countries has been, explicitly or implicitly, influenced by Char's strong and diverse poetry—from his love poems, noble and erotic, to his poems of resistance and poetic revolution. His tone dominated French poetry during the middle of the century, beginning with his *Moulin premier* (First Mill) and *Le Marteau sans maître* (The Hammer with No Master), the latter set to music by Pierre Boulez. Through his powerfully expressed wartime notebook of courage, *Feuillets d'Hypnos* (Leaves of Hypnos, or Hypnos Waking, in two different translations); the majestic panoply of poems in *Fureur et mystère* (Furor and Mystery); the love poems and vivid local settings of *Les Matinaux* (The Dawnbreakers) and *Le Nu perdu* (Nakedness Lost), Char showed a seigneurial impatience and force that modified our view of the long-suffering romantic poet and lent a particular momentum to his writing: "J'ecris brièvement. Je ne puis guère *m'absenter* longtemps" (I write in brief. I can't *absent* myself for long).[1] Many of us—critics, poets, and translators alike—have tried to emulate Char's marriage of concision and presence.

There was, and is, a great deal of affection for this generation of poets. Several among them demonstrate a lyricism that appealed to readers who would not have been content with the bareness that was to follow. Added to that, the intense involvement of Char, des Forêts, and others in the Resistance lends them a larger-than-life stature, as does the exile of various writers from their native countries to France in this period, such as that of Edmond Jabès from Egypt. The influence of Jabès is marked, partly through the realization of his strong links with past French poetry and poetics—no one in the twentieth century has been closer to Stéphane Mallarmé than Jabès, whose work turns, as did Mallarmé's, around the

idea of the book. Jabès's dialogic form and intense moral questioning, which speak not just to the diasporic experience but to the overwhelming problems of contemporary political life, seem more urgent than ever.

The influx of Francophone writers from Algeria, Haiti, Martinique, the Maghreb, Canada, and other countries increased during this period, as did their influence: we have only to think of Mansour, who was born in England and was half Egyptian; of Edmond Jabès and Andrée Chédid, also Egyptian; of Aimé and Suzanne Césaire, from Martinique; of Mohammed Dib from Algeria; of Dora Maar, who was half Yugoslavian; and of so many other poets of this era. Cultural cross exchanges strengthened the form and content, the import and impact of French poetry in the twentieth century. French poetry became so infused by poetic spirit beyond the Hexagon that it could never again be accused of parochialism. During the years surrounding the war, the frontiers of the French poetic establishment finally began to open to what we might think of as a great otherness—women poets and poets from other lands. That spirit of generosity has become increasingly felt.

Note

1. René Char, *Feuillets d'Hypnos*, in *Fureur et mystère* (Paris: *Poésie*/Gallimard, 1967), p. 94.

Claude de Burine 1931–

NIÈVRE, FRANCE

F ollowing in the tradition of the Surrealists, de Burine's poetry and several essays employ impassioned metaphor and an effusion of imagery to illustrate the joys and sorrows of human existence. The landscape of her native Nièvre inspires much of her writing, and although she has won many of the country's most important literary prizes, she remains practically unknown outside of France. What is most singular about her strangely haunting work is a kind of "mysterious, troubling presence in the fields, flowers, trees, country folk," which she refers to frequently. From the age of five, she says, she had wanted to bring the moonlight back into her poetry: she is not far from doing just that. Her first collection appeared in 1955, but it was not until 1995 that a collection of her work appeared in English translation. Principal works: *L'Allumeur de réverbères,* 1963; *Hanches,* 1969; *Le Passeur,* 1976; *La Servante,* 1980; *Le Voyageur,* 1991; *Le Visiteur,* 1991; *Le Passager,* 1993; *Le Pilleur d'étoiles,* 1997.

Te saluer

Te saluer
Comme on lance un bouquet d'œillets
L'été
Sur des dalles fraîches.

Prononcer ton nom
Comme on allume un feu
Dans une rue déserte.

Te toucher
Comme on touche le pain
Quand lui seul fait vivre.

Mais quand j'aurai

Mais quand j'aurai fermé les yeux
Que vous serez sous les violettes
Ou les ronces comme moi
Que les nuages au-dessus de nous
Se feront se déferont comme nous,
Qui parlera pour nous?
Qui dira: «Toi, tes yeux,
Sont la couleur de la rêverie
Et des jeunes ardoises
Au printemps des pluies.

Et toi: ta peau
Est la grive qui chante,
Tes mains sont ma chaleur
Et la fièvre de l'été
Qui porte ton nom».

Le temps va où il veut
Pose son habit de jonquilles
Et d'eau où il veut,
Nous n'avons rien
Qu'une aile de papillon qui sèche
Contre les vitres de la nuit.
Nous ne sommes rien qu'une poussière

Greet You

Greet you
The way carnations are thrown
In summer
On keen slabs.

Name you
The way a fire is lit
In an empty street.

Touch you
The way bread is touched
When it alone brings life.

— MARTIN SORRELL

But When I Have

But when I have closed my eyes
When you lie beneath the violets
Or brambles like me
When the clouds above us
Will take shape and crumble like us,
Who will speak for us?
Who will say: "You, your eyes
Are the colour of dreaming
And young slates
Which tile the Spring of rains.

And you: Your skin
Is the thrush singing,
Your hands my warmth
And summer's fever
Which bears your name."

Time goes where it will
Puts down its costume of jonquils
And water where it will,
We have nothing more
Than a butterfly wing drying
Against night's windows.
We are nothing more than a dust

Sous les lèvres avides du vent.
Seul le langage
Est le bronze qui dure.

———————————

Le Cristal automatique

allo allo encore une nuit pas la peine de chercher c'est moi l'homme des cavernes
 il y a les cigales qui étourdissent leur vie comme leur mort il y a aussi l'eau verte
 des lagunes même noyé je n'aurai jamais cette couleur-là pour penser à toi j'ai

Inside the avid lips of the wind.
Only language
Is lasting bronze.

—MARTIN SORRELL

Aimé Césaire 1913–
MARTINIQUE

A poet and a politician, Césaire gave up on European claims of universalism early on and instead chose to redefine the relationship between colonized and colonizer. He left Martinique for Paris in 1931 to prepare for the École normale supérieure at the Lycée Louis-le-Grand. There he met the future president of Senegal, Léopold Sédar Senghor; together with Césaire's childhood friend Léon-Gontran Damas they founded the student journal *L'Étudiant noir*. Césaire contributed an article against assimilation that incorporated his term *négritude*, which would come to describe a movement of black writers and intellectuals interested in preserving a positive racial identity. He was a member of the French Communist Party until he founded the Parti progressiste martiniquais. Greatly revered, he also served as mayor of Fort-de-France. His poetic work, imbued with strongly Surrealist overtones, has an unusual power. In particular, his *Cahier d'un retour au pays natal* has inspired a major current of Francophone expression in poetry and prose. Principal works: *Cahier d'un retour au pays natal*, 1939; *Tropiques*, 1941; *Les Armes miraculeuses*, 1946; *Ferrements*, 1960; *Cadastre*, 1961; *Moi laminaire*, 1982.

The Automatic Crystal

hello hello night again don't worry about it this is your caveman speaking grass-
   hoppers whose life is as dizzy as their death green lagoon water even drowned
   that will never be my colour thinking of you I have to pawn all my words a

267

déposé tous mes mots au mont-de-piété un fleuve de traîneaux de baigneuses
dans le courant de la journée blonde comme le pain et l'alcool de tes seins allo
allo je voudrais être à l'envers clair de la terre le bout de tes seins a la couleur et
le goût de cette terre-là allo allo encore une nuit il y a la pluie et ses doigts de
fossoyeur il y a la pluie qui met ses pieds dans le plat sur les toits la pluie a
mangé le soleil avec des baguettes de chinois allo allo l'accroissement du cristal
c'est toi . . . c'est toi ô absente dans le vent et baigneuse de lombric quand
viendra l'aube c'est toi qui poindras tes yeux de rivière sur l'émail bougé des
îles et dans ma tête c'est toi le maguey éblouissant d'un ressac d'aigles sous
le banian

An neuf

      Les hommes ont taillé dans leurs tourments une fleur
      qu'ils ont juchée sur les hauts plateaux de leur face
      la faim leur fait un dais
      une image se dissout dans leur dernière larme
      ils ont bu jusqu'à l'horreur féroce
      les monstres rythmés par les écumes
En ce temps-là
il y eut une
inoubliable
métamorphose
      les chevaux ruaient un peu de rêve sur leurs sabots
      de gros nuages d'incendie s'arrondirent en champignon
      sur toutes les places publiques
      ce fut une peste merveilleuse
      sur le trottoir les moindres réverbères tournaient leur tête
        de phare
      quant à l'avenir anophèle vapeur brûlante il sifflait dans les jardins
En ce temps-là
le mot ondée
et le mot sol meuble
le mot aube
et le mot copeaux
conspirèrent pour la première fois

_____

whole stream of bathing beauties in their sleds as the day goes by gold as the bread and wine of your breasts hello hello I'd like to be on the earth's bright underside the tip of your breasts looks and tastes like that earth hello hello night again the rain has gravedigger fingers the rain tripping over itself on the roofs the rain ate the sun with chopsticks hello hello in growth of a crystal it's you . . . it's you oh absence in the wind and serpentine bather at dawn you'll set the river of your eyes on the enamel of the islands slipping by and in my head you're the dazzling maguey tree of the tide of eagles under the banyan

—MARY ANN CAWS AND PATRICIA TERRY

New Year

    Out of their torments men carved a flower
    which they perched on the high plateaus of their faces
    hunger makes a canopy for them
    an image dissolves in their last tear
    they drank foam rhythmed monsters
    to the point of ferocious horror
In those days
there was an
unforgettable
metamorphosis
    on their hooves the horses were rearing a bit of dream
    fat fiery clouds filled out like mushrooms
    over all the public squares
    there was a terrific pestilence
    on the sidewalks the smaller streetlamps were rotating their lighthouse
        heads
    as for the anophelic future it was hissing in the gardens a scorching vapor
In those days
the word shower
and the word topsoil
the word dawn
and the word shavings
conspired for the first time

—CLAYTON ESHLEMAN AND ANNETTE SMITH

Redonnez-leur . . .

Redonnez-leur ce qui n'est plus présent en eux,
Ils reverront le grain de la moisson s'enfermer dans l'épi et s'agiter sur
   l'herbe.
Apprenez-leur, de la chute à l'essor, les douze mois de leur visage,
Ils chériront le vide de leur cœur jusqu'au désir suivant;
Car rien ne fait naufrage ou ne se plaît aux cendres;
Et qui sait voir la terre aboutir à des fruits,
Point ne l'émeut l'échec quoiqu'il ait tout perdu.

Le Martinet

   Martinet aux ailes trop larges, qui vire et crie sa joie autour de la maison. Tel est le coeur.

René Char 1907–1988
ÎLE-SUR-LA-SORGUE, FRANCE

C har believed above all in the power of poetry and human morality. He was greatly admired by writers, philosophers, and painters of many nations and remains a towering poetic figure. His philosophy confronted political and moral uncertainties with a conviction born of action and thought. He was born in Île-sur-la-Sorgue, where his father was mayor; the family name was Charlemagne. Char published *Ralentir travaux* with Éluard and Breton in 1930 but left the Surrealists in 1935, finding their games and group experiments irrelevant to his thinking. From the front in Alsace, he played a leading part in the Resistance, becoming known as "le Capitaine Alexandre." After 1950, he concentrated on his writing and befriended the painters Joan Miró, Georges Braque, Viera da Silva, and a host of others. Principal works: *Arsenal,* 1929; *Artine,* 1930; *Le Marteau sans maître,* 1934; *Moulin premier,* 1936; *Seuls demeurent,* 1945; *Les Matinaux,* 1950; *Fureur et mystère,* 1948; *Commune Présence,* 1964; *Retour amont,* 1966; *Le Nu perdu,* 1971; *La Nuit talismanique,* 1972; *Aromates chasseurs,* 1979; *Les Voisinages de Van Gogh,* 1985; *Éloge d'une soupçonnée,* 1988.

Restore to Them . . .

Restore to them what they have no longer.
They will see again the harvest grain enclosed in the stalk and swaying on the
    grass.
Teach them, from the fall to the soaring, the twelve months of their face,
They will cherish their emptiness until their heart's next desire;
For nothing is shipwrecked or delights in ashes;
And for the one who can see the earth's fruitful end,
Failure is of no moment, even if all is lost.

—MARY ANN CAWS

The Swift

Swift whose wings are too wide, who spirals and cries out his joy around the house. The heart is like that.

Il dessèche le tonnerre. Il sème dans le ciel serein. S'il touche au sol, il se déchire.

Sa repartie est l'hirondelle. Il déteste la familière. Que vaut dentelle de la tour?

Sa pause est au creux le plus sombre. Nul n'est plus à l'étroit que lui.

L'été de la longue clarté, il filera dans les ténèbres, par les persiennes de minuit.

Il n'est pas d'yeux pour le tenir. Il crie, c'est toute sa présence. Un mince fusil va l'abattre. Tel est le coeur.

Toute vie . . .

Toute vie qui doit poindre
achève un blessé.
Voici l'arme,
rien,
vous, moi, réversiblement
ce livre,
et l'énigme
qu'à votre tour vous deviendrez
dans le caprice amer des sables.

Le Mortel Partenaire

à Maurice Blanchot

Il la défiait, s'avançait vers son coeur, comme un boxeur ourlé, ailé et puissant, bien au centre de la géométrie attaquante et défensive de ses jambes. Il pesait du regard les qualités de l'adversaire qui se contentait de rompre, cantonné entre une virginité agréable et son expérience. Sur la blanche surface où se tenait le combat, tous deux oubliaient les spectateurs inexorables. Dans l'air de juin voltigeait le prénom des fleurs du premier jour de l'été. Enfin une légère grimace courut sur la joue du second et une raie rose s'y dessina. La riposte jaillit sèche et conséquente. Les jarrets soudain comme du linge étendu, l'homme flotta et tituba. Mais les poings en face ne poursuivirent pas leur avantage, renoncèrent à

He dries up the thunder. He sows in the quiet sky. If he touches the ground, he breaks.

The swallow is his counterpart. He detests her domesticity. What good is the tower's lace?

He will pause in the darkest crevice. None is more stringently lodged than he.

In the long brilliance of summer, he slips through the shutters of midnight into shadow.

No eyes can hold him. His presence is all in his cry. A slender gun is going to strike him down. The heart is like that.

—PATRICIA TERRY

Every Life . . .

Every life, as it dawns,
kills one of the injured.
This is the weapon:
nothing,
you, me, interchangeably
with this book,
and the riddle
that you, too, will become
in the bitter caprice of the sands.

—JAMES WRIGHT

The Mortal Partner

for Maurice Blanchot

He challenged her, went straight for her heart, like a boxer—trim, winged, powerful—centered in the offensive and defensive geometry of his legs. His glance weighed the fine points of his adversary who was content to break off fighting, suspended between a pleasant virginity and knowledge of him. On the white surface where the combat was being held, both forgot the inexorable spectators. The given names of the flowers of summer's first day fluttered in the June air. Finally a slight grimace crossed the adversary's cheek and a streak of pink appeared. The riposte flashed back, brusque and to the point. His legs suddenly like linen on the line, the man floated, staggered. But the opposing fists

conclure. À présent les têtes meurtries des deux battants dodelinaient l'une contre l'autre. À cet instant le premier dut à dessein prononcer à l'oreille du second des paroles si parfaitement offensantes, ou appropriées, ou énigmatiques, que de celui-ci fila, prompte, totale, précise, une foudre qui coucha net l'incompréhensible combattant.

Certains êtres ont une signification qui nous manque. Qui sont-ils? Leur secret tient au plus profond du secret même de la vie. Ils s'en approchent. Elle les tue. Mais l'avenir qu'ils ont ainsi éveillé d'un murmure, les devinant, les crée. Ô dédale de l'extrême amour!

Vers l'arbre-frère aux jours comptés

Harpe brève des mélèzes,
Sur l'éperon de mousse et de dalles en germe
—Façade des forêts où casse le nuage—,
Contrepoint du vide auquel je crois.

La Chambre dans l'espace

Tel le chant du ramier quand l'averse est prochaine—l'air se poudre de pluie, de soleil revenant—, je m'éveille lavé, je fonds en m'élevant; je vendange le ciel novice.

Allongé contre toi, je meus ta liberté. Je suis un bloc de terre qui réclame sa fleur.

Est-il gorge menuisée plus radieuse qua la tienne? Demander c'est mourir!

L'aile de ton soupir met un duvet aux feuilles. Le trait de mon amour ferme ton fruit, le boit.

Je suis dans la grâce de ton visage que mes ténèbres couvrent de joie.

Comme il est beau ton cri qui me donne ton silence!

did not pursue their advantage, refusing to conclude the match. Now the two fighters' battered heads nodded against each other. At that instant the first must have purposely pronounced into the second's ear words so perfectly offensive, or appropriate, or enigmatic, that the latter let fly a lightning bolt, abrupt, complete, precise, which knocked the incomprehensible fighter out cold.

Certain beings have a meaning that escapes us. Who are they? Their secret resides in the deepest part of life's own secret. They draw near. Life kills them. But the future they have thus awoken with a murmur, sensing them, creates them. O labyrinth of utmost love!

—NANCY KLINE

To Friend-Tree of Counted Days

Brief harp of the larches
On mossy spur of stone crop
—Façade of the forest,
Against which mists are shattered—
Counterpoint of the void in which
I believe.

—WILLIAM CARLOS WILLIAMS

Room in Space

Such is the wood-pigeon's song when the shower approaches—the air is
   powdered with rain, with ghostly sunlight—
I awake washed, I melt as I rise, I gather the tender sky.

Lying beside you, I move your liberty.
I am a block of earth reclaiming its flower.

Is there a carved throat more radiant than yours? To ask is to die!

The wing of your sigh spreads a film of down on the leaves. The arrow of my
   love closes your fruit, drinks it.

I am in the grace of your countenance which my darkness covers with joy.

How beautiful your cry that gives me your silence!

—W. S. MERWIN

Lutteurs

Dans le ciel des hommes, le pain des étoiles me sembla ténébreux et durci, mais dans leurs mains étroites je lus la joute de ces étoiles en invitant d'autres: émigrantes du pont encore rêveuses; j'en recueillis la sueur dorée, et par moi la terre cessa de mourir.

Lied du figuier

Tant il gela que les branches laiteuses
Molestèrent la scie, se cassèrent aux mains.
Le printemps ne vit pas verdir les gracieuses.

Le figuier demanda au maître du gisant
L'arbuste d'une foi nouvelle.
Mais le loriot, son prophète,
L'aube chaude de son retour,
En se posant sur le désastre,
Au lieu de faim, périt d'amour.

Fighters

In the sky of men the bread of stars seemed to me shadowy and hardened but in their narrow hands I read the jousting of these stars, inviting others: still dreaming emigrants from the deck; I gathered up their golden sweat and because of me the earth stopped dying.

—THOMAS MERTON

Lied of the Fig Tree

So much it froze that the milky branches
Hurt the saw, and snapped in the hands.
Spring didn't see the gracious ones turn green.

From the master of the felled, the fig tree
Asked for the shrub of a new faith.
But the oriole, its prophet,
The warm dawn of his return,
Alighting upon the disaster,
Instead of hunger, died of love.

—GUSTAF SOBIN

Andrée Chedid 1920–
CAIRO, EGYPT

A poet, playwright, and novelist, Chedid devoted her work to an exploration of the human condition, particularly that of a non-French woman; she is noted for her evocative and sensual descriptions of the Orient. Born to Lebanese parents, Chedid began writing early. She published her first poems, written in English, under a pseudonym. At fourteen she traveled in Europe but returned to Cairo to enroll at American University. Although she had cherished an ambition to become a dancer, Chedid married at twenty-two and had two daughters. In 1946 she moved to Paris and published her first collections

Épreuves du poète

En ce monde
Où la vie
Se disloque
Ou s'assemble

Sans répit
Le poète
Enlace le mystère

Invente le poème
Ses pouvoirs de partage
Sa lueur sous les replis.

Regarder l'enfance

Jusqu'aux bords de ta vie
Tu porteras
Ses fables et ses larmes
Ses grelots et ses peurs

Tout au long de tes jours
Te précède ton enfance
Entravant ta marche
Ou te frayant chemin

Singulier et magique
L'œil de ton enfance
Qui détient à sa source
L'univers des regards.

———————————————

of poetry. Principal works: *Textes pour une figure*, 1949; *Terre et poésie*, 1956; *Contre-chant*, 1969; *Visage premier*, 1972; *Fraternité de la parole*, 1975; *Cavernes et soleils*, 1979; *L'Enfant multiple*, 1989; *Territoires du souffle*, 1999.

Trials of the Poet

In this world
Where our life
Falls apart,
Or reshuffles

The poet
Unendingly
Hugs the unknown

Inventing the poem
Its powers of sharing
Its light in the depths.

—ROSEMARY LLOYD

Looking at Childhood

To your life's final borders
You'll carry your childhood
Its stories, its tears
Its toys and its fears

Through all of your days
You follow your childhood
It hobbles your pace
As it shows you the way

Unique as a spell
The eye of your childhood
Holds in its well
The world of the gaze.

—ROSEMARY LLOYD

Solde

Pour Aimé Césaire

J'ai l'impression d'être ridicule
dans leurs souliers
dans leur smoking
dans leur plastron
dans leur faux-col
dans leur monocle
dans leur melon

J'ai l'impression d'être ridicule
avec mes orteils qui ne sont pas faits
pour transpirer du matin jusqu'au soir qui déshabille
avec l'emmaillotage qui m'affaiblit les membres
et enlève à mon corps sa beauté de cache-sexe

J'ai l'impression d'être ridicule
avec mon cou en cheminée d'usine

Léon-Gontran Damas 1912–1978
GUYANA

O ne of the three founders of the *négritude* movement of black intellectuals and writers, Damas was more interested in valorizing his African heritage than in bringing about reconciliation with the West. He moved to Paris in 1929 to pursue studies in Russian and Japanese but soon changed to law and letters. While in Paris, he met the other two future coleaders of négritude, Aimé Césaire and Léopold Sédar Senghor, who also collaborated with him on the review *L'Étudiant noir* (1935). Damas then began publishing his poems and political works. His pamphlet *Retour de Guyane* was judged subversive by the Guyanese government and burned. This censure, however, did not prevent him from later being elected a deputy in Guyana's National Assembly. Principal works: *L'Étudiant noir,* 1935; *Pigments,* 1937; *Poèmes nègres sur des airs africains,* 1948; *Black Label,* 1956; *Pigments névralgiques,* 1972.

On Sale

For Aimé Césaire

I feel ridiculous
in their shoes
in their tux
their starched shirt
their detachable collars
their monocle
their top hat

I feel ridiculous
with my big toes not made
to sweat from morning to evening undress
swaddling clothes weakening my members
taking the G-string beauty from my body

I feel ridiculous
with my neck in a stovepipe

avec ces maux de tête qui cessent
chaque fois que je salue quelqu'un

J'ai l'impression d'être ridicule
dans leurs salons
dans leurs manières
dans leurs courbettes
dans leur multiple besoin de singeries

J'ai l'impression d'être ridicule
avec tout ce qu'ils racontent
jusqu'à ce qu'ils vous servent l'après-midi
un peu d'eau chaude
et des gâteaux enrhumés

J'ai l'impression d'être ridicule
avec les théories qu'ils assaisonnent
au goût de leurs besoins
de leurs passions
de leurs instincts ouverts la nuit
en forme de paillasson

J'ai l'impression d'être ridicule
parmi eux complice
parmi eux souteneur
parmi eux égorgeur
les mains effroyablement rouges
du sang de leur ci-vi-li-sa-tion

Par la fenêtre ouverte à demi

sur mon dédain du monde
une brise montait
parfumée au stéphanotis
tandis que tu tirais à TOI
tout le rideau

Telle
je te vois
te reverrai toujours
tirant à toi

with these headaches that stop
when I greet someone

I feel ridiculous
in their drawing rooms
in their manners
in their curtseys
all their grimaces

I feel ridiculous
with the stuff they tell
until in the afternoon they serve you
a little hot water
and some cakes with colds

I feel ridiculous
with the theories they spice
to the taste they need
their passions
their instincts open nightly,
like a mattress

I feel ridiculous
complicitous with them
a pimp with them
a killer with them
my hands frightful red
with the blood of their ci-vi-li-za-tion

—MARY ANN CAWS

Through the Half-Opened Window

on my disdain of the world
a breeze was rising
perfumed with stephanotis
while you drew towards YOURSELF
the whole curtain

Such
do I see you
shall I always see you
drawing towards yourself

tout le rideau du poème
où
Dieu que tu es belle
mais longue à être nue

———————————————

Je parle dans tous les âges

Attention, la perle au fond des siècles futurs aux roues de cuivre hurlantes, qui sont les anciens, la perle est dans son écaille vivante sur la table où l'ancêtre rompt le granit chaque matin, qui dure des siècles, pour la nourriture des fils à venir aux places marquées, vêtus d'astres, et celle des fils morts habillés de pierre.

Attention, la perle est dans le creux de la seule main, au croisement des rayons sous le ciel solide qui ne pèse pas lourd dans ta gorge, vieux buveur!

À ma voix familière tu me reconnais et cette main c'est la mienne, tu n'y peux rien, tu ris, vieux toucheur de mondes, mais j'ai saisi la perle et te voilà détrôné, tout en bas.

Va-t'en régner sur les peuples nomades et les douces nations pastorales, j'ai l'œil aussi sur tes vieux bergers et ils en savent long sur la nuit de ta bouche.

the whole curtain of the poem
where
God you are lovely
but so long getting naked

—MARY ANN CAWS

René Daumal 1908–1944
ARDENNES, FRANCE

D aumal's work remained all but unknown until after his death. Founder of the journal *Le Grand Jeu* (1928–1930), he was primarily a visionary. He experimented at an early age with carbon tetrachloride; his use of the drug inspired his essay "Une expérience fondamentale" (1930), which follows his consciousness from drug-enhanced insight to a rational understanding of these perceptions. He was also influenced by, and wrote on, Eastern religions. Daumal was a relentless seeker of truth. In the later part of his life, he met and worked with the spiritual leader Gurdjieff. Principal works: *Le Contreciel*, 1936; *Poésie noire, poésie blanche*, 1954.

I Speak in All Ages

Watch out, the pearl in the depth of future centuries, the old ones, their copper wheels screeching, the pearl rests in its living shell on the table where the ancestor smashes the granite every morning, centuries long, to feed the sons to come in the places signaled, dressed with stars, and the dead sons robed in stone.

Watch out, the pearl is in the hollow of the only hand, at the crossing of rays under the solid sky not weighing much in your throat, old drinker!

You recognize me by my familiar voice and this hand is mine, you can do nothing, you laugh, old toucher of worlds, but I've seized the pearl and there you are dethroned, cast down.

Go reign over model peoples and gentle pastoral nations, I am keeping an eye on your old shepherds too, and they know a lot about the night of your mouth.

Attention, le fil indéfini des siècles tient tout entier dans cette perle qui est ma face et ma fin.

Le Mot et la mouche

Un magicien avait coutume de divertir son monde du petit tour que voici. Ayant bien ventilé la chambre et fermé les fenêtres, il se penchait sur une grande table d'acajou et prononçait attentivement le mot «mouche». Et aussitôt une mouche trottinait au milieu de la table, tâtant le vernis de sa petite trompe molle et se frottant les pattes de devant comme n'importe quelle mouche naturelle. Alors, de nouveau, le magicien se penchait our la table et prononçait encore le mot «mouche». Et l'insecte tombait raide sur le dos, comme foudroyé. En regardant son cadavre à la loupe, on ne voyait qu'une carcasse vide et sèche, ne renfermant aucun viscère, aucune humeur, aucune lueur dans les yeux à facettes. Le magicien regardait alors ses invités avec un sourire modeste, quêtant les compliments, qu'on lui accordait comme il se doit.

J'ai toujours trouvé ce tour assez misérable. A quoi aboutissait-il? Au commencement, il n'y avait rien, et à la fin il y avait un cadavre de mouche. La belle avance! Il fallait encore se débarrasser des cadavres—encore qu'une vieille admiratrice du magicien les collectionnât, quand elle pouvait les ramasser à la dérobée. Cela faisait mentir la règle: «jamais deux sans trois». On attendait une troisième proféation du mot «mouche», qui eût fait disparaître sans traces le cadavre de l'insecte; ainsi toutes choses à la fin eussent été comme au commencement, sauf dans nos mémoires, déjà bien assez encombrées sans cela.

Je dois préciser que c'était un assez médiocre magicien, un raté qui, après s'être essayé avec aussi peu de bonheur à la poésie et à la philosophie, avait transporté ses ambitions dans l'art des prestiges; et même là, il lui manquait encore quelque chose.

Watch out, the indefinite thread of centuries is complete in this pearl which is my face and my end.

—MARY ANN CAWS

Poetry and Thought

A magician was in the habit of amusing his public with the following little trick. Having well aired the room and closed the windows, he would lean over a large mahogany table and carefully pronounce the world "fly." And immediately a fly would be trotting about in the middle of the table, testing the polish with its soft little proboscis and rubbing its front legs together like any natural fly. Then the magician would lean over the table again, and once again pronounce the word "fly." And the insect would fall flat on its back, as if struck by lightning. Looking at the corpse through a magnifying glass, one could see only a dry and empty carcass, no innards, no life, no light in the facetted eyes. The magician would then look at his guests with a modest smile, seeking compliments which were duly paid him.

I have always thought this was a pretty pathetic trick. Where did it lead? At the beginning there was nothing, and at the end there was the corpse of a fly. Such progress. And one still had to get rid of the corpses—although there was an aging lady admirer of the magician who collected them, whenever she could pick them up unnoticed. It disproved the rule: where there's two there's always three. One expected a third utterance of the word "fly" which would have made the insect's corpse disappear without a trace; in that way things would have been the same at the end as they were at the beginning, except in our memories, which are quite cluttered enough without that.

I must add that he was a fairly mediocre magician, a failure who, having tried his hand at poetry and philosophy without much luck, transferred his ambitions to the art of wonders; and even there he didn't really come up to scratch.

MICHAEL WOOD

O la grande apposition du monde

O la grande apposition du monde

un champ de roses près d'un
champ de blé et deux enfants rouges dans le champ voisin du champ de roses et
un champ de maïs près du champ de blé et deux saules vieux à la jointure; le
chant de deux enfants roses dans le champ de blé près du champ de roses et deux
vieux saules qui veillent les roses les blés les enfants rouges et le maïs

Le bleu boit comme tache
L'encre blanche des nuages
Les enfants sont aussi mon
Chemin de campagne

Quai gris

Quai gris d'où tombe l'appât de neige
Le jour décline dans sa coïncidence

Michel Deguy 1930–
PARIS, FRANCE

One of the younger French postwar poets, Deguy was influenced by his studies in philosophy and literature. Central to his belief that the poem is a process of becoming is the French word *comme*, or "like," whereby two opposing elements may be brought together without eliminating their difference. Deguy taught philosophy at the Université Saint-Denis (Paris VIII) until 1968 and has since taught literature there. He founded many reviews, among them *Po&sie* (in 1977), which he continues to edit. He has traveled widely as one of the leading representatives of French poetry and is noted for his essays on other poets, especially Mallarmé, and on poetic theory. Principal works: *Fragments du cadastre*, 1960; *Oui dire*, 1966; *Tombeau de Du Bellay*, 1973; *Vingt poètes américains* (with Jacques Roubaud), 1980; *Gisants*, 1985; *Arrêts fréquents*, 1990; *A ce qui n'en finit pas: Thrène*, 1995; *La poésie n'est pas seule*, 1998; *La Raison poétique*, 2000; *L'Énergie du désespoir, ou d'une poétique continuée par tous les moyens*, 2002.

O Great Apposition of the World

O great apposition of the world
                                        a rose field near a wheat field and
two red children in the field bordering on the rose field and a corn field near the
wheat field and two old willows where they join; the song of two rose children in
the wheat field near the rose field and two old willows keeping watch over the
roses the wheat the red children and the corn

The blue blots like a spot
The white ink of clouds
Children are also my
Country path

—CLAYTON ESHLEMAN

Grey Pier

Grey pier from where the snow bait falls
The day declines into its coincidence

289

L'homme et la femme échangent leur visage
Le vin est lent sur le tableau
A passer dans son sablier de verre
Et l'artiste rapide au cœur par symboles
Doué de confiance hésite:
La pierre est-elle plus belle dans le mur?

Qui quoi

Il y a longtemps que tu n'existes pas
Visage quelquefois célèbre et suffisant
Comment je t'aime Je ne sais Depuis longtemps
Je t'aime avec indifférence Je t'aime à haine
Par omission par murmure par lâcheté
Avec obstination Contre toute vraisemblance
    Je t'aime en te perdant pour perdre
Ce moi qui refuse d'être des nôtres entraîné
De poupe (ce balcon chantourné sur le sel)
Ex-qui de dos traîné entre deux eaux
        Maintenant quoi
        Bouche punie
Bouche punie cœur arpentant l'orbite
Une question à tout frayant en vain le tiers

Le Mur . . .

    Le mur est massif, de pierre pleine, dur, fini; pourtant il suinte Le mur est lisse, neuf et vieux, durable, et pourtant il est lézardé, et par la faille sourd et glisse une goutte, une bête, une mousse Le mur accomplit son rôle, il borde, il bouche, il sépare, il dérobe, il obstrue, et pourtant est-ce à lui de le faire, il protège, il soutène l'insecte à 100%, il se lamente, il adosse la décision, il est compté jusqu'à l'os, il transperce les eaux, il vient de laisser passer la main qui inscrivait, il met mortel en tête

           Ici   est tombé
           Ici   a   vécu
           Ici   est mort
           Ici   a   passé

The man and the woman exchange their faces
The wine is slow on the painting
To pass through its hourglass
And the artist quick to the heart through symbols
Gifted with confidence hesitates:
Is the stone more beautiful in the wall?

—CLAYTON ESHLEMAN

Who What

For a long time you have not existed
Face occasionally celebrated and sufficient
How I love you I don't know For a long time
I've been loving you indifferently I love you to hate
Through an omission through a murmur through cowardice
Obstinately Against all likelihood
    I love you in losing you in order to lose
This me who refuses to be one of us carried away
From the stern (this jig-sawed balcony over the salt)
Ex-who dragged by the back between surface and depth
        Now what
        Punished mouth
Punished mouth heart surveying the orbit
A question for all wearing the third thing in vain

—CLAYTON ESHLEMAN

The Wall . . .

    The wall is massive, of solid stone, hard, finished; yet it oozes The wall is smooth, new and old, durable, and yet it is cracked, and through the fault welling and sliding a drop, a beast, a moss The wall performs its role, it borders, it blocks, it separates, it conceals, it obstructs, and yet must it do it, it protects, it upholds the insect 100%, it laments, it offers the decision backing, it is reckoned to the bone, it pierces the waters, it has just allowed the inscribing hand to pass through, it makes one mortal in one's mind

Here	fell
Here	lived
Here	died
Here	passed

—CLAYTON ESHLEMAN

Ici souvent je suis

And
and they die
and you die
and we die
and she / he / it dies
and you again
and I die

Ici souvent je suis un peu comme encore un
Peu et je vais pleurer à tout moment était-ce
Deux millions trois cent dix mil neuf cent trente-deux
Sept cent vingt quatre mil huit cent soixante-quatre
Il m'a semblé que soudain je faillis pleurer
Quand en finirons-nous avec

Ainsi parlant il se tendait vers son fils, le magnifique Hector Mais l'enfant sur le
sein de nourrice à belle ceinture / Se rejeta criant, l'aspect de son père l'effraye, Il
a peur du bronze et la crête en crins de cheval / terrible au sommet du casque il la
voit s'agiter / Éclatent de rire son père sa noble mère / Aussitôt de sa tête il retirait
son casque, le magnifique Hector / Et il le posa sur terre complètement brillant /
Alors son fils il l'embrassa il le prit dans ses bras / Il dit invoquant Zeus et les
autres dieux /

Encore un instant Monsieur le bourreau
Il n'y en a plus que pour un instant
Encore un instant Monsieur le bourreau
Parce que ça brille, la scène, parce que
Ça monte aux yeux le jour ému en pleurs
En pleurs aux yeux qui vont quitter cela
Qui ne l'ont pas non plus connu avant

Tout ce qu'il va falloir emporter
L'offre se tient, ce dont on fut privé
Un dieu ramasse le monde à ses bras
Qu'il ne savait pas Il doit repartir

Comme   Si
De   Rien
N'   Était

Here Often I Am

And
and they die
and you die
and we die
and she / he / it dies
and you again
and I die

Here often I am a little like still a
Little and I could cry at any moment was it
Two million three hundred ten thousand nine hundred thirty-two
Seven hundred twenty-four thousand eight hundred sixty-four
It seemed to me that suddenly I was about to cry
When will we have done with

Speaking thusly he was stretching toward his son, magnificent Hector But the child at the breast of the nurse with a beautiful sash / Drew back crying, his father's looks terrify him, He is afraid of bronze and the horsehair crest / terrible at the top of the helmet he sees it move / His father his noble mother burst out laughing / At once he took his helmet from his head, magnificent Hector / And he placed it on the ground shining all over / Then his son he kissed him he took him in his arms / He said invoking Zeus and the other gods /

Just a moment more executioner
It will be over in an instant
Just a moment more executioner
Because it shines, the scene, because
It goes to the eyes the day moved to tears
To tears in the eyes that are going to leave all that
That were not even aware of it before

All that one will have to take away
The offer holds, what we were deprived of
A god gathers the world at his arms
That he did not know He must go back
As   If
There   Were
Nothing   To It

—CLAYTON ESHLEMAN

La Ballade

En ce temps-là, façons de feinte et de tendresse, la peste ayant figure d'ennui dans les villes, c'était plusieurs abris, caches d'amour contre l'amour et de franchise contre le mal: aller parler, très peu, avec une femme apte à redisparaître, se mettre nus les visages, abaissant les mains, un téléphone suffisait, ou parfois sur un lit, échange d'autopsies, la nudité se faisait lente, grâce à l'autre, je demandais puis-je venir on ne s'aimera plus dans la ville occupée, si tu es triste, c'était des entresols, recès d'insouci, plus mentaient les discours publics et privés plus montait le goût de vœux rompus dans une intimité de hasard, l'ennemi dans la place nous amenait à nous trahir, c'était aveux risqués aléatoires, et maintenant j'attends que le dégoût se relâche pour reprendre le stylo.

The Ballad

In those days, ways of feinting and of tenderness, the plague having the face of
boredom in the cities, it was many shelters, caches of love against love and of
candor against evil: to go speak, very little, with a woman apt to redisappear, to
make one's faces naked, lowering hands, a phone was enough, or sometimes on a
bed, an exchange of autopsies, the nakedness was slowing down, thanks to the
other, I was asking can I come we won't love each other any more in the occupied
city, if you're sad, it was mezzanines, carefree refuges, the more the public and
private speeches lied the more the taste for broken vows rose up in a chance
intimacy, the enemy on our own grounds led us to betray each other, these were
risky uncertain confessions, and now I wait for disgust to let go in order to take
up the pen again.

—CLAYTON ESHLEMAN

René Depestre 1926–
JACMEL, HAITI

A novelist and poet, Depestre enjoyed early fame and success. *Étincelles*
was published in 1945, when the young writer was only nineteen. In his
newspaper, *La Rûche*, and his poetry, Depestre regularly railed against
his government and the American occupation of Haiti. Love, the poet asserted,
cannot exist without political freedom. Depestre was eventually detained for his
opinions and activities. A general student strike ensued, and Depestre became
one of the heroes of the so-called bloodless revolution that forced the Haitian
government to resign. The new president, however, encouraged Depestre to leave
Haiti, offering him a scholarship to the Sorbonne in 1947. He was not permitted
to return to Haiti until 1957. Frustrated once again with his country, Depestre left
for Cuba, where he remained for twenty years. In 1979 he moved to France and
took a post at UNESCO. Shortly thereafter he broke with the negritude move-
ment in favor of a more traditional utopian humanism. Principal works: *Un arc-*

Romancero d'une petite lampe

Il n'y a de salut pour l'homme
Que dans un grand éblouissement
De l'homme par l'homme je l'affirme
Moi un nègre inconnu dans la foule
Moi un brin d'herbe solitaire
Et sauvage je le crie à mon siècle
Il n'y aura de joie pour l'homme
Que dans un pur rayonnement
De l'homme par l'homme un fier
Elan de l'homme vers son destin
Qui est de briller très haut
Avec l'étoile de tous les hommes
Je le crie moi que la calomnie
Au bec de lièvre a placé
Au dernier rang des bêtes de proie
Moi vers qui toujours le mensonge
Braque ses griffes empoisonnées
Moi que la médiocrité poursuit
Nuit et jour à pas de sanglier
Moi que la haine dans les rues
Du monde montre souvent du doigt
J'avance berger de mes révoltes
J'avance à grands pas de diamant
Je serre sur mon coeur blessé
Une foi si humaine que souvent
La nuit ses cris me réveillent
Comme un nouveau-né à qui il faut
Donner du lait et des chansons
Et tendrement la nuit je berce
Mon Hélène ma foi douce ma vie tombe
En eaux de printemps sur son corps
Je berce la dignité humaine
Et lui donne le rythme des pluies
Qui tombaient dans mes nuits d'enfant
J'avance porteur d'une foi

en-ciel pour l'Occident chrétien, 1966; *Pour la révolution, pour la poèsie*, 1974; *Alléluia pour une femme jardin*, 1981; *Éros dans un train chinois*, 1990; *Hadriana dans tous mes rêves*, 1990; *Le Mât de cocagne*, 1998; *Ainsi parle le fleuve noir*, 1998.

Ballad of a Little Lamp

There is hope for man
Only in man's great dazzling
For man I affirm it
Me, an unknown nigger in the crowd
Me, a solitary blade of grass
And wild I cry out to my century:
There will be joy for man
Only in man's pure radiance
For man
Man's proud leap towards his destiny
Blazing high
With the star of all men
I cry it out I whom hare-lipped
Slander has placed
In the last rank of beasts of prey
Me, towards whom falsehood always
Aims his poisoned claws
Me, whom mediocrity pursues
Night and day with wild-boar steps
Me, at whom hate often points his finger
In the streets of the world
I go forward, shepherd of my revolts
I go forward with great diamond-steps
I clasp to my wounded heart
A faith so human that often
At night its cries awaken me
As a newborn who must
Be given milk and songs
And at night tenderly I lull
My Helen, my gentle faith, my life falls
In waters of Spring over her body
I lull human dignity
And give it the rhythm of the rains
That fell in my child-nights
I go forward carrier of a faith

Insulaire et barbue bêcheur
D'une foi indomptable indomptée
Non un grand poème à genoux
Sur la dalle de la douleur
Mais une petite lampe haïtienne
Qui essuie en riant ses larmes
Et d'un seul coup d'ailes s'élève
Pour être à tout jamais un homme
Jusqu'aux confins du ciel debout
Et libre dans la verte innocence
    De tous les hommes!

Occident chrétien mon frère terrible
Mon signe de croix le voici:
Au nom de la révolte
Et de la justice
Et de la tendresse

Ainsi soit-il!

———————————————

Islander and bearded toiler
For an unconquerable faith unconquered
Not a great poem on its knees
Before the slab of sorrow
But a little Haitian lamp
That wipes away its tears while smiling
And with one beat of its wings
Rises for ever and ever a man
As far as the ends of the sky upright
And free in the green innocence
  Of all men!

Christian West my terrible brother
Here is my sign of the cross
In the name of revolt
And of justice
And of tenderness

Amen!

—JOAN DAYAN

Mohammed Dib 1920–
TLEMCEN, ALGERIA

One of the most highly regarded of the Maghrebian poets, Dib explores, in his enigmatic, sensuous work, meanings seemingly beyond words and, in the subterfuge of his elliptical remarks, engages in what has come to be known as postcolonial counterdiscourse. Dib, Mouloud Mammeri, Mouloud Feraoun, and Kateb Yacine formed a literary group alternately referred to as the "Generation of '52," to mark the year Mammeri's and Dib's first novels appeared, and the "Generation of '54," to mark the start of the war for independence in Algeria. In 1959 Dib moved to France, where he con-

A un voyageur

à Pierre Seghers

1. *lieu de mémoire*

entre les maisons du jour
et les feux de dernière main
ressac de splendeurs sur les collines
dont la cendre colporte le souvenir
la saison a flambé derrière toi
le soleil s'écaille à te chercher
c'est le temps opaque de la terre
c'est le temps de la suie étalée
un archipel noir et perdu
de doutes se hâte de souffler
la dernière lampe allumée
qui délire dans les dunes du nord

2. *pour vivre*

l'or de la fatigue peut-être
l'arme candide muette plus loin

l'entre-temps d'une neige
annoncée à cris dévorants

ce songe de vérité peut-être
son aurore aux mains de louve

tu vas avec d'autres gestes
recevoir ton exil d'une blancheur
habitée par quelques oiseaux

-----

tinues to reside. He is also a successful novelist. Principal works: *L'Ombre gardienne*, 1961; *Formulaires*, 1970; *Omneros*, 1978; *Feu, beau feu*, 1979; *Ô vive*, 1987; *L'Enfant jazz*, 1998; *Le Coeur insulaire*, 2000.

To a Voyager

to Pierre Seghers

1. *place of memory*

between the houses of the day
and the fires of last-hand
surf of splendors on the hills
whose ash spreads memory
the season blazed behind you
the sun peeled looking for you
it's the opaque time of earth
it's the time of spreading soot
an archipelago, black and lost
in doubt hastens to blow out
the last lit lamp
that wanders in the dunes of the north

2. *to live*

the gold of fatigue, perhaps
the candid arm mute further on

the interval of a snowfall
announced to devouring screams

this dream of truth perhaps
its dawn with she-wolf hands

you are going with other gestures
to receive your exile from a whiteness
inhabited by a few birds

—RONNIE SCHARFMAN

Il n'est que temps

Il n'est que temps de remonter au soleil,
Le feu de son alcool purifie l'air
On le boit à longs traits pour oublier celle
Revenue la nuit déchirer le cœur
Dire adieu de sa main enfantine,
Une chandelle parfois tenue en l'air
Qu'elle souffle comme à regret
Mais sans s'attarder davantage
Ni qu'on la voie disparaître.

C'est elle encore souriant debout
Parmi les asters et les roses
Dans la pleine lumière de sa grâce
Fière comme elle fut toujours
Elle ne se fait voir qu'en rêve
Trop belle pour endormir la douleur
Avec tant de faux retours
Qui attestent son absence.

Louis-René des Forêts 1918–2000

PARIS, FRANCE

D es Forêts was a novelist, painter, and translator who, as Albert Camus and many other writers maintained, had a significant impact on the direction of French literature. After publication of *Les Mendiants* (1943), his novel *Le Bavard* (1946) caused a minor sensation in France for questioning the positions of its narrator, writer, and readers. His work, which pointed to the inadequacy of words and art to capture memory and life, would inspire Marguerite Duras and other writers. Des Forêts founded the journal *L'Éphemère* with Yves Bonnefoy, André du Bouchet, and Claude Esteban. During World War II he was involved in the Resistance. He also served as a literary adviser to the publisher Robert Laffont (1944–1946) and worked for Gallimard. Principal works: *Les Mégères de la mer*, 1967; *Poèmes de Samuel Wood*, 1988; *Face à l'immémorable*, 1993; *Ostinato*, 1997.

It Is High Time

It is high time to go back to the sun,
The fire of its alcohol purifies the air
We drink it down lustily in order to forget
The one who came in the night to tear open our heart
And to bid us farewell with her child's hand,
A candle sometimes held in the air
Which she blows out regretfully
But without tarrying further
And without our seeing her disappear.

She is also the one we see smiling, standing
Amid the roses and the aster
In the full light of her gracefulness
Proud as she always was
She only lets herself be seen in dreams,
Too beautiful to let sorrow sleep
With so many false returnings
Which only bear witness to her absence.

Non, elle est là et bien là,
Qu'importe si le sommeil nous abuse
Il faut se brûler les yeux,
Endurer cette douce souffrance,
Ébranler, perdre même la raison,
Détruire ce qui viendrait à détruire
L'apparition merveilleuse
Accueillie comme on tremble
A la vue d'un visage saisi par la mort
Dans le dernier éclat de sa fleur.

Elle est là pour veiller sur nous
Qui ne dormons que pour la voir
Quand par honte, par peur de nos larmes
Nous ne songeons le jour qu'à fuir dehors
Non sans guetter là aussi son retour
Et c'est en quête d'un mauvais refuge
Nous abrutir sous le soleil qui brûle.

Ce que le cœur reconnaît, la raison le nie.
Un rêve, mais est-il rien de plus réel qu'un rêve?
Faut-il se résigner à vivre sans rêver
Que l'enfant aimantée vers ses lieux familiers
Vient dans ce jardin de roses, et chaque nuit
Revient emplir la chambre de sa flamme candide
Qu'elle nous tend comme une offrande et une prière?

Ces visions n'étaient qu'une erreur de l'oubli,
Leur charme sèchement rompu nous enseigne que
Revendiquer son bien n'est pas l'avoir.
Fini donc, fini ce leurre entretenu
Elle n'est pas où nous croyions la voir
Ni là où nous ne serons pas davantage.
Muets tout au fond de la terre
Qui, sauf à se donner le change,
Pourrait désormais nous entendre
Comme au temps des amours heureuses
Où nous étions de vivantes personnes
A l'écoute du moindre aveu sur nos lèvres
Mais libres de parler ou de se taire?

No, she is there, really there,
What matter if sleep beguiles us,
We must burn out our eyes,
Endure the sweet suffering,
Shake, lose, even, our reason,
Destroy anything that would come to destroy
The wonderful vision
Welcomed as one trembles
At the sight of a face seized by death
In the final splendour of its flowering.

She is there to keep watch over us,
Who only sleep to catch sight of her,
When through shame, through fear of our tears,
We flee outdoors at daytime,
Though there too we wait for her return,
And seek illicit refuge
In the bright sun's stultifying blaze.

What the heart recognizes, reason denies.
A dream, but is anything more real than a dream?
Must we learn to live without dreaming
That the child, drawn toward the places she knew,
Comes into the rose garden, and nightly
Fills our bedroom with her pure flame
Which she brings toward us like an offering and a prayer?

These visions were only the delusions of forgetfulness,
Their charm, brutally broken, teaches us
That what we long for we do not have.
Finished, then, finished the illusion we maintained
She is not where we thought we saw her
Nor where we also will never be.
Silent in the depths of the ground
Who, except through willing deception,
Will ever hear us then
As in the time of our happy loves
When we were living people
Attentive to the slightest avowal on our lips
But free to speak or be still?

Feindre d'ignorer les lois de la nature,
Réincarner en songe la forme abolie,
Prêter au mirage les vertus d'un miracle
Est-ce pour autant faire échec à la mort?
Tout au plus douter, qu'elle nous sépare,
Que soit un fait le fait de n'être nulle part.

Irréparable cassure. Prenons-en acte.
Nous voilà désolés la vie durant,
Notre mémoire ouverte comme une blessure,
C'est en elle que nous la verrons encore
Mais captive de son image, mais recluse
Dans cette obscurité dévorante
Où, pour lier son infortune à la nôtre,
Nous rêvions d'aller nous perdre ensemble
Toute amarre tranchée, et joyeux peut-être
Si le pas eût été moins dur à franchir,
Ne faire qu'un avec elle dans la mort
Choisie comme la forme parfaite du silence.

A s'unir au rien, le rien n'engendre rien.
S'il faut vivre éveillé aux choses vivantes,
Craignons plutôt que le chagrin ne s'apaise
De même que vient à faiblir la mémoire
Cesser de souffrir en cessant de la voir
Nous rejoindre la nuit favorable aux rencontres
Serait comme laisser le cœur s'appauvrir
Par deux fois dévasté, et désert.

Pretending to ignore the laws of nature,
Resurrecting in dream the obliterated form,
Giving to illusion the virtues of a miracle,
Does any of this make death less triumphant?
At the very most, let us doubt that death can separate,
Or that the fact of being nowhere is a fact.

Irreparable break: let us take full measure of it.
Here we will be in sorrow our whole life through,
Our memories open like a wound,
It is here that we will find her once more
But a prisoner of her image, a recluse
In that all-consuming darkness
In which, to bind her misfortune to our own,
We dreamed of losing ourselves together,
The cables cut, and full of joy perhaps,
Had the step been less hard to take:
One with her in death,
Chosen as the perfect form of silence.

Coupling with nothing, nothing engenders nothing.
If we must live awake to living things,
Let us rather fear that our sorrow subside
As memories weaken and grow dull.
To suffer no more, seeing her no more
On those nights that welcomed her returning
Would be to let the heart grow poor,
Twice devastated, and alone.

—JOHN NAUGHTON

Toast en réponse

Aux défis de l'impossible.
À deux déserts si distants.
À la lumière qui les sépare.
Aux gemmes incertaines de l'abîme.
À la vérité d'une approche éperdue.
À la médiation du feu.
À l'inacceptable. À la reconnaissance.
À l'échange. À la réparation.
À la migration ensemble.
Au commun accès.
À toi. À moi.

La Création de soi

Mes bêtes de la nuit qui venaient boire à la surface,
j'en ai harponné qui fuyaient,
je les ai conduites à la maison.
Vous êtes ma chair et mon sang.
Je vous appelle par votre nom, le mien.

André Frénaud 1907–1993

MONTCEAU-LES-MINES, FRANCE

Frénaud studied law and philosophy at the University of Lvov, where he served as a teacher. He also worked in the Ministry of Public Works before enlisting in the military in 1940. Soon after joining the war, he was captured and imprisoned; he wrote his first poetry collection in a German prisoner-of-war camp. In 1942, after two years in captivity, Frénaud returned to Paris to join the Resistance. In his work, Frénaud combatted his profound pessimism by identifying with the joyful facets of life. Principal works: *Les Rois mages*, 1966; *Il n'y a pas de paradis*, 1962; *L'Étape dans la clairière*, 1966; *La Sainte face*, 1968; *Depuis toujours déjà*, 1970; *Notre inhabileté fatale*, 1979; *La Sorcière de Rome*, 1979; *Haeres*, 1982; *Nul ne s'égare*, 1986; *Les Gloses à la sorcière*, 1995.

Toast in Response

To impossible challenges.
To two so distant deserts.
To the light separating them.
To the uncertain jewels of the abyss.
To the truth of a crazed approach.
To the meditation of fire.
To the unacceptable. To thankfulness.
To exchange. To restoration.
To migration together.
To the shared access.
To you. To me.

—MARY ANN CAWS

Self-Creation

When they surfaced to drink,
I harpooned some of those night beasts of mine,
As they tried to get away.
I brought them back to the house.
You are my flesh and blood.
I call you by your name, my own.

Je mange le miel qui fut venin.
J'en ferai commerce et discours, si je veux.
Et je sais que je n'épuiserai pas vos dons,
vermine habile à me cribler de flèches.

Les Paroles du poème

Si mince l'anfractuosité d'où sortait la voix,
si exténuant l'édifice entrevu,
si brûlants sont les monstres, terrible l'harmonie,
si lointain le parcours, si aiguë la blessure
et si gardée la nuit.

Il faudrait qu'elles fussent justes et ambiguës,
jamais rencontrées, évidentes, reconnues,
sorties du ventre, retenues, sorties,
serrées comme des grains dans la bouche d'un rat,
serrées, ordonnées comme les grains dans l'épi,
secrètes comme est l'ordre
que font luire ensemble les arbres du paradis,
les paroles du poème.

I eat the honey that was venom.
I'll barter and broadcast it if I like.
And I know I won't exhaust your gifts,
You vermin who know how to pierce me with arrows.

—MICHAEL SHERINGHAM

The Words of the Poem

So narrow the crack whence came the voice,
so forbidding the edifice glimpsed,
such flaming monsters, such terrible harmony,
so long the path, so keen the wound
and the night so protected.

They need to be just and ambiguous,
never seen before, evident, recognized,
spewed out, held back, spewed out,
packed tight as the seeds in the rat's mouth,
tight and trim as the seeds on an ear of corn,
secret as the order
that makes the trees of paradise gleam together,
the words of the poem.

—MICHAEL SHERINGHAM

Jean Grosjean 1912–
PARIS, FRANCE

A poet and translator, Grosjean was a Catholic priest from 1939 to 1950. His translations include the New Testament, the Koran, and Greek tragedies by Sophocles and Aeschylus. Grosjean was taken prisoner in World War II. His first book, *Terre du temps,* was published shortly after the war, its publication greatly aided by André Malraux. Grosjean was on the board of *La Nouvelle Revue Française* from 1967 to 1986. In 1968 his *Élégies* won the Prix

L'Aïeul

Joachaim est sans doute au fond du jardin. On ne s'occupe plus guère de lui. Si impérieux autrefois, il a fini par accepter tant d'événements imprévus qu'on ne lui demande plus son avis. Jeune il semblait faire peu de cas de ses bonheurs. Les premiers ennuis l'ont trouvé impavide. Puis les déceptions ont été inavouables : il a plié d'un air distrait.

Il ne sait plus les jours ni les heures. Assis sous le poirier, près des pendoirs de raphia, il lit le livre des hymnes. Il s'étonne, il s'émeut. Le soleil d'un soir précoce pose une gaieté dérisoire sur les premières feuilles mortes et sur les dernières roses.

Sa vie il en est comme déjà dépossédé. On dirait qu'elle vient de le quitter en l'éclaboussant. Mais le texte est une herbe insolente au milieu du chemin. Les phrases chantonnent comme le vent quand les ronces l'éraflent :

> *L'étrangeté du monde met mon cœur en feu.*
> *Certes personne ne dure longtemps.*
> *Ô ce peu de jours que tu nous donnes.*
> *On erre quelques saisons parmi les apparences*
> *avant d'entrer dans la disparition.*

Joachim lève la tête comme s'il avait entendu des nuages se prendre dans les ramures. Et il s'aperçoit qu'un jeune homme se tient près de lui. Alors il répète tout haut ce qu'il vient de lire :

> *On erre quelques saisons parmi les apparences*
> *avant d'entrer dans la disparition,*

mais en même temps il se souvient du jour où ils avaient arrêté la charrette en forêt. Toute la famille s'était reposée dans l'ombre entre les taches de soleil. N'en restait-il que ce grand jeune homme pour revenir le voir ?

Le jeune homme ne sait que dire quand il rencontre ainsi le deuil atavique de sa race. Il esquisse un sourire et il a sur le visage l'enluminure du couchant.

des Critiques. Principal works: *Hypostases*, 1950; *Le Livre du juste*, 1952; *Fils de l'homme*, 1958; *Hiver*, 1964; *Élégies*, 1967; *La Gloire*, 1969; *La Lueur des jours*, 1991; *Cantilènes*, 1998; *Si peu*, 2001; *Les Vasitas: Poèmes*, 2001.

The Ancestor

Joachim must be in the garden. They're not concerned with him any more. He who was always so imperious, finally accepted so many unexpected events that his opinion no longer counted. In his youth he took his good fortune for granted. The first problems found him untroubled. Then he couldn't admit his disappointments: he gave in looking absent-minded.

He no longer counts the days or the hours. Seated under the pear tree, close to the raffia hangers, he reads the hymnal. He is astonished, excited. The sun of an early evening casts a mocking gaiety over the first dead leaves and the last of the roses.

It's as if he were already dispossessed of his life. It seemed to have just left, splattering him. But the text is an insolent weed in the middle of the road, intoning its sentences, like the wind when the brambles rake through it.

> *The strangeness of the world sets my heart afire.*
> *Surely no one lasts for long.*
> *Oh! these few days you allow us.*
> *You wander a few seasons among the illusions*
> *before you disappear,*

Joachim raises his head as if he's heard clouds getting caught in the branches. He notices a young man standing near him. Then he repeats aloud what he had just read:

> *You wander a few seasons among the illusions*
> *before you disappear,*

but at the same time he remembers the days when they'd stopped their cart in the forest. The whole family had rested in the shade between the patches of sunlight. Was this tall young man the only one left to come back to see him?

The young man doesn't know what to say when he meets the atavistic sorrow of his race. There's a faint smile on his face, illuminated by the setting sun.

—MARY ANN CAWS AND PATRICIA TERRY

Désert à l'essai

Il s'est éloigné des villages. Vers le soir il a atteint le désert, il s'y est enfoncé. Il s'est livré au mutisme de l'espace. Il n'a guère dormi. Les constellations tournaient lentes. Puis toutes les veilleuses du ciel se sont éteintes dans la pâleur de l'aube.

Adossé à une pierre froide il a regardé naître la lumière. Il a senti monter une tiédeur, puis sourdement la fièvre. Ne pas manger.

La chaleur qui gagne. Les yeux offensés par l'éclat du jour. Il faut des creux d'ombre pour survivre, et changer de place suivant l'heure.

Jusqu'à ce que le soleil se fiche vibrant comme une flèche dans le zénith. L'azur blessé à mort. Le chaos du sol prêt à tomber dans le puits d'en haut et l'âme dans l'inconscience.

Que d'instants à l'attache. Mais rien de changeant comme eux. Le scorpion sous la roche. Un souffle avec ses pieds de poussière ou une lapidation de sable.

Et le soleil lassé lui-même. Désarmée de rayons sa braise encore en suspens, puis tombée d'un coup.

Alors la nuit de nouveau avec sa froidure sous un ciel de pierreries tremblantes et le sillage des météorites.

L'insomnie jusqu'au petit matin, jusqu'à l'abîme d'un sommeil sans rêve et ne revenir à soi qu'au plein jour.

Devant moi l'étendue de l'avenir. Derrière moi infranchissables les parois du passé. Fermer les yeux. T'attendre.

Le silence. Ou presque. Ton pas est pourtant léger.

Trial Desert

He had left the villages far behind. Toward evening he reached the desert, he went deep into it. He gave himself over to the stubborn silence of space. He scarcely slept. The constellations revolved slowly. Then all the night lights of the sky went out in the pallor of dawn.

Leaning against a cold stone, he saw the light being born. He felt a warmth rising, then, underneath it, fever. Do not eat.

Heat is taking over. The blaze of day hurts the eyes. Only in hollows of shadow can you survive, finding another as the light shifts.

Until, quivering like an arrow, the sun has stabbed the zenith. The sky fatally wounded. The chaos of the ground about to fall into the well above and the soul into unconsciousness.

So many instants one after another. Nothing is as changeable as they. The scorpion under the rock. A breath of wind's feet of dust or stoning by sand.

And even the sun is tired. Stripped of its rays, its embers still suspended, then suddenly fallen.

Then night again with its chill under a sky of trembling jewels and the wake of meteorites.

Sleeplessness until the first light of dawn, until the abyss of a dreamless sleep, absent from oneself until broad daylight.

Before me stretches the future. Behind me, unscalable, the walls of the past. Closing my eyes. Waiting for you.

Silence. Or almost. But your step is very light.

— MARY ANN CAWS AND PATRICIA TERRY

Eugène Guillevic 1907–1997
CARNAC, FRANCE

A poet who opposed Surrealism in favor of dialectical materialism, Guillevic was interested in visual poetics, using various geometric shapes in his poems as things in themselves. He was thirty-five when his first book, *Terraqué*, was published in 1942, with great success. During World War II he joined the Communist Party; in the 1950s some felt his Marxist sympa-

Quand il eut regardé

Quand il eut regardé de bien près tous les monstres
Et vu qu'ils étaient faits tous de la même étoupe,

Il put s'asseoir tranquille dans une chambre claire
Et voir l'espace.

Il tremblait devant la lumière
Et tremblait devant les rameaux.

Il n'était pas content des fenêtres
Et se méfiait des oiseaux.

Il n'avait pu
Être davantage.

Parlant à la poupée
Dont les yeux rappelaient
Ceux qu'il ne trouvait pas

Et dont les bras tendus
Avaient été cassés
Par lui, un autre soir.

Puisque le goût du crime était trop fort pour lui
Et que pourtant détruire était son grand besoin,

Il dut bon gré mal gré occuper ses journées
A faire avec ses yeux du vide autour de lui.

Allongé sur la mousse et voyant que ce jour
N'aurait pas de pareil,

thies gave a particular slant to his verse. Guillevic was a distinguished translator of German poets, notably Georg Trakl. Principal works: *Exécutoire*, 1947; *Gagner*, 1949; *Trente et un sonnets*, 1954; *Carnac*, 1961; *Inclus*, 1963; *Sphère*, 1963; *Avec*, 1966; *Euclidiennes*, 1967; *Ville*, 1969; *Paroi*, 1970; *Du domaine*, 1977; *Autres*, 1980; *Trouées*, 1981; *Requis*, 1983; *Art poétique*, 1989; *Le Chant*, 1990; *Maintenant*, 1993; *Possibles futurs*, 1996.

When He'd Looked Hard

When he'd looked hard at all the monsters
And seen that all were made of the same old rags,

He could sit down calmly in a bright room
And see space.

He trembled at the light
And trembled at the boughs.

He chafed at the windows
And distrusted the birds.

He'd been unable to
Be more.

Speaking to the doll
Whose eyes reminded him
Of those he couldn't find

And whose arms,
Held out one evening
He had broken.

Since for him crime tasted too strong
Though he greatly needed to destroy

Like it or not, he had to kill time
By razing the world with his eyes.

Stretched out on the moss and seeing that this day
Would be unique,

Il rêvait que, blessé, des mains l'avaient touché
Puis lavé avec l'eau qui coulait de la roche.

Je ne parle pas

Je ne parle pas pour moi,
Je ne parle pas en mon nom,
Ce n'est pas de moi qu'il s'agit.

Je ne suis rien
Qu'un peu de vie, beaucoup d'orgueil.

Je parle pour tout ce qui est,
Au nom de tout ce qui a forme et pas de forme.
Il s'agit de tout ce qui pèse,
De tout ce qui n'a pas de poids.

Je sais que tout a volonté, autour de moi,
D'aller plus loin, de vivre plus,
De mieux mourir aussi longtemps
Qu'il faut mourir.

Ne croyez pas entendre en vous
Les mots, la voix de Guillevic.

C'est la voix du présent allant vers l'avenir
Qui vient de lui sous votre peau.

―――――――――――――――――

He dreamed that hands had touched his wounds,
Had washed them with the water from the rock.

—HOYT ROGERS

I Don't Speak

I don't speak for myself,
I don't speak in my name,
it's not a question of me.

I'm nothing but
a little life, a lot of pride.

I speak for all that is,
in the name of all that has form and no form.
It's a question of all that weighs
and all that's weightless.

I know that everything that surrounds me
longs to go further, to live more intensely,
to die more fully, if dying
is what must be done.

Don't think you hear inside you
the words and the voice of Guillevic.

It's the voice of the present moving towards the future,
the voice of the present sounding from under your skin.

—DENISE LEVERTOV

———————————

Je suis la terre et l'eau

Je suis la terre et l'eau, tu ne me passeras pas à gué, mon ami, mon ami

Je suis le puits et la soif, tu ne me traverseras pas sans péril, mon ami, mon ami

Midi est fait pour crever sur la mer, soleil étale, parole fondue, tu étais si clair, mon ami, mon ami

Tu ne me quitteras pas essuyant l'ombre sur ta face comme un vent fugace, mon ami, mon ami

Le malheur et l'espérance sous mon toit brûlant, durement noués, apprends ces vieilles noces étranges, mon ami, mon ami

Tu fuis les présages et presses le chiffre pur à même tes mains ouvertes, mon ami, mon ami,

Tu parles à haute et intelligible voix, je ne sais quel écho sourd traîne derrière toi, entends, entends mes veines noires qui chantent dans la nuit, mon ami, mon ami

Anne Hébert 1916–2000

QUEBEC, CANADA

lthough Hébert is perhaps best known for her novels, she was an
extremely accomplished poet and playwright as well. Her cousin Hec-
tor de Saint-Denys was a preeminent Quebecois poet; through him
Hébert became acquainted with the literary circles in Quebec. Her first collection
of poems, *Les Songes en équilibre* (1942), was immediately popular. After her
cousin's early death in 1943, Hébert became more interested in exploring themes
of escape from what she perceived as the stultifying weight of Quebecois society
and tradition. In the mid-1950s she left Quebec for Paris, though she died in
Montreal. Principal works: *Le Tombeau des rois*, 1953; *Mystère de la parole*, 1960;
Le Jour n'a d'égal que la nuit, 1994; *Poèmes de la main gauche*, 1997.

I Am Earth and Water

I am earth and water, you will not pass me, will not ford me, my friend, my
friend

I am the well and the thirst, you will not cross me without danger, my friend,
my friend

Noon exists to burst above the sea, flaunted sun, melted word, you were so
bright, my friend, my friend

You will not leave me wiping the shadow on your face like a transient wind,
my friend, my friend

Sorrow and hope beneath my burning roof, knotted tightly, learn these
strange old couplings, my friend, my friend

You flee these omens and press the pure number against your open hands, my
friend, my friend,

You speak out and intelligibly loud, I don't know what deaf echo trails behind
you, hear, hear my black veins singing in the night, my friend, my friend

Je suis sans nom ni visage certain; lieu d'accueil et chambre d'ombre, piste de songe et lieu d'origine, mon ami, mon ami

Ah quelle saison d'âcres feuilles rousses m'a donnée Dieu pour t'y coucher, mon ami, mon ami

Un grand cheval noir court sur les grèves, j'entends son pas sous la terre, son sabot frappe la source de mon sang à la fine jointure de la mort

Ah quel automne! Qui donc m'a prise parmi des cheminements de fougères souterraines, confondues à l'odeur du bois mouillé, mon ami, mon ami

Parmi les âges brouillés, naissances et morts, toutes mémoires, couleurs rompues, reçois le coucher obscur de la terre, toute la nuit entre tes mains livrée et donnée, mon ami, mon ami

Il a suffi d'un seul matin pour que mon visage fleurisse, reconnais ta propre grande ténèbre visitée, tout le mystère lié entre tes mains claires, mon amour.

Terre originelle

Pays reçu au plus creux du sommeil
L'arbre amer croît sur nous
Son ombre au plus haut de l'éveil
Son silence au cœur de la parole
Son nom à graver sur champ de neige.
Et toi, du point du jour ramené,
Laisse ce songe ancien aux rives du vieux monde
Pense à notre amour, l'honneur en est suffisant
L'âge brut, la face innocente et l'œil grand ouvert.
L'eau douce n'est plus de saison
La femme est salée comme l'algue
Mon âme a goût de mer et d'orange verte.
Forêts alertées rivières dénouées
    chantent les eaux-mères de ce temps
Tout un continent sous un orage de vent.
Et route, bel amour, le monde se fonde comme une ville de toile
S'accomplisse la farouche ressemblance du cœur
Avec la terre originelle.

I have no fixed name or face; waiting room and darkroom, track of dreams and place of origin, my friend, my friend

Oh what a season of red leaves God has given me in which to lay you down, my friend, my friend

A great black horse races over the riverbanks, I hear his hoofbeats beneath the earth, his shoe strikes the source of my blood at the slender fetlock of death

Oh, what an autumn! Who then has taken me amidst the motion of subterranean ferns, mixed with the odor of wet wood, my friend, my friend

Among the scrambled ages, births and deaths, all memories, colors shattered, receive the shadowed setting of the earth, all night given and delivered into your hands, my friend, my friend

It took only one morning for my face to flower, acknowledge your own great darkness visited, all the enigma bound between your bright hands, my love.

—MARILYN HACKER

Earth at Its Origin

Land received in the hollowest of sleep
The bitter tree grows upon us
Its shadow at the highest waking
Its silence in the heart of speech
Its name to engrave on the field of snow.
And you, brought back from the break of day,
Leave this ancient dream on the old world shores
Think of our love, its honor is enough.
Brute age, pure face and eyes wide open.
Sweet water is no longer in season
Woman is salty like seaweed
My soul has the taste of sea and green oranges.
Forests alerted rivers unknotted
    sing the mother-waters of this weather
A whole continent under a storm of wind.
And road, lovely friend, the world melts like a town of cloth
Now comes about the heart's wild likeness
To earth at its origin.

—MARY ANN CAWS

Mavena

Ni oui, ni non : elle est entière.
Une barque : il suffit pour qu'elle se taise.
Les poissons viennent à elle comme le rêve.

Elle plonge ses bras dans l'eau pour s'endormir.
Quand elle s'éveille, de petites gouttes tombent de ses doigts, rient
Sur le sol : ce sont ses yeux, ce sont toutes les couleurs.
C'est pourquoi, devant les oiseaux, elle s'enferme dans la peur.

Trois prairies vertes te guettent dans son corps.
Dès qu'elle désire se trouver quelque part, ses mains y sont déjà.
Elle dissimule le vent dans les vagues.

Elle se demande pourquoi elle devrait, comme le sable, s'écouler entre
les doigts, puisqu'elle est belle, même sans marcher sur son haleine.
Si tu la caressais, elle s'écoulerait entre tes doigts comme le sable.
Sais-tu maintenant pourquoi j'aime tant le sable ?

Elle n'a même pas besoin de se taire pour tout dire.
Elle ne sait pas ce qu'elle désire lorsqu'elle regarde à travers les longs
rameaux des cerfs.
Si tu savais . . .

Radovan Ivsic 1921–
ZAGREB, CROATIA

The writings of Ivsic, a poet and playwright, were banned in Croatia not only by the Nazis during the Occupation but also by the postwar Croatian government. In 1954 Ivsic moved to Paris and joined the Surrealist movement. He collaborated on Surrealist exhibitions and on the reviews *BIEF, La Brèche,* and *L'Archibras.* His poems began to appear in print in France after 1960, illustrated by such artists as Joan Miró and Toyen (Marie Cermínová). In 1972 he founded the publishing house Éditions Maintenant. Collections of his poetry finally appeared in Croatia in 1974. Principal works: *Le Roi Gordogane,* 1968; *Mavena,* 1972; *Autour ou dedans,* 1974.

Mavena

Neither yes nor no: she is entire,
A boat: she just has to keep silent.
Fish come to her as does dream.

She plunges her arms in water to go to sleep.
When she awakes, little drops fall from her fingers, laughing
On the ground: they are her eyes, all colors.
That's why, in front of the birds, she closes herself off in fear.

Three green prairies watch you in her body.
As soon as she desires to be somewhere, her hands are already there.
She hides the wind in the waves.

She wonders why she should, like the sand, slip between
the fingers, because she is lovely, even without walking on her breath.
If you caressed her, she would slip between your fingers like sand.
Now do you know why I so love sand?

She doesn't even need to be silent to say everything.
She doesn't know what she desires when she looks through the long
branches of the deer.
If you knew . . .

Sur sa lèvre, le jour s'égare dans la nuit.
Elle ne se retournera pas.
Les fougères.

Lorsqu'elle a soif, jamais elle n'éveille l'eau.
Le silence à l'orée de la forêt peureuse.
Voit-elle les étoiles, ou les étoiles la voient-elle? C'est ce qui la trouble.

Elle respire.
Elle dort.
Elle écoute.

Ce qu'elle entend dans un coquillage ne lui suffit pas.
Elle est dans une crique.
De l'ombre à belles dents.

Ce qu'elle semble m'avouer et ce qu'elle me confie: si tu fermes les yeux, ferme-
les vraiment et ouvre-toi.
Ne regarde pas avant de voir.
Oublie que tu oublies.

Des souvenirs, elle ne garde que les couleurs. Elle n'a jamais rien caché d'autre.
Lorsqu'elle lève une paupière, les papillons éclatent sur l'eau, les chenilles rouges
couvrent la forêt.
Mais que s'élève l'autre paupière . . .

Son sourire écarte les fleurs. Elle sait ce que les fleurs ont oublié.
Seule, elle ne sera jamais tout à fait nue.

Qui est-elle?

On her lips, the day goes lost in the night.
She won't turn around.
The ferns.

When she is thirsty, never does she awaken the water.
Silence at the border of the fearful forest.
Does she see the stars, or do the stars see her? That's what troubles her.

She breathes.
She sleeps.
She listens.

What she hears in a shell isn't enough for her.
She is in a creek.
Shadow with lovely teeth.

What she seems to confess to me and what she confides in me: if you close your
    eyes, close them really and open yourself.
Don't look before seeing.
Forget that you forget.

From memories, she keeps only the colors. She has never hidden anything else.
When she opens an eyelid, the butterflies burst upon the water, the red
    caterpillars cover the forest.
But if the other eyelid opens . . .

Her smile pushes the flowers away. She knows what the flowers have forgotten.
Alone, she will never be completely naked.

Who is she?

—MARY ANN CAWS

Le Miroir et le mouchoir

« *Nous rassemblerons les images et les images des images jusqu'à la dernière qui est blanche et sur laquelle nous nous accorderons.* » —*Reb Carasso*

Mardohai Simhon prétendait que le mouchoir de soie qu'il portait, autour du cou, était un miroir.

« Regardez, disait-il, ma tête est séparée de mon corps par un foulard. Qui oserait me contredire si je déclarais que je me promène avec, au-dessous du menton, un miroir noué ?

Le mouchoir reflète un visage et vous croyez qu'il est de chair.

La nuit est le miroir. Le jour est le foulard. Lune et soleil sont figures réfléchies ; mais mon véritable visage, mes frères, où l'ai-je égaré ? »

A sa mort, on découvrit qu'il avait une large cicatrice à la nuque.

Edmond Jabès 1912–1991

CAIRO, EGYPT

A poet and aphorist, Jabès focused on the mysteries and risks he found inherent in writing, employing an oblique style, and refused to associate with any literary group. In 1930 he left Cairo for Paris to pursue studies in literature at the Sorbonne. He soon abandoned his classes, however, and returned to Cairo, where he took up an extended correspondence with Max Jacob, who became his greatest literary inspiration. In 1945, a year after the poet's death, Jabès published his letters to Jacob. Jabès was active in the Resistance and fought with the British in Palestine. In 1957 he was forced to leave Cairo during the Suez Crisis. He became a French citizen in 1967 and resided in Paris. Principal works: *Je bâtis ma demeure: Poèmes, 1943–1957*, 1959; *Le Livre des questions*, 1963; *Le Livre de Yukel*, 1964; *Retour au livre*, 1965; *Yaël*, 1967; *Elya*, 1969; *Aely*, 1972; *El, ou le dernier livre*, 1973; *Ça suit son cours*, 1975; *Le Livre des ressemblances*, 1976; *Le Soupçon le Désert*, 1978; *Du désert au livre: Entretiens avec Marcel Cohen*, 1980; *L'Ineffaçable l'Inaperçu*, 1980; *Le Petit Livre de la subversion hors de soupçon*, 1982; *Récit*, 1983; *Dans la double dépendance du dit*, 1984; *Le Livre du dialogue*, 1984; *Le Parcours*, 1985; *Le Livre du partage*, 1987; *Un Étranger avec, sous le bras, un livre de petit format*, 1989; *Le Seuil*, 1990; *Le Livre de l'hospitalité*, 1991.

Mirror and Scarf

"We will gather images and images of images up till the last, which is blank. This one we will agree on."
—Reb Carasso

Mardohai Simhon claimed the silk scarf he wore around his neck was a mirror.

"Look," he said, "my head is separated from my body by a scarf. Who dares give me the lie if I say I walk with a knotted mirror under my chin?

"The scarf reflects a face, and you think it is of flesh.

"Night is the mirror. Day the scarf. Moon and sun reflected features. But my true face, brothers, where did I lose it?"

At his death, a large scar was discovered on his neck.

Une discussion, entre rabbins, s'engagea sur le sens qu'il fallait donner à cette anecdote.

Reb Alphandery, en sa qualité de doyen, prit le premier la parole.

«Un double miroir, dit-il, nous sépare du Seigneur; de sorte qu'en cherchant à nous voir, Dieu Se voit et que, cherchant à Le voir, nous ne voyons que notre visage.

— L'apparence n'est-elle que le reflet de l'objet qu'un jeu de miroirs nous renvoie? demanda Reb Éphraïm. Tu fais, sans doute, allusion à l'âme, Reb Alphandery, dans laquelle nous nous mirons. Mais le corps est le lieu de l'âme, comme la montagne est le lit de la source. Le corps a brisé le miroir.

— La source, reprit Reb Alphandery, dort sur la cime. Le rêve de la source, comme elle, est d'eau. Il coule pour nous. Nos songes nous prolongent.

Ne te souviens-tu pas de cette phrase de Reb Alsem : «Nous vivons le rêve de la création qui est le rêve de Dieu ; au soir, nos songes viennent s'y blottir, comme des moineaux dans le nid.»

Et Reb Hames n'a-t-il pas écrit : «Oiseaux de nuit, mes songes explorent l'immense songe de l'univers endormi.»?

— Le rêve est-il le limpide discours des facettes d'un bloc de cristal, reprit Reb Éphraïm? Le monde est de verre, on le devine à sa brillance, la nuit ou le jour.

— La terre tourne dans un miroir. La terre tourne dans un mouchoir, répondit Reb Alphandery.

— Le mouchoir du dandy à la vilaine cicatrice, dit Reb Éphraïm.

> («*La parole est dans le souffle, comme la terre est dans le temps.*»
> Reb Mares.)

Et Yukel dit :

Le baluchon du Juif errant contient la terre et plus d'une étoile.

«Ce qui contient est soi-même contenu», disait Reb Mawas.

L'histoire que je vous ai contée, comme les commentaires qu'elle inspira seront consignés dans le livre du regard. L'échelle nous presse de nous dépasser. Là est son importance. Mais, dans le néant, où la poser?

> («*Dieu est sculpté.*»
> Reb Moyal.)

The meaning of this anecdote was discussed by the rabbis.

Reb Alphandery, in his authority as the oldest, spoke first.

"A double mirror," he said, "separates us from the Lord so that God sees Himself when trying to see us, and we, when trying to see Him, see only our own face."

"Is appearance no more than the reflections thrown back and forth by a set of mirrors?" asked Reb Ephraim. "You are no doubt alluding to the soul, Reb Alphandery, in which we see ourselves mirrored. But the body is the place of the soul, just as the mountain is the bed of the brook. The body has broken the mirror."

"The brook," continued Reb Alphandery, "sleeps on the summit. The brook's dream is of water, as is the brook. It flows for us. Our dreams extend us.

"Do you not remember this phrase of Reb Alsem's: 'We live out the dream of creation, which is God's dream. In the evening our own dreams snuggle down into it like sparrows in their nests.'

"And did not Reb Hames write: 'Birds of night, my dreams explore the immense dream of the sleeping universe' "?

"Are dreams the limpid discourse between the facets of a crystal block?" continued Reb Ephraim. "The world is of glass. You know it by its brilliance, night or day."

"The earth turns in a mirror. The earth turns in a scarf," replied Reb Alphandery.

"The scarf of a dandy with a nasty scar," said Reb Ephraim.

> (*"Words are inside breath, as the earth is inside time."*
> —Reb Mares)

And Yukel said:

"The bundle of the Wandering Jew contains the earth and more than one star."

"Whatever contains is itself contained," said Reb Mawas.

The story I told you, as well as the commentaries it inspired, will be recorded in the book of the eye. The ladder urges us beyond ourselves. Hence its importance. But in a void, where do we place it?

> (*"God is sculpted."*
> —Reb Moyal)
> —ROSMARIE WALDROP

Soleilland

Un pays où les écriteaux ont des ongles
N'entre pas qui veut
Où les pierres sont hors des paupières ravagées de la terre
L'ombre y risque
le matin Les branches combien de nœuds de soif de fruits les immobilisent
depuis les racines
Un pays une ville au bas d'un mur
où des enfants jouent à traquer l'air
à crever les grands yeux bleus de l'air
où les filles soulèvent leur robe d'eau-de-vie
à minuit
Mon amour un pays une ville une chambre
que l'huile des croisées prolonge
que le quartz du soir tombant délimite
où les verrous sont des écrins de clé des songes
sur lesquels tu écris ton nom
où l'eau coule entre les doigts
lorsque fléchit la lampe
Mon amour un pays une ville une chambre un lit
L'univers y germe en frondes d'araignée semelles de lynx
On entend la vie gonfler les veines
du silence
Toute chose se tâte et se complaît
dans sa forme
Mon amour un pays une ville une chambre un lit un mort
qui circule
quand tout se tait
Je ne t'ai jamais parlé de lui
mon frère mon allié
seul à se souvenir
à égrener indéfiniment le chapelet glacé de l'âme
La douleur met le feu
à l'ombre Les tempes s'irisent
à leur insu
Mon amour un pays une ville une chambre un lit un mort
un toit
Cendrillon réveille des bracelets de fête dans le fleuve
avec son pied nu
L'orchestre fait éclater des fèves d'orgie d'or
autour des chevelures grisées

Sunland

A country where the billboards have claws
Not just anyone can enter
Where the stones are outside earth's ravaged eyelids
Shadows there take a chance on
morning How many knots of thirst for fruit immobilize the branches
from the roots up
A country a town at the foot of a wall
where children play at catching the wind
at blinding the big blue eyes of the wind
where girls hike up their schnappsy dresses
at midnight
My love a country a town a room
prolonged by the oil of casements
cut short by the quartz of evening setting in
where the bolts are lock-boxes with dream keys
on which you write your name
where water runs between the fingers
when the lamp begins to flicker
My love a country a town a room a bed
The universe sprouts there in spider fronds lynx-pads
We hear life inflating the veins
of silence
All things take measure of themselves and rejoice
in their own form
My love a country a town a room a bed a dead man
which opens out
when nothing sounds
I never spoke to you about him
my brother my ally
the only one who remembers
who tells indefinitely the frozen beads of his soul
Pain sets fire
to shadows His temples become irridescent
unawares
My love a country a town a room a bed a dead man a
    roof
Cinderella rouses festive rings on the river
with her naked foot
The orchestra makes gold orgy-beans glitter
on heads of grizzled hair

On tue comme on chante
Une fille a perdu sa traîne de myrtils de nonchalance
et l'alouette de ses soucis
Les saisons dans les miroirs
abattent leurs cartes truquées
Mon amour un pays une ville une chambre un lit un mort
un toit un collier
La faute n'est pas au voile d'arête qu'on écorche
ni à la perle réfugiée dans le grenier
Le marin a la rime facile
Son amie exhibe des boucles de cornes de requin
et une ceinture de lames de faon
Mon amour un pays une ville une chambre un lit un mort
un toit
J'ai rendu le collier
Mon amour un pays une ville une chambre un lit un mort
Le toit s'est écroulé
Mon amour un pays une ville une chambre un lit
Le mort est enterré
Mon amour un pays une ville une chambre
Le lit est défait
Mon amour un pays une ville
La chambre est vide
Mon amour un pays
Quelle était cette ville
Mon amour notre amour
sans pays

———————————

We kill the same way we sing
A girl has lost her train of don't-care berries
and the lark of her anxieties
The mirrored seasons
throw down their marked cards
My love a country a town a room a bed a dead man
a roof a necklace
The fault is not with the fish-bone veil that we flay
nor with the pearl seeking refuge in the attic
The sailor has no trouble rhyming
His girl displays shark's-fin buckles
and a layered belt of fawn
My love a country a town a room a bed a dead man
a roof
I have returned the necklace
My love a country a town a room a bed a dead man
The roof has fallen in
My love a country a town a room a bed
The dead man is buried
My love a country a town a room
The bed is unmade
My love a country a town
The room is empty
My love a country
What town was it
My love our love
without a country

—KEITH WALDROP

Parle . . .

Cet espace il te faut l'abandonner à sa propre fructification. Tu n'y entres pas, il est ce qui se délègue au-devant de toi mais l'entrevue est silencieuse. Parle, si tu veux, mais par voix d'arbre ou d'herbe ; c'est-à-dire : ne pratique pas l'imposture, ne mélange pas l'esprit à ce donné si pur.

Abandonne ces directions qui vont pourrir en terre ; sois la simple résonance de la flèche qui te traverse sans fin.

Prière

Que l'innocence demeure
qu'il lui soit donné de pouvoir se perdre dans l'inutilité de ce monde
qu'elle soit suffisamment forte pour oublier de le clamer
que dans son silence où elle éclaire il n'y ait pas d'obstacle à son silence
qu'elle soulève ce monde las et danse dans sa poussière
que son sourire de fleur soit à jamais inscrit sur mes lèvres lorsqu'elles deviendront givre
qu'elle soit l'innocence à jamais.
Que d'aucuns puissent s'en saisir qui voudront sauter hors du bourbier

Pierre-Albert Jourdan 1924–1981

PARIS, FRANCE

Jourdan spent his entire professional career as chief of the Paris public transportation system. Although he published very little during his lifetime, his friends included such notable literary figures as Henri Michaux and René Char; the latter inspired his first poetry collection in 1961. In 1975 Jourdan founded the journal *Port-des-singes,* which attracted contributions by Yves Bonnefoy, Lorand Gaspar, Philippe Jaccottet, and Jacques Réda. Jourdan's paintings and photographs were collected in a volume entitled simply *Pierre-Albert Jourdan* (1984). He died in Caromb, in the Vaucluse. Principal works: *La Langue des fumées,* 1961; *Le Matin,* 1976; *Fragments,* 1979; *L'Angle mort,* 1980; *L'Entrée dans le jardin,* 1981; *Les Sandales de paille* (preface by Yves Bonnefoy), 1987; *Le Bonjour et l'adieu* (preface by Philippe Jaccottet), 1991.

Speak . . .

You have to leave this space to its own fruition. You don't enter it, it sends itself before you but the interview is silent. Speak, if you like, through the voice of a tree or a grass; that is: don't practice imposture, don't mix your mind into what is so pure.

Give up this guidance which will rot in the ground; be just the resonance of the arrow endlessly traversing you.

—MARY ANN CAWS

Prayer

Let innocence remain
let it know how to be lost in the uselessness of this world
let it be strong enough to forget to say that
let there be no obstacle to its silence in the silence where it shines
let it lift this tired world and dance in its dust
let its flower smile be inscribed always on my lips when they become frost
let it be innocence forever.
Let no one wanting to leap out from the mire seize it

qu'elle soit ; ce que de toujours l'affirme ce dialogue de terre et de ciel à l'écart des chemins imposés

qu'elle soit cette folie, suffisamment sourde, receleuse de source pour que tant de soifs s'y abreuvent.

Amen.

————————————

Ma déraison d'être

le désespoir a trois paires de jambes
le désespoir a quatre paires de jambes
quatre paires de jambes aériennes volcaniques absorbantes symétriques
il a cinq paires de jambes cinq paires symétriques
ou six paires de jambes aériennes volcaniques
sept paires de jambes volcaniques
le désespoir a sept et huit paires de jambes volcaniques
huit paires de jambes huit paires de chaussettes
huit fourchettes aériennes absorbées par les jambes

let it be; affirmed always by this dialogue of earth and sky to the side of paths imposed

let this madness be, deaf enough, keeper of the spring to quench so many thirsts.

Amen.

—MARY ANN CAWS

Gherasim Luca 1913–1994
BUCHAREST, ROMANIA

L uca, an artist and creator of *livres-objets* (book-objects), invented "cubo-mania," a Surrealist technique in which a larger image is cut into smaller squares and reassembled in random order. Just before the adoption of communism, France served as political and literary model to Romania. Luca and his fellow poet Gellu Naum therefore had little trouble promoting Surrealism in their country. The movement thrived in Romania until the onset of communism. Luca's first works were written in his mother tongue, but he later turned to French. He moved to Paris in 1952 and committed suicide in 1994. Principal works: *Héros-limite*, 1970; *Le Chant de la carpe*, 1973; *Paralipomènes*, 1976; *Théâtre de bouche*, 1984; *La Proie s'ombre*, 1991; *La voici la voix silencieuse*, 1996.

My Folly of Being

despair has three pairs of legs
despair has four pairs of legs
four pairs of light volcanic absorbent symmetrical legs
it has five pairs of legs five symmetrical pairs
or six pairs of light volcanic legs
seven pairs of volcanic legs
despair has seven or eight pairs of volcanic legs
eight pairs of legs eight pairs of socks
eight light forks absorbed by the legs

il a neuf fourchettes symétriques à ses neuf paires de jambes
dix paires de jambes absorbées par ses jambes
c'est-à-dire onze paires de jambes absorbantes volcaniques
le désespoir a douze paires de jambes douze paires de jambes

il a treize paires de jambes
le désespoir a quatorze paires de jambes aériennes volcaniques
quinze quinze paires de jambes
le désespoir a seize paires de jambes seize paires de jambes
le désespoir a dix-sept paires de jambes absorbées par les jambes
dix-huit paires de jambes et dix-huit paires de chaussettes
il a dix-huit paires de chaussettes dans les fourchettes de ses jambes
c'est-à-dire dix-neuf paires de jambes
le désespoir a vingt paires de jambes
le désespoir a trente paires de jambes
le désespoir n'a pas de paires de jambes
mais absolument pas de paires de jambes
absolument pas absolument pas de jambes
mais absolument pas de jambes
absolument trois jambes

La Fin du monde: Prendre corps

Je te narine je te chevelure
je te hanche
tu me hantes
je te poitrine
je buste ta poitrine puis te visage
je te corsage
tu m'odeur tu me vertige
tu glisses
je te cuisse je te caresse
je te frissonne
tu m'enjambes
tu m'insupportable
je t'amazone
je te gorge je te ventre
je te jupe
je te jarretelle je te bas je te Bach
oui je te Bach pour clavecin sein et flûte

it has nine forks symmetrical in its nine pairs of legs
ten pairs of legs absorbed by its legs
in other words eleven pairs of absorbent volcanic legs
despair has twelve pairs of legs twelve pairs of legs

it has thirteen pairs of legs
despair has fourteen pairs of light volcanic legs
fifteen fifteen pairs of legs
despair has sixteen pairs of legs sixteen pairs of legs
despair has seventeen pairs of legs absorbed by the legs
eighteen pairs of legs and eighteen pairs of socks
it has eighteen pairs of socks in the forks of its legs
in other words nineteen pairs of legs
despair has twenty pairs of legs
thirty pairs of legs.
despair doesn't have any pairs of legs
not a single pair of legs
absolutely not absolutely no legs
absolutely not a single leg
absolutely three legs

—MICHAEL TWEED

The End of the World: To Embody

I nostril you I hair you
I hip you
you haunt me
I breast you
I breast your bust then visage you
I corsage you
you odor me you dizzy me
you slide
I thigh you I caress you
I shiver you
you leg across me
you unbearable me
I amazon you
I neck you I stomach you
I skirt you
I garter you I stocking you I Bach you
yes I Bach you for harpsichord breast and flute

je te tremblante
tu me séduis tu m'absorbes
je te dispute
je te risque je te grimpe
tu me frôles
je te nage
mais toi tu me tourbillonnes
tu m'effleures tu me cernes
tu me chair cuir peau et morsure
tu me slip noir
tu me ballerines rouges
et quand tu ne haut-talon pas mes sens
tu les crocodiles
tu les phoques tu les fascines
tu me couvres
je te découvre je t'invente
parfois tu te livres

tu me lèvres humides
je te délivre et je te délire
tu me délires et passionnes
je t'épaule je te vertèbre je te cheville
je te cils et pupilles
et si je n'omoplate pas avant mes poumons
même à distance tu m'aisselles
je te respire
jour et nuit je te respire
je te bouche
je te palais je te dents je te griffe
je te vulve je te paupières
je te haleine
je t'aine
je te sang je te cou
je te mollets je te certitude
je te joues et te veines

je te mains
je te sueur
je te langue
je te nuque
je te navigue
je t'ombre je te corps et te fantôme

I trembling you
you seduce me you absorb me
I dispute you
I risk you I climb you
you brush by me
I swim you
But you you whirlwind me
you graze me you surround me
you flesh me leather skin and bite
you black slip me
you red ballet slipper me
and when you don't high heel my senses
you crocodile them
you seal you fascinate them
you cover me
I discover you I invent you
sometimes you deliver yourself

you damp lips me
I deliver you and I delirious you
you delirious me and passionate me
I shoulder you I vertebra you I ankle you
I eyelash and pupil you
and if I don't shoulder blade before my lungs
even at a distance you armpit me
I breathe you
day and night I breathe you
I mouth you
I palate you I teeth you I fingernail you
I vulva you I eyelid you
I breath you
I groin you
I blood you I neck you
I calf you I certitude you
I play you and vein you

I hand you
I sweat you
I tongue you
I nape you
I navigate you
I shadow you I body you and ghost you

je te rétine dans mon souffle
tu t'iris

je t'écris
tu me penses

Si l'attendrissant souvenir

Si l'attendrissant souvenir du verre brisé dans son oeil ne sonne l'heure à la cloche qui parfume le bleu si las d'aimer la robe soupirante qui l'enveloppe le soleil qui pourrait d'un moment à l'autre éclater dans sa main rentre ses griffes et s'endort à l'ombre qui dessine la mante religieuse grignotant une hostie mais si la courbe qu'agite la chanson pendue au bout de l'hameçon s'enroule et mord au coeur le couteau qui la charme et la colore et le bouquet d'étoiles de mer crie sa

I retina you in my breath
you iris you

I write you
you think me

—MARY ANN CAWS

Dora Maar
(Henriette Theodora Markovitch) 1907–1997
TOURS, FRANCE

A photographer and painter, Maar spent her childhood in Argentina before returning to her native France. Settling in Paris, she worked as a set photographer for the filmmaker Jean Renoir and became involved with the Surrealist movement. She was a companion to Georges Bataille. It was on the terrace of Les Deux Magots that Picasso asked Paul Éluard to introduce Maar to him. The two entered into a relationship that lasted from 1936 to 1942, through both the Spanish Civil War and World War II, dark years for Picasso. During this time he painted his famous *Guernica,* which Maar photographed in all its stages. She was popularly known as Picasso's "Weeping Woman." After their separation she lived the life of a recluse, in Paris and Provence. "After Picasso," she once explained, "only God." She continued to paint and write.

If the Touching Memory

If the touching memory of broken glass in his eye does not sound the hour from the bell perfuming the blue if tired of loving the sighing dress surrounding him with sun that could from one moment to the next burst apart in his hand pulls in its claws and sleeps in the shadow sketching the praying mantis nibbling on a host but if the curve stirred up by the song hung from the end of the snail should wrap itself around biting the heart charming it and coloring it and the

détresse dans la coupe le coup de langue de son regard éveille la ratatouille
tragique du ballet des mouches dans le rideau de flammes qui bout sur le bord de
la fenêtre

Les Grandes Constructions

Les grandes constructions, face au soleil, le ciel égal, sont visibles de la
    chambre tout au sommet du paysage.
Je ne bouge pas.
C'est ainsi que je faisais autrefois, j'alourdissais tout.
Pressée par la solitude il s'agissait d'imaginer l'amour

le temps passe
Aujourd'hui un dimanche de la fin du mois
Mars 1942 à Paris les chants des oiseaux domestiques
sont comme de petites flammes bien visibles brûlant calmement
dans le silence. Je suis désespérée
Mais il ne s'agit pas de moi

Les grandes constructions face au soleil, le ciel égal,
je les vois de ma chambre au sommet du paysage
Je ne bouge pas.
C'est ainsi que j'ai toujours fait. J'alourdissais tout

Aujourd'hui c'est un autre paysage dans ce dimanche de la fin
du mois de mars 1942 à Paris le silence est si grand que les
chants des oiseaux domestiques sont comme des petites flammes bien visibles.
    Je suis désespérée

Mais laissons tout cela

_____

bouquet of stars of the sea shrieking its distress in the cup the verbal blast of its gaze awakens the tragic ratatouille of the ballet of flies in the curtain of flames boiling on the window ledge

—MARY ANN CAWS

These Tall Constructions

These tall constructions facing the sun in the cloudless sky are visible from the
    room at the top of the landscape.
I do not move.
That is what I used to do, weighing everything down.
Pressed by solitude it was a matter of imagining love

time passes
Today a Sunday at the month's end
March 1942 in Paris the songs of the tame birds
are like little flames burning calmly you can see
in the silence. I am desperate
But it isn't a question of me

These tall constructions facing the sun in the cloudless sky,
I see them from my room at the top of the landscape
I do not move.
This is what I have always done. I weighed down everything

Today it's another landscape in this Sunday at the end
of the month of March 1942 in Paris the silence is so great
that the songs of the tame birds are like little flames you can see.
    I am desperate

But forget it

—MARY ANN CAWS

Je veux dormir avec toi

Je veux dormir avec toi coude à coude
Cheveux entremêlés
Sexes noués
Avec ta bouche comme oreiller.
Je veux dormir avec toi dos à dos
Sans haleine pour nous séparer
Sans mots pour nous distraire
Sans yeux pour nous mentir
Sans vêtements.
Je veux dormir avec toi sein contre sein
Crispée et en sueur
Brillant de mille frissons
Mangée par l'inertie folle de l'extase
Ecartelée sur ton ombre
Martelée par ta langue
Pour mourir entre les dents cariées de lapin
Heureuse.

Papier d'argent

Je veux vivre à l'ombre de ton visage
Plus hostile que le bois
Plus vigilant que Noé

Joyce Mansour 1928–1986
BOWDEN, ENGLAND

Mansour was one of the few prominent female poets associated with the Surrealist movement. Her caustic, subversive, and humorous verse explored taboo subjects, mainly sexual. Mansour, of Egyptian heritage, spent her childhood in Cairo and was nicknamed "l'enfant du conte orientale" by André Breton. She began publishing in *Actes Sud* in 1950, and her work continues to influence new generations of feminists as well as Lebanese and Francophone writers. Principal works: *Crisis*, 1954; *Déchirures*, 1955; *Rapaces*, 1960; *Carré blanc*, 1965; *Ça*, 1970; *Faire signe au machiniste*, 1977.

I Want to Sleep with You

I want to sleep with you side by side
Our hair intertwined
Our sexes joined
With your mouth for a pillow.
I want to sleep with you back to back
With no breath to part us
No words to distract us
No eyes to lie to us
With no clothes on.
To sleep with you breast to breast
Tense and sweating
Shining with a thousand quivers
Consumed by ecstatic mad inertia
Stretched out on your shadow
Hammered by your tongue
To die in a rabbit's rotting teeth
Happy.

—MARY ANN CAWS

Tinfoil

I want to live in the shade of your face
More hostile than wood
More vigilant than Noah

Penché sur les flots
Je veux creuser des routes dans les lunaires collines
De ton corps
Allumer des feux dans le creux de tes paupières
Savoir te parler et partir quand il est temps
Encore
Je veux vivre lentement dans le jeu de ton décor
Flotter entre mère et père
Tel le sourire de l'écho dans la pénombre
Dévêtue
Etre l'étincelle de l'oreiller
Entendue par le sourd qui se croit seul
Cannibale
Je veux titiller de désespoir sous ta langue
Je veux être lys sur ton ombre légère
Et me coucher éblouie sous l'araignée
Bonne nuit Irène
C'est l'heure

Rappelle-toi

Rappelle-toi
Le vol saccadé de mon cœur
Ton émoi
Le froissement de mes poils
Quand je ris avec toi
Le vent farci d'odeurs
Qui précède mon corps en feu
L'épais caoutchouc gris des molles soirées de l'hiver
Quand nous écoutions les rats carillonner
En mangeant des coquelicots
Toi et moi.

L'Orage tire une marge argentée

L'orage tire une marge argentée
Dans le ciel
Et éclate dans un immense spasme englué
Sur la terre.
L'écume flottante

Attending to the Flood
I want to forge new routes in your body's
Moon hills
Light fires in the hollows of your eyelids
Know how to speak to you and when to leave
In good time
I want to live slowly in the movement of your scenery
Float between mother and father
Like echo's smile in shaded light
Undressed
Be the pillow's spark
Heard by the deaf man who thinks he's alone
Cannibal
I want despair to whet your lifted tongue
I want to be the lily on your light shadow
And lie down dazzled under the spider
Good night Iris
It's time

—MARTIN SORRELL

Remember

Remember
The jolting flight of my heart
Your excitement
The way my hair ruffles
When I laugh with you
The wind stuffed with smells
Coming before my body aflame
The rubbery grey thickness of the winter evenings
When we heard the rats jingling around
Eating poppies
You and me.

—MARY ANN CAWS

The Storm Sketches a Silver Margin

The storm sketches a silver margin
In the sky
And bursts in a great sticky spasm
On the ground.
The floating foam

Envolée de la mer en déroute
Vient rafraîchir nos visages défaits
Et nos corps qui se cachent
Dans la sombre tiédeur de nos désirs endormis
Se dressent.
Notre sieste harcelée de punaises
Prend fin
Et le court lapement des vagues
Sur la plage où danse l'azur
S'est tu, mon amour
Et il pleut.

———————————

Rêve à Barcelone

Je suis couchée avec un homme dans un lit qui est à l'extrémité d'une grande salle. Tout au long des murs court un relief grec, comme au Parthénon. Par une petite porte à l'autre bout de la salle arrive une chose, une sorte de sculpture

Cast up by the receding sea
Comes to cool our tired faces
And our bodies hiding
In the tepid dark of our sleeping desires
Stand up straight.
Our nap the lice have plagued
Ends
And the brief lapping of the waves
On the beach where the azure dances
Has fallen quiet, my love,
And it's raining.

—MARY ANN CAWS

Meret Oppenheim
(Elizabeth Oppenheim) 1913–1985
BERLIN, GERMANY

A photographer, poet, painter, and sculptor, Oppenheim is best known for her sculpture *The Fur-Lined Teacup* (1936), which launched her into immediate fame and became an icon of Surrealism. This work was photographed by Man Ray. In 1937 Oppenheim left Paris to study in Basel, in an attempt to catch up with her growing international reputation. She quickly fell into a depression that lasted seventeen years. In the 1950s she began to work again and in the 1960s was rediscovered as a mature artist who had retained loyal ties to Dadaism and Surrealism. She died in Paris. Principal works: *Ma gouvernante, my nurse, mein Kindermächen*, 1936; *Le Couple*, 1956; *Meret Oppenheim: Defiance in the Face of Freedom* (an anthology), 1989.

Dream in Barcelona

I am lying down with a man in a bed at the far end of a large room. All along the walls there runs a Greek relief, as in the Parthenon. Through a little door at the other end of the room there comes something, a sort of paranoid sculpture

paranoïde (elle rappelle des figures de Salvador Dali), mais qui prend des proportions gigantesques dès qu'elle a franchi la porte, et elle remplit la salle jusqu'au plafond. Construction amorphe, elle se termine en un endroit en soulier de dame; la construction marche sur le soulier qui se trouve à un bout et sur la pointe de quelque chose comme un nez. Je dis à l'homme avec qui je suis couchée que je ne l'aime plus. Il dit: Alors prends-toi un de ces Grecs! Je me lève, je vais jusqu'au mur, et je tire la jambe d'un des jeunes hommes en marbre. Il descend du mur. Nous partons ensemble, nous nous promenons dans un paysage. L'homme près duquel je marche devient subitement mon père. Nous marchons côte à côte sur un plateau. Plus bas, sur les pentes poussent des sapins dont on ne voit pourtant que les faîtes. Mon père montre un groupe de ces sommets de sapins (sur le versant sud) qui sont fortement agités et dit: «C'est là-bas que j'ai connu ta mère.» Je dis: «Là-bas est mon meurtrier!»

Je descends la pente, je crois qu'il s'agit maintenant du versant nord, jusqu'au pied de ces sapins. Là est assis, appuyé à un tronc, un homme sur le retour d'âge, vêtu sportivement, avec une veste de tweed de couleur rouille, les cheveux gris et courts. Il dirige un couteau vers moi. De l'extrémité de l'index d'une main je touche la pointe du couteau, de l'autre index l'extrémité de la poignée, je retourne le couteau et m'apprête à poignarder cet homme quand mon père, à côté de moi, dit: «Ça ne se fait pas.» Sur quoi je donne un coup à l'homme, si bien qu'il dévale la pente. Il roule sur lui-même tout en se touchant le front avec l'index et il a l'air du serpent Ouroboros qui se mord la queue.

———————————

(like the figure of Salvador Dalí), but which takes on gigantic proportions as soon as it gets through the door, filling the room to the ceiling. An amorphous construction, it ends in one place like a woman's shoe; the construction is walking on the shoe at that end and on the point of something like a nose. I say to the man I am lying down with that I don't love him any longer. He says: "Then go take one of those Greeks!" I get up, go toward the wall, and pull at the leg of one of those young men in marble. He gets down from the wall. We leave together, we walk along in some countryside. The man I am walking with suddenly becomes my father. We are walking side by side on a plateau. Lower there are some fir trees only the tops of which are visible. My father points out one cluster of these fir tree tops (on the south slope) which are tossing about, and says: "Over there is where I knew your mother." I say: "Over there is my murderer!"

I descend the slope, I think now it's the north face, down to the foot of those fir trees. There, sitting against a tree trunk is an aging man, dressed very sportily, with a rust-colored tweed jacket, his grey hair very short. He draws a knife on me. With the tip of my index finger, I touch the point of the blade, and with the other index finger the end of the handle. I turn the knife around and get ready to stab this man when my father, beside me, says: "That just isn't done." At which I stab the man, who falls down the slope. He rolls over on himself, touching his forehead with his index finger and looks like the Ouroboros serpent biting his tail.

—MARY ANN CAWS

Valentine Penrose 1898–1978
CONDOM-SUR-BAÏSE, FRANCE

P enrose was part of the Surrealist movement in the 1920s and was adept at the creation of remarkable images through the automatic process. In 1925 Valentine Boué married Roland Penrose, who, with David Gascoyne, is credited with bringing Surrealism to London. The three moved to Spain in 1936 during the Spanish Civil War. Penrose later produced a graphic biography of Erzsébet Bathory, the sixteenth-century Hungarian countess who had hundreds of young women put to death, believing that bathing in their blood would enable her to keep her beauty and youth (*Erzsébet Bathory: La Comtesse san-*

La Pluie retrouvant

La pluie retrouvant ce qui est perdu
le soleil trouvant ce qui luit
grandes compagnes de ma vie.
Sur la terre qui est brune
moi aussi j'ai trouvé place.

Aux sphères entières
mouvant les tourments
par mes pas dorés je monte et descends.

Et s'y tiennent debout les eaux comme des lames
et plongerai ma lame au profond des citernes
sous mes yeux faux témoins au pays de mon être
dans la salle dormant à ma propre lumière
parmi tous les miroirs dont je me souviendrai.

À mes carreaux

À mes carreaux nul n'a dansé
l'équateur a laissé la neige
sans venues l'appel des brasiers.

Au balcon sans fleurir les bouteilles de cendres
de grive d'or sont perdus les pouvoirs
dessein de terre terne guise
cette fois est toutes les fois
les épées sont remises
et si hantées les plantes au coin d'air ont douté.

Mais heureuse la dame peut toute au ciel bouger
et les nuits linges filants aux ronces courant
fleurs de cendre de ce côté sûr bien attisées
le lierre le vent le lierre le vent.

glante, 1962). Principal works: *Herbe à la lune*, 1935; *Le Nouveau Candide*, 1936; *Sorts de la lueur*, 1937; *Dons de féminines*, 1951; *Les Magies*, 1972.

The Rain Finding Once More

The rain finding once more what is lost
the sun finding what shines
great companions of my life.
On the brunette earth
I too have found my place.

      To the entire spheres
      moving the torments
through my gilded steps I go up go down.

And there the waters stand like blades
and I plunge mine in the cisterns' depths
under my eyes false witness to the country of my being
in the room sleeping by my own light
among all the mirrors I shall remember.

—MARY ANN CAWS

At My Windows

      At my windows no one has danced
      the equator has left the snow
      placeless the summons of embers.

At the balcony unblooming the bottles of ash
of golden thrush are lost the powers
earth's drawing dull dress
this time is every time
the swords are put back
so haunted the nearby air plants have doubted.

But lucky the lady can move all in the sky
and the nights streaking linen thorns running
ash flowers on this side well lit
ivy wind ivy wind.

—MARY ANN CAWS

Qualités d'apôtre

Lire et chanter est une chose propre tandis que parler c'est des minutes.

J'ai parlé et mon être brave a gémi.

J'ai joué peu et j'ai mal fini.

Parce que la fin c'est la fin d'une chose et quand je m'apercevrai que j'existe, je dirai : « La neige a commencé de tomber ce matin. »

J'ai vu très clair pendant que le ciel me regardait.

Et, parmi ces brouillards liquides, j'ai pensé qu'entre elles deux il n'y avait que chansons.

Alors, merveilleusement bien, j'ai couru vers la ferme en sifflant et mon cœur plus digne que la poussière a crié sous vos pas.

Mais, comme je n'ai jamais vu d'apôtre, je ne pourrai pas sortir d'ici. Aussi, avec un zèle sans pareil, mon âme simple et nonchalante a prononcé ces mots :

« Chose sucrée que la vanille ! »

Poème amoureux

À l'ombre du tapis chatoyant, ah ! pourquoi, tendre inspirée, avez-vous trié les fibres intimes de mon cœur ? n'avez-vous donc jamais surpris le clignotement instinctif et forain de la corporation centrale de mon âme ? croyez-vous donc que la moralité fidèle soit un secret que l'on souffre particulièrement ?

Est-ce que mes regards salubres ne crèveront plus sous l'influence aride de vos prunelles sombres ?

Gisèle Prassinos 1920–
ISTANBUL, TURKEY

Prassinos was born in Turkey to Greek parents who moved the family to France in 1922. André Breton and Paul Éluard discovered her poetry in 1934 when it first appeared in the Surrealist journal *Minotaure*. The two declared that her works at the age of fourteen proved the efficacy of automatic writing. They dubbed her the "ambiguous schoolgirl." Éluard praised the poet for her childlike ethics, her imagination, and her ability to create moments of purity in the face of centuries of rationalization. Principal works: *Une demande en mariage*, 1935; *La Sauterelle arthritique* (preface by Éluard), 1935; *Le Feu maniaque* (preface by Éluard), 1939; *Trouver sans chercher*, 1975.

Apostle Qualities

Reading and singing are good, while speaking is just minutes.
I spoke and my honest self moaned.
I seldom played and I finished badly.
Because the end is the end of something, when I see I exist, I'll say: "Snow started to fall this morning."
I saw things very clearly while the sky was looking at me.
And, among these damp mists, I surmised that between the two of them there were only songs.
Then, in wondrous spirits, I ran whistling toward the farm, and my heart more worthy than the dust shouted under your steps.
But, since I've not seen an apostle, I won't be able to leave here. So, in an unparalleled eagerness, my simple and nonchalant soul said these words:
"How sweet vanilla is!"

—MARY ANN CAWS

Loving Poem

In the shadow of the gleaming carpet, ah! why, tender inspired one, have you sorted out the intimate fibers of my heart? haven't you ever surprised the instinctive and foreign blinking of the central corporation of my soul? so do you think that faithful morality is a secret that we particularly suffer from?

Will my health-giving gazes never again collapse under the arid influence of your somber eyes?

Non, ce n'est pas, ce ne sera jamais, car je veille socialement à l'unanime capacité des organes originaux et je sais qu'en prenant la supériorité générale de l'organisation prophétique, votre cœur n'osera jamais réserver le mien.

Donc, en vous fixant révérences et filatures, je vous dis fumistement ces paroles gémissants : « craignons les sens ».

Un jour

Un jour
Il y aura autre chose que le jour
Une chose plus franche, que l'on appellera le Jodel
Une encore, translucide comme l'arcanson
Que l'on s'enchâssera dans l'oeil d'un geste élégant
Il y aura l'auraille, plus cruel

No, it isn't and never will be, for I keep a social watch over the unanimous capacity of the original organs, and I know that by taking on generally the superiority of prophetic organization, your heart will never dare to reserve mine.

So, by fixing upon you curtsies and spinnings, I moan these words at you, as a hoax: "let's fear the senses."

—MARY ANN CAWS

Boris Vian 1920–1959
VILLE D'AVRAY, FRANCE

Vian was a musician, jazz critic, singer and songwriter, opera librettist, novelist, short-story writer, and playwright. He was a favorite among existentialist and post-Surrealist groups in Paris, and his plays were closely linked to the Theater of the Absurd. He wrote his first novel in ten days for a publisher looking for a new best-selling American author. Acquainted with Miles Davis and Dizzie Gillespie, Vian used their experiences as a background on American race relations for the book. He was twenty-six when *J'irai cracher sur vos tombes* (1946) appeared, published under the pseudonym Vernon Sullivan. The book was phenomenally successful, selling one hundred thousand copies, and Vian's real identity was soon exposed. In 1959 the book was made into a film; Vian died of a heart attack while watching the preview. Principal works: *Cantilènes en gelée*, 1949; *Je voudrais pas crever*, 1962.

One Day

One day
There won't be just the day
There'll be something more candid, we'll call it the Jodel
And something else, too, translucent as turpentine
We'll insert in our eyes with an elegant gesture
There'll be the orpack, more cruel

Le volutin, plus dégagé
Le comble, moins sempiternel
Le baouf, toujours enneigé
Il y aura le chalamondre
L'ivrunini, le baroique
Et tout un planté d'analognes
Les heures seront différentes
Pas pareilles, sans résultat
Inutile de fixer maintenant
Les détails précis de tout ça
Une certitude subsiste : un jour
Il y aura autre chose que le jour.

Pourquoi que je vis

Pourquoi que je vis
Pourquoi que je vis
Pour la jambe jaune
D'une femme blonde
Appuyée au mur
Sous le plein soleil
Pour la voile ronde
D'un pointu du port
Pour l'ombre des stores
Le café glacé
Qu'on boit dans un tube
Pour toucher le sable
Voir le fond de l'eau
Qui devient si bleu
Qui descend si bas
Avec les poissons
Les calmes poissons
Ils paissent le fond
Volent au-dessus
Des algues cheveux
Comme zoizeaux lents
Comme zoizeaux bleus
Pourquoi que je vis
Parce que c'est joli.

The bendbind, more jaunty
The apogee, less endless
The ruckub, eternally snow clad
There will be the chalamonder
The ivrunini, the baroqueme
A whole planting of analittles
The hours will be different
Not all the same, with no result
No point in fixing now
Exactly what it'll be like
But one thing's for sure: one day
There won't be just the day.

—ROSEMARY LLOYD

What for Do I Live Then

What for do I live then
What for do I live then
For the lemony leg
Of a blond woman
Leaning on the wall
In the blazing sun
For the round sail
Of a pointed in the port
For the shadow of the shades
The icy coffee
You drink in a tube
To touch the sand
See the water's depths
That grow so blue
That go so low
With the fish
The calm fish
Grazing on the depths
Flying above
The seaweed hairs
Like birdies slow
Like birdies blue
Why I live
It's so nice.

—ROSEMARY LLOYD

4

1946–1966:
The Death of André Breton, the
Beginning of *L'Éphémère*

Yves Bonnefoy, André du Bouchet, Bernard Collin, Jacques Dupin,
Jacques Garelli, Lorand Gaspar, Édouard Glissant, Philippe Jaccottet,
Claire Lejeune, Claire Malroux, Robert Marteau, Abdelwahab Meddeb,
Gaston Miron, Bernard Noël, Anne Perrier, Anne Portugal, Jacques
Réda, Jude Stéfan, Salah Stétié

The postwar years of French poetry were marked by a new
openness. Raymond Queneau's experimental works of
this period: his *Exercices de style* (1947), *Bâtons, chiffres et
lettres* (1950), and *Un conte à votre façon* (1967) follow the tradition of
Mallarmé's unique book *Le Livre,* whose individual sheets could be rear-
ranged at will. In this open work, the reader becomes an active partici-
pant—playing an authorial role in the rearrangement of description and
narrative. Americans such as Charles Olson, Louis Zukofsky, Robert
Duncan, and George Oppen stress the major theme of openness—a long-
ing for a dogma-free order—and emphasize the crucial tempos of human
breathing. In France, a poetics based on breath had had a brief run with
the theoretician André Spire (in America its influence remains strong
with Charles Olson's "Projectivism" and its descendants). Of course, the
heavy shadow of World War II hangs over all the work of this period,
French and American: it is frequently tinged with despair, the intricate
play of matter and open form notwithstanding.

Founded in 1960 by Queneau and François Le Lionnais, OULIPO (an
acronym for OUvroir de LIttérature POtentielle, or Workshop of Poten-
tial Literature) was the serious/playful working/playing ground of the

Pataphysical College (dedicated to the Science of Imaginary Solutions, following the principles of Alfred Jarry). OULIPO formulated its textual work as the dialogic and flexible structure of endless combinations of form and vocabulary, multiplying possibilities ad infinitum. The poem is protean, always potentially capable of changing shape. It is less a question of the author-poet speaking than of language playing itself out. Self-imposed formal constraints were the high wire on which the Oulipians performed: the most famous narrative example, *La Disparition*, by Georges Perec, was written without the single most essential vowel in the French language—the letter *e*. Oulipians called such experiments Creative, not Created. Jacques Roubaud, Michelle Grandgaud, and many others included in this anthology have engaged in Oulipian experiments.[1]

Francis Ponge, author of a long text entitled *La Fabrique du pré* (The Making of the Pré), was fascinated by the precision and materiality of language. He creates what he calls *objeu* (a combination of *objet* and *jeu*, the French words for "object" and "game"), in which the poet stresses the visuality of words, taking, as he says, the side of things (*Le Parti-pris des choses*).[2] Ponge's *Proêmes* follows in the tradition of the prose poem but moves beyond it, exploring its process and form—his "Mûres" (Blackberries) plays on the blackness of dots (the periods at the ends of sentences), which the poet describes as "ripe. . . ." Here, ripeness is all. Ponge is a classic French precision painter—in words. In the United States, the approach closest to his was probably that of the Objectivists flourishing in the 1930s, chief among them George Oppen, Louis Zukofsky, and Charles Reznikoff, and more recently, the New York School, including Frank O'Hara and James Schuyler, who focused on "Das Ding an Sich," the Thing in Itself, or things as they are.[3]

Jean Follain also took the side of things. Follain's *Objets* (1955) expressed the poetry of still life, as had Reverdy's short prose poems of 1915–1917 (often composed with the paintings of Juan Gris in mind) and Max Jacob's *Cornet à dés* (The Dice Cup) of the same period. The still life as poem-object had in fact been made concrete in André Breton's "*poèmes-objets*" well before Ponge's *objeu*. One sees in this poetic lineage the tradition of French still-life painting, as exemplified by Matisse, Braque, and other masters.

Yves Bonnefoy's poems in *Pierre écrite* (1964) also work as still lifes, inscribing themselves on the *Written Stone* of the title. Bonnefoy, a translator as well as a poet, translates Shakespeare into French. He is also an art historian gifted with an extraordinary analytic power, moving gracefully and effortlessly from the baroque to the present. A classic contemporary, he writes with extensive knowledge and a no less passionate curiosity.

In 1966, two years after the publication of *Pierre écrite*, Michel Deguy

published his *Actes*. Although the poet explores locations as diverse as his styles of writing, his sense of place is unremittingly strong, whether he is writing about Brittany or Baltimore. This period of French poetry demonstrates an extraordinary geographical scope: from Martinique, Édouard Glissant's *Sel noir;* from Haiti, René Depestre's *Un arc-en-ciel pour l'Occident chrétien;* from Tunisia, Abdelwahab Meddeb's *Tombeau d'Ibn Arabi;* from Yugoslavia and Corsica, Jacques Garelli's *Prendre appui;* from Transylvania and Tunisia, Lorand Gaspar's *Sol absolu;* from Quebec, Gaston Miron's *L'Homme rapaillé;* from Lebanon, Salah Stétié's *Fièvre et guérison de l'icône;* from Belgium, Claire Lejeune's *ELLE;* from Switzerland, Philippe Jaccottet's *Airs*. Largesse indeed.

Notes

1. See Warren Motte, ed., *OULIPO: A Primer of Potential Literature* (Normal, Ill.: Dalkey Archives, 1988).
2. Francis Ponge, *Le Parti pris des choses* (Taking the Side of Things) (Paris: Gallimard, 1942).
3. For Objectivism, see *The New Princeton Encyclopedia of Poetry and Poetics*, ed. Alex Preminger and T. V. F. Brogan (Princeton: Princeton University Press, 1993), pp. 848–849. On James Schuyler and the New York School, see the *Encyclopedia of American Poetry*, ed. Erich Haralson (Chicago: Fitzroy Dearborn, 2001), pp. 506–507, 650–652.

Yves Bonnefoy 1923–
TOURS, FRANCE

A beloved contemporary poet in France, Bonnefoy is also an essayist and art historian who has produced numerous translations of Shakespeare. Surrealism had a great impact on his work; after the war he founded the review *La Révolution la nuit* and became briefly involved in the Surrealist movement. He studied math and philosophy at the University of Poitiers and at the Sorbonne, after moving to Paris in 1944. Bonnefoy also edited the review *L'Éphémère* with Louis-René des Forêts, Gaëton Picon, André du Bouchet, and Jacques Dupin, and later with Paul Celan and Michel Leiris. In 1981 he was awarded the Grand prix national de la poésie by the Académie française. He is a leading scholar on Baudelaire, Rimbaud, Poussin, and Giacometti, among many other artists, as well as on the baroque era, and has held the *Chaire d'Etudes comparées de la fonction poétique* at the Collège de France. Principal works: *Du mouvement et de l'immobilité de Douve,* 1953; *Hier régnant desert,* 1958; *Pierre écrite,* 1964; *Dans le leurre du seuil,* 1975; *Ce qui fut sans lumière,* 1987; *Début et fin de la neige,* 1991; *Les Planches courbes,* 2001.

Le Livre, pour vieillir

Étoiles transhumantes; et le berger
Voûté sur le bonheur terrestre; et tant de paix
Comme ce cri d'insecte, irrégulier,
Qu'un dieu pauvre façonne. Le silence
Est monté de ton livre vers ton cœur.
Un vent bouge sans bruit dans les bruits du monde.
Le temps sourit au loin, de cesser d'être.
Simples dans le verger sont les fruit mûrs.

Tu vieilliras
Et, te décolorant dans la couleur des arbres,
Faisant ombre plus lente sur le mur,
Étant, et d'âme enfin, la terre menacée,
Tu reprendras le livre à la page laissée,
Tu diras, C'étaient donc les derniers mots obscurs.

Une voix

Nous vieillissions, lui le feuillage et moi la source,
Lui le peu de soleil et moi la profondeur,
Et lui la mort et moi la sagesse de vivre.

J'acceptais que le temps nous présentât dans l'ombre
Son visage de faune au rire non moqueur,
J'aimais que se levât le vent qui porte l'ombre

Et que mourir ne fût en obscure fontaine
Que troubler l'eau sans fond que le lierre buvait.
J'aimais, j'étais debout dans le songe éternel.

À la voix de Kathleen Ferrier

Toute douceur toute ironie se rassemblaient
Pour un adieu de cristal et de brume,
Les coups profonds du fer faisaient presque silence,
La lumière du glaive s'était voilée.

Je célèbre la voix mêlée de couleur grise
Qui hésite aux lointains du chant qui s'est perdu

The Book, for Growing Old

Transhumant stars; and the shepherd bending
Over earthly happiness; and peace
Such as this insect's intermittent cry,
Shaped by a humble god. Silence
Has climbed from your book towards your heart.
A noiseless wind stirs in the world's noise.
Time smiles in the distance, ceasing to be.
Simple is the ripe fruit in the orchard.

You will grow old
And, fading amid the color of the trees,
Casting a slower shadow on the wall,
Being at last, in your soul, the threatened earth,
You will take the book up where you had left it,
You will say, These were the last obscure words.

—RICHARD PEVEAR

A Voice

We were growing old. He was the leaves, I was the flowing spring.
He was a sliver of sun, I was the depth underneath.
He was death, and I was the wisdom to live.

Time showed his face in the shadows, the face of a faun;
His laughter did not mock us, and I accepted time.
I loved how the wind rose, shouldering the dark,

Loved how even dying in the deep black spring
Would barely stir the pool where the ivy drank.
I loved: I stood submerged in the endless dream.

—HOYT ROGERS

To the Voice of Kathleen Ferrier

All sweetness all irony gathered
For a farewell of crystal and of mist,
The deep iron blows yielded almost silence,
The light of the blade was veiled.

I sing the voice mixed with grey
Lingering far from the song now lost

Comme si au delà de toute forme pure
Tremblât un autre chant et le seul absolu.

O lumière et néant de la lumière, ô larmes
Souriantes plus haut que l'angoisse ou l'espoir,
O cygne, lieu réel dans l'irréelle eau sombre,
O source, quand ce fut profondément le soir!

Il semble que tu connaisses les deux rives,
L'extrême joie et l'extrême douleur.
Là-bas, parmi ces roseaux gris dans la lumière,
Il semble que tu puises de l'éternel.

La Neige

Elle est venue de plus loin que les routes,
Elle a touché le pré, l'ocre des fleurs,
De cette main qui écrit en fumée,
Elle a vaincu le temps par le silence.

Davantage de lumière ce soir
À cause de la neige.
On dirait que des feuilles brûlent, devant la porte,
Et il y a de l'eau dans le bois qu'on rentre.

La Tâche d'espérance

C'est l'aube. Et cette lampe a-t-elle donc fini
Ainsi sa tâche d'espérance, main posée
Dans le miroir embué sur la fièvre
De celui qui veillait, ne sachant pas mourir?

Mais il est vrai qu'il ne l'a pas éteinte,
Elle brûle pour lui, malgré le ciel.
Les mouettes crient leur âme à tes vitres givrées,
Le dormeur des matins, barque d'un autre fleuve.

As if beyond all pure form
There were to tremble another song, the absolute.

Oh light and nothing of light, oh tears
Smiling above all anguish or hope,
Oh swan, real place in the unreal somber water,
Oh spring, when it was profoundest dusk!

You seem to know both shores,
Utter joy and utter grief.
Over there, among those grey reeds in the light,
You seem to drink deeply from what never ends.

—MARY ANN CAWS

The Snow

It has come from further than the roads,
It has touched the meadow, the ochre of the flowers,
With that hand that writes in smoke,
It has vanquished time through silence.

More light this evening
Because of the snow.
You would think the leaves in front of the door were burning,
And there is water in the wood we bring in.

—JOHN NAUGHTON

The Task of Hope

It is dawn. Has this lamp, then, finished
Its task of hope, hand placed
In the clouded mirror, on the fever
Of the one who kept watch, not knowing how to die?

But it is true that he has not put it out,
It still burns for him, in spite of the sky.
The seagulls screech their soul at your frost-covered
Window, morning sleeper, boat from another river.

—JOHN NAUGHTON

Pierre ou eau

         . . . en avant
    du centre
       serré
    comme pierre un instant

    ou eau.

         . . . l'oubli
    au centre
    où
      pierre
    un instant ou eau

    a été serrée.

         . . . et immobile
après le centre.

André du Bouchet 1924–2000

PARIS, FRANCE

D
u Bouchet moved to the United States in 1941 to earn his B.A. at Amherst and his M.A. at Harvard, where he also served as a teaching fellow. He published an important monograph on Alberto Giacometti. His poetry, unlike any other, is remarkable for its spaciousness and depth. Du Bouchet was a close friend of Yves Bonnefoy, Claude Esteban, and Louis-René des Forêts, founding the journal *L'Éphémère* with them. He translated works by William Shakespeare, Friedrich Hölderlin, Gerard Manley Hopkins, James Joyce, Osip Mandelstam, Boris Pasternak, Laura Riding, and Paul Celan. Principal works: *Air*, 1951; *Dans la chaleur vacante*, 1961; *Où le soleil*, 1968; *Giacometti*, 1969; *Qui n'est pas tourné vers nous*, 1972; *L'Incohérence*, 1979; *Laisses*, 1979; *Rapides*, 1980; *Peinture*, 1983; *Aujourd'hui c'est*, 1984; *Ici en deux*, 1986; *Cendre tirant sur le bleu*, 1991; *Axiales*, 1992; *Pourquoi si calmes*, 1996; *D'un trait qui figure et défigure*, 1997; *L'Ajour*, 1998.

Stone or Water

> ... ahead
of the center
> gripped
like stone an instant

or water.

> ... forgetfulness
at the center
where
> stone
an instant or water

has been gripped.

> ... and motionless
after the center.

. . . le cœur de la montagne sera pierre

ou eau.

La Lumière de la lame

Ce glacier qui grince

pour dire
la fraîcheur de la terre

sans respirer.

——————

Comme du papier à plat sur cette terre,
ou un peu au-dessus de la terre,

comme une lame je cesse de respirer. La nuit
je me retourne, un instant, pour le dire.

A la place de l'arbre.

A la clarté des pierres.

J'ai vu, tout le long du jour,
la poutre sombre et bleue qui barre le jour se soulever pour nous rejoindre
dans la lumière immobile.

——————

Je marche dans les éclats de la poussière
qui nous réfléchit.

Dans le souffle court
et bleu
de l'air qui claque

loin du souffle

l'air tremble et claque.

... the heart of the mountain will be stone
or water.

—HOYT ROGERS

The Light of the Blade

This glacier that creaks

to utter
the cool of the earth

without breathing.

=====

Like paper flat against this earth,
or a bit above the earth,
like a blade I stop breathing. At night I return to
myself, for a moment, to utter it.

In place of the tree.
In the light of the stones.

I saw, all along the day,
the dark blue rafter that bars the day rise up to reach us in the motionless light.

=====

I walk in the gleams of dust
that mirror us.

In the short blue
breath
of the clattering air

far from breath

the air trembles and clatters.

—PAUL AUSTER

Fraction

Le lointain est moins distant que le sol, le lit mordant
de l'air,

      où tu t'arrêtes, comme une herse, sur la terre
rougeoyante.

Je reste au-dessus de l'herbe, dans l'air aveuglant.

Le sol fait sans cesse irruption vers nous,

                                sans que je m'éloigne
     du jour.

                                Rien,
aujourd'hui, n'est foulé.   Je ne subsiste pas
   dans l'air nu.

Sur cette route qui grandit.

———————————————

Perpétuel *voyez* physique
17/5

Ligne droite, rang de nageurs, cent pieds par ligne, l'oratio pedestris, la langue
qui se traîne, va par terre, l'autre est la langue ailée, l'autre est l'hirondelle, vous

Fraction

Far off is less distant than the ground, the biting bed
of air,
      where you stop, a harrow on the reddening
earth.

I remain above the grass, in the blinding air.

The ground erupts ceaselessly towards us,
                            without my moving off
    from the day.

                                Nothing
today, is trampled.   I don't subsist
    in the naked air.

On this road growing.

—MARY ANN CAWS

Bernard Collin 1927–
PARIS, FRANCE

Collin, a poet and artist, lives in Paris. He has been publishing his highly original texts since 1960 with Mercure de France, Christian Bourgois, and Fata Morgana. His most recent books have been published by Éditions Ivréa. Principal works: *Perpétuel* voyez *physique,* 1996; *Les Milliers, les millions et le simple,* 1999; *Les Globules de Descartes,* 2003.

Perpetual *Look* Physics
17/5

    Straight line, row of swimmers, a hundred feet to a line, *l'oratio pedestris,* the tongue dragging itself along, goes over the earth, the other is the winged tongue,

379

n'aurez plus besoin de poser le pied, je rêve de marcher c'est vrai, de marcher et de boire, et quand vous aurez bu impossible de marcher, et je rêve de terre, de la terre tout près, de la terre tout à fait dessus, se touchant l'un sur l'autre, que je rêve de poser la main à cet endroit, la main avant le pied, et vous marcherez pendant cinq cents jours et la langue descendra vers vous, je rêve que je voyais les arbres sauter par petits bonds, et des lignes de trois mille pas, on allait boire dans ce jardin, et tous les oiseaux venaient se poser à son tour, sur les branches longues et droites, pas d'autre figure que le pied suivant l'autre, et les deux sur la même ligne, à pieds joints par bonds comme les moineaux. Une fourmi se hâte sur le parquet, on vous l'a dit, on vous redira, ces choses n'ont pas d'importance, une vieille fourmi sèche de quelle taille? Vous avez lu qu'en Éthiopie on élève des fourmis aussi grandes qu'un grand chien, grattant le sable jour et nuit pour trouver de l'or et capables de mettre en pièces un homme qui viendrait les voler, les livres sont pleins de mensonges, six pattes à un chien qui fait des provisions, l'abondance de la fourmi ne produit aucune richesse, l'abondance, l'abondance

———————————

the other is the swallow, you won't need to put down your foot any more, I dream of walking, that's true, walking and drinking, and when you've drunk impossible to walk, and I dream of the earth, the earth right there, the earth completely on top, touching one atop the other, that I dream of putting my hand there, the hand before the foot, and you will walk for five hundred days and the tongue will descend towards you, I dream that I saw the trees leaping by little jumps, and lines of three thousand steps, we were going to drink in that garden, and all the birds were coming to rest one after the other, on the long straight branches, no other figure than the foot following the other one, and both on the same line, feet together leaping like sparrows. An ant rushes over the floor, they told you, they'll tell you again, these things have no importance, an old dry ant of what size? You've read that in Ethiopia they raise ants as big as a big dog, scratching the sand day and night to find gold and able to pull a man to pieces should he come to rob them, the books are full of lies, six paws for a dog who goes to get groceries, the ant's abundance produces no treasures, abundance, abundance

—MARY ANN CAWS

Jacques Dupin 1927–
PRIVAS, FRANCE

Along with Philippe Jaccottet, Yves Bonnefoy, and André du Bouchet, Dupin was one of the foremost French poets of the 1950s and remains among the most respected poets today. Like them, he is concerned with the interrelations of language and art; Georges Braque, among other artists, illustrated his work. Dupin was born in the Ardèche, a mountainous region that turns up in his work; he is fascinated with the relationships between landscapes and people. At the end of the war, he moved to Paris. As an art historian, he is celebrated for his major works on Joan Miró, Alberto Giacometti, and many other artists. From 1956 to 1981 he worked at the Galerie Maeght. Principal works: *Gravir*, 1963; *L'Embrasure*, 1969; *Dehors*, 1975; *Une apparence de soupirail*, 1982; *Contumace* 1986; *Chansons troglodytes*, 1989; *Rien encore, tout déjà*, 1990; *Echancré*, 1991; *Le Grésil*, 1996; *Écart*, 2000.

Même si la montagne

1

Même si la montagne se consume, même si les suivants s'entretuent . . . Dors, berger. N'importe où. Je te trouverai. Mon sommeil est l'égal du tien. Sur le versant clair paissent nos troupeaux. Sur le versant abrupt paissent nos troupeaux.

2

Dehors, les charniers occupent le lit des fleuves perdus sous la terre. La roche qui se délite est la sœur du ciel qui se fend. L'événement devance les présages, et l'oiseau attaque l'oiseau. Dedans, sous terre, mes mains broient des couleurs à peine commencées.

3

Ce que je vois et que je tais m'épouvante. Ce dont je parle, et que j'ignore, me délivre. Ne me délivre pas. Toutes mes nuits suffiront-elles à décomposer cet éclair? O visage aperçu, inexorable et martelé par l'air aveugle et blanc!

4

Les gerbes refusent mes liens. Dans cette infinie dissonance unanime, chaque épi, chaque goutte de sang parle sa langue et va son chemin. La torche, qui éclaire et ferme le gouffre, est elle-même un gouffre.

5

Ivre, ayant renversé ta charrue, tu as pris le soc pour un astre, et la terre t'a donné raison.

L'herbe est si haute à présent que je ne sais plus si je marche, que je ne sais plus si je suis vivant.

La lampe éteinte est-elle plus légère?

6

Les champs de pierre s'étendent à perte de vue, comme ce bonheur insupportable qui nous lie, et qui ne nous ressemble pas. Je t'appartiens. Tu me comprends. La chaleur nous aveugle . . .

Even If the Mountain

1

Even if the mountain is consumed, even if the survivors kill each other . . . Sleep, shepherd. It doesn't matter where. I will find you. My sleep is the equal of yours. On the bright slope our flocks are grazing. On the abrupt slope our flocks are grazing.

2

Outside, charnel-houses fill the beds of rivers lost beneath the earth. The rock, stripped of its foliage, is sister of the cleaving sky. Event precedes prediction, bird attacks bird. Inside, under the earth, my hands are grinding colors that have hardly begun.

3

That which I see, and do not speak of, frightens me. What I speak of, and do not know, delivers me. Does not deliver me. Will all my nights be enough to decompose this bursting light? O inexorable seen face, hammered by the blind white air!

4

The sheaves refuse my bonds. In this infinite, unanimous dissonance, each ear of corn, each drop of blood, speaks its language and goes its way. The torch, which lights the abyss, which seals it up, is itself an abyss.

5

Drunk, having overturned your plow, you took the plowshare for a star, and the earth agreed with you.

The grass is so high now I no longer know if I am walking, I no longer know if I am alive.

Does the darkened lamp weigh any less?

6

The stone fields stretch on out of sight, like this unbearable happiness that binds us, that does not resemble us. I belong to you. You understand me. The warmth blinds us . . .

La nuit qui nous attend et qui nous comble, il faut encore décevoir son attente pour qu'elle soit la nuit.

7

Quand marcher devient impossible, c'est le pied qui éclate, non le chemin. On vous a trompés. La lumière est simple. Et les collines proches. Si par mégarde cette nuit je heurte votre porte, n'ouvrez pas. N'ouvrez pas encore. Votre absence de visage est ma seule obscurité.

8

Te gravir et, t'ayant gravie — quand la lumière ne prend plus appui sur les mots, et croule et dévale, — te gravir encore. Autre cime, autre gisement.

Depuis que ma peur est adulte, la montagne a besoin de moi. De mes abîmes, de mes liens, de mon pas.

9

Vigiles sur le promontoire. Ne pas descendre. Ne plus se taire. Ni possession, ni passion. Allées et venues à la vue de tous, dans l'espace étroit, et qui suffit. Vigiles sur le promontoire où je n'ai pas accès. Mais d'où, depuis toujours, mes regards plongent. Et tirent. Bonheur. Indestructible bonheur.

Commencer

Commencer comme on déchire un drap, le drap dans le pli duquel on se regardait dormir. L'acte d'écrire comme rupture, et engagement cruel de l'esprit, et du corps, dans une succession nécessaire de ruptures, de dérives, d'embrasements. Jeter sa mise entière sur le tapis, toutes ses armes et son souffle, et considérer ce don de soi comme un déplacement imperceptible et presque indifférent de l'équilibre universel. Rompre et ressaisir, et ainsi renouer. Dans la forêt nous sommes plus près du bûcheron que du promeneur solitaire. Pas de contemplation innocente. Plus de hautes futaies traversées de rayons et de chants d'oiseaux, mais des stères de bois en puissance. Tout nous est donné, mais pour être forcé, pour être entamé, en quelque façon pour être détruit, — et nous détruire.

The night awaits us, fills us, again we must disappoint its waiting, in order that it become the night.

7

When walking becomes impossible, it is the foot that shatters, not the path. You were deceived. The light is simple. And the hills near. If, by mistake, I knock at your door tonight, do not open it. Do not open it yet. The absence of your face is my only darkness.

8

To climb you, and having climbed you—when the light is no longer supported by words, when it totters and crashes down—climb you again. Another crest, another lode.

Ever since my fears came of age, the mountain has needed me. Has needed my chasms, my bonds, my step.

9

Vigils on the promontory. Not to go down. To be silent no longer. Neither passion nor possession. Comings and goings in full view, within the narrow space, which is sufficient. Vigils on the promontory to which I have no access. But from which I have looked down, always. And drawn. Happiness. Indestructible happiness.

—PAUL AUSTER

Begin Like Tearing

Begin like tearing the sheet in whose folds you watched yourself sleeping. The act of writing as rupture, and the cruel engagement of the spirit and the body in a necessary succession of ruptures, drifts and burnings. Throw it all down on the table, with all its fight and breath, and consider this gift of self an imperceptible displacement that is almost of indifference to the universal balance. Tear, restore, and so renew. In the forest we are nearer to the woodcutter than to the lonely wanderer. No innocent contemplation. No high trees threaded with rays and birdsong, but blocks of potential firewood. All is given to us, but to be driven, to be breached, in one sense destroyed—and to destroy us.

—STEPHEN ROMER

Il y a

Il y a quelque part, pour un lecteur absent, mais impatiemment attendu, un texte sans signataire, d'où procède nécessairement l'accident de cet autre ou de celui-ci, dans le calme, dans l'obscénité, dans le dédoublement de la nuit écarlate, silence

trait pour trait superposable à ce qui, du futur sans visage, déborde le texte et dénude sa foisonnante et meurtrière illisibilité.

J'ai cru rejoindre

J'ai cru rejoindre par instants une réalité plus profonde comme un fleuve la mer, occuper un lieu, du moins y accéder de manière furtive, y laisser une empreinte, y voler un tison, un lieu où l'opacité du monde semblait s'ouvrir au ruissellement confondu de la parole, de la lumière et du sang. J'ai cru traverser vivant, les yeux ouverts, le nœud dont je naissais. Une souffrance morne et tolérable, un confort étouffant se trouvaient d'un coup abolis, et justifiés, par l'illumination fixe de quelques mots inespérément accordés. Nous coïncidions hors du temps mais le temps pliait les genoux et si je ne le maîtrisais pas dans sa course, du moins commandais-je alors à ses fulgurantes éclipses . . . Je l'ai cru. Le battement de l'abîme scandait abusivement l'offrande de rosée au soleil, dehors, sur chaque ronce.

Il respire avant d'écrire

Il respire avant d'écrire . . . Puis il écrit sans respirer, toute une nuit, un autre respirant pour deux. Un seul respirant pour tous : cordée tendue dans la mort, dans la transgression, dans le cahotant quotidien qui les ressaisit et qui les borde.

Et de rire! Lequel d'entre nous? Aveugle de naissance. Attaqué par ses outils. Le monde est à ses pieds, désœuvré, grésillant. Il ne l'ignore pas mais demeure immobile. Et silencieux. Comme un arbre dans le soleil.

De la contorsion du pitre à la distorsion du supplice, ces pratiques mènent le corps. Sans le garantir contre le procès inverse. Sordide, foudroyant . . .

Entre le coma et la transparence, seule, peut-être, la haie d'une phrase, vive, le souffle d'une haie, l'ombre haletante d'un loup . . .

386

There Exists

There exists somewhere, for a reader who is absent but impatiently awaited, a text without a signature from which the accident of this or that necessarily proceeds, in calm, in obscenity, in the unfolding of scarlet night, silence

feature for feature superimposable on whoever, from the faceless future, overflows the text and lays bare its spreading and murderous unreadability.

—STEPHEN ROMER

At Instants I Thought

At instants I thought I merged with a deeper reality like a river the sea, occupied a place—at least acceded to it with stealth—left an imprint on it, stole a firebrand from it, a place where the opacity of the world seemed to open onto the rustle and mingle of word, light and blood. I thought I crossed, alive and wide-eyed, the node where I was born. A grey and tolerable longsufferingness, a smothering comfort, were abolished at a blow, and justified, by the steady illumination of a few words that fitted against all hope. We collided outside of time, but time knelt down and if I did not master it on its course, then at least I ordered its lightning eclipses . . . so I thought. The throbbing of the abyss punctuated like abuse the dew's offering to the sun, outside, on each barb.

—STEPHEN ROMER

He Breathes before Writing

He breathes before writing . . . then he writes without breathing, for a whole night, while another breathes for two. One breathing for all: a cord stretched in death, in transgression, in the daily jolting that seizes and binds them round.

And laughter! Who among us? Blind from birth. Attacked by his tools. The world lies at his feet, idle, sputtering. He is aware of it but remains still. Like a tree in the sun.

From the contortion of the clown to the distortion of the rack, these practices train the body. Without guaranteeing against the inverse process. Sordid, dumbfounding . . .

Between coma and transparency, only the hedgerow of a phrase, live, the breath of a hedgerow, the panting shadow of a wolf . . .

—STEPHEN ROMER

Il m'est interdit

Il m'est interdit de m'arrêter pour voir. Comme si j'étais condamné à voir en marchant. En parlant. A voir ce dont je parle et à parler justement parce que je ne vois pas. Donc à donner à voir ce que je ne vois pas, ce qu'il m'est interdit de voir. Et que le langage en se déployant heurte et découvre. La cécité signifie l'obligation d'inverser les termes et de poser la marche, la parole, avant le regard. Marcher dans la nuit, parler sous la rumeur, pour que le rayon du jour naissant fuse et réplique à mon pas, désigne la branche, et détache le fruit.

Quand il est impossible

Quand il est impossible d'écrire un mot, de faire tenir debout une brique sur la mer. De coucher sur la table un copeau d'amour de la langue . . .

Tout commence.

L'impossibilité d'écrire se fend, se découple. D'écrire ce qui n'a pas encore été écrit, ce qui l'a toujours été, dans la trame et le souffle d'un seul. Dans l'attente et la surdité de tous. Et de personne . . .

Ecrivant sans écrire, je suis moins attablé qu'attelé, que garrotté à cette longue planche de châtaignier qui bourgeonne, qui convoque les braises et les signes. Qui m'humilie. Qui me chasse.

Dehors souffle un vent fort, et froid. Une buse, haut dans le ciel, vire et s'immobilise. Je marche en boitant, j'écris en boitant. Par les collines, dans la rue, dans le vide, je balbutie, je griffonne les airs que me soufflent, ou me refusent, les arbres et les gens, les nuages, les oiseaux, la lumière . . .

I Am Forbidden

I am forbidden to stop to see. As if I were condemned to see while walking. While speaking. To see what I speak, and to speak precisely because I do not see. Thus to show what I do not see, what I am forbidden to see. What language, unfolding, strikes and discovers. Blindness signifies the obligation to invert the terms, and to posit walking and word before the eyes. To walk in the night, to speak through din and confusion, so that the shaft of the rising day fuses and answers my step, designates the branch, and picks the fruit.

—PAUL AUSTER

When It Is Impossible

When it is impossible to write a word, to have a brick stand straight up on the sea. To lay on the table a shaving of the love of language . . .

Everything begins.
The impossibility of writing splits in two, undoes. To write what isn't yet written what has always been written, in the breath and texture of a single person. In the waiting and the deafness of everyone. And of no one . . .

Writing without writing, I am less seated at a table than harnessed, than shackled to this long board of chestnut budding, calling on embers and signs. That shames me. That chases me.

Outside a strong wind is blowing, cold. A buzzard, high in the sky, spins about and stops still. I walk limping, I write limping. Through the hills, in the street, in the void, I stammer, I scribble the airs that blow at me or reject me, the trees and the people, the clouds, the birds, the light . . .

—MARY ANN CAWS

Démesure de la poésie

Le poème est ce qui n'a ni nom, ni repos, ni lieu, ni demeure : fissure à l'œuvre se mouvant. Inutile de le circonscrire hors de paysages connus dans quelque zone aux pensées interdite, horizon d'antinature ou alors achevé au terme de son dépassement. Il hante notre espace car il est notre temps. Insaisissable en chacune de ses figures qui ne surgit que pour lier sa tendance naissante à d'imprévisibles successions, le poème sécrète sa propre histoire comme l'avion traceur ses spirales irréductibles dans leur lecture linéaire à ce que fut dans l'azur ce point blanc. Prenant appui sur l'explosion étoilée du langage, ressassant l'amorce naissante de l'événement, sortant le geste de ses fonctionnels usages, le coupant de ses thématiques intentions, le poème fait qu'après lui l'homme foudroyé demande aux pages l'abri et le repos d'une histoire, le modèle entrevu parfait de la pierre bleue sur un visage, l'impossible clef. Sans rémission.

Jacques Garelli 1931–

BELGRADE, YUGOSLAVIA

A poet and philosopher, Garelli has been a professor at Yale University, New York University, and the University of Amiens. He has frequently lectured and written on the work of the French phenomenologist Maurice Merleau-Ponty. His poetry, dense and suggestive, is often illustrated by painters and sculptors. Garelli currently lives in Paris and Corsica. Principal works: *Brêche*, 1966; *Les Dépossessions*, 1968; *Prendre appui*, 1968; *Lieux précaires*, 1972, *L'Ubiquité d'être*, 1986; *Archives du silence*, 1989.

Excess of Poetry

The poem is what has neither name, nor rest, nor place, nor home: fissure moving towards the work. Useless to circumscribe it beyond landscapes unknown in some zone forbidden to thoughts, horizon of antinature or then finished when it has gone past. It haunts our space for it is our time. Ungraspable in each of its figures, only surging forth to link its emerging tendency to unpredictable successions, the poem secretes its own history as the airplane traces irreducible spirals in their linear reading to what was in the azure this white point. Leaning against the starry explosion of language, masticating the emerging bait of the event, pulling the gesture out of its practical uses, cutting it off from its thematic intentions, the poem makes the one it has astonished ask for shelter in its pages and the repose of a story, the perfect model, just glimpsed, of the blue stone on a face, the impossible key. Without remission.

—MARY ANN CAWS

Joueur de flûte

Joueur de flûte, j'ai tant erré dans les terres d'ombre
et je ne sais pas ton visage.
Le tintement liquide des cloches de troupeau
tout ce large au soir qui vient sur les cailloux
écailles et bris d'une ancienne mémoire
désastres lointains, départs imminents
pourquoi ces grappes maintenant si légères
et j'écoute adossé à un ciel très pâle
les morts qui connurent tous les sons de l'air
tant de rouages que meut la transparence
et je sens dans la bouche les dents rouges de l'âme

> tourbillon de danse, sifflement d'aile
> porteur de vie et d'égarements
> toi la Règle, toi l'Erreur,
> la juste tension des larmes,
> le goût âpre de la langue brûlée—

Lorand Gaspar 1925–

EASTERN TRANSYLVANIA (IN MAROVÁSÁRHELY,
NOW TIRGU-MURES, ROMANIA)

Gaspar is a doctor as well as a translator, photographer, and travel writer. In 1943 he began university studies in Budapest but was deported to a German labor camp in 1944 during the Nazi occupation of Hungary. He escaped in 1945 and surrendered to a French military unit in Pfullendorf, Germany. After moving to France, he became a surgeon and worked in Jerusalem, Bethlehem, and Tunisia. In 1966 he began publishing his poetry. Gaspar has translated works by Rainier Maria Rilke, Georges Séféris, János Pilinszky, and D. H. Lawrence. Principal works: *Le Quatrième État de la matière*, 1966; *Gisements*, 1968; *Sol absolu*, 1972; *Approche de la parole*, 1978; *Corps corrosifs*, 1978; *Égée, Judée*, 1980; *Feuilles d'observation*, 1986; *La Maison près de la mer*, 1992; *Amandiers*, 1996.

Flute Player

Flute player, I've roamed so far in shadowed lands
and I do not know your face.
The liquid ringing of the herd's bells
all this open sea at evening that comes over the pebbles
scales and fractures of an ancient memory
far-off disasters, imminent departures
why these grape bunches now so light
and I listen leaning against a very pale sky
to the dead who knew all the sounds of the air
so many cog-wheels that transparency drives
and in my mouth I feel the red teeth of the soul

> whirlwind of dance, whistling of wing
> carrier of life and wanderings
> you the Rule, you the Error,
> the just tension of tears,
> the tart taste of my burnt tongue

—RONNIE SCHARFMAN

Minoen récent I
(Aiguières d'Hagia Triada)

Dauphins, poulpes, poissons
fraîcheur de lin, de roseaux, d'oliviers
tremblement du jour dans une couleur
joie d'une ligne qui bouge encore
et je rêve à cette main entre milliards
de mains, étonnée, heureuse—
et je ne sais quoi, un pigment
qui fait que l'âme respire,
que voit la vie, ces choses qui
viennent à mes doigts
et mourront une fois encore—

Late Minoan I
(Ewers of Hagia Triada)

Dolphins, octopi, fish
cool of linen, of reeds, of olive trees
trembling of the day in a color
joy of a line that still moves
and I dream of this hand among billions
of hands, astonished, happy—
and I don't know what, a pigment
that causes the soul to breathe,
that life sees, these things that
come to my fingers
and will die one more time—

—RONNIE SCHARFMAN

Édouard Glissant 1928–
MORNE-BEZAUDIN, MARTINIQUE

Glissant is perhaps best known for his theoretical work *Caribbean Discourse* (1981), in which he postulates a new Caribbean identity based on neither negritude nor Western culture, both of which he rejects. His formulation of ethnicity serves as a basis for his poetry and occasionally he writes in Creole. In 1945 Glissant relocated to France to study philosophy and ethics at the Sorbonne. He aided Aimé Césaire in his election campaign and was prohibited from leaving France because of his efforts on behalf of Antillean independence. In 1965 he finally returned to his native Martinique to teach philosophy. There, in 1974, he began the Institut martiniquais d'études, a private school teaching Martiniquan culture and history. He has taught at Louisiana State University and at the Graduate School of the City University of New York, as a distinguished professor. In 1980 he took a position with UNESCO. Principal

Pour Mycéa

Ô terre, si c'est terre, ô toute-en-jour où nous sommes venus. Ô plongée dans l'éclat d'eau et la parole labourée. Vois que tes mots m'ont déhalé de ce long songe où tant de bleu à tant d'ocre s'est mis. Et vois que je descends de cette nuit, entends

*   *   *

Si la nuit te dépose au plus haut de la mer
N'offense en toi la mer par échouage des anciens dieux
Seules les fleurs savent comme on gravit l'éternité
Nous t'appelons terre blessée ô combien notre temps
Sera bref, ainsi l'eau dont on ne voit le lit
Chanson d'eau empilée sur l'eau du triste soir
Tu es douce à celui que tu éloignes de ta nuit
Tel un gravier trop lourd enfoui aux grèves de minuit
J'ai mené ma rame entre les îles je t'ai nommée
Loin avant que tu m'aies désigné pour asile et souffle
Je t'ai nommée Insaisissable et Toute-enfuie
Ton rire a séparé les eaux bleues des eaux inconnues

*   *   *

Je t'ai nommée Terre blessée, dont la fêlure n'est gouvernable, et t'ai vêtue de mélopées dessouchées des recoins d'hier

Pilant poussière et dévalant mes mots jusqu'aux enclos et poussant aux lisières les gris taureaux muets

Je t'ai voué peuple de vent où tu chavires par silences afin que terre tu me crées

Quand tu lèves dans ta couleur, où c'est cratère à jamais enfeuillé, visible dans l'avenir

*   *   *

J'écris en toi la musique de toute branche grave ou bleue
Nous éclairons de nos mots l'eau qui tremble
Nous avons froid de la même beauté
Le pays brin à brin a délacé cela qu'hier
Tu portais à charge sur ta rivière débordée

works: *Un Champ d'îles,* 1953; *La Terre inquiète,* 1954; *Sel noir,* 1959; *Le Sang rivé,* 1960; *Pays rêvé, pays réel,* 1985; *Poétique de la relation,* 1990; *Introduction à une poétique du divers,* 1996.

For Mycea

O earth, if it is earth, O earth all-in-daylight where we came. O dive into flashing water and labored speech. See that your words have hauled me out of that long dream where so much blue and so much ochre were mixed. And see that I come down from that night, hear

* * *

If the night deposits you at the sea's high line
Do not offend the sea in you by running ancient gods aground
Only flowers know how to climb eternity
We call you wounded earth O how brief our time
Will be, like the water whose bed cannot be seen
Song of water piled on the water of that sorrowful evening
You are sweet to the one you distance from your night
Like a too-heavy pebble buried on the shores of midnight
I aimed my oars between the islands I named you
Long before you assigned me sanctuary and breath
I named you Ungraspable and All-Fled-Away
Your laughter separated the blue waters from the unknown waters

* * *

I named you wounded Earth, whose rift is ungovernable, and I clothed you in threnodies uprooted from the recesses of yesterday

Crushing dust and hurtling down my words to the pens and pushing the mute gray bulls to the edges

I dedicated to you a people of the wind where, in your silence you capsize so that earth, you create me

When you rise in your color, where there is a crater ever in leaf, visible in the future

* * *

I write in you the music of every branch, grave or blue
With our words we shed light on the water that trembles
We are cold with the same beauty
Strand by strand the country has unlaced what yesterday
You took up on your overflowing stream

Ta main rameute ces rumeurs en nouveauté
Tu t'émerveilles de brûler plus que les vieux encens

*   *   *

Quand le bruit des bois tarit dans nos corps
Étonnés nous lisons cette aile de terre
Rouge, à l'ancrée de l'ombre et du silence
Nous veillons à cueillir en la fleur d'agave
La brûlure d'eau où nous posons les mains
Toi plus lointaine que l'acoma fou de lumière
Dans les bois où il acclame tout soleil et moi
Qui sans répit m'acharne de ce vent
Où j'ai conduit le passé farouche

*   *   *

L'eau du morne est plus grave
Où les rêves ne dérivent
Tout le vert tombe en nuit nue
Quelle feuille ose sa pétulance
Quels oiseaux rament et crient
Dru hélé de boues mon pays
Saison déracinée qui revient à sa source
Un vent rouge seule pousse haut sa fleur
Dans la houle qui n'a profondeur et toi
Parmi les frangipanes dénouée lassée
D'où mènes-tu ces mots que tu colores
D'un sang de terre sur l'écorce évanoui
Tu cries ta fixité à tout pays maudit
Est-ce ô navigatrice le souvenir

*   *   *

Plus triste que la nuit où l'agouti s'arrête
Sa patte droite est lacérée d'un épine
Au point où le jour vient il s'acasse et s'entête
Il lèche la blessure et referme la nuit
Ainsi je penche vers mes mots et les assemble
A la ventée où tu venais poser la tête
En ce silence auquel tu voues combien de fêtes
Ta veille ton souci ton rêve tes tempêtes
La volée où tu joues avec le malfini
Les éclats bleus du temps dont tu nous éclabousses
Alors les mots me font brûler mahogany

Your hand stirs these murmurs together like something new
You marvel that you burn more than ancient incense

*   *   *

When the noise of the woods runs dry in our bodies
Surprised, we read this wing of red earth
Anchored in shadow and silence
We make sure to gather the agave flower
The burn of the water where we place our hands
You, more distant than the light-mad acoma
In the woods where it acclaims any sun, and I
Who restlessly hound that wind
Where I drove the intractable past

*   *   *

The mountain water is more solemn
Where dreams do not drift
All the green falls in naked night
What leaf dares its petulance
What birds stroke their wings and cry out
Thick, hailed out of the mud, my country
Uprooted season that returns to its source
A solitary red wind sends up its flower
In the swell that has no depth and you
Among the frangipani trees, unraveled worn out
Where do you find these words you color
With earthen blood on the withered bark
You cry your fixity to every accursed country
O navigatrix is this the remembrance?

*   *   *

Sadder than the night when the agouti stops short
His right paw lacerated by a thorn
As day arrives he shakes with stubborn scorn
He licks the wound and closes up the night
Likewise I lean unto my words, assemble them
In the windswept space you came to rest your head
That silence where you dedicate your feasts
Your vigil and your care, your dream your storms
The volley of your play with what goes wrong
The bright blue sparks of time you splash us with
My words, then, make me burn mahogany

La ravine où je dors est un brasier qu'on souche
Le jour en cette nuit met la blessure qui nous fit

*   *   *

Je n'écris pas pour te surprendre mais pour vouer mesure à ce plein d'impa-
tience que le vent nomme ta beauté. Lointaine, ciel d'argile, et vieux limon, réel

Et l'eau de mes mots coule, tant que roche l'arrête, où je descends rivière
parmi les lunes qui pavanent au rivage. Là où ton sourire est de la couleur des
sables, ta main plus nue qu'un vœu prononcé en silence

*   *   *

Et n'est que cendre en brousses tassée
N'est qu'égarement où le ciel enfante
L'eau d'agave n'apaise pas la fleur timide
Les étoiles chantent d'un seul or qu'on n'entend
Au quatre-chemins où fut rouée la sève
A tant qui crient inspirés du vent
Je hèle inattendue errance
Tu sors de la parole, t'enfuis
Tu es pays d'avant donné en récompense
Invisibles nous conduisons la route
La terre seule comprend

The ravine where I sleep a deeply rooted furnace
This day in night opens the wound that made us

* * *

    I do not write to take you by surprise but to give measure to this flood of impatience that the wind names your beauty. Far away, clay sky, and ancient silt, real
    And the water of my words flows, until the rock stops it, when I come down the stream among the moons that strut along the bank. There where your smile is the color of the sands, your hand more naked than a vow pronounced in silence

* * *

And it is only ash settled in the underbrush
It is only straying where the sky gives birth
The agave water does not appease the timid flower
The stars sing of a single gold that is unheard
At the crossroads where the sap was beaten out
Of so many who cry out inspired by the wind
I hail unexpected wandering
You go out from speech, slip away
You are the country of the past given in recompense
Invisible we travel the road
The earth alone understands

—BRENT HAYES EDWARDS

Philippe Jaccottet 1925–
MOUDON, SWITZERLAND

A noted translator, Jaccottet has rendered in French works by Homer, Rainier Maria Rilke, Robert Musil, and Thomas Mann, as well as the complete works of Friedrich Hölderlin. He first began translation work while living in Lausanne, Switzerland. In 1953 he moved to Grignan, in southern France. His own writing combines the principles and lessons of literary criticism and translation and depicts humans in relation to elements in the

Sérénité

L'ombre qui est dans la lumière
pareille à une fumée bleue

Sur les pas de la lune

M'étant penché en cette nuit à la fenêtre,
je vis que le monde était devenu léger
et qu'il n'y avait plus d'obstacles. Tout ce qui
nous retient dans le jour semblait plutôt devoir
me porter maintenant d'une ouverture à l'autre
à l'intérieur d'une demeure d'eau vers quelque chose
de très faible et de très lumineux comme l'herbe :
j'allais entrer dans l'herbe sans aucune peur,
j'allais rendre grâce à la fraîcheur de la terre,
sur les pas de la lune je dis oui et je m'en fus . . .

Je me redresse avec effort

Je me redresse avec effort et je regarde:
il y a trois lumières, dirait-on.
Celle du ciel, celle qui de là-haut
s'écoule en moi, s'efface,
et celle dont ma main trace l'ombre sur la page.

L'encre serait de l'ombre.

Ce ciel qui me traverse me surprend.

402

natural world. Jaccottet has won the Grand Prix de Poésie de Paris (1986), the Grand Prix National de Traduction (1987), and the Prix Pétrarque (1988). Principal works: *Requiem*, 1947; *L'Effraie et autres poésies*, 1953; *L'Ignorant*, 1958; *Airs*, 1967; *Leçons*, 1969; *Paysages aves figures absentes*, 1970; *A la lumière d'hiver*, 1977; *Pensées sous les nuages*, 1983; *La Semaison*, 1983; *A travers un verger*, 1984; *Cahier de verdure*, 1990.

Serenity

The shadow within the light
like blue smoke

—MARTIN SORRELL

In the Steps of the Moon

Tonight, leaning at the window,
I saw that the world was weightless,
and its obstacles were gone.
All that holds us back in the daytime
seemed bound to carry me now
from one opening to the other,
from within a house of water
towards something weak and bright
as the grass I was about to enter,
fearless, giving thanks for earth's freshness,
in the steps of the moon I said
yes and then off I went . . .

—EDWARD LUCIE-SMITH

With Effort, I Sit up and Look Outside

With effort, I sit up and look outside:
you might say there are three lights.
Light in the heavens, light from there
that flows in me and fades,
light's shadow that my hand is tracing on the page.

Shadow turns to ink.

Surprise runs through me like this sky.

On voudrait croire que nous sommes tourmentés
pour mieux montrer le ciel. Mais le tourment
l'emporte sur ces envolées, et la pitié
noie tout, brillant d'autant de larmes
que la nuit.

Pensées sous les nuages

—Je ne crois pas décidément que nous ferons ce voyage
à travers tous ces ciels qui seraient de plus en plus clairs,
emportés au défi de toutes les lois de l'ombre.
Je nous vois mal en aigles invisibles, à jamais
tournoyant autour de cimes invisibles elles aussi
par excès de lumière . . .
                            (À ramasser les tessons du temps,
on ne fait pas l'éternité. Le dos se voûte seulement
comme aux glaneuses. On ne voit plus
que les labours massifs et les traces de la charrue
à travers notre tombe patiente.)

—Il est vrai qu'on aura peu vu le soleil tous ces jours,
espérer sous tant de nuages est moins facile,
le socle des montagnes fume de trop de brouillard . . .
(Il faut pourtant que nous n'ayons guère de force
pour lâcher prise faute d'un peu de soleil
et ne pouvoir porter sur les épaules, quelques heures,
un fagot de nuages . . .
Il faut que nous soyons restés bien naïfs
pour nous croire sauvés par le bleu du ciel
ou châtiés par l'orage et par la nuit.)

—Mais où donc pensiez-vous aller encore, avec ces pieds usés?
Rien que tourner le coin de la maison, ou franchir,
de nouveau, quelle frontière?

(L'enfant rêve d'aller de l'autre côté des montagnes,
le voyageur le fait parfois, et son haleine là-haut
devient visible, comme on dit que l'âme des morts . . .

We like to believe our torment
helps heaven show clear. But torment
overcomes those wistful flights, and pity
drowns all, shining with as many tears
as night.

—HOYT ROGERS

Clouded Skies

—I am not convinced we shall ever make that journey
across the many skies becoming clearer and clearer,
carried away in defiance of all the laws of shadow.
I cannot see us as invisible eagles
for ever circling the peaks invisible themselves
in the excess of light . . .
                            (Picking up the broken bits of time
will not construct eternity. We learn to stoop, that is all,
like the gleaners. Now we see
only the massive ploughlands and the marks of the plough
across our patient tomb.)

—True, we have seen little of the sun lately
and it is less easy to hope under such an amount of cloud,
the mountain platform billows with too much fog . . .
(But how nearly destitute of strength we must be
if we let go for want of a bit of sun
and are incapable of shouldering
a fardel of clouds for an hour or so . . .
And we must be very naive still
to think ourselves saved by the blue of the sky
or punished by storms and night.)

—Where else did you think you were going on your worn feet?
Only rounding the house or crossing
a border—which?—again?

(The child dreams of going to the other side of the mountain.
A traveller may, and his breath up there
shows, as they say that the souls of the dead . . .

On se demande quelle image il voit passer
dans le miroir des neiges, luire quelle flamme,
et s'il trouve une porte entrouverte derrière.
On imagine que, dans ces lointains, cela se peut:
une bougie brûlant dans un miroir, une main
de femme proche, une embrasure . . .)

Mais vous ici, tels que je vous retrouve,
vous n'aurez plus la force de boire dans ces flûtes de cristal,
vous serez sourds aux cloches de ces hautes tours,
aveugles à ces phares qui tournent selon le soleil,
piètres navigateurs pour une aussi étroite passe . . .

On vous voit mieux dans le crevasses des labours,
suant une sueur de mort, plutôt sombrés
qu'emportés vers ces derniers cygnes fiers . . .

— Je ne crois pas décidément que nous ferons encore ce voyage,
ni que nous échapperons au merlin sombre
une fois que les ailes du regard ne battront plus.

Des passants. On ne nous reverra pas sur ces routes,
pas plus que nous n'avons revu nos morts
ou seulement leur ombre . . .
                Leur corps est cendre,
cendre leur ombre et leur souvenir; la cendre même,
un vent sans nom et sans visage la disperse
et ce vent même, quoi l'efface?
                Néanmoins,
en passant, nous aurons encore entendu
ces cris d'oiseaux sous les nuages
dans le silence d'un midi d'octobre vide,
ces cris épars, à la fois près et comme très loin
(ils sont rares, parce que le froid
s'avance telle une ombre derrière la charrue des pluies),
ils mesurent l'espace . . .
                Et moi qui passe au-dessous d'eux,
il me semble qu'ils ont parlé, non pas questionné, appelé,
mais répondu. Sous les nuages bas d'octobre.
Et déjà c'est un autre jour, je suis ailleurs,

We ask ourselves what image he sees passing
in the mirror of the snows, what flame he sees glimmering,
and whether he finds a door half open at the back.
We imagine that in those distances it might be so:
a candle burning in a mirror, the hand
of a woman close, an opening . . .)

But you, such as I find you here,
you will no longer have the strength to drink from those crystal flutes,
you will be deaf to the bells of those high towers,
blind to those beacons that turn as the sun turns,
unfit for the navigation of such narrow straits . . .

Easier to imagine you labouring in crevasses of clay
sweating the death-sweats, foundering,
not lifted up towards those proud and final swans . . .

—I am not convinced we shall make that journey now
nor escape the shadow of the axe
once the wings of sight have ceased to beat.

Passers-by. We shall not be seen on these roads again
any more than we have ever seen our dead
or even their shades . . .
                Their bodies are ash,
ash their shades and their memory and the ashes themselves
a nameless faceless wind disperses them
and the wind itself, what effaces it?
                    Nonetheless
in passing we shall have heard again and still
these bird-cries under the clouds
in the silence of an empty October noon,
these scattered cries, near and yet seeming very far away
(they are rare because the cold
advances like a shadow behind the ploughing rain),
they measure space . . .
              And passing underneath them
it seems to me they have spoken, not asked anything or called
but answered. Under the low clouds of October.
Already it is another day and I am elsewhere,

déjà ils disent autre chose ou ils se taisent,
je passe, je m'étonne, et je ne peux en dire plus.

———————————————

Illettrée

Illettrée. Je n'ai jamais pu lire qu'entre les lignes. Ailleurs, il n'y avait rien. Que les os, la cage. Quand j'eus dévoré les entrailles, bu le sang, il fallut bien se rendre à la carcasse . . . C'est là, dans la secrète école vertébrale que j'appris tout, l'existence de rien. Je me retrouvai seule sur la grande voierie. Désarmée.

Étant toi je serai guérie de cette agonie originelle que ton existence même secrète en moi. Se ravir, il n'y a pas d'autre remède à la fatalité de notre faille.

already they are saying something else or have fallen silent.
I pass, I am amazed, I can say nothing more about it.

—MARK TREHARNE AND DAVID CONSTANTINE

Claire Lejeune 1926–
HAVRÉ, BELGIUM

A poet and essayist, Lejeune experienced early in her career a mystical revelation in which the idea of an "I" writing itself presented itself to her. She founded two journals in Geneva: *Les Cahiers internationaux de symbolisme* (1962) and *Réseaux* (1965). The latter is an interdisciplinary review dealing with moral and political philosophy, which Lejeune continues to edit. She also established an interdisciplinary center for philosophical studies, the Centre interdisciplinaire d'études philosophiques de l'Université de Mons-Hainaut. In 1984 she received the Prix Canada—Communauté française de Belgique de littérature for her body of work. Principal works: *La Gange et le feu*, 1963; *Le Pourpre*, 1966; *La Geste*, 1966; *Le Dernier Testament*, 1969; *ELLE*, 1969 (revised, 1994).

Illiterate

Illiterate. I could never read except between the lines. Anywhere else there never was anything. Except the bones, the cage. When I'd devoured the entrails and drunk the blood, I had to attack the carcass . . . And there it was, in the secret vertebral school that I learned everything, the existence of nothingness. I found myself all alone on the great way. Unarmed.

Being you I shall be cured from this original agony that your very existence secretes in me. To be ravished: there's no other remedy for the fatality of our fault.

—MARY ANN CAWS

Où donc

Où donc sera le texte coronaire?

Issue du livre : couronnement? Sacre? Massacre?

Couronne précipice où le livre vient à bout de quête. Ultime contraction où le royaume éclate, où le tiers s'ingénie . . .

Senti jusqu'à ces temps le livre comme une tension croissante dont il se ferait feu et sang : le livre ma guerre. Ce matin saisi ma vie comme une pièce ronde, un franc qui se serait battu de mon métal. Reçu le sceau du livre pour acquit de mon intégrité. Je suis loisible.

Se saluer c'est l'œuvre du septième jour.

La Mort, j'en parle

La mort, j'en parle
Comme je parlerais de pesetas ou de dollars,
Moi qui n'ai jamais mis le pied en Amérique,
Moi qui porte une Espagne vierge en mon sang
Comme un goût de grenade éclatée,
Moi qui n'ai jamais mangé de grenade . . .

Je parle de la mort
Comme je décline mon nom;
C'est une très vieille habitude,
C'est la mort, quand on en parle . . .

Mais il y a celle dont on ne parle pas
Parce qu'elle est nue et qu'on ne peut pas l'habiller.
La mort enfoncée comme un poing dans l'oreiller
Et qui est le dernier visage de ma mère.

Et celle qui s'épanouit au dedans,
M'aspire, m'absorbe, se nourrit de moi
Et qui est mon autre Vie.

La mort dont on ne parle pas.

So Where

So where will the crowning text be?

Issued from the book: coronation? Consecration? Desecration?

Crown cliff where the book arrives at quest's end. Ultimate contraction where the realm explodes, where the third devises . . .

Felt up until now the book as a growing tension from which it would make itself fire and blood: the book my war. This morning seized my life like a round coin, a franc which might have been hammered from my metal. Received the seal of the book as a receipt of my integrity. I am free.

To greet yourself, that's the work of the seventh day.
—RENÉE LINKHORN AND JUDY COCKRAN

Death, I Speak of It

Death, I speak of it
Just as I would speak of dollars and pesetas
Though I have never set foot in America,
Though in my blood there flows a virgin Spain
Like the flavor of a ripe pomegranate,
Though I have never tasted pomegranate . . .

I speak of death
As I pronounce my name;
It is a very old habit,
It is deathly to speak of it . . .

Yet there is a kind that no one speaks of
Because it is naked and cannot be clothed.
Death sunk like a fist in a pillow:
The last look on my mother's face.

Then there is a kind that blossoms inside,
Breathes me in, absorbs me, feeds on me,
The kind that is my other Life.

The kind of death that no one speaks of.
—RENÉE LINKHORN AND JUDY COCKRAN

Rendez-vous en juin

pour Marilyn Hacker

L'arc des roses autour du gazon, leurs joues pâles
Laissant à peine sourdre l'angoisse du sang
Et derrière l'arc des roses l'arc des bancs, loges
D'où contempler leur candeur offerte au soleil
Glissant sur elles comme sur une page
Où bientôt les mots ne compteront plus
Le soleil grille les mots superflus
Qui le tiennent à distance, il brûle
En bon jardinier ce qu'il a fait s'épanouir
Ainsi tu fus en juin ma première morte
Le suc de ton cerveau emporté par l'abeille
Vers les rayons d'une ruche étoilée
Mon premier vrai poème peut-être
La chair tiédit les bancs mais nul vide
Ne flotte après le départ du couple enlacé
Les enfants jouent à prendre la petite maison
Rouge en haut de l'escalier jaune vif

Claire Malroux ca. 1930s

ALBI, FRANCE

A poet, translator, and critic, Malroux has a keen interest in American and British poetry, which serves as an inspiration for her own work. She has translated into French works by Charlotte Brontë, Emily Dickinson, Wallace Stevens, and Derek Walcott. In 1995 she was awarded the Grand Prix National de la Traduction. She has also won the Prix Maurice Edgar Coindreau and the Prix Laure Bataillon. Malroux is on the editorial board of *Po&sie* and on the jury of the Prix Nelly Sachs, a prize for poetry translation. Some of her collections have appeared under the pseudonym Claire Sara Roux. Principal works: *A l'arbre blanc,* 1968; *Les Orpailleurs,* 1978; *Au bord,* 1981; *Aires,* 1985; *Entre nous et la lumière,* 1992 (as Claire Sara Roux); *Edge,* 1996; *Soleil de jadis,* 1998; *Suspens,* 2001.

Appointment in June

for Marilyn Hacker

Roses curve around the lawn, their pale cheeks
Barely letting the blood's anguish well up
And beyond the roses' curve, the curve of benches, loges
To contemplate their candor, offered to the sun
Which slides across them, as across a page
Whose words soon will no longer matter
The sun broils superfluous words
Which keep it at bay. Good gardener
It burns what it has first brought to bloom
And so my first death was your death in June
The nectar of your brain borne off by bees
Toward the rays of a starry hive
Perhaps you were my first real poem
Flesh warms the benches but no emptiness
Shimmers when the embracing couple leaves
Children play at capturing the small
Red house atop a bright yellow ladder

Pendus à la rampe comme des vieillards
Une fille en brodequins croque une pomme
De son bourdonnement le trafic rassure
Y aura-t-il toujours des hommes pour embrasser
L'espace de leurs bras même bruyants?
Et de l'herbe, des roses pâles pour apaiser
Leur fuite en tumulte dans le néant?
Y aura-t-il toujours une figure penchée
Pour déchiffrer l'écriture du mystère
Bienveillant d'un matin d'été?
Quelqu'un quelque chose pour lui donner
Ailleurs un nouveau rendez-vous?

Il y a la guerre ou la paix

Il y a la guerre ou la paix
La paix comme une douleur
quand se prolonge l'attente d'on ne sait quoi
La grêle tombe sur la bâche d'une charrette abandonnée
et cela fait un roulement de tambour
Quelques enfants blottis
y resteront pendant des heures qui ne furent
peut-être que des minutes ou même des secondes
Le ciel est de plomb, une absence
sans forme ni contenu ni couleur ni odeur
les cloue sur ces planches
Reviendront-ils
de cet écrasement
de cet enfoncement
dans le coeur boueux oublieux de la terre

Toutes les haleines

Toutes les haleines (me mentais-je)
dans mon haleine   toutes les fleurs
pour aiguiser mes yeux   toutes les
mers pour flâner dans mon sang
et du corps à corps avec le spectre
du vent la vie reverdissait toujours
mêlée aux boucles de la mort   mais quelle
mémoire planait   de prés et d'aurochs

Hanging over its ramp like bent old men
A girl in laced boots bites into an apple
The drone of passing cars is comforting
Will there always be people to embrace
In the enclosure of their blood-loud arms?
And grass, pale roses to calm
Their clamorous flight into the void?
And will there always be a figure bent
Over decoding the benevolent
Mystery of a summer morning?
Someone something to establish somewhere
A place to meet again?

—MARILYN HACKER

There's War or There's Peace

There's war or there's peace
Peace like a kind of sorrow
when the wait for who knows what prolongs itself
Hail rattles the tarp on an abandoned cart
where it rumbles like a drum
Some children huddled inside
will stay there for hours which were only
minutes, perhaps; perhaps only seconds
The sky is leaden; an absence
without form, content, color, odor
nails them to the planks
Will they return
from that crushing
from that sinking
into the muddy, forgetful heart of the earth?

—MARILYN HACKER

Every Breath

Every breath (I lied to myself)
in my own breath   every flower
will sharpen my eyes   every ocean
will wander in my blood
and struggling skin on skin against the specter
of the wind life always grew green again
tangled in death's curls   but what
memory hovered   of fields and of bison

à l'aurore   tournant vers la nuit leur
mufle orange et vers eux une à une
les étoiles nageaient et elles creu-
saient creusaient d'insupportables
rides.

———————————————

Je consens que tout s'efface

Je consens que tout s'efface
Si survient la source qui surgit
En jet : joie où le fleuve jaillit
Même s'il n'est de nous nulle trace
Après que les pas auront passé
Même si nulle part une rayure
Ne reste comme un sillon laissé
   Au verso de l'emblavure
   Voici le champ levé haut
Le chemin que tracent nos planètes
Le lait convoité tant de miettes
Qu'aucune main n'amasse là-haut.

———————————————

at dawn   turning their orange muzzles
back toward night while at them one by one
swam stars and they fur-
rowed furrowed unbearable
lines

—MARILYN HACKER

Robert Marteau 1925–
POITOU, FRANCE

A poet, novelist, translator, and art critic, Marteau has written exten-
sively on Marc Chagall. He spent an extended period in Quebec, where
he became very involved in literary circles. He now lives in Paris.
Principal works: *Royaumes,* 1962; *Travaux sur la terre,* 1966; *Sibylles,* 1971; *Ce qui
conseille crie,* 1989; *Liturgie,* 1992; *Louange,* 1996; *Régistre,* 1999; *L'Étoile dans la
vitre,* 2001.

I Consent That Everything Vanishes

I consent that everything vanishes
If the fount arises which surges
In spray: joy where the current gushes
Even if no trace of us remains
After the tracks shall have passed
Even if nowhere a remnant
Remains like a furrow left
    Beneath the sown meadow
    Behold the field aloft
The pathway our planets trace
The coveted milk so many crumbs
Which no hand gathers up there.

—JOHN MONTAGUE

Sur des traces oubliées

Sur des traces oubliées, dans des lieux innommés, je vois le chœur des pleu-
reuses, sur les rives sud, je regarde les demeures en ruine, dans le matin frais,
j'admire celle, qui porte le masque de la douleur, les morts traversent la noire
passerelle, et cueillent les fruits du silence, la pluie hachure la grise lumière, j'ai
dit, oui, je viendrai, sans ruse, ni bouclier, ainsi j'ai répondu, à celle qui parlait,
d'un cœur coupé, traquée, à découvert, sur la plaine, les quatre vents apportaient
des messages opposés, elle dit, je me diviserai, je serai neuve, comme le soleil,
chaque jour.

Je prends le chemin

Je prends le chemin, qui mène au jardin de l'erreur, je joue avec les noms,
derrière le bosquet de la vérité, je bois là où l'enfant ramasse ses dés, je me cache
dans le hallier, où tremble la gazelle, le loup couvre le chant du berger, une brise
époussette mon corps, dans le jour noir, l'averse remplit le lac, qui sépare les deux
pays, je bois dans une coupe de Sumer un vin conservé, dans une amphore
d'argile, enfouie sous terre, depuis des millénaires, la vieille coupe, fossile du
paradis, exhale une haleine, que je flaire mortelle.

Abdelwahab Meddeb 1946–
TUNIS, TUNISIA

A poet, novelist, essayist, and translator, Meddeb writes in French and
has translated many Arabic texts, with special emphasis on Sufist
work. He left Tunisia to study French, art, and history at the Sorbonne.
From 1974 to 1988 he served as literary adviser to Éditions Sindbad. From 1988 to
1991 he directed the journal *Intersignes* and served as its Arabic translator. Med-
deb has also worked as a consultant at UNESCO and as a visiting professor at the
University of Geneva, Yale University, and the Sorbonne. He currently lives in
Paris. Principal works: *Talismano,* 1979, 1987; *Phantasia,* 1986; *Tombeau d'Ibn
Arabi,* 1987; *Les Dits de Bistami,* 1989; *La Gazelle et l'enfant,* 1992.

On Forgotten Tracks

On forgotten tracks, in unnamed places, I see the chorus of mourners, on the
south banks, I look at homes in ruin, in the cool morning, I admire her, who
wears the mask of pain, the dead cross the black footbridge, and pluck the fruits
of silence, the rain crisscrosses the grey light, I said, yes, I'll come, without ruse,
or shield, that's how I replied, to her who spoke, with a cut heart, hunted,
without cover, on the plain, the four winds brought contradictory messages, she
says, I will divide myself, I will be new, like the sun, each day.

—CHARLOTTE MANDELL

I Take the Path

I take the path, that leads to the garden of error, I play with names, behind the
grove of truth, I drink where the child gathers up his dice, I hide in the thicket,
where the gazelle trembles, the wolf drowns the shepherd's song, a breeze dusts
my body, in the black day, the downpour fills the lake, that separates the two
countries, in a Sumerian goblet I drink a wine preserved, in an amphora of clay,
buried underground, for millennia, the ancient goblet, fossil from paradise, gives
off a breath, that I scent as mortal.

—CHARLOTTE MANDELL

La Marche à l'amour (extraits)

Tu as les yeux pers des champs de rosées
tu as des yeux d'aventure et d'années-lumière
la douceur du fond des brises au mois de mai
            . . .
tu viendras tout ensoleillée d'existence
la bouche envahie par la fraîcheur des herbes
le corps mûri par les jardins oubliés
où tes seins sont devenus des envoûtements
tu te lèves, tu es l'aube dans mes bras
où tu changes comme les saisons
je te prendrai marcheur d'un pays d'haleine
à bout de misères et à bout de démesures
je veux te faire aimer la vie notre vie
            . . .
puis les années m'emportent sens dessus dessous
je m'en vais en délabre au bout de mon rouleau
des voix murmurent les récits de ton domaine
à part moi je me parle
que vais-je devenir dans ma force fracassée
ma force noire du bout de mes montagnes
pour te voir à jamais je déporte mon regard
je me tiens aux écoutes des sirènes
dans la longue nuit effilée du clocher de Saint-Jacques

Gaston Miron 1928–1996

SAINTE-AGATHE-DES-MONTS, QUEBEC, CANADA

Miron was a leading contemporary Quebecois poet and a militant for the cause of independence. For forty years he avidly defended Francophone rights and participated in the Mouvement de libération populaire, the Parti socialiste québécois, the Mouvement pour l'unilinguisme français au Québec, and the Front du Québec français. Miron was also an editor and helped found the publishing house Éditions de l'Hexagone and the journals *Liberté* and *Parti pris* in the 1960s. His *L'Homme rapaillé* (1970) contains all of his poetic works.

The Walk toward Love

Your eyes are the grey of fields of dew
of adventure and light years
the sweetness back of the breezes in May

. . .

you will come all sunstruck with existing
your mouth invaded by the coolness of grass
your body ripened by the forgotten gardens
where your breasts work their magic spells
you arise, you are dawn in my arms
where you change like the seasons
walking in a country of breath I'll take you
at the end of miseries at the end of excesses
I want to make you love life our life

. . .

then the years will take me upside down
I go off disheveled at my wit's end
voices murmur the tales of your realm
I speak to myself as an aside
what shall I become in my shattered strength
my dark strength of my mountains' end
to see you forever I transport my gaze
I keep listening to sirens
in the long narrow night of the Saint Jacques tower

et parmi ces bouts de temps qui halètent
me voici de nouveau campé dans ta légende
tes grands yeux qui voient beaucoup de cortèges
les chevaux de bois de tes rires
tes yeux de paille et d'or
seront toujours au fond de mon cœur
et ils traverseront les siècles

je marche à toi, je titube à toi, je meurs de toi
lentement je m'affale de tout mon long dans l'âme
je marche à toi, je titube à toi, je bois
à la gourde vide du sens de la vie
à ces pas semés dans les rues sans nord ni sud
à ces taloches de vent sans queue et sans tête
je n'ai plus de visage pour l'amour
je n'ai plus de visage pour rien de rien
parfois je m'asseois par pitié de moi
j'ouvre mes bras à la croix des sommeils
mon corps est un dernier réseau de tics amoureux
avec à mes doigts les ficelles des souvenirs perdus
je n'attends pas à demain je t'attends
je n'attends pas la fin du monde je t'attends
dégagé de la fausse auréole de ma vie

and among these panting ends of time
here I remain again in your legend
your great eyes upon many processions
the wooden horses of your laughter
your eyes of straw and gold
will remain forever in the depths of my heart
and they will traverse the ages

I walk to you, I stagger to you, I die from you,
slowly I collapse completely in my soul
I walk to you, I stagger to you, I drink
from the empty gourd of the meaning of life
to these steps sown in the streets without north or south
to these gusts of wind without tail or head
I have no more face for love
no face for anything anything
sometimes I sit down with pity for myself
I open my arms to the cross of sleep
my body is a last net of loving twitches
the thread of lost memories in my fingers
I don't wait for tomorrow I wait for you
I'm not waiting for the world to end I'm waiting for you
disengaged from the false halo of my life

—MARY ANN CAWS

Bernard Noël 1930–

SAINTE-GENEVIÈVE-SUR-AGENCE, FRANCE

Silent for nearly ten years after the publication of his first book, *Extraits du corps,* in 1958, Noël is now considered one of the finest poets and prose writers of his generation. After 1971, he devoted himself entirely to his writing, including many essays on painters, and began to publish regularly with Fata Morgana, P.O.L., and Gallimard. Principal works: *Le Château de Cène,* 1969;

Portrait

où est la lettre?

cette question vient d'un mourant
puis il se tait

tant qu'un homme vit
il n'a pas besoin de compter sa langue
quand un homme meurt
il doit rendre son alphabet

de chaque mort
nous attendons le secret de la vie
le dernier souffle emporte
la lettre manquante

elle s'envole derrière le visage
elle se cache au milieu du nom

Angers

un château noir et blanc fait la différence
la nuit du temps devenue pierre et tours rondes
passante image moins vive qu'un visage
qu'est-ce que l'unique quelle est sa nature
toute tissée de forme et de point de vue
tu regardes le tu sous la chevelure
le mortel désir replié dans son nid
un lourd minuit d'hiver couvre l'élan
la rencontre se casse au bord de la rue

Une messe blanche, 1970; *Souvenirs du pâle*, 1971; *D'une main obscure*, 1980; *L'Été de langue morte*, 1982; *La Chute des temps*, 1983; *La Castration mentale*, 1994; *Le Reste du voyage*, 1997; *La Langue d'Anna*, 1998.

Portrait

where is the letter?

asks the dying man
before going silent

as long as a man lives
there is no need to justify his tongue
when a man dies
he must return his alphabet

from each death
we await the secret of life
the last breath carries
the missing letter

it vanishes behind the face
it hides within the name

—MICHAEL TWEED

Angers

a black and white castle makes all the difference
time's night turned to stone and circular towers
an image that passes less alive than a face
define the unique reveal its nature
all woven of form and angle of vision
you watch the you that's under the hair
mortal desire in its nest tucked away
heavy winter midnight covering the outburst
the meeting shatters on the edge of the street

—ROSEMARY LLOYD

Toutes les choses de la terre

Toutes les choses de la terre
Il faudrait les aimer passagères
Et les porter au bout des doigts
Et les chanter à basse voix
Les garder les offrir
Tour à tour n'y tenir
Davantage qu'un jour les prendre
Tout à l'heure les rendre
Comme son billet de voyage
Et consentir à perdre leur visage

———————————

Anne Perrier 1922–

LAUSANNE, SWITZERLAND

Perrier is a major voice in Swiss poetry. Her husband, Jean Hutter, is director of the publishing house Payot-Lausanne. Perrier's work has appeared under her husband's imprint, as has Philippe Jaccottet's. Although she studied the classics and French literature, her poetry is most inspired by her love of music. She has won many literary prizes and has been widely translated. Principal works: *Selon la nuit*, 1952; *Pour un vitrail*, 1955; *Le Livre d'Ophélie*, 1979; *Oeuvre poétique, 1952–1994*, 1996; *La Voie nomade*, 2000.

All Earth's Things

All earth's things
You have to love them passing
And bear them on your fingers' ends
And sing them quietly
Keep them give them
In turn not hold on to them
More than a day take them
And now give them up
Like your ticket for the trip
And just let them go

—MARY ANN CAWS

427

Vu de ce côté-ci

de l'horizon il se
produit forcément
une accélération
du coeur vers la nuit
on ne souhaite pas
d'autres passages
vers d'autres lumières
et s'il nous est possible
vous voyez bien des peines à croire
vous voyez bien des mots
des mouvements
sitôt créés
avec la bouche

et sur le formulaire le soir
on biffe
les inscriptions signalétiques

Vu de ce côté-ci

«vu de ce côté-ci
il y avait cet homme dont la profession
est de porter les morts dans leurs appartements
il me regarda si civilement
si vif en son regard glissait l'intelligence

Anne Portugal 1949–

ANGERS, FRANCE

A contemporary lyric poet, Portugal currently lives and works in Paris. Her work is at once feminist, highly experimental, and enormously influential on other poets. She has contributed to the reviews *Po&sie, If, Action poétique,* and *Banana split,* among others. She has also translated the work of Emily Dickinson and contemporary poets Stacy Doris and Barbara Guest. Principal works: *Les Commodités d'une banquette,* 1985; *De quoi faire un mur,* 1987; *Nude,* 1988; *Le Plus Simple Appareil,* 1992.

Seen from Over Here

from the horizon there
is an unavoidable
acceleration of the
heart toward the night
one does not wish for
other passages
toward other lights
and if we can
you see the trouble believing
you see the words
the movements
as soon as they're created
by mouth

and on the evening questionnaire
one crosses out
descriptive entries

—NORMA COLE

Seen from Over Here

"seen from over here
there was this man whose profession
is taking the dead from their apartments
he looked at me so civilly
so alert into his gaze intelligence slipped

j'ai besoin dit Suzanne d'écrire son nom
j'ai besoin dit Suzanne de lui porter ces lettres mes stations

chronique d'une année de misère

pardon ce bain
est habitable en toute saison
même si le coeur (plus besoin de battements)
saute et saute en l'air
pourquoi je reste au bord du bassin
pourquoi je reste»

Chaque case

chaque case a sa voisine
et le soulèvement des photographes
ou surveillants de mer
marque des scores
au-dessus du tableau

il faudrait deux jumeaux
deux cavaliers
pour traverser la zone

venus seuls
sans savoir
et dans le champ de mine
passer sans rien qui saute
sans savoir
les sabots près des détonateurs
et des petits graviers plus chevauchants

I need said Susannah to write his name
I need said Susannah to take him these letters my stations

chronicle of a year of misery

pardon this bath
is livable all year round
even if the heart (need beat no more)
leaps and leaps in the air
why I stay on the edge of the pool
why I stay"

—NORMA COLE

Every Shack

every shack has its girl-next-door
and the surge of photographers
or maritime observers
marks their scores
above the painting

needed are two twins
two horsemen
to cross the zone

came alone
unaware
and in the minefield
crossing with nothing exploding
unaware
clogs near the detonators
and the denser fine gravel

—NORMA COLE

———————————————

Distance de l'automne

Puis tel soir de septembre après tous ces jours lumineux,
Le soleil n'est plus qu'un chasseur entre les landes de nuages;
Il guette et la forêt se retire en elle-même,
A distance du rayon froid.
Des craquements veillent partout sur le silence
Et la mûre dans les taillis tend ses grappes noires à personne.
Ce sera donc la nuit dans une heure. Le ciel
Très pâle se réserve et ne touche plus l'herbe ni les eaux
Qui se retournent vers la profondeur oblique.
Buvez, doux animaux.

Amen

Nul seigneur je n'appelle, et pas de clarté dans la nuit.
La mort qu'il me faudra contre moi, dans ma chair, prendre comme une
    femme,
Et la pierre d'humilité que je dois toucher en esprit,
Le degré le plus bas, la séparation intolérable
D'avec ce que je saisirai, terre ou mains, dans l'abandon sans exemple de ce
    passage—

Jacques Réda 1929–
LUNÉVILLE, FRANCE

A tireless and inveterate walker, Réda gathers material for his writing from his peregrinations around Paris. The writer has characterized his books as walking tours through narrative, in which his characters are monuments. From 1987 to 1995 Réda served as editor-in-chief of the *Nouvelle Revue Française*. He is also a contributor to *Jazz* magazine. Principal works: *Amen*, 1968; *Récitatif*, 1970; *Les Ruines de Paris*, 1977; *L'Improviste*, 1980; *Hors les murs*, 1982; *L'Herbe des talus*, 1984; *Celle qui vient à pas léger*, 1985; *Châteaux des courants d'air*, 1986; *Recommendations aux promeneurs*, 1988; *Retour au calme*, 1989; *Le Sens de la marche*, 1990; *La Liberté des rues*, 1997; *La Course*, 1999; *Moyens de transport*, 2000.

Autumn Distance

And then one September evening, after these luminous days,
The sun is only a hunter between the moors and the clouds;
Lying in wait as the forest withdraws into itself,
At a distance from the chill ray.
Crackings everywhere keep watch over the silence
And the blackberry in the thicket proffers its black bunches
To nobody.
It'll be dark in an hour. The sky,
Very pale, holds back, and no longer touches the grass
Or the waters which return to the slanted depth.
Drink, gentle animals.

—STEPHEN ROMER

Amen

I call on no saviour, there's no gleam in the night.
The death I need to put against my flesh, like a woman,
Is the stone of humility I must touch in spirit.
The lowest rung, the intolerable severance
From what I shall clutch at, earth or hand, in the unexampled abandon of this
    period—

Et ce total renversement du ciel qu'on imagine pas.
Mais qu'il soit dit ici que j'accepte et ne demande rien
Pour prix d'une soumission qui porte en soi la récompense.
Et laquelle, et pourquoi, je ne sais point:
Où je m'agenouille il n'est foi, ni orgueil, ni espérance,
Mais comme à travers l'oeil qu'ouvre la lune sous la nuit
Retour au paysage impalpable des origines,
Cendre embrassant la cendre et vent calme qui la bénit.

Viande de boucherie par Loti

apparition de la mer verte un soir
par-delà les dunes sous un ciel rare
sous la neige le vieux prunier s'est
affaissé dans l'enfance des jardins
          ô main du temps
et les bœufs pleins de sang se sont abattus
aux coups de massue en plein front attaché

And this unsuspected, total inversion of the sky.
But let it be said here that I accept and ask nothing
Against a submission that contains its recompense.
Which, and why, I do not know:
Where I kneel is neither faith, pride, nor hope,
But rather, passing through the night moon's opened eye
A return to the untouchable country of origins,
Ash embracing ash with a calm wind blessing it.

—STEPHEN ROMER

Jude Stéfan 1930–
PONT-AUDEMER, FRANCE

S téfan, a poet, novelist, and essayist, has produced numerous short-story collections and engravings. He studied French, law, and philosophy and went on to teach French, Latin, and Greek in Bernay. Latin poetry and Renaissance literature have both inspired his writing. The author of *Lettres tombales* (1987), Stéfan has received both the Prix Max Jacob and the Grand Prix de Poésie de la Ville de Paris (2000). Principal works: *Cyprès*, 1967; *Aux chiens du soir*, 1979; *Suites slaves*, 1983; *Laures*, 1984; *Alme Diane*, 1986; *A la Vielle Parque*, 1989; *Stances*, 1991; *Povrésies*, 1997; *Épodes, ou, poèmes de la desuétude*, 1999; *Génétifs: Poèmes*, 2001; *La Muse province: 76 proses en poèmes*, 2002.

Butcher's Meat by Loti

apparition of the green sea one evening
beyond the dunes beneath a rare sky
under the snow the old plum-tree has
sunk into the childhood of gardens
        o hand of time
and the blood-engorged steers have collapsed
under bludgeon blows across their brows attached

435

au sol par une boucle après long beuglement
    contre l'immonde sacrifice
    nous les corps de poussière
       mort, pitié

Emma Zola à Wimbledon supposons

j'ai embrassé j'ai remercié juliette récamier
    un siècle trop tard
    grâce à david et au baron gérard
    nantie d'un trop mince pertuis
    elle n'en fut que plus aimée
une aiguille transperçait son chignon
vos mains voulaient redresser sa tête
puis descendre au long de sa tendresse
en même temps que sa robe festonnée
à ses pieds nus aux bords de la piscine
l'air doux de ses yeux bruns sa bouche carmin
à sa place n'ayant aimé qu'une fille camier
beauté vulgarité dans le temple du blanc
    vert tennis

Harengs et bouleaux

Trois harengs
et quatre arbres
quatre arbres sur le pré
sous des monceaux de nuées
l'un défeuillé et l'autre ébréché
l'un ployé et l'autre tout entier
encore offert aux vents
sous des nuées bigarrées
trois harengs dans un plat
près d'un bol en porcelaine
à midi pour le déjeuner
et quatre arbres roux
dressés au soleil décoloré
le soir en automne

to the ground by a thong after long bellowing
    against the impure sacrifice
    we bodies of dust
        death, pity

—MARILYN HACKER

Emma Zola at Wimbledon Let's Say

I kissed I thanked juliette récamier
      a century too late
    thanks to david and to baron gérard
    equipped with a too-narrow channel
    she was only loved the more for it
a needle pierced her chignon
your hands wanted to straighten her head
then descend the length of her tenderness
along with her beribboned dress
to her bare feet at the edge of the pool
the mild look of her brown eyes her carmine lips
having only loved in her place a coked-up girl
beauty vulgarity in the temple of white
      tennis green

—MARILYN HACKER

Herrings and Birch Trees

Three herrings
and four trees
four trees in the meadow
under heaps of clouds
one leafless and one split
one bent and one whole
still offered to the winds
under the many-coloured clouds
three herrings on a plate
near a porcelain bowl
at noon for luncheon
and four russet trees
standing in the pale sun
at evening in autumn

437

trois harengs morts
et quatre arbres là.

Le Jardin de l'un

Il faut l'escargot il faut le liseron
Il faut le froid feuillage et sa rosée
Les murs aussi posés dans la lumière
Et le tissage de nos mains dans la lumière
Sous l'angle dessiné et blanc des amandiers
Où dorment un peu nos impasses — tout cela
Notre respiration
Qui va dans l'infini se nuire et nous dissoudre

Ici je suis. « La lune est mon enfant » (la lune ?)
Comme cela fut dit
Ma toute nuit si tendre par l'éclat
Très doucement mon épouse, ma fille

three dead herrings
and four trees there.

—EDWARD LUCIE-SMITH

Salah Stétié 1929–
BEIRUT, LEBANON

Stétié is a poet, essayist, art critic, and diplomat. In Beirut he founded the cultural weekly *L'Orient littéraire,* which he directed from 1956 to 1961. The review forged an important link between literary innovations in the West and those nascent in Oriental and Arabic writing. He served as a permanent delegate from Lebanon to UNESCO (1965–1982), as ambassador to Morocco (1985), and later as a diplomat to The Hague. In 1995 he received the Grand Prix de la Francophonie, given by the Académie française. Principal works: *L'Eau froide gardée,* 1973; *Fragment: Poème,* 1978; *Inversion de l'arbre et du silence,* 1980; *L'Autre Côté brûlé du très pur,* 1992; *Fièvre et guérison de l'icône,* 1998.

The Garden of the One

The snail is necessary the bindweed is necessary
The cold leaves and their dew
The walls too placed in the light
And our hands' weaving in the light
Beneath the etched white angle of the almond trees
Where our stalemates sleep a while—all that
Our breathing
Launched into the infinite to drown itself and dissolve us

Here I am. "The moon is my child" (the moon?)
As it was once said
My nocturnal one so tender in outbursts
Very gently, my spouse, my daughter

Dans ce lit de roches rompues, muscles noués
Lit de violence naturelle et draps du vent
Cirque de pierre malheureuse et conque fille
Sur qui passe et repasse
L'ombre du rapace inconnu de la mort

Voici enfin l'arrivée des nuages
En qui se fait et se défait la lampe fille
Déjà née de demain ô lampe rouge
En verticalité de jour nocturne
Sur la maison de feu des fous du rêve
Leurs draps tordus comme des nébuleuses
Leurs yeux délégation d'oiseaux vers le centre

Ma fille ma colombe
À toi de toi par toi l'étranglement
Cette lampe de givre
Toi-même à demi dénudée sous la feuille
De ce jardin de l'Un
Où va ta nuit aimer ta transparence
Mille fois mon cœur cela brille
Cicatrice incicatrisable et qui palpite
À toi de toi par toi l'étranglement
Sous bien de pluie tombée
En qui sommeil avec le soleil nous dormons

———————————————

In this bed of broken rocks, knotted muscles
Bed of natural violence and sheets of wind
Crater of woeful stone and conch daughter
Over which comes and goes
The shadow of death's unknown raptor

At last here come the clouds
In which the lamp undoes and redoes itself daughter
Already born of tomorrow O red lamp
Sheer height of nocturnal day
On the house of fire of the dream-maddened
Their sheets twisted like nebulae
Their eyes a delegation of birds toward the center

My daughter my dove
To you through you from you the constriction
That lamp of frost
Yourself half-naked beneath the leaf
In this garden of the One
Where your night goes to love your clarity
A thousand times my heart this shines
Un-scarred-over scar which palpitates
To you through you from you the constriction
Beneath so much fallen rain
In that slumber with the sun in which we sleep

—MARILYN HACKER

5

1967–1980:
The Explosion of the Next Generation

Anne-Marie Albiach, Marie-Claire Bancquart, Silvia Baron Supervielle, Martine Broda, Nicole Brossard, Danielle Collobert, Claude Esteban, Marie Étienne, Dominique Fourcade, Michelle Grangaud, Emmanuel Hocquard, Hédi Kaddour, Vénus Khoury-Ghata, Abdellatif Laâbi, Annie Le Brun, Marcelin Pleynet, Jacqueline Risset, Jacques Roubaud, Paul de Roux, Claude Royet-Journoud, Habib Tengour, Franck Venaille

Younger poets have always gathered around established poets they respect and emulate: René Char, as we have seen, influenced an earlier generation of poets in these years, and Yves Bonnefoy, Philippe Jaccottet, Bernard Noël, and Michel Deguy formed, as they do now, the center of French poetic activity, serving as inspirations for future generations. For the most part, the poetry in France during this period reflected neither nostalgia nor prophecy but a celebration of everydayness.

The deliberate minimalism of language in much poetry of this time stands in contrast to the lush verbiage of Saint-John Perse in books like *Éloges, Amers,* and *Exil.* There developed in this period a sensible uncertainty, not about where poetry was going but about where to locate the enthusiasm that had infused previous works. As Danielle Collobert phrased it, a kind of "not knowing on what to open energy" emerged.[1]

The endless and frequently joyous experiments of the most forward-looking of these poets—Jacques Roubaud (translated here by Rosmarie Waldrop), Michelle Grangaud (translated here by Rosemary Lloyd and Paul Lloyd), Emmanuel Hocquard, Olivier Cadiot, Pierre Alféri, Anne-Marie Albiach, and Claude Royet-Journoud—are frequently cited in North America. They are the pillars of the ongoing transatlantic exchange.

Important differences notwithstanding, these French poets might be considered the equivalent of the American L=A=N=G=U=A=G=E poets (Bruce Andrews, Charles Bernstein, Clark Coolidge, Lyn Hejinian, Susan Howe, Michael Palmer, Bob Perelman, Leslie Scalapino, Ron Silliman, and others). In L=A=N=G=U=A=G=E poetry, the emphasis falls, heavily, on the word itself, its constituent parts made salient and not permitted to retreat before meaning, hence the dramatic and eye-catching separation of letters in the movement's original title. We remember, too, the short-lived, vital French-language Lettrist movement of the 1960s, led by the Romanian Isidore Isou, which emphasized the drama of the individual letter.[2] In their consideration of the material of the word as all-important, and in their insistence upon the relation of the stuff of words to other words, the French and American poets mentioned here represent a completely different way of looking at poetry and prose.

The poet Anne-Marie Albiach, for example, is quite outspoken in her distrust of the lyric mode. She requires of poetry a "propelling gesture" or projective force that permits both breathing in the poem (hence space) and an upward spiraling movement, as if the poem were the constrained and limited equivalent of what we used to think of as the sublime. It is not about knowing, as she says in an interview with Jean Daive, but about something else entirely: "I hate knowledge. Passion is what I have."[3] Of the multitude of living facts, only the essentials are present in the poet's work, lest these facts stand in the way of the poem itself.

Albiach's often difficult writing is influenced by Pierre-Jean Jouve's blasphemous verses in "Lamentations au cerf," by Georges Bataille's notions of cruelty, and by Antonin Artaud's claims for his Theater of Cruelty. She advocates a "theatre that divides, at once lyric, ornamental and cruel in the development of its discourse."[4] Her refusal to write "after" anyone's work and her insistence on writing only " 'after' the mark they have left in me" can be read in an interesting relation with the recent poetry journal entitled L'Instant après. What is inscribed by such a mark is not a school or an ism but rather some trace—again visible or audible, suggestive but not controlling.

The writing of Emmanuel Hocquard is of special interest to the contemporary reader. The poet's questioning of language and representation is central in all his work. In Hocquard's collection Les Élégies (1990), the fragmentary had come to dominate in what has been called his "archaeological mode."[5] And by 1994, his work would become linked with Jean Baudrillard's theory of the simulacrum or simulation—the creation of the real through conceptual or "mythological" models having little connection to or origin in reality. In 1989, Hocquard founded his Bureau sur l'Atlantique, an association that serves to further relationships between

French and American poets—a mode of expansion and exchange that is common to the majority of the poets included in this volume.

Notes

1. In Norma Cole, *Cross-Cut Universe: Writing on Writing from France,* trans. Norma Cole (Providence: Burning Deck, 2002), p. 41.

2. See the extraordinary volume *Poésure et peintrie* (Marseille: Musée de Marseille, 1993).

3. Cole, *Cross-Cut Universe,* p. 24.

4. Cole, ibid., p. 31.

5. Term used in Glenn Fetzer's " *(Le) Voyage Reykjavik* and Emmanuel Hocquard's 'Poetics of Simulacra,' " *French Literary Studies* 28 (Lincoln: University of Nebraska Press, 2002), pp. 1–14. In a note, he introduces Hocquard's "Il rien" (from *Un privé à Tanger*), which alludes to the strategy of the Objectivist poet Charles Reznikoff, who gathers archival details and makes them into verse, without intervening therein (p. 7, n. 4).

Anne-Marie Albiach 1937–

SAINT-NAZAIRE, FRANCE

A lbiach is celebrated as a highly experimental poet. Along with Claude Royet-Journoud and Michel Couturier, she founded the journal *Siècle à mains*. Her seminal translation of Louis Zukofsky's *"A"*-9 first appeared in the review. During the 1960s Albiach lived in London. Principal works: *Flammigère*, 1967; *État*, 1971; *Césure: Le Corps*, 1975; *Le Double*, 1975; *Objet*, 1976; *Anawratha*, 1984; *Mezza voce*, 1984; *Figure vocative*, 1985; *Le Chemin de l'ermitage*, 1986; *Travail vertical et blanc*, 1989.

Le Chemin de l'ermitage
(extraits)

La vie parallèle des horizons de corps déjà vécus, les liens se dénouent dans une trajectoire,
laissant au silence une dynamique de force ou de destruction.

Les contours d'une délinéation s'exercent sur le visage masqué et les membres, enserrent les poignets et leurs anneaux, le cou et sa chaîne. Luxure des premières heures; lumière sur la levée des paupières, distinctes dans les couleurs. Sous la dentelle de la coiffe, les cheveux teintés argent «émergent dans une floraison de saisons inouïes».

Face à eux, complices dans le lieu privilégié, de blanc et de ceinture précise dans le flou de la jupe, elle vérifie de deux mains le point exact du masque, où le féminin et le masculin s'exaspèrent; dans la pénombre du double, ils regardent avec apaisement, une fragilité dans leurs jabots d'un bleu évanescent : un songe indécis s'empreint d'elle à eux; dans l'attente, une blancheur irradie nos pulsions.

Comment pénétrer dans cette luminosité qui annule le spectateur le plus ardent. Deux ardeurs, l'une blanche, l'autre écarlate, séparées par le rideau d'une distance que les occlusions temporelles auraient travaillée.

Cela se situe dans une mémoire immédiate.

Un enjeu traverse les positions, de part et d'autre d'un reflet, alors qu'elle s'astreint à des mouvements altérant cette immobilité.

Ils interrogent leurs regards. Ils ne sauraient dire que ce qui avait été immobile le demeurerait, et se précipitent dans l'univers de l'instant qui porterait ce masque d'un présent ludique.

Elles ne sauraient plus qui il est, lui dont le regard donnait puissance d'entendre ces paroles étrangères et qu'il ne tenait que d'une passion lacérée ou parfaite — «mes lèvres sur tes lèvres»— et une mutité déjouée, cette irrépréhensible absence. La vélocité du hasard dans la froideur d'une fièvre, l'éblouissement.

The Hermitage Road

Parallel life of corporeal horizons already lived—the ties loosen along a trajectory, leaving to silence a dynamic of power or of destruction.

The contour of an outline constrains the masked face and the limbs, encloses wrists and wristlets, neck and neck band. Lewdness of earliest hours; light on lifting eyelids, distinct in color. Under the lace cap, silver-tinted hair "emerges in a flowering of unsuspected seasons."

Facing these accomplices in their preferred setting, soft skirts white and trimly belted, she verifies with both hands the precise point of the mask, where feminine and masculine become exacerbated. In the penumbra of the double, they look on with calm, a fragility in their frills of evanescent blue. An uncertain dream issues from her to them, a whiteness meanwhile irradiating our impulses.

How pierce this luminosity, which cancels the most ardent spectator. Two ardors, one white, the other scarlet, separated by the curtain of a distance fashioned as by time's occlusions.

All that in an immediate memory.

A stake plays the positions, meandering a reflection, while she keeps to motions that alter this immobility.

They question their eyes. They'd be unable to say that what had been immobile would remain so, and they rush headlong into the world of the instant, which would wear this mask of a playtime present.

They could no longer know who he is, whose eyes gave power to understand these foreign words, power from nothing but a passion, rent or perfect—"my lips on your lips"—and a frustrated dumbness, this irreproachable absence. Speed of chance in the chill of a fever, vertigo.

—KEITH WALDROP

449

Contrefable d'Orphée

Voiler la sainte face
de ma femme.
Pouvoir me retourner sans tuer des abeilles.

N'avoir pas suscité
risque de leurre
en descendant l'ombre déclive de la mort.

Etre encore au jeune moment
où des sucs de bourgeons
naissaient parmi les lèvres d'Eurydice.

Grouper bêtes et astres
autour d'un chant ductile
aux cris de procession et d'aube.

C'est fini: le dieu sec
a capturé la fraîcheur de mes vignes.
Je hais l'avidité de la vendangeuse qui va
derrière
au même pas que moi

Marie-Claire Bancquart 1932–

AUBIN, FRANCE

Bancquart is a poet, novelist, and literary scholar. A professor emerita at the Sorbonne, Paris IV, she has written authoritatively on the works of Guy de Maupassant, Jules Vallès, and Anatole France. Among the many prizes she has won are the Prix Max Jacob (1978), the Grand Prix de l'Essai de la Ville de Paris, and the Grand Prix de Critique de l'Académie Française. Principal works: *Proche*, 1972; *Cherche-terre*, 1977; *Mémoire d'abolie*, 1978; *Partition*, 1981; *Opportunité des oiseaux*, 1986; *Opéra des limites*, 1988; *Sans lieu sinon l'attente*, 1991; *Dans le feuilletage de la terre*, 1994; *La Paix saignée*, 1999; *Rituel d'emportement*, 2002; *Anamorphoses*, 2003.

Counterfable of Orpheus

To veil the saintly face
of my wife.
Able to turn around without killing bees.

Not to have set
a possible trap
by going down death's sloping shadow.

To be at that young moment still
when bud sap
rose in Eurydice's lips.

To gather beasts and stars
round beckoning song
with marching sounds and sounds of dawn.

It's over; the dry god
has captured the freshness of my vines.
I hate the wine-harvester's greed as she
follows
dogging my steps

coupant les grappes de mes notes entre ses dents
pour barbouiller ses joues de fards interdits à mes lèvres.

Je marche dans la solitude des livres

Je marche dans la solitude des livres :
mon cœur gèle
avec ces mémoires gelées.

La vent tape au volet.

Novembre.

Il a fallu toute une vie pour que le craquement du bois suscite une attente
    essentielle.

Au-delà du jardin
au-delà du temps devant nous
il y a les bogues tombées de châtaignes
le feu des feuilles dans la brume
les fenêtres violettes.

Exactement novembre.

Toute chose à sa place.

Cependant l'inconnu est proche
comme un oiseau inquiet.

Retour d'Ulysse

Ulysse tue les prétendants près d'un fragile bol de lait
qu'une servante
aux seins désormais traversés de flèches
serrait
tout blanc.

Surprise dans les yeux des cadavres.

Surprise au cœur d'Ulysse :
avoir tant erré pour trouver ce retour,
sa femme à peine reconnue, la servante massacrée par erreur.

biting through the bunches of my notes
smearing her cheeks with rouge my lips aren't allowed.

—MARTIN SORRELL

I Walk in the Solitude of Books

I walk in the solitude of books:
my heart ices over
with those memories iced over.

The wind pounds on the shutter.

November.

It took a whole life for the cracking of wood to arouse a crucial anticipation.

Beyond the garden
beyond the time before us
there are the fallen husks of chestnuts
the fire of leaves in the fog
the purple windows.

Exactly November.

Everything in its place.

And yet the unknown is nearby
like an anxious bird.

—MARY ANN CAWS

Return of Ulysses

Ulysses kills the suitors close to a fragile bowl of milk
which a servant
with breasts henceforth pierced by arrows
was clasping
in its whiteness.

Surprise in the corpses' eyes.

Surprise in Ulysses's heart:
that great odyssey for such a homecoming,
a wife barely recognised, a servant butchered in error.

Il se reprend. Tendresse
du métier à tisser
du lit
du soleil sur le lait.

Le long périple aux monstres
c'est
maintenant
le doigt qui suit au bord du bol un rivage toujours d'exil

la figure qui se regarde
en étroit liquide

et ce qu'il faut de ciel pour bleuir le lait autour d'elle.

———————————————

He collects himself. Tenderness
of the loom
of the bed
the sun on milk.

The long voyage crowded with monsters
now
is
a finger tracing exile's endless shore around the bowl's rim

the face reflected
in confines of liquid

and enough blue sky to tint the milk around it.

—MARTIN SORRELL

Silvia Baron Supervielle 1934–
BUENOS AIRES, ARGENTINA

Baron Supervielle's first poems were written in Spanish, her native tongue. In 1961 she moved from Argentina to Paris. There she worked at the bookstore La Hune, at Éditions Gallimard, and at the Centre culturel argentin. She also undertook translation work for UNESCO. During this time she was not writing her own poetry; after a long silence, she began writing in French and translating French and Spanish. Baron Supervielle was the first to translate Marguerite Yourcenar into Spanish. Invited by the French embassy to participate in conferences in Buenos Aires, she returned to Argentina in 1997. Principal works: *La Distance de sable*, 1983; *Lectures de vent*, 1988; *L'Or de l'incertitude*, 1990; *L'Eau étrangère*, 1993; *Le Livre du retour*, 1993; *La Frontière*, 1995; *Après le pas*, 1997; *La Ligne et l'ombre*, 1999.

455

Ici l'heure

ici l'heure
ne garde
ni n'égare

ici l'herbe
se repose
des ruines

que j'arrive
ou que je parte

rien ne se
modifie

ne change
l'éternité

de l'invisible
maître
du désert

je suis
l'inassouvi
désir

j'ai prononcé
la syllabe
de ton nom

j'ai ressenti
les lueurs
de tes yeux

j'ai reconnu
l'éclipse
de ta face

sans relâche
je dresse
un échafaudage

Here Time

here time
neither holds
nor loses

here grass
finds rest
from ruins

whether I come
or whether
I go

nothing is
altered

no change
to eternity

of the invisible
lord
of the desert

I am
the unfulfilled
desire

I have pronounced
the syllable
of your name

I have experienced
the gleam
of your eyes

I have recognized
the eclipse
of your face

without relief
I build
a scaffold

dont la planche
s'effondre
après le pas

j'ai abandonné
ma langue
et j'ai marché
longtemps

même le rythme
de mon pas
je le quittais

même le son
de mon silence
je le perdis

même à moi
revenue
je reste partie

———————————

whose boards
collapse
behind our steps

I have abandoned
my tongue
and have walked
through ages

even the rhythm
of my steps
I left behind

even the sound
of my silence
has gone astray.

even returned
to myself
I remain
away.

—ROSEMARY LLOYD

Martine Broda 1947–
NANCY, FRANCE

A poet and essayist, Broda is perhaps best known for her love poems. She has also written on and translated Pierre-Jean Jouve and Paul Celan. In 1979, after serving as a high school teacher for nine years, Broda began work with the Centre national de la recherche scientifique, in the Centre de poétique comparée. In 1992 she joined the Centre de recherches sur les arts et le langage. Principal work: *Grand Jour,* 1994.

Je lave

je lave
ce que j'ai ramassé
dans la lumière et ce désert
de larmes je mange
mes yeux brûlants

Je voulais te l'avouer

je voulais te l'avouer
à travers des mots sans larmes

tandis que sous

je t'aime

une rose de l'horizon

depuis que je te connais

je porte un renoncement je porte
joues d'enfant de l'inconnu

le nom du poème

———————————————

I Wash

I wash
what I have picked up
in the light and this desert
of tears I eat
my burning eyes

—MARY ANN CAWS

I Wanted to Tell You

I wanted to tell you about it
in words not weeping

while under

I love you

a horizon rose

since I've known you

I've had a fresh start I've had
the look of someone unfamiliar

the name of the poem

—MARY ANN CAWS

Nicole Brossard 1943–
MONTREAL, CANADA

A poet, essayist, and novelist, Brossard is at the center of feminist and postmodernist writing in Canada. She is an active organizer of literary conferences and events, and her works exemplify radical experiments in both form and style. Brossard founded and edited the journal *Barre du jour* in

Je veux revoir cette séquence

ainsi que la porno délibérée du vent
symbolique et *d'ailleurs en tout cas*
peau un mot m'a suffi : virtuelles
traverse nos versions de la voix
et jouissance, cela m'est radical
comme la pensée qui saisit son élan
le cerveau : que d'inscriptions
de la corniche à la cornée
───────── transversales

bouche, j'écris j'éprouve et je pense
acquise, j'oublie **une émotion singulière**
dans le tournoi je cultive l'identité
de l'amour et d'indice dès lors
j'accoste / so close
in to your ─────────── brain
sans traduction / in Time / je me souviens
et viens d'un seul élan : paysage excite

cities get closer : l'épaule, le verdict
une fois et je pleure, autour
plus près, je risque de dos le souvenir
cervicales / et braise baiser les cuisses
et d'existence : il m'a fallu un dé,
une histoire pour continuer / get closer
l'amour lesbien jour de *gerbe*
ma semblable de connivence : musique

1965 and began another, *Les Têtes de pioche,* in 1976. Between 1975 and 1976 she produced the play *Some American Feminists.* In 1991 she won the Prix Athanase-David for lifetime achievement and in 1994 entered the Académie des lettres du Québec. Principal works: *Le Centre blanc/poèmes,* 1965–1975; *Mordre en sa chair,* 1966; *Double impression/poèmes et textes,* 1967–1984, 1978; *L'Écho bouge beau,* 1968; *Suite logique,* 1970; *Amantes,* 1980; *Installations,* 1989; *Langues obscures,* 1992; *Vertige de l'avant-scène,* 1997; *Au présent des veines,* 1999; *L'Anthologie de la poésie des femmes au Québec de 1892–1988* (coeditor with Lisette Girouard), 2002; *Poèmes à dire la francophonie: 38 poètes contemporains* (editor), 2002.

I Want to Revise This Sequence

as well as the wind's deliberate pornography
symbolic and *besides anyway*
skin a word were enough for me: virtual
crossing our versions of the voice
and pleasure, that's at the root of it for me
like the thought which grasps its thrust
the brain: so many transversal
from the corniche to the cornea
_____ inscriptions

mouth, I write, I test out and I think
acquired, I forget a unique emotion
in the tournament I cultivate the singularity
of love and symptom therefore
I accost/si proche
dans ton _____ cerveau
with no translation/dans le Temps/I remember
and come in one rush: excited landscape

les villes s'approchent: the shoulder, the verdict
once and I weep, around
closer, I risk remembrance from behind
cervical / and smouldering kiss thighs
and of existence: I needed a thimble
a story to continue/d'approcher
l/over les/bian day of *sheaves*
my kind my accomplice: music

profils et miroir, je travaille
à l'horizon
explore et n'en reviens jamais
sans savoir si j'ose le paradoxe :
transformer *la* volûte, *la* flamme
la synthèse
aucun texte ne m'aura, j'en conviens
convoque (minimum ton visage)
sans quoi je tourne au ralenti trop
fluide pour ne pas être coulée / goutte

ici (la fiction) *l'échine* lorsque
les cils *doucement la matière à écriture*
la tension va venir ainsi que ton épaule
m'a verticalement éblouie je poursuis
sel conquête et sommeil / quelques mots :
je veux revoir cette séquence
nous nues genoux enlacées en un mot
radicalement

profiles and mirror, I work
on the horizon

explore and don't ever return from there
without knowing if I'll dare the paradox:
to transform *the* scroll, *the* flame
the synthesis
no text will have me, I agree to it
convoke (at least your face)
without which I turn in slow motion too
fluid not to flow/ a drop

here (the fiction) the *spine* when
eyelashes *softly writing material*
tension will build the way your shoulder
vertically dazzled me I pursue
salt conquest sleep/ a few words:
I want to revise this sequence
us naked knees enlaced in a word
radically

—MARILYN HACKER

Danielle Collobert 1940–1978
ROSTRENEN, FRANCE

C ollobert's family took part in the Resistance during World War II. Her
work, largely contained in her notebooks, details her commitment to
political activism and to her writing. She was associated with the
National Liberation Front in Algeria during that country's war for independence.
Collobert moved to Paris at the age of nineteen. A translation of her notebooks
appeared in *Zazil #1*, and her poetry appeared in the journal *Tripwire #2*. She
committed suicide in 1978. Principal works: *Cahiers*, 1956–1978; *Meurtre*, 1964; *Il
donc*, 1976.

Je temps de quoi

je temps de quoi
l'étalement
vague roulée à regard
inlassable du je liquide repéré rouge
fragments imperceptibles à petit œil du temps vision nulle
sur l'espace jamais plus d'un grand champ
le reste ouvert au vogueur les visions célestes
sucer des phrases nourriture sans dents
je broyeur sons syllabes magma secousses telluriques
ou gagné par le raz de marée perdu pied dans sous-sol syntaxe
jours de passion
lumière des veines qui vient
en surface l'articulation
je dis ardent énergie le cri ou comme brûle jamais dit

Dont le soleil

dont le soleil parfois musique sur grand ciel d'ouvert
à plat dos l'écarté
l'écartelé probable à plaisir tirant sur la lancée du supportable
de ce côté là d'assez profond l'écrit sur corps
je gravant du sablonneux l'instant effacé
pousser la fièvre aux lèvres résonnantes le gong
ou rhombe bourdonnant fuyant la tête
ou tambours de survie
ou sec désert poussière bombes
et toujours léchant les flammes le corps de peur
je d'insecte vivant cloué au mur
cherchant vivant à souffrance plus
se la rêvant même nocturne
en vue du définitif

I Time of What

I time of what
the flood
wave riding a gaze
unflaggingly from I liquid marked red
fragments imperceptible to the little eye of time vision useless
on space never more than a large field
the rest open to the drifter the celestial visions
sucking nourishment from sentences toothless
I grinder sounds syllables magma tremors
or beaten by the tidal wave adrift in substratum syntax
days of passion
light of veins unveiled
on the surface the articulation
I said energy blazing the scream or as burns left unsaid

—MICHAEL TWEED

For Which the Sun

for which the sun sometimes music on vast sky of open
flat on its back the isolate
the severed probably just for fun drawing upon the thrust of the bearable
from that side from deep enough the writing on the body
I etching of the sandy the instant effaced
pushing the fever to the resonating lips the gong
or a buzzing bull-roarer fleeing the head
or drums of survival
or dry desert dust bombs
and the flames always licking the body of fear
I of insect living nailed to the wall
seeking living to suffer more
dreaming it nightly
in light of the definitive

—MICHAEL TWEED

Le Soir venu

Le soir venu, on se prépare pour un voyage
qui n'aura jamais lieu puisque bien sûr on ne part pas
mais c'est quand même chaque soir un moment
très extraordinaire car avant de tout quitter il faut
mettre en ordre sa maison et chacune de ses pensées
qui prenaient tant de place et n'en garder qu'une
ou deux, les plus légères, pour son bagage

le soir venu, c'est comme si quelqu'un
qui n'est pas vous disposait de chaque chose
à votre place, mais sans vous faire souffrir, juste
pour vous aider et l'on se prend, dieu sait pourquoi,
à aimer ce compagnon sans visage et quand il faut
partir on voudrait presque l'embrasser, lui qui ne
s'en va pas, et l'on reste avec lui, très tard, sous les ombrages.

Claude Esteban 1935–

PARIS, FRANCE

A poet, essayist, and translator, Esteban has translated the works of García Lorca and Paz, as well as those of Quevedo, Góngora, and Machado. From 1974 to 1981 he directed the review *Argile* and from 1984 to 1993 headed the poetry division of Flammarion. He is currently a professor of Spanish at the Sorbonne. He is also the president of the Maison des Écrivains, where he resides. Principal works: *Terres, travaux du coeur*, 1979; *Le Nom et la demeure*, 1985; *Élégie de la mort violente*, 1989; *Quelqu'un commence à parler dans une chambre*, 1995; *Janvier, février, mars*, 1999; *Morceaux de ciel, presque rien: Poèmes*, 2001.

Once Evening's Fallen

Once evening's fallen you prepare for a voyage
which will never take place because of course you don't leave
and yet all the same every evening it's a very exceptional
moment because before leaving it all you must
put your house in order and all of your thoughts
that took up so much space and keep back just one
or two, those that weigh least, to go in your baggage

once evening's fallen, it's as if someone
else took care of all this, doing all this
in your place, but without hurting your feelings, just
to help you and you find yourself, though you never know why,
loving that faceless companion and when you have to leave
you could almost embrace him, he who does not leave,
and you stay on with him, very late, in the shadows.

—ROSEMARY LLOYD

Cauchemars

Premièrement. La Maison est restée là-bas, il part à sa recherche, reconnaît le quartier mais la nuit est tombée tandis qu'il suit les rues parallèles à la Mer, celles qui vont vers l'Ouest. Comme il ne trouve rien il prend le sens inverse, c'est-à-dire les rues parallèles au Palais, celles qui vont au Sud. Mais entre-temps, préoccupé de la méthode il oublie ce qu'il cherche ou ce qu'il cherche a disparu, s'est transformé, ou la nuit est vraiment trop noire : la Maison demeure introuvable.

Sauf une fois. Il la découvre en fête, des inconnus, d'anciens amis circulent et sourient. Le jardin en revanche est désert, près de l'étang un écriteau branlant porte son nom.

— Tu vois, fait remarquer un invité à Cook, tu n'es pas oublié.

Deuxièmement. Il s'apprête au voyage. Seul partir compte. Hélas! sur le quai de la gare ses bagages l'entourent comme des bornes qui s'opposent. Plusieurs cas se présentent.

Il arrive en retard. Le train au loin ne montre plus que sa fumée tandis que sur le quai sa silhouette à lui est une borne qui s'ajoute.

Il est à l'heure. Comment s'y prendre? Le poids le rend perplexe. Le train démarre. Sans lui.

Il est monté heureux. Tous ses bagages autour de lui sont ses petits. Hélas hélas! il s'est trompé de train, il est monté en queue, bref le bon train démarre. Sans lui.

Il est monté heureux en tête. Le train a démarré mais son voisin bizarre se répand sur le siège. Laissant là ses bagages Cook circule, détendu, vers l'arrière. Le paysage le distrait tant et si bien qu'il prend la place, qu'il absorbe le train dont

Marie Étienne 1938–
MENTON, FRANCE

É tienne spent part of her adolescence in Vietnam and Africa. After moving to Paris, she became assistant to the poet Antoine Vitez, a job she held for ten years. Many of her works are dedicated to him. Étienne has also served on the board of the reviews *Action poétique* and *La Quinzaine littéraire*. She is currently a member of the Poetry Committee of the Centre national du livre. Principal works: *La Longe*, 1981; *Lettres d'Idumée*, 1982; *Katana: La Clef du sabre*, 1993; *Anatolie*, 1997; *Roi de cent cavaliers*, 2002.

Nightmares

First of all. The House has remained in its old spot, he goes in search of it, recognizes the neighborhood but night has fallen while he's been following the streets parallel to the Sea, those which go West. Since he's found nothing he goes in the opposite direction, that is, the streets parallel to the Palace, those which go South. But meanwhile, preoccupied by how to go about it, he forgets what he's looking for or what he's looking for has disappeared, has shifted shapes, or the night is really too black: the House is nowhere to be found.

Except once. He discovers it with a party in full swing, unknown people and former friends mill around and smile. The garden on the other hand is deserted, near the pond a rickety signboard bears his name.

—You see, one of the guests remarks to Cook, you aren't forgotten.

Second of all. He's getting ready for a trip. All that counts is leaving. Unfortunately, his suitcases surround him on the station platform like barriers to prevent it. Several possibilities present themselves.

He arrives late. From far off, all that can be seen of the train is its smoke while on the platform his own silhouette is one more barrier.

He's on time. How should he go about it? The weight stymies him. The train starts off. Without him.

He gets on happily. All the suitcases around him are his children. Too bad too bad! He's gotten on the wrong train, he's gotten on the end of the train, in short, the right train leaves. Without him.

He gets on happily at the head of the train. The train starts off, but his peculiar neighbor spreads himself out over the seat. Leaving his luggage there. Cook wanders, relaxed, towards the rear of the train. The landscape distracts him

les derniers wagons suivent la courbe de la voie. Et disparaissent. Cook est seul dans le paysage.

Il atteint la falaise d'où un avion doit l'enlever en volant bas sans atterrir. Un ami porte les bagages, l'avion surgit. Des mains saisissent ses effets, s'en dessaisissent dans la mer. Cook a la peine au cœur.

Un jour enfin il vole, il voit les sources et les monts, les saules et les fleuves, les lavandières sur les berges.

— Que ne suis-je léger, pense-t-il.

Dans l'arc-en-ciel où il s'inscrit il abandonne ses bagages. Et monte.

––––––––––

Ensembles

ensembles ici, spacieux : ainsi
groupés à l'orée du pré ouvrant sur le côté gauche de la cour un frêne entre
    deux saules debout les uns contre les autres (mais ne s'appuyant pas) très
    élancés souffles différents légèretés différentes verts pas les mêmes argents de
  · temps à autre se touchent les cimes

so thoroughly that it takes the place of, that it absorbs the train whose last cars follow the curve of the tracks. And disappear. Cook is alone in the countryside.

He reaches a cliff where a plane is to pick him up flying low without landing. A friend is carrying his luggage, the airplane looms up. Hands seize his possessions, and then let them drop into the ocean. Cook is heartbroken.

Finally one day he takes off, he sees the springs and the mountains, the willows and the rivers, the washerwomen on the riverbanks.

—If only I were light, he thinks.

In the rainbow where he registers he abandons his luggage. And gets on board.

—MARILYN HACKER

Dominique Fourcade 1938–
PARIS, FRANCE

A poet and art critic, Fourcade began publishing his poetry in 1961. He wrote steadily until 1970, at which point he fell silent for thirteen years. When he took it up again, he adopted an entirely different mode. His work published after 1983 relies on wordplay and neologisms and is simultaneously philosophical and process-oriented. He wrote on Matisse (*Écrits et propos sur l'art*) and was the Commissaire de l'Exposition Henri Matisse, 1904–1917, at the Centre Georges Pompidou. Principal works: *Épreuves du pouvoir*, 1961; *Nous du service des cygnes*, 1970; *Le Ciel pas d'angle*, 1983; *Rose-déclic*, 1984; *Son blanc du un*, 1986; *Xbo*, 1988; *Outrance utterance et autres élégies*, 1990; *Décisions ocres*, 1992; *Il*, 1994; *Le Sujet monotype*, 1997; *Est-ce que je peux placer un mot?* 2001.

Ensembles

ensembles here, spacious: thus
grouped at the edge of the meadow that opens to the left of the courtyard an ash
    between two willows standing against one another (but not leaning on each
    other) very slender different breath different lightness greens not the same
    silvers now and then touch their tips

en pendant
deux grands saules contre lesquels se blottit le parfum d'un noyer et devant eux
    mais disjoint un frêne encore

dans la cour même cinq jeunes tilleuls immobiles pur sang intranquilles

dans l'autre cour, celle où est la citerne à gaz, le buddleia (subspontané, ô fleur
    de terrain vague) est un ensemble à lui seul, à haute fréquence
particules lilas sont ivres de papillons fragrance solitude

contenance

derrière la maison, le long de la rivière cette fois
un entrelacs frêne saule auquel
on ne sait qui, le saule sans doute, a consenti
projetant, comme il se fait toujours, en arc par-dessus l'eau — libellules héliport
calopteryx virgo, métal vert violet de l'aile obscure, non, bleu violet obscur
    obscur, c'est à nervures, et rose clair segmenté de leurs ventres
demoiselle ophtalmique éros (trempe tes yeux gonflés dans l'eau de la rivière
    pendant que je soulève)
ensemble — les libellulidées — au programme le plus léger du monde, le moins
    piloté, le plus escadrille — à ne rien faire que l'amour (en las, ou cœur
    copulatoire), et pondre, et broyer un moucheron cette suite a lieu sur une
    brindille en surplomb, ou variablement voler —
au monde

et tout au fond du pré le long de l'autre bras d'eau une ligne, un contour
de saules-élévations de saules et d'aulnes alternés dont certains morts

ingresque et pas

saules
parfois les ailes jointes au-dessus de l'abdomen
sur perchoirs
libellules êtres de soleil, ou crépusculaires
comment osent jeunes poules d'eau marcher sur nénuphars
masses, il y a quelque chose de plus crémeux dans les saules que dans les autres
    apparences
d'où vient leur stabilité en vol? d'un système cybernétique sûrement (vous avez
    vu les plaques pileuses sur leur prothorax?), ou d'une plate-forme inertielle

counterpointing
two tall willows against which the scent of a walnut huddles and in front of
    them but apart an ash again

in the courtyard itself five young restless immobile pure-blood lindens

in the other courtyard, the one with the gas cistern, the buddleia
    (subspontaneous, oh flower of vacant lots) is an ensemble in itself, at high
    frequency
lilac particles drunk on butterflies fragrance solitude

bearing

behind the house, along the river this time
an ash willow interlace, to which
one — the willow perhaps — consented
projecting, as it always does, in an arc over the water — dragonfly heliport
calopteryx virgo, green violet metal of dark wing, no, blue violet dark dark, it's
    got ribs, and the segmented light pink of their abdomens
ophthalmic damselfly eros (dip your swollen eyes in the water of the river while
    I raise)
ensemble — the dragonflideas — with the lightest agenda in the world, the least
    piloted, the most squadronized — making nothing but love (in a circle, or
    copulatory heart), and laying eggs, and nibbling a gnat this sequence occurs
    on an overhanging reed, or for variety, flying —
in the world

and at the far end of the meadow along the other branch of the river a line, a
    contour
of willow-heights of alternating willows and alders some of which dead

ingresque and not

willows
sometimes the wings join on top of the abdomen
perched
dragonflies beings of the sun, or crepuscular
how dare young moorhens walk across lilypads
masses, there's something more creamy about the willows than about other
    appearances
what stabilizes their flight? a cybernetic system, no doubt (you've seen the hairy
    plates on their pro-thoraxes?), or an inertial platform (or maybe from a

(ou encore, d'un gyrolaser avec accéléromètre), sinon comment filer d'un trait, puis être en vol stationnaire, pour se trouver planant avec virage sur l'aile — d'une turbulence !

saules sont seuls à connaître des inversions de vibrations

les libellules — charge alaire légère et grande surface portante classée secret défense — sont un ensemble — dont les ailes antérieures et postérieures ne fonctionnent pas ensemble

frêne : qui est mâle, qui est femelle dans le jeu puissant, lointain des frênes

essai sur l'obsession : saules n'ont que des épures

d'obsessions

contenance

ingresque et pas

P.S. : je dis à Degas que le soir, en rentrant, ma femme peut lire sur mon visage si c'est le personnage du saule que j'ai le plus travaillé, ou le rôle frêne, ou celui du martin-pêcheur parti dans la lune-Stieglitz, ou encore celui, tout en postcombustion, de la l.ll.l. .

———————————

gyrolaser with accelerometer), if not, how can they zoom forward, then stop
dead in stationary flight, to end up gliding, a banking on wing — what
turbulence!
willows alone experience the inversions of vibrations
dragonflies — with light lift and large carrying surface classified defense secret
    — are an ensemble — the front and back wings of which don't work together
ash: which is male, which is female in the powerful distant game of the ashes
essay on obsession: willows have only the sketches
of obsessions
bearing
ingresque and not

P.S. I tell Degas that in the evening, when I come home, my wife can read on my
face whether it was the character of the willow that I'd worked on the most, or the
ash act, or that of the kingfisher gone into the Stieglitz moon, or even the one, in
total post-combustion, of the dra-fly-gone.

—COLE SWENSEN

Michelle Grangaud 1941–
ALGIERS, ALGERIA

G rangaud is a specialist in anagrams. Her work makes use of these and
many other experimental techniques. In 1995 she joined the OULIPO
(Ouvroir de Littérature Potentielle), comprising writers from around
the world who are interested in investigating literary constraints and experimenta-
tion. She is currently a member of the editorial board of the review *Poë&sie*. Principal
works: *Mémento-framents*, 1987; *Renaître*, 1990; *Stations*, 1990; *Geste*, 1991; *Jours le
jour*, 1994; *Formes de l'anagramme*, 1995; *Poèmes fondus*, 1997; *État civil*, 1998.

Translators' Note

Michelle Grangaud drew inspiration from the play on words and num-
bers of the OULIPO group in producing her 1995 collection of poems
entitled *Formes de l'anagramme*. In this book she creates poems in which

each line offers a different anagram of such thirty-two-letter titles as "Isidore Ducasse comte de Lautréamont." Raising the stakes even higher, she arranges these anagrams so as to create one of the most difficult and complicated of all the fixed-form poems: the sestina. This form is composed of six stanzas, each of six lines, followed by an envoi of three lines. Although rhyme is usually not used in a sestina, the end words recur in a constantly shifting but fixed pattern. If we assign each end word a number from 1 to 6, the following pattern is created:

Stanza 1 123456   Stanza 2 615243
Stanza 3 364125   Stanza 4 532614
Stanza 5 451362   Stanza 6 246531
Envoi 246

The envoi also contains the other end words in this pattern, 135. Because each line is an anagram, translating word for word would obviously have little sense. We therefore decided that the only way to transfer Granguad's anagrammatical poems into English would be to write a sestina in homage to her, taking as our thirty-two-letter starting point one of her own titles. In her poem, Grangaud was able to use as end words the four cardinal points: English does not allow that, so we have chosen instead the words *inside, outside,* and *under,* plus three elements of the natural (and poetic) world as our other end words: *star, cloud,* and *moon.* We have followed her lead in removing all punctuation.

—PAUL LLOYD AND ROSEMARY LLOYD

Michelle Grangaud Creating Anagrams

clang lace rug anhingas dream ragtime
thundering mice-clan lams a garage rag
a gaggle man charms granite lunar dice
grail claim hung near grand acme stage
an angel must chair arming ragged lace
rage curls again changing metal dream

turn a manacle arches a giggling dream
cage land manager rushing arc lag time
gain drachma stage merging lunar lace
a mugging canal is cleaner than glad rag
alarm lunging arch earned magic stage
nag urge a calm manner—lights raga dice

as Marg ran a light lugger can name dice
unlace gal stagger in a charming dream
niggling a caldera charm me an ur-stage
sear a chum clang a grin dangle ragtime

479

Isidore Ducasse comte de Lautréamont

méduse l'auditoire mets sac à côté nord
et mise du crocodile dans ta mare ouest
démode du croissant au court à demi est
toast à taire consomme le décideur sud
sors ta mince camelote du désert oui-da
monte maturité à la corde cuisse de dos

conduit le sommet au Tati à créer de dos
accoutume-toise : méditer salades nord
détourne-toi du commerce assis là et da
contracte l'idiome dur de masse à ouest

castle ring dare gleam again munch rag
girl sang a mad march tune gearing lace

nag nag chum in a garret rides a glum lace
rugger male alas can't mar hanging dice
an eager man-child acts ruling game rag
gar-angling games leach curtain dream
and can gauge charm in larger slag time
Michigan grudge race ran all man stage

dig Gaul man girl harem er cancan stage
glaring chart manages maiden rug lace
girdle an acre harm a gnu clang gas time
charm a strange lama lugging near dice
a gaming gang caller untrace his dream
laughter claims game in grand cane rag

angel music can mar regain the glad rag
alleged marching arum can ring a stage
gang chuting angels alarm a rice dream
strangling a mug made rain charge lace
gurgling ale a strange man a charm dice
ginger gala Ra can charm sun glade time

change guard time signal near calm rag
Graham gull dice-man in range arc stage
gale cringing asthma rung a lace dream

—PAUL LLOYD AND ROSEMARY LLOYD

Isidore Ducasse comte de Lautréamont

I am more cursed at close a dent outside
a sluice meet roused a distracted moon
some toadies direct moat clause under
o I must care seamed a rose tinted cloud
lo our coast master educated me inside
so tailed mouse can't deem dour ice star

Timo acted on cue released sodium star
idle man adores succor at meet outside
a mad or electrocuted mouse sat inside
ate delicious creams rate dusted moon

comme sa décision dérate ta rotule sud
adulte du sans mémoire accorde-toi est

situe dam le contour de ma croisade est
conte le traumatisme coi du rasé de dos
modèle de saut ton moi si caractère sud
miette accumule des oasis radote nord
admets le concert du soir à mardi ouest
immole ton étude s'écrit courses à dada

commente la cause sois de tout Derrida
souris au médicament coloré daté d'est
décide des mots à courir l'amante ouest
acclame ton truisme au soir d'été de dos
couds la tête assidue mérite coma nord
incise ta dermatose morale de coût sud

et commande l'écriteau d'os à sortie sud
considère la tasse comme toiture du da
cuis le camaïeu de mots et torsade nord
accommode l'autorité de sardine US est
commets la couture de raisin à et de dos
décommande aussi le tricot rade ouest

cascade le moto de dire terminus ouest
déçois le tas à trou de commentaire sud
acclimate ton trousseau de rime de dos
soude la contumace d'iris motte réséda
cuisine de coteau mords le matador est
détruis cocotte malade au messie nord

décroise la sciée du tam-tam nord-ouest
amortis le roc est ce demain d'ouate sud
tic tiré da essore la communauté de dos

———————————————

carouse dammit see a rose tinted cloud
aside I too must lead soccer team under

diced tomatoes rule SE coast I am under
do sluice middle ear seemed to count a star
smite its oar Comus deed a neater cloud
reduce lot actress moaned I am outside
titmice use suet groaned a cradled moon
dour comma elected us at a store inside

outdoor metal creases mute cad inside
so I met a cloud or I'm a tested case under
a lee dead dust occurs emits ire at moon
cue cede true minds so I doom a late star
aunt tossed ice cream or medal outside
indeed mutters a core a moist sea cloud

I made mud roots—can seat eeriest cloud
a curt mead loots out same creed inside
I ate dame cauldron's rest come outside
I am a Celtic rose do toasted muse under
mount mid-tour ace see a sole diced star
Maud sits out Dee cit a clear red moon

clue I said rated comet used trade moon
I use test score to read and mime a cloud
me me I do I do sue trace Tuscan lode star
O door lets eat EU cream custard inside
I must close a door taste ace dime under
a mist cure arose comet landed outside

add muscle outside rise tea crate moon
Satie ice ode starts memo under a cloud
o lace meet true doom inside a scud star.

—PAUL LLOYD AND ROSEMARY LLOYD

À Noël
(extraits)

I

À Noël, Cyrille a introduit les loups dans la
maison
Où les trouve-t-il.
Ils chantent quarante minutes
entre singe et chat.
Fragments de meute échos bouts de distances
Depuis je les écoute plusieurs
Ces loups, Viviane, chantent autour des points.
Faut-il qu'ils entrent dans la pièce pour entendre
tomber la neige.
Des tas de petites vies juxtaposées.
Si je *vous* écrivais au passé j'aurais l'impression
de mentir.
Reviendrez-vous le jour de l'an?

II

Qu'est-ce qui vide un nom de sa substance.
Quelle sorte de grammaire serait une grammaire

Emmanuel Hocquard 1940–

TANGIERS, MOROCCO

A poet, novelist, professor, editor, and translator, Hocquard has written on subjects ranging from Greek and Latin classics to Objectivism. With the painter Raquel, he founded and served as an editor of the small press Orange Export Ltd. He also edits the series *Un bureau sur l'Atlantique*, dedicated to translating the works of contemporary American poets. He coedited two large anthologies of new American poets with Claude Royet-Journoud: *21 + 1: Poètes américains d'aujourd'hui* (1986) and *49 + 1: Nouveaux poètes américains* (1991). Principal works: *Album d'images de la Villa Harris*, 1978; *Les Élégies*, 1990; *Théorie des tables*, 1992; *Tout le monde se ressemble: Une anthologie de poésie contemporaine*, 1995; *Un test de solitude: Sonnets*, 1998; *Ma haie*, 2001.

At Christmas

I

At Christmas, Cyrille brought the wolves into the
house.
Where does he find them.
They sing for forty minutes
at the bitching hour.
Part of a pack, echoes, scraps of distance
Ever since I've listened to them for several
These wolves, Viviane, sing around the points.
Do they need to enter the room to hear the snow
falling.
Heaps of little lives in juxtaposition.
If I wrote to *you* in the past tense I would feel I
was lying.
Will you be back on New Year's Day?

II

What empties a name of its substance.
What kind of grammar would a grammar

sans questions
et sur quoi portent les questions.
Vous n'êtes pas une question mais entourée de
sortes de questions.
Est-ce qu'il neige comment hurlent les loups.
Oui, Viviane.
Ne répondant à aucune question
pourrait-on dire que oui et être sont un.
Maintenant oui.
« J'avais l'impression de comprendre. »
Oui
pourrait être le mot manquant.

III

Viviane est Viviane, oui.
La tautologie ne dit pas tout mais oui.
Oui et tout ne sont pas équivalents. Chaque oui
comble l'espace du langage, qui ne forme pas pour
autant un tout.
On n'obtiendrait pas une somme en additionnant
ces oui.
Et si on supprimait *tout* de notre vocabulaire.
Ces loups ne chantent pas en chœur.
L'espace que remplissent leurs bouts de voix est
un espace brisé.
Des tas de petits espaces juxtaposés
chantent
autour des points.

XXV

J'écris cela pour écrire ceci. Ce qui est écrit l'est
deux fois.
Ce que *vous* lisez est-il deux ?
Entre deux il y a un champ dont la forme tourne
entre nous.
Ce trou est sans mesures.
Autour de ce trou, le chant des oiseaux comprend
le jour se lève un 11 avril.
La nuit est contenue dans le silence de la chèvre
noire et blanche est morte.

without questions be
and what are the questions about.
You are not a question, but surrounded by kinds
of questions.
Is it snowing how do wolves howl.
Yes, Viviane.
Not answering any question
could one say that yes and to be are one.
Now yes.
"I felt I understood."
Yes
could be the missing word.

III

Viviane is Viviane, yes.
Tautology does not say all but yes.
Yes and all are not equivalents. Every yes fills the
space of language, which for all that does not
form a whole.
One would not obtain a sum by adding up these
yeses.
What if we subtracted *all* from our vocabulary.
Those wolves do not sing in chorus.
The space filled by their scraps of voices is a
broken space.
Heaps of little spaces in juxtaposition
sing
around the points.

XXV

I write that in order to write this. What is written
is so twice over.
What *you* read, is it two?
Between two there is a field whose form turns
between us.
This hole is boundless.
Around this hole, the song of the birds
comprehends day breaks on one 11th of April.
Night is contained in the silence of the black and
white goat is dead.

Les lignes de mots sont pliées ainsi.
Deux restent n'a pas de fin
ou Viviane le prix à payer.
Grammaire et fiction sont un.

Trois leçons de morale

I

Regardons autour de nous.
Tous nos camarades ont un nom;
tous les objets,
tous les animaux de nos gravures
ont un nom pour les désigner.

Toutes les personnes,
tous les animaux,
toutes les choses
ont un nom.

II

Si on vous dit:
dessinez une orange . . .
Vous demandez:
une orange verte, mûre, grosse, petite, ronde?

Pour la dessiner exactement
il faut vous dire comment elle est.
Les mots: verte, mûre, etc.
qu'on ajoute au nom orange
et qui disent ses qualités
bonnes ou mauvaises
sont des adjectifs qualificatifs.

Les mots qui disent comment sont les personnes
lex animaux et les choses
sont des adjectifs qualificatifs.

III

Si je dis:
Une hirondelle vole,
on me comprend.

The lines of words are folded this way.
There is no end to two remain
or Viviane the price to pay.
Grammar and fiction are one.

—ROSMARIE WALDROP

Three Moral Tales

I

Let's look around ourselves.
All our companions have a name;
all objects,
all the animals in our engravings
are indicated by a name.

All the people,
all the animals,
all things
have a name.

II

If someone tells you:
draw an orange . . .
You ask what kind:
green, ripe, large, small, round?

To draw it exactly
you must be told what it's like.
The words: green, ripe, etc.
that are added to the name orange
and which tell of its qualities
good or bad
are modifiers.

The words which tell what persons
animals and things are like
are modifiers.

III

If I say:
A swallow flies,
I am understood.

Si je dis:
Une hirondelle rase,
on me demande:
Elle rase quoi?
La rue,
le toit,
le pré?

Il me manque un renseignement.
Par exemple:
Une hirondelle rase le toit.
Il a suffi d'ajouter le complément.

Ainsi, parfois,
le verbe a besoin d'un complément.

———————————

If I say:
A swallow skims,
I am asked:
Skims what?
The street,
the rooftop,
the meadow?

I need more information.
For example:
A swallow skims the rooftop.
It was enough to add the complement.

Thus sometimes
the verb needs a complement.

—MICHAEL PALMER

Hédi Kaddour 1945–
TUNIS, TUNISIA

Kaddour is a critic and a contributor to such journals as the *American Poetry Review*. His poems have appeared in the *New Yorker*, the *Paris Review*, *Poetry*, *Poetry International*, *Prairie Schooner*, and *Verse*. He has been director of the Atelier d'écriture at the Centre d'études poétiques and currently teaches literature, drama, and creative writing in Lyon, in addition to writing a theater column. Principal works: *La Fin des vendanges*, 1989; *La Chaise vide*, 1993; *Jamais une ombre simple*, 1994; *L'Émotion impossible*, 1994; *Les Fileuses*, 1995; *Passage au Luxembourg: Poèmes*, 2000.

Le Chauffeur

Qu'est-ce qui rôde autour du chauffeur
Qui a quitté son autobus, s'est assis
Place de l'Opéra au bord du trottoir
Et glisse dans la douceur de n'être
Déjà plus que ses larmes ? Les passants
Qui se penchent sur une tristesse
Commune et présentable aimeraient
Qu'il leur dise que le vent naguère
Savait venir de la forêt vers une robe,
Ou qu'un jour son frère lui a lancé
Même ton ombre ne voudra plus de toi.
Les pieds dans l'eau, le chauffeur
Ne sait que répéter : *ce travail est dur*
Et le monde n'est pas complaisant.

Variations

Elle sait aussi qu'il avait dit : « *Les autres*
chient du marbre », et qu'il jouait
parfois en plein, disons, bordel (c'est
dans *Amadeus*), ça donne, *Ah! vous dirai-je,*
du goût à la douceur des notes, entre marches
et feintes, où le temps ne fait pas de cadeau :
elle joue, *ré, mi, do, tou-our-ment,* un *mi*
d'un quart de temps dans un grand mot,
pour dire le bon faux pas, et le silence
n'est pas une forme qui s'éloigne : c'est pour
tout rassembler quand le traversent les fulgurantes
exactitudes, l'arpège de l'autre main. Plus tard,
la roue du cœur, l'ivresse, les mots fêlés,
ou tenir les étoiles ! Ce soir *Ah! vous dirai-je,*
ce n'est que le début de la course et déjà
le reflet ironique de soi, tandis que l'utopie
discrètement se tient derrière la lampe dans
les mains de maman, ce soir, le temps est un octave.

The Bus Driver

What has gotten into the bus driver
Who has left his bus, who has sat down
On a curb on the Place de l'Opéra
Where he slips into the ease of being
Nothing more than his own tears? The passers-by
Who bend over such a shared and
Presentable sorrow would like him
To tell them that the wind used to know
How to come out of the woods towards a woman's dress,
Or that one day his brother said to him
Even your shadow wants nothing to do with you.
His feet in a puddle, the bus driver
Can only repeat: *This work is hard
And people aren't kind.*

—MARILYN HACKER

Variations

She already knows that he had said *"The rest of them
shit marble"* and that he sometimes played
in, shall we say, disorderly houses (it's
in *Amadeus*), which produced *Ah, vous dirais-je,*
a taste with the notes' sweetness, between marches
and flourishes, where time gives nothing away:
she plays, *re mi do tou-our-ment,* a *mi*
that's a quarter-note in a big word,
to utter the right misstep, and silence
is not a figure walking away: it's there to
bring everything together when it's crossed
by fiery certainties, the other hand's arpeggios. Later
the heart's wheeling, drunkenness, shattered words,
or holding on to stars. Tonight *Ah, vous dirais-je,*
is only the start of the race, and already
the ironic reflection of herself, while utopia
stays discreetly behind the lamp in
mama's hands, tonight, time is an octave.

—MARILYN HACKER

493

Elle lançait sa vieille vaisselle

Elle lançait sa vieille vaisselle à la lune
qui répare les assiettes ébréchées
ravaude le linge des noces
et classe par ordre de tristesse les photos jaunies par le regard de la lampe

Tout l'univers se partageait les taches ménagères de ma mère
les vents adverses soufflaient dans les tiroirs
négociaient dans ses volets
et balayaient vers la ville les miettes de rêves qu'elle grignotait dans son sommeil

Mère si négligente
sur ta corde de linge séchaient les nuages au blanc douteux
qui suscitaient le sarcasme des rossignols et attristaient le soleil
tu signalais leur disparition aux gendarmes quand le vent les entrainaient
par-delà de la vallée
le traitant de voleur de draps et de bétail
puis retirait ta plainte quand les nuages te revenaient brouillard accroupi
sur ton seuil

L'Automne précéda l'été

L'automne précéda l'été d'un jour
des jardiniers vigilants coupèrent plus tôt que prévu les cils humides de

Vénus Khoury-Ghata 1935–

BEIRUT, LEBANON

A n intellectual poet and novelist, Khoury-Ghata has used many genres to depict both her everyday life and the cruelty and destruction of war. She has also written on the tension between French and Lebanese Arabic, the "Franbanais." She was born to a Francophone father and a mother she referred to as "illiterate in two languages." She moved to France in 1972. In 1980 she won the Prix Apollinaire for her *Les Ombres et leurs cris* (1980). Principal works: *Monologue du mort*, 1986; *Fables pour un peuple d'argile*, 1992; *Anthologie personnelle*, 1997; *Elle dit*, 1999; *La Voix des arbres*, 1999; *Compassion des pierres: Poèmes*, 2001.

She Used to Throw Her Old Crockery

She used to throw her old crockery at the moon
which mends chipped plates
darns wedding sheets
and sorts lamplight-yellowed snapshots by degrees of sadness

The whole universe shared my mother's household chores
contrary winds blew into her bureau drawers
bargained between her shutters
and swept towards town the dream-crumbs she nibbled in her sleep

Negligent mother
clouds of a dubious whiteness dried out on your clothesline
provoking the nightingales' sarcasm and saddening the sun
you reported them missing to the police when the wind carried them out of
the valley
called the wind a thief of sheets and cattle
then withdrew your complaint when the clouds came home to you, fog kneeling
on your doorstep.

—MARILYN HACKER

Autumn Preceded Summer

Autumn preceded summer by one day
vigilant gardeners cut the passionflowers' damp lashes earlier than

495

la passiflore
et les horloges tricotèrent des nuits plus étroites

Un vent jaune teignit les façades des forêts
les arbres cessèrent de pleurer
et les balançoires pleines de fillettes et de merles s'arretèrent dans un
grand froissement de jupons et d'ailes

Novembre avait banni les larmes
des anges compatissants léchèrent les eraflures des petits genoux

---

Le Portrait du Père

Le portrait du père
a pris sa place sur le mur
derrière moi
Je suis seul
dans ma chambre close
Ma femme est partie travailler
Pourtant
une main vient me caresser la nuque

expected
and the clocks knit narrower nights.

A yellow wind dyed the forests' façades
the trees stopped weeping
and the swings full of little girls and robins stopped moving
with a great rustling of wings and petticoats

November had banished tears
compassionate angels licked the small scraped knees

— MARILYN HACKER

Abdellatif Laâbi 1942–
FEZ, MOROCCO

A playwright and translator of Arabic literature, Laâbi also became a left-wing militant. With Mohammed Khaïr-Eddine and Mostefa Nissaboury he founded the review *Souffles*. The journal was banned in 1972, and Laâbi was sentenced to ten years in prison. He was finally freed in 1980 and settled in France in 1985. Principal works: *Le Soleil se meurt*, 1992; *L'Étreinte du monde*, 1993; *Le Spleen de Casablanca*, 1996; *Fragments d'une genèse oubliée*, 1998; *Poèmes périssables*, 2000.

The Portrait of the Father

The portrait of the father
has taken its place on the wall
behind me
I am alone
in my closed room
My wife has gone to work
Yet
a hand comes to caress my neck

497

doucement
telle une plume d'oiseau
Le goût de l'enfance
me monte à la bouche

Demain sera le même jour

Demain
sera le même jour
Je n'aurai vécu que quelques instants
le front collé à la vitre
pour accueillir le carrousel du crépuscule
J'aurai étouffé un cri
car personne ne l'aura entendu
en ce désert
Je me serai mis
dans la position du foetus
sur le siège de ma vieille solitude
J'aurai attendu
que mon verre se vide à moitié
pour y déceler le goût du fiel
Je me serai vu
le lendemain
me réveillant et vaquant
Atrocement semblable

————————————————

gently
like a bird's feather
The taste of childhood
rises to my mouth

—PIERRE JORIS

Tomorrow Will Be the Same Day

Tomorrow
will be the same day
I will have lived but a few instants
forehead glued to the window pane
to welcome dusk's merry-go-round
I will have stifled a cry
because nobody will have heard it
in this desert
I will have curled up
in fetal position
on the seat of my old solitude
I will have waited
for my heart to be half empty
to detect there a taste of bile
I will have seen myself
the next day
waking up and going about
Atrociously similar

—PIERRE JORIS

———————————

Annie Le Brun 1942–
RENNES, FRANCE

A poet, essayist, polemicist, and editor, Le Brun joined the Surrealist group in 1963. Her literary heroes are libertines of all epochs, notably Alfred Jarry, André Breton, and the Marquis de Sade. It was Le Brun who, along with others such as Paul Éluard, drew the connection between Sur-

Des rites

Le lieu et la formule reculent avec l'écho à la reconquête des territoires en friche. On ne cessera de les poursuivre à bride abattue dans la direction du point de fuite de ce qui nous échappe à plaisir.

Au début de chaque saison du corps, les nomades se rassemblent pour mieux se séparer.

Aucun mot n'est prononcé sur la lande frémissante tandis que les enfants jouent à saute-mouton sur leur destin. Des cordons ombilicaux sont distribués aux plus jeunes d'entre eux pour qu'ils se familiarisent avec les joies du lasso.

Les cérémonies de séparation se déroulent dans l'air raréfié de novembre. Par intermittence, on projette quelques images fugitives sur les brouillards incestueux dont les plus décisives particules restent en suspension dans l'atmosphère.

A l'aide de subtils frôlements, on soigne les blessures occasionnelles (dues à la lenteur inévitable de certains voyages), par exemple la méconnaissance temporaire de la partie sud-est de la pensée. Les pratiques magiques auxquelles on a recours en pareille circonstance ont pour résultat d'arrêter l'amoncellement des cercles concentriques tétanisés : ceux-ci se détachent progressivement les uns des autres. On assiste à un gonflement spectaculaire des distances intérieures. Et brusquement, la partie autrefois malade devient visible, palpable, sautillante, étincelante, de nouveau impatiente d'envahir.

Lentement se déploient des présences de proie. Les fouets claquent l'échine de l'air. Et la lande disparaît sous les routes qui poudroient. De jeunes ventres ont irrémédiablement brisé leurs amarres.

Nous n'arpenterons plus les champs de l'amour, nous les relierons à la mer.

realism and the marquis de Sade's writings, recognizing in both a concern with the liberation of desire and primitive instincts. Le Brun edited de Sade's complete works, in addition to those of Raymond Roussel. Le Brun has also worked with fellow poets Radovan Ivsic and Georges Goldfayn and the painter Toyen through Éditions Maintenant. Principal works: *Les Mots font l'amour*, 1970; *Les Pâles et Fiévreux Après-midis des villes*, 1972; *Tout près, les nomades*, 1972; *Les Écureuils de l'orange*, 1974; *Annulaire de lune*, 1977; *Lâchez tout*, 1977; *Les Châteaux de la subversion*, 1982; *A distance*, 1984; *Appel d'air*, 1988.

Rituals

The place and the formula recede with the echo to win back the fallow lands. We won't stop pursuing them at a gallop, towards the vanishing point of what wants to escape.

At the beginning of each of the body's seasons, the nomads gather so as to scatter apart.

Not a word is pronounced on the trembling land while the children play at leapfrog on their destiny. Umbilical cords are distributed to the youngest among them so they can become familiar with the joys of the lasso.

The ceremonies of separation take place in the rarefied air of November. Intermittently, a few fugitive images are projected on the incestuous fogs whose most decisive particles remain suspended in the atmosphere.

The slightest touches care for the occasional wounds (due to the inevitable slowness of some voyages), for example, for the temporary misrecognition of the southeastern part of thought. The magical practices used in such circumstances succeed in stopping the accumulation of the tetanized concentric circles: gradually, these detach from each other. There is a spectacular swelling of interior distances. And suddenly, the part that was sick becomes visible, palpable, leaping, sparkling, once again impatient to invade.

Slowly the presences of the prey spread out. Whips lash the spine of the air. And the heath disappears under the powdery roads. Young stomachs have broken forth from their cables forever.

We shall no longer stride along the fields of love, we shall link them to the sea.

— MARY ANN CAWS

Des fêtes

Mes dents ont arraché des cubes de rire, des sorties d'école de rire, des bouteilles de rire, des camions de rire, des parallélépipèdes de rire, des ascenseurs de rire, des caisses de rire, des cônes de rire, des meules de rire, des valises de rire, des coques de rire, des volières de rire, des boîtes de rire, des boules de rire, voilà ce que mes dents ont arraché à la ficelle blanche du désespoir.

On ne rit d'ailleurs que pour manger le morceau d'espace qui nous manque.

Sous des fondrières gonflées de joie menaçante, les pieds des nomades déchirent le papier de la marche, leurs cils lacèrent la cellophane de la vue, les clous de leur attention crèvent le tympan paraffiné des paroles. Les mots ne s'envoleront plus ; ils sont empalés sur place.

Dans ces conditions, le feu au carton des caresses et les pièces du corps détachées, détachables, glissant à califourchon sur les méridiens des instants fuyards. Vos yeux s'éloignent à l'heure où les seins vont boire. Je cours sur la place déserte de votre dos, mes os s'en vont en ricochets sur le miroir de vos muscles. Debout et nus, parviendrons-nous à essayer jusqu'à l'épuisement les robes vertes, sourdes, salées, les chapeaux terrifiants, mauves, gluants, victorieux, les gants jaunes, matinaux, bleu-canard, sanglants, les cravates neigeuses, sinistres, oranges, grises, minuscules, bien frappées, les pantalons indigo, glacés, lilas, galvaudés, sous les pelisses précieuses, blanches, tumescentes, sombres, souveraines de notre complicité qui fait trembler d'inutilité première les agiles muqueuses des mains ?

Les seules fêtes sont souterraines comme le désespoir. On y joue à traquer la balle folle de ce qui est et de ce qui n'est pas.

Les seules fêtes sont hasardeuses comme le désespoir. Effacent-elles totalement l'histoire des grandes famines qui les ont précédées ?

Les seules fêtes sont fatales comme le désespoir. Elles assoiffent de vide ; mieux, elles sont un appel du vide.

Les seules fêtes sont évasives comme le désespoir. Elles flottent un court instant au-dessus du toboggan des veines.

L'avenir ne partira pas en voyage.

Les fêtes comme le désespoir le mettent à mort. Car les fêtes vont aussi vite que le désespoir.

Festivals

My teeth have ripped out cubes of laughter, school-leavings of laughter, bottles of laughter, trucks of laughter, parallapipeds of laughter, elevators of laughter, crates of laughter, cones of laughter, millstones of laughter, suitcases of laughter, eggshells of laughter, aviaries of laughter, boxes of laughter, bowling balls of laughter, that's what my teeth have ripped from the white thread of despair.

Besides we only laugh to eat the bit of space we lack.

Under quagmires swollen with menacing joy, the nomads' feet tear up the paper of the walk, their eyelashes lacerate the cellophane of vision, the nails of their attention split the parafin tympanum of speech. Words will no longer fly off: they are impaled in their place.

In these conditions, the fire in the cardboard of caresses and the detachable, detached body pieces mount astride the noons of the fleeing instants. Your eyes take their distance at the moment when the breasts go to drink. I run along the deserted domain of your back, my bones make ricochets on the mirror of your muscles. Standing naked, shall we try on until we are exhausted those green, deaf, and soiled dresses, those terrifying, mauve, sticky, and victorious hats, those yellow, matinal, canary-blue, and bloody gloves, those snowy, sinister, orange, and tiny, grey, well-tailored ties, under the precious, white, tumescent, somber and sovereign coverings of our complicity that make the agile mucous membranes of the hands tremble from a primary uselessness?

The only festivals are subterranean like despair. People play at tracing the crazed ball of what is and is not.

The only festivals are chancy like despair. Will they totally efface the story of the great famines which preceded them?

The only festivals are fatal like despair. They are thirsty with emptiness; better, they are a summons to emptiness.

The only festivals are elusive like despair. They float for a brief instant above the toboggan of veins.

The future will not leave for a trip.
Festivals, like despair, put it to death. For festivals go as quickly.

—MARY ANN CAWS

Dans la lumière du jour

Je suis claire dit-elle. Je suis claire comme les rumeurs de l'aube. Je suis le miroir, je m'efface

— et dans la vallée un matin laiteux pousse des berges de la rivière jusqu'au seuil, jusqu'aux toits des maisons molles de sommeil

— à sa naissance le jour est partagé entre le bonheur de la prairie et la lumière tardive de l'étang

Je suis dit-elle, je suis dans la lumière du jour

Marcelin Pleynet 1933–

LYON, FRANCE

Pleynet is a historian, essayist, art critic, and prolific poet. Along with Philippe Sollers, he was the director and executive officer of the review *Tel quel* (1962–1982). Publishing such writers as Julia Kristeva, Roland Barthes, Michel Foucault, Jacques Derrida, and Luce Irigaray, the review was the primary outlet for emerging poststructuralist thought in the 1960s and 1970s. After 1982, Pleynet and Sollers shifted their participation to another review, *L'Infini*. From 1987 to 1998 Pleynet held the aesthetics chair at the École nationale supérieure des beaux-arts de Paris. Principal works: *Provisoires amants des nègres*, 1962; *Paysages en deux, suivis de Les Lignes de la prose*, 1964; *Comme*, 1965; *Lessives du loup*, 1966; *L'Enseignement de la peinture*, 1971; *Fragments de choeur: Vers et proses*, 1984; *Plaisir à la tempête*, 1987; *Art de voir, art d'écrire*, 1988; *Les Modernes et la tradition*, 1990.

In the Daylight

I am transparent, she says. Transparent like the sounds of dawn. I am the mirror, I stand aside

—and in the valley a milky morning pushes the shores of river to the threshold, to the roofs of the houses soft with sleep

—at its birth, the day is divided between the gladness of the meadow and the late light of the pool

I am she says, I am in the light of day

—MARY ANN CAWS

M. S. 1544

A contempler
Pour être tout

mais quand au but —
que ceux que tient
par ton regard —
qui de la terre —
pris du regard —
petit objet —
plutôt au temps —
plutôt le nom —
mais si à tous —
que dans la voix —
ainsi voit-on —
pour ouvrir l'autre —
que si en moi —
qu'en te —

le contraire —
ou le rapport —
sachant que tout —
et si en toi —

Jacqueline Risset 1936–
BESANÇON, FRANCE

A poet and translator, Risset is best known for her French translations of Dante's works, in particular the *Inferno*, *Purgatorio*, and *Paradiso* (1985–1990), for which she received the Académie française award for translation. She has also written several biographies of Dante. Risset's other work includes an Italian translation of Francis Ponge's poetry. She moved to Italy to pursue advanced studies and now teaches at the University La Sapienza in Rome. Principal works: *Jeu*, 1971; *Mors*, 1976; *La Traduction commence*, 1978; *Sept passages de la vie d'une femme*, 1985; *L'Amour de loin*, 1988; *Petits éléments de physique amoureuse*, 1991.

M. S. 1544

For consideration
To be all things

but when at end —
so those that hold
on by your look —
who of the earth —
took for the look —
little object —
sooner in time —
sooner in name —
but if for all —
than in the voice —
one sees therefore —
to open the other —
that if in me —
that of it you —

the reverse —
or the relation —
knowing that everything —
and if in you —

tu vois —
que voir —
ainsi dit-il
de qui — et de qui l'œil —
tant qu'autre n' —
ne pourra donc —
quand tout midi ? —
qui la pensée —

moins plus plus plus —
en un moment —
tant je qu'en il —
tel —

    *Maurice Scève

---

you see —
that seeing —
as thus he says
of whom — and of whom the eye —
so long as no other —
will thus be unable —
when every twelve o'clock?
who thought —

less more more more
in a moment —
as much in me as he —
as —

—JENNIFER MOXLEY

Jacques Roubaud 1932–
CALUIRE-ET-CUIRE, FRANCE

A mathematician, poet, novelist, translator, and essayist, Roubaud terminated his studies in literature at the age of twenty-two to devote himself to mathematics. Early in the 1960s, while working on both a book of poetry and a thesis in set theory, he found that logic and mathematical strategies informed his poetic creation. In 1966, at Raymond Queneau's invitation, he joined the literary group OULIPO (Ouvroir de Littérature Potentielle), which experiments extensively with poetic styles and modes. His translation work includes modern American and Japanese poetry, and his essays champion poetry and recount the history of its forms. Principal works: *Trente et un au cube*, 1973; *Autobiographie chapitre X*, 1977; *Une anthologie de poésie américaine: Vingt poètes américains* (with Michel Deguy), 1980; *Dors*, 1981; *Quelque chose noir*, 1986; *La Vieillesse d'Alexandre*, 1986; *Le Grand incendie de Paris*, 1989; *Anthologie du sonnet français: Soleil du soleil*, 1990; *La Forme d'une ville change plus vite hélas que le coeur des humains*, 1999.

Méditation du 8/5/85

Soir après soir
Le vecteur de lumière traverse
La même vitre
S'éloigne
Et la nuit
L'emporte
Où tu te ranges
Invisible
Dans l'épaisseur

Lumière, par exemple

Lumière, par exemple. noir.
Verres.
Bouche fermée. s'ouvrant à la langue.
Fenêtre. réunion de craies.
Seins. puis bas. la main s'approche. pénètre.
Écarte
Lèvres frayées. à genoux.
Lampe, là. mouillée.
Regard empli de tout.

Dans cet arbre

Descends et dors   dans cet arbre, dans cet arbre.
Repousse la terre   dans cet arbre, dans cet arbre.
Écope la terre   dans cet arbre, dans cet arbre.
Désinvente le noir   dans cet arbre, dans cet arbre.
Reconstruis des jambes   dans cet arbre, dans cet arbre.
Décline les poussières   dans cet arbre, dans cet arbre.
Coupe la lumière   dans cet arbre, dans cet arbre.
Emplis les orbites   dans cet arbre, dans cet arbre.
Écris, écris toi vivante   dans cet arbre.

Certaine manière je

d'une certaine manière je voudrais
me dessaisir. mais d'abord réfuter

Meditation of 8/5/85

Evening after evening
A vector of light crosses
This same windowpane
And fades
Night
Carries it off to
Where you
Invisible
Adapt to denseness

—ROSMARIE WALDROP

Light, for Example

Light, for example. black.
Panes.
Closed mouth. opens to the tongue.
Windows. chalked in rows.
Breasts. farther down. the hand approaches. enters.
Spreads
Parted lips. on knees.
A lamp, there. wet.
The eye overflows.

—ROSMARIE WALDROP

In This Tree

Come down and sleep   in this tree, in this tree.
Push back the earth   in this tree, in this tree.
Scoop out the earth   in this tree, in this tree.
Disinvent the dark   in this tree, in this tree.
Rebuild your legs   in this tree, in this tree.
Decline the dust   in this tree, in this tree.
Cut the light   in this tree, in this tree.
Fill the orbits   in this tree, in this tree.
Write, write yourself alive   in this tree.

—ROSMARIE WALDROP

A Way I

in a way i would not
to proceed. but first refute

ces ongles. puisqu'ils ne débordent pas
dont les pentes à la lumière s'apparentent
en cela qu'il faut bien nommer d'un nom.
et peut-être déduisant du blanc
posé à la porte face pour face.   n'est ce
à dire que. la ligne scintillera
tracée dans l'or géométrique   ou si

d'ici et là j'arrache mes yeux
en ayant soin de bien essuyer
le monde. pour qu'ils ne lui refusent rien.

Une glace de

il mange une glace de couleur
qui n'a pas envergure de montagne
moyenne.   ni moyenne de montagne
ni quoi que ce soit qui tienne ou arrange
des continents pour soi.

mais ajoutent ses yeux tels qu'ils rétractent
la terre. ou changement de domicile
sous une surface de petite grandeur
abîmée. par des résines possibles
et verveines.   au devant des mots par accrochage.

Partout les

partout
sous les objets la
verdure
dommageable. du
bout de musique ils
s'entourent et du bout de musique ils
passent la verdure à la
langue. ainsi que la
toupie sur
le sable. la
farine. elle peinait sur
la mémoire de la ligne

those nails. as they do not reach over
which silent slopes pairing with the light
into that which must be named with a name.
deducing from something white maybe
settling by the door and face to face.   is it
but to say that. the line must go on shining
drawn into gold geometry.   or if

here and now i tear out my eyes
as i make sure i'll wipe carefully
the world, so that they refuse nothing to it.

—JACQUES ROUBAUD

Ice In

he is eating some ice with colour
which has no average breath
of mountain   nor average mountain
nor anything that would hold or arrange
continents in itself.

but adding his eyes such as they retract
the earth. or change location
under a small sized surface
damaged. by resins possibly
or verbena.   ahead of words hanging up.

—JACQUES ROUBAUD

Everywhere the

everywhere
under objects
grass
detrimental. with
an extremity of music they
surround themselves and with an extremity of music
they bend the grass with their
language. thus the
top spins over
sand. or
flour. it used to toil
along the memory of a line

derrière
la verdure
dommagée. le cercle
en bout de musique.

Il pleut

À Charlotte Borel, à l'occasion de certaine absence de stress hydrique

— Je crois qu'il pleut, mais il ne pleut pas.
— Tu crois qu'il pleut et tu affirmes qu'il ne pleut pas ?
— Oui.
Je crois qu'il pleut mais je sais que je me trompe.
— Comment le sais-tu ?
— Là n'est pas la question. La question est : je crois qu'il pleut,
Mais j'ai tort.
— Qui dit que tu as tort ?
— Moi.
— Mais si tu as tort de croire qu'il pleut,
Si tu sais que tu as tort de croire qu'il pleut
Comment peux-tu croire qu'il pleut ?
Réponds-moi sincèrement.
— Il pleut ?
— Non.
— Tu vois !
— Je vois qu'il ne pleut pas. Mais je ne vois pas comment tu peux
Dire que tu crois qu'il pleut
Et comment tu peux
Dire en même temps que cette croyance est erronée. Je ne peux
Pas le croire.

— Je crois que je crois qu'il pleut et que je sais qu'il ne pleut pas.
— Bien.
— Si je crois que je crois ce que je crois, je le crois.
— Bien.
— Personne ne croit que et en même temps que ne pas.
— Que quoi ? que ne pas quoi ?
— N'importe quoi : qu'il pleut, par exemple.

behind
grass
damaged. a circle
at the end of music.

—JACQUES ROUBAUD

It Is Raining

To Charlotte Borel, on the occasion of a certain absence of moisture-induced stress

—I believe that it is raining, but it is not.
—You believe that it is raining and assert that it is not?
—Yes.
I believe that it is raining but I know that I am mistaken.
—How do you know?
—That is not the issue. The issue is: I believe that it is raining
But I am wrong.
—Who says that you are wrong?
—I do.
—But if you are wrong to believe that it is raining,
If you know that you are wrong to believe that it is raining
How can you believe that it is raining?
I need a straight answer.
—Is it raining?
—No.
—You see!
—I see that it is not raining. But I do not see how you can
Say that you believe that it is raining
And how you can
At the same time say that this belief is mistaken. I cannot
Believe it.

—I believe that I believe it is raining and that I know it is not.
—Fine.
—If I believe that I believe what I believe, I believe it.
—Fine.
—No one believes that and at the same time that not.
—That what? that what not?
—Whatever: that it is raining, for example.

—Bon.

—Si je crois que je crois à tort qu'il pleut,

Autrement dit si je crois qu'il pleut bien que ce ne soit pas le cas qu'il pleut,

Il s'ensuit que je crois que je crois qu'il pleut

Et au même moment que ce n'est pas le cas qu'il pleut

Et il s'ensuit alors que je crois simultanément qu'il pleut

Et qu'il ne pleut

Pas. Mais puisque personne n'a jamais cru en même temps qu'il pleuvait et qu'il
    ne pleuvait pas, il est impossible que je croie que je crois qu'il pleut

Tout en sachant qu'il ne pleut pas.

—En effet.

—Et pourtant je le crois.

—Tu crois quoi ?

De toute façon, il pleut.

Le Passé

Elle lui dit : « Il fait très beau. »

Donc

il faisait beau.

S'il fait beau, il ne fait pas nécessairement très beau.

Si elle avait dit « il fait beau »

aurait-il pu comprendre qu'elle avait, potentiellement

en quelque sorte,

dit

« il fait beau, *mais* il ne fait pas très beau » ?

Non.

« Il fait beau » n'aurait annoncé de sa part aucune réticence.

Mais il n'aurait pas entendu non plus dans un

« il fait beau »

(si elle avait dit « il fait beau »)

« il fait beau, il fait même très beau ».

« Il fait beau »

n'aurait annoncé

de sa part

aucune insistance.

Cependant si, ayant dit « il fait beau »

—Go on.
—If I believe that I believe wrongly that it is raining,
In other words if I believe that it is raining even though it is not the case that it
    is raining,
It follows that I believe that I believe it is raining
And at the same time that it is not the case that it is raining.
And it thus follows that I simultaneously believe that it is raining
And that it is
Not. But given that no one has ever at the same time believed that it was raining
    and that it was not, it is impossible that I believe that I believe that it is
    raining
Knowing full well that it is not.
—To be sure.
—And yet I believe it.

—You believe what?

In any event, it is raining.

—RICHARD SIEBURTH AND FRANÇOISE GRAMET

The Past

She said to him: "It is very nice out."
Therefore
it was nice out.
If it is nice out, it is not necessarily very nice out.
If she had said "it is nice out"
could he have understood that she had, as it were,
potentially
said
"it is nice out, *but* it is not very nice out"?
No.
"It is nice out" would not have signaled any reservations on her part.
But neither would he have heard in her
"it is nice out"
(if she had said "it is nice out")
"it is nice out, it is even very nice out."
"It is nice out"
would not have signaled
any insistance
on her part.
All the same if, having said "it is nice out"

517

(ce qui n'avait pas été le cas)
elle avait ajouté « il fait même très beau »
cela aurait-il voulu dire qu'elle aurait pensé
qu'en disant seulement
« il fait beau » elle n'avait pas été assez précise,
qu'elle n'avait pas assez affirmé
la beauté du temps ?
Sans doute.
Mais aurait-elle pu dire
« il fait très beau, il fait même très beau » ?
Non.
Pourquoi ?
Ça ne se dit pas. Si elle avait dit
« il fait même très beau » après avoir dit
« il fait très beau »
elle aurait appliqué l'opérateur « même » à l'énoncé
« il fait très beau ». Mais quand on dit
« il fait très beau » on ne dit en aucun cas
qu'il fait beau mais pas très beau,
ce qu'on pourrait vouloir ajouter à l'énoncé « il fait beau »
avec autant de vraisemblance que « il fait même très beau »
et il s'ensuit qu'inapplicable est ce « même »
à l'énoncé
« il fait très beau ».

—Vraiment ?

Et il faisait beau ?

—Il faisait beau.

———————————————

(which had not been the case)
she had added "it is even very nice out"
would this have meant that she thought
that by simply saying
"it is nice out" she had not been precise enough,
that she had not sufficiently asserted
how nice the weather was?
Probably.
But could she have said
"it is very nice out, it is even very nice out"?
No.
Why?
It is simply not said. If she had said
"it is even very nice out" after having said
"it is very nice out"
she would have applied the qualifier "even" to the utterance
"it is very nice out." But when one says
"it is very nice out" in no case does one say
it is nice out but not very nice,
which added on to the utterance "it is nice out"
would be as unlikely as "it is even very nice out"
and it follows that this "even" cannot apply
to the utterance
"it is nice out."

—Really?

And was it nice out?

—It was.

—RICHARD SIEBURTH AND FRANÇOISE GRAMET

Labeur du jour

Comme si c'était nous que le jour halait
si difficilement aux premières heures du matin,
comme si le jour peinait en nous
plus encore que dans le brouillard, et que le souffle
qui agite les feuilles des arbres et porte
un vol de pigeons d'une extrémité du ciel à l'autre
ne parvenait pas à animer en nous un paysage
encore voué à la nuit et à la pétrification,
et derrière les carreaux du monde, alors,
n'est plus qu'un fardeau pesant et gris
qu'il va falloir jeter sur l'épaule
et porter en butant sur chaque obstacle,
les yeux loin du ciel et de l'espace ouvert.

Encore le froid

Peupliers agités par le vent froid
dans la lumière basse, arasée,
la terre recluse en elle-même,
quelques feuilles encore sur le bouleau,
lampions éteints, un train passe au loin
évoquant le froid de la limaille,

Paul de Roux 1937–

NÎMES, FRANCE

D e Roux is a poet, translator, freelance writer, and editor in Paris. His work is based on the quotidian, a preference for the daily being central to contemporary French poetry. De Roux founded the journal *La Traverse* (1969–1974). Principal works: *Entrevoir*, 1980; *Les Pas*, 1984; *Le Front contre la vitre*, 1987; *Poèmes des saisons*, 1989; *Poèmes de l'aube*, 1990; *La Halte obscure*, 1993; *Le Soleil dans l'oeil*, 1998; *Allers retours: Poèmes*, 2002.

The Day's Labor

As if it were us the day were hauling
so painfully in the early hours of the morning,
as if the day labored in us
more even than in the fog, and the breeze
which shakes the leaves
and sweeps a flight of pigeons across the whole sky
could not revive the landscape in us
still vowed to darkness and petrifaction,
and beyond the panes the world
is merely a heavy grey burden
which we have to shoulder and carry
tripping on every obstacle
eyes turned from the sky and open spaces.

—STEPHEN ROMER

The Cold Again

Poplars shaken in the cold wind,
in a low, curtailed light,
the earth withdrawn into itself,
a few dull leaves on the birch;
a remote train passes,
conveying the coldness of iron,
and the station with its icy winds

la gare au courant d'air glacial
où l'on a accompagné un ami, où les quais vides
sont la piste crissante vers les étoiles cachées.

Localité

une discrimination angulaire
accompagne la proposition

le nom que je donne à un corps

mettre au clair l'usage
bouche ouverte dans l'abandon

« une autre grammaire »

where you dropped off a friend, and where the empty platform
is a whistling track to the hidden stars.

—STEPHEN ROMER

Claude Royet-Journoud 1941–
LYON, FRANCE

R oyet-Journoud is a poet more interested in literal transcriptions of
reality than in metaphorical, musical, or other descriptions of the
world. Along with Anne-Marie Albiach and Michel Couturier, he
founded and directed the review *Siècle à mains* (1963–1970). The three published
such poets as Louis Zukofsky, Edmond Jabès, Serge Gavronsky, and John Ash-
bery, in addition to contributing their own works. Royet-Journoud also edited
two volumes of American poetry with Emmanuel Hocquard: *21 + 1: Poètes
américains d'aujourd'hui* (1986) and *49 + 1: Nouveaux poètes américains* (1991).
Principal works: *Le Renversement,* 1972; *La Notion d'obstacle,* 1978; *La Lettre de
Symi,* 1980; *Les Objets contiennent l'infini,* 1983; *Une méthode descriptive,* 1986;
Milieu de dispersion, 1986; *Porte de voix,* 1990; *Les Natures indivisibles,* 1997.

Locality

an angular discrimination
accompanies the proposition

the name I give to a body

to make clear the usage
mouth gaping in surrender

"another grammar"

la distance paraissait grande
au bord du canal
sans mesure ni exploitation

Secrète au grand jour

> « . . . *Toujours plus lente, et tes gestes pris peu à peu dans la glu d'une étrange torpeur,*
> *immobile enfin, tellement perdue que ma voix ne peut plus t'atteindre . . .* »
> —*Gustave Roud*

ÉTAT I

NOIRE,   telle âme en exil   s'achemine lentement vers
la mort.   Voici l'hiver.   Le corps des mendiants se tord sur
une bouche de métro.   Ce n'est pas ce froid que je crains ni la
faim du ventre bien que mendiant à ton seuil,   les membres
bleus. C'était mon histoire déjà   vivre pour t'aimer me perdre
dans la nuit de ma ceinture.

it seemed a great distance
to the brink of the canal
unreckoned and put to no use

—KEITH WALDROP

Habib Tengour 1947–
MOSTAGANEM, ALGERIA

Tengour is one of the foremost contemporary Maghrebian poets. His work focuses on the postcolonial and nomadic condition of his people. Tengour's father was a militant nationalist, and when Tengour was five, the family moved to France to escape persecution by the police. After studying sociology and anthropology, Tengour returned to Algeria to complete his national service. His writing concerns issues of identity and the invention of a narrative structure beyond traditional French lyric form. Principal works: *Tapapaktaques, la poésie-île*, 1976; *La Nacre à l'âme*, 1981; *Schistes et Tahmad II*, 1983; *Sultan Galiev, ou la rupture de stocks*, 1985; *L'Épreuve de l'Arc*, 1990.

Secret in Broad Daylight

> "... *Always slower, and your gestures caught little by little in the glue of a strange torpor, finally unmoving, so lost that my voice can't reach you any longer* ... "
> —*Gustave Roud*

STATE I

BLACK,   such a soul in exile   slowly makes its way towards
death.   Here's winter.   The body of the beggars twists at
a subway opening.   It's not this cold that I fear or the stomach's hunger
although a beggar at your threshold,   my limbs blue.
It was already my story   to live to love you to lose myself
in the dark of my belt.

Je me suis masqué au moment de l'accueil.
Les amants ont souffert une passion, se sont séparés.
Gardes-tu en mémoire mon aimée cette agonie déployée dans l'
écume rose du matin
la fenêtre dans la mer demeure-t-elle reconnaissante?

ÉCLATANTE   l'   âme au comble du désir
elle tourbillonne dans un ciel pur
se protège des regards envieux   libre

C'est un été qui porte une moisson bénie   offrande

Comment nos cœurs se sont-ils égarés dans la maison?

Il y avait un serpent pour garder le seuil   éconduire
tous étrangers.   Il y avait une telle impatience dans nos
corps épris...   et l'été qui allait finir dans la peine.

Mais dans l'instant les amoureux chantent   dansent
ne cessent de s'éblouir dans la lumière.

BLANCHE   l'âme qui s'est reniée dans son âme tremblée
elle glisse sans ivresse sur le corps étendu   à mi-chemin
(il dit : j'étais celui qui était mort   t'attendait
dans mon cœur il y avait ton empreinte depuis longtemps
elle dit : ma vie était vide   tu ne l'as pas remplie)
se discerne une trace qui est triste   que tu cherches
à effacer   C'est en vain que tu regardes ton visage   dans
le miroir de la salle de bains   Que regardes-tu   la bête
terrassée...   gémissante la bête aux grands yeux blessés
Elle dit : mon cœur a eu si mal   tu n'as rien su faire,
pauvre cœur qui ne voit pas   son âme saigner   à blanc

INQUIÈTE   mais reine mon âme dirige une cohorte d'anges
blessés au talon.   Elle exhorte son armée boiteuse au martyre
comme s'il s'agissait d'aller cueillir   dans les terrains de
parcours les premières fleurs du printemps.   Elle se trouble à
la vue du sang qui parsème les champs mal cultivés.   L'été va
bientôt venir tout incendier dans la plaine.   L'âme a ses
refuges haut dans la montagne   (jadis la tribu y fut enfumée)
J'ai survécu aux massacres mais mon cœur a   oublié le
battement familier des paupières,   et le supplice.

I put on my mask at the moment of welcome.
The lovers have suffered a passion, have separated.
Do you keep in your memory my beloved this agony unfolded in the rose
spray of morning
the window in the sea does it remain grateful?

GLEAMING   the   soul at the height of desire
it whirls about in a pure sky
protects itself from envious glances   free

It's a summer wearing a blessed harvest   offering

How   could   our   hearts   have   gotten   lost   in   the   house?

There was a snake to watch over the threshold   to turn away
all strangers.   There was such an impatience in our
bodies in love . . .   and the summer that would end in sorrow.

But right now the lovers are singing   are dancing
never ceasing to be dazzled in the light.

WHITE   the soul who denied itself in its trembled soul
it slides undrunken over the body stretched out   half-way
(he says: I was the one who was dead   waited for you
in   my   heart   had   been   your   imprint   for   a   long   time
she says: my life was empty   you didn't fill it)
a trace can be seen so sad   that you try
to wipe out   in vain you look at your face   in the
mirror of the bathroom   What are you looking at   the beast
laid low . . .   moaning the beast with the great wounded eyes
She says: my heart hurt so much   you couldn't do anything,
poor heart that doesn't see   its soul bleeding   white

DISTURBED   but queen my soul directs a cohort of angels
wounded in the heel.   It exhorts its limping army to martyrdom
as if it were a matter of going to gather   in the traversed
terrains the first spring flowers.   It is disturbed at the sight of the blood
sprinkled over the ill-cultivated fields.   Soon the
summer will come to burn all up in the plain.   The soul has its
refuges high in the mountain   (formerly the tribe was smoked in there)
I've survived the massacres but my heart has   forgotten the
familiar beating of eyelids,   and the torture.

Après si longue absence,
le cœur ne raconte plus ses exploits.
La veilleuse a cligné avant de s'éteindre au-dessus de

nos têtes flottantes.

La nuit est tombée   bleu   dans le jardin.

AVEUGLE   âme a perdu son cœur aimant ;
elle trébuche dans la peine.   Elle a mal à son cœur.
Elle s'agite   comme un coq égorgé sur le trottoir.
Elle a trop mal pour le dire à   tout le monde.
Elle est amoureuse à genoux   et nue !
Dans le crépuscule il y a des voix distinctes   du sang.
Ils sont nombreux — abandonnés — à tendre l'oreille   ou le
couteau   à chercher un chien dans la clairière   du feu.
Avec l'été tous nos amis sont partis.
Que de souvenirs . . .
Au moment de l'adieu ta vie devient transparente   aussi
peut-elle se
regarder sans peine.

ÉTAT II

NEUVIÈME heure   s'empare de mon âme l'étrangère
s'acheminant dans l'hiver et la faim   blême
au pas d'une porte   là tu te plies dans la nuit
pour consulter ta vie   celle transcrite
celle où   tu grelottais d'aimer si fort
devant la porte close   mesurais les heures
tu ne savais comment   découvrir ton âme
ni accueillir la peine dans le   cœur délaissé
passé la douzième heure   consulte sa mémoire
pour en saisir encore l'   agonie
revoir la mise en scène d'un désir   décédé
le matin les surprenait   écumant et rose
par la fenêtre bleue   le corps gonflé de joie
et la belle endormie   le jour   l'étrangère

ÉTRANGÈRE   corps scarifié   âme bleue
elle s'offre tourbillon au comble de l'   été
légère la vague éclate à la face du   ciel
bénis   les cœurs dilatés dans la lumière
cœurs égarés dans la blanche maison   là

After such a long absence,
The heart no longer tells its exploits.
The night light blinked before going out over

                                                   our drifting heads.
The night fell   blue   in the garden.

BLIND   soul has lost its loving heart;
it stumbles in sorrow.   Its heart is pained.
It thrashes about   like a cock its throat cut on the sidewalk.
It's too pained to say it to   everyone.
It is loving on its knees   and naked!
In the twilight there are distinct voices   of blood.
They are numerous — left behind — to bend the ear   or take out a
knife   to look for a dog in the clearing   of fire.
With the summer all our friends have left.
Such memories . . .
At the instant of farewell your life turns transparent   and so
it can look
at itself without grief.

STATE II

NINTH hour   the stranger takes hold of my soul
making its way in winter and hunger   pale
at a doorstop   there you bend over in the night
to consult your life   the one transcribed
the one where   you shivered from loving so
before the closed door   you counted the hours
you didn't know how   to discover your soul
nor to welcome sorrow in the   abandoned heart
past the twelfth hour   consults its memory
to grasp again the   agony
to see once more the setting of a desire   deceased
the morning surprised them   foamy and rose
through the blue window   the heart swollen with joy
and the lovely sleeping one   the day   the stranger

STRANGER   scarred body   blue soul
she offers herself tornado at the height of the   summer
lightly the wave splashes in the face of the   sky
blessed   the hearts dilated in the light
hearts lost somewhere in the white house   over

bas   en   bordure   de   la   mer   où   dansent   des   rayons
il y avait une garde secrète   familière
cette impatience   /lustres   l'été
commençant   été   il allait finir tel
enfer   des rêves exprimés
inaccomplis   ne reste que la tension sourde
des cœurs ballottés de gares routières   en
paradis   cœurs éblouis dans le merveilleux
instant d'   abandon inconnu   étrange bleue

BLEUE   la transe emporte l'âme incandescente
loin de   la ville où se pavanent nos rêves lourds
d'avoir rêvé à haute voix   échangé
leurs secrets au grand jour   c'est la jument Borâq
elle s'élève ailée ivre et tremble de s'   approcher
elle me regarde dans l'âme et l'   âme silencieuse
vainement   le cœur ravive l'empreinte   effacée
voilà qu'à nouveau ta vie s'étend dans le   vide
dans l'œil   qui cerne la tristesse de la bête
que tu interroges   elle ne répond pas
à terre le ciel   manteau qui couvre mal
le soir c'est un saignement   elle reste muette
transportée dans le vide de son âme   guérie
se confond avec sa veine   incandescente

INCANDESCENTE mon âme   / . . . incandescente/   aurore
dans la paume de l'aurore   cœur aimant
un galet se fendille   comme aimant
sur la grève   l'aurore distingue une intaille
remous roses et caresses portent le cœur à l'   âme
aurores successives auront poli la   texture
d'où vient que la nacre s'y dépose   étincelle
au premier rai sur la grève   parmi les galets
celui-là seul dressé au soleil dans le   blanc
de l'été   — vis-à-vis des chansons —   terrasses
une saison   nos âmes sont blanches de feu
sur la terrasse aveugle se réjouissent   chaux vive
vagues et brises murmurent dans le bleu de l'   intaille
ton regard   /écho à la mer   cœur   aurore

AURORE   une puis l'autre les cordes lâchent   Celles Noueuses
de maléfices   . . . réintègrent   l'œil bas   le repaire

there   at   the   edge   of   the   sea   where   the   rays   dance
there was a secret familiar   guard
this impatience   /candelabra   summer
beginning   summer   it was going to end a
hell   of the dreams told
unaccomplished   there remains only the dulled tension
of the hearts tossed about in the bus stations   in
paradise   hearts dazzled in the marvelous
instant of   unknown abandon   strange blue

BLUE   the trance bears away the incandescent soul
far from   the town where our heavy dreams strut
from having dreamed aloud   exchanged
their secrets in broad daylight   it's the Borâq mare
she rises winged tipsy and trembles at coming   closer
she looks in my soul and the   silent soul
vainly   the heart brings back to life the imprint   effaced
look how once more your life stretches forth into the   void
in the eye   which envelops the sadness of the beast
whom you question   she doesn't reply
on the earth the sky   a cloak scarcely covering
the evening something's bleeding   she stays silent
transported in the emptiness of her soul   healed
mingling with her vein   incandescent

INCANDESCENT my soul   / . . . incandescent/   dawn
in the dawn's palm   loving heart
a pebble splits open   as if loving
on the sand   dawn singles out a gem
rose tremors and caresses bear the heart to the   soul
successive dawns will have polished the   texture
how is it that the mother of pearl settles there   spark
at the first ray upon the sand   among the pebbles
this one alone standing in the sun in the   white
of summer   — facing the songs —   terraces
a season   our souls are white with fire
on the blind terrace are rejoicing   limestone
waves and breezes murmuring in the blue of the   gem
your gaze   /echoing the sea   heart   dawn

DAWN   one then the other the cords slip   Those Knotted
with evil spells   . . . reintegrate   the eye low   the repair

531

lorsque les deux amants se réveillent   il fait grand jour
dans le secret de leur âme   la table est servie
j'ai bien dormi   /dit-il/   tu dors très bien   /dit-elle/
c'est bon quand l'amour est violent   comme tu le fais
je n'ai rien fait dit-il   c'est un coup du destin
ce n'est pas mon corps et nous allons   en mourir
pour l'instant les deux lits étaient joints   la fenêtre
donnait dans le rêve à venir   rose   bleu   et musc
l'été dans son apogée   les enchantait
ce décor tombé les âmes sans   cœur
se tourmentent à l'   écoute la romance dénouée
et Celles dans l'aurore   au guet   déjà mains noueuses

Au pays des morts (extraits)

> Tiresias. — *Pourquoi donc, malheureux, abandonner ainsi la clarté*
> *du soleil et venir voir les morts en ce lieu sans douceur?*
> —*Odyssée*, XI

Ombres 1

Tous ces morts

lequel d'entre nous ira les interroger

nous faudra-t-il encore une hécatombe
et des larmes
pour que la route sous la terre nous soit tracée

à moins que ce vent qui nous déchire ne
nous ait fait perdre raison

au point de ne plus nous soucier de la rencontre

Ombres 2

Tous ces morts
quels noms invoquer dans le cercle

les mains tendues pour une prière d'adieu
du bout des lèvres

when the two lovers wake up   it is broad daylight
in the secret of their soul   the table is set
I slept well   /he says/   you sleep very well   /she says/
it's good when love is violent   as you make it
I did nothing he says   it's a trick of fate
it's not my body and we shall   die from it
for the moment the two beds were joined   the window
opened on the dream to come   rose   blue   and musk
the summer at its apogee   enchanted them
this setting once struck the souls without   a heart
torment each other in   listening to the romance unknotted
and Those in the dawn   watching   already knotted hands

—MARY ANN CAWS

In the Country of the Dead

TIRESIAS: *Why then, o unfortunate one, thus abandon the sunlight
and come to see the dead in this ungentle place?*
—*The Odyssey*, XI

Shadows I

All these dead

who among us will question them

will it still require a massacre
and tears
for the road beneath the earth to be traced for us

unless this wind that rips into us has
made us lose our reason

to the one point that we don't care about the meeting

Shadows 2

All these dead
what names should be called in the circle

hands extended for a prayer of parting
but reluctantly

on ne se lamente plus comme autrefois

tant de gens disparaissent chaque jour que le cœur
refuse d'enregistrer la douleur

est-ce là métamorphose

Ombres 3

Tous ces morts
que l'on ne voit jamais
était-il dans leur destin de mourir

femmes enfants jeunes gens vieillards et combattants
beaucoup sont semblables au pauvre Alpénor
pas même fichus de garder l'équilibre

les journaux leur consacrent parfois une rubrique
malgré la censure

on dit qu'ils sont nombreux alors on les oublie

Ombres 10

Tous ces morts
qui lentement se retirent de notre vie
que leur avons-nous offert durant tout ce temps
des mots trop décousus pour faire naître le poème
mots retenus par le remords ou cette peur
suspendue devant nos yeux
depuis l'aube des temps selon le dire ancien
des mots qui nous deviennent obscurs à l'usage
on s'interroge parfois sur les célébrations
leur faste n'allume pas l'étrange désir de mémoire

---

we don't wail the way we used to

so many people die each day that our hearts
refuse to register grief

is this a metamorphosis

Shadows 3

All these dead
whom we never see
was it part of their destiny to die

women children youths old men and soldiers
many are like poor Alpenor
not even able to keep their balance

the newspapers sometimes grant them a column
despite the censors

we say that they are numerous so we forget them

Shadows 10

All these dead
who slowly slip out of our lives
what have we offered them in all this time
words too unraveled to give birth to the poem
words held back by regret or that fear
suspended before our eyes
since the dawn of time as the old saying goes
words whose usage becomes obscure to us
we ask ourselves sometimes about the celebration
their splendor fails to illuminate our strange desire for memory

—MARILYN HACKER

Éloge de Robert Desnos

Parfois nous rêvons de jeunes femmes brunes un peu folles avec lesquelles il serait bon d'écouter Coltrane et Ornette Coleman jusqu'à des heures impossibles du petit matin le jour se lèverait sur des taffetas des brocarts des étoles — mais que ceci ne laisse pas supposer je ne sais quelle déliquescence nocturne — nous aurions fait l'amour selon les règles ancestrales avec quelque peu de perversité froide voire de distanciation je ne veux pas que vous m'aimiez me direz-vous vous deviendriez mon semblable Pareils à des gisants, non des cadavres, non deux bêtes accouplées le chiffre de vos lèvres sur mes hanches tel le carmin de vos ongles et de mon sang qui éclatera à midi.

Maintenant

Maintenant ils me disent que je ressemble aux enfants du mois d'août qui creusent des fossés dérisoires contre un château qui s'en effondrera. A peine enlevé le sable glisse, gicle, petite pluie qui me traverse et j'abandonne bientôt, yeux brûlés, les épaules recouvertes, les enfants pensent à la curée prochaine. Je n'ai même plus la force l'envie de tenter le dialogue Trahi désemparé que peut l'alcool sinon hâter l'échéance les coups de pelle vont pleuvoir J'aborde à la douleur que je narguais du haut de mon bonheur factice ils vont bientôt m'interroger, réclamer des éclaircissements je leur confie la date de mon suicide sans cesse reportée depuis neuf ans. Solitaire, guère solidaire je me débats mais je

Franck Venaille 1936–

PARIS, FRANCE

Venaille turned to poetry writing after having fought in the Algerian war and has written extensively on his war experiences. Venaille began and directed two magazines, *Chorus* (1968–1974) and *Monsieur Bloom* (1978–1981). His *La Descente de l'Escaut* won the Prix Mallarmé, Prix Wallonie-Bruxelles, and Grand Prix de Poésie de la Ville de Paris. Venaille has also done much radio work for France Culture. Principal works: *La Tentation de la sainteté,* 1985; *L'Apprenti foudroyé,* 1986; *Cavalier cheval,* 1989; *Les Enfants gâtés,* 1989; *Le Sultan d'Istamboul,* 1991; *La Halte belge,* 1994; *La Descente de l'Escaut,* 1995; *Capitaine de l'angoisse animale,* 1998.

In Praise of Robert Desnos

Sometimes we dream of young brunettes, a little mad, with whom it would be lovely to listen to Coltrane and Ornette Coleman into all hours, with the dawn rising on taffeta, brocades, stoles, but don't let anyone imagine some sort of nocturnal deliquescence—we'd have made love by ancestral rules with a bit of cold perversity, even distancing I don't want you to love me, you will say, for then you'd be like me Like those statues stretched out, not cadavers, not two beasts coupled the cipher of your lips on my hips like the scarlet of your nails and of my blood that will splash at noon.

—MARY ANN CAWS

Now They Tell Me

Now they tell me I'm like those August children digging ridiculous ditches next to a castle that will collapse from them. Scarcely is the sand taken away when it slides, spurts, scattering a light rain over me, and soon I give up, my eyes burned, my shoulders covered over, and the children are thinking about the next quarry. I don't even have the strength the desire to try any dialogue. Betrayed, vulnerable, what can alcohol do except hasten the moment when the spade will rain its blows upon me? I land in the pain that I was mocking from the height of my factitious happiness they are going to question me soon, demand clarification I hand over to them the date of my suicide which has been endlessly put off for

n'insulte personne (il faut dire que le sable commence à m'étouffer) la plage oscille ils vont bientôt enfumer mon terrier. Je t'aimais Un lit n'est qu'un lit et le sable ne grince pas, voici les cris les coups, cette fois-ci je suis *définitivement* blessé.

---

the last nine years. Solitary, not at all companionable, I struggle but don't insult anyone (I must say the sand is beginning to stifle me) the beach is wavering soon they will smoke out my burrow. I loved you A bed is only a bed and the sand isn't creaking, here come the cries the blows, this time I am *definitively* wounded.

—MARY ANN CAWS

6

1981–2002:
Young Poetry at the End of the Millennium

Pierre Alféri, Tahar Bekri, Olivier Cadiot, Jean Frémon, Liliane Giraudon, Guy Goffette, Michel Houellebecq, Franck André Jamme, Jean-Michel Maulpoix, Robert Melançon, Pascalle Monnier, Nathalie Quintane, Valérie-Catherine Richez, Amina Saïd, Christophe Tarkos, André Velter

I n the last two decades of the twentieth century, the explosion of new poetries was nothing short of remarkable. The pre-1966 heritage was far from forgotten; rather, it was capitalized upon in ever more ingenious ways. From Emmanuel Hocquard to the youngest writer included here, Pierre Alféri, the entire range of poetic possibilities has a distinctly optimistic tinge—perhaps for the reason that the darkest chapters of the century now lay fully two generations behind—though the era of rapid globalization has brought its own set of problems and challenges.

Poetic exchange remains the transatlantic currency for French, British, and American poets of various ages. Michel Deguy and Jacques Roubaud's anthology *Vingt poètes américains* (1980) is a testament to the power and importance of this exchange between like-minded poets working in different languages. Also in the 1980s, Emmanuel Hocquard and Raquel set up their Orange Export Ltd. In 1986, Hocquard edited, with Claude Royet-Journoud, *21 + 1: Poètes américains d'aujourd'hui* and, in 1991, *49 + 1: Nouveaux poètes américains,* further indications of a new openness to cross-Atlantic translation.

Openness in the realm of publication is reflected in the proliferation of little magazines in the last decades, some short-lived, some lasting. Consider Michel Deguy's *Po&sie,* which was founded in 1977 and continues strong today, its editorial board comprising such highly respected poets as Claire Malroux and Jacques Roubaud and such overseas correspondents as Pierre Joris, Christopher Middleton, and Nathaniel Tarn. And consider *L'Action poétique,* edited by Henri Deluy and founded by André Parinaud and Jacques Darras, with the poet Marie Étienne on its editorial board. A recent issue of the journal *Autrement,* entitled *Zigzag poésie: Formes et mouvements: L'Effervescence,* is filled with challenging pieces about performance poetry and debates concerning a few recent writings ("écritures") and poetry anthologies; several poems from that issue were chosen for this volume.[1]

Little poetry magazines continue to flourish in France, often subsidized by the government's literary agency. They bear such titles as *Doc(k)s, Double-Change, Java, Lungfull!, Nioques,* and *If*—pronounced "eef," referring, first, to the conditional *if,* second, to Le Château d'If, an infamous island prison where inmates inscribed their names on stone walls, and, third, to the yew from which bows for string instruments are created. Although these magazines are, in large part, defined by their differences, they belong to an international literary community that includes editors and writers associated with American publications such as *Chain, The Germ, Issue, Mirage,* and *Talisman.* The journal *Fence* has deliberately established itself on both sides of the Atlantic, with an equal number of editors on each shore; such a bold venture gives new luster to poetry. On the North American side of the Atlantic, we think of the endlessly experimental and venerable publishing house Burning Deck and its Série d'Écriture(s), edited by Rosmarie and Keith Waldrop, renowned among publishers and translators of poetry for their enduring optimism and hospitality—especially to emerging and lesser-known poets.

The rapid development of digitizing practices—which acted as a sort of leveler, allowing these smaller journals to succeed—raises serious questions about individual property: Who owns a poem, its translation, its presentation? But the open, intercontinental dialogue that characterized the last two decades of the twentieth century was ultimately able to transcend anxieties about globalization and technology. These changes do not obscure the art but indeed permit a greater participation in the literary process. Editors, poets, readers, and translators have all tried here to maintain a common goal: a poetics of possibility.

Note

1. *Zigzag poésie: Formes et mouvements: L'Effervescence,* ed. Frank Smith and Christophe Fauchon (Paris: Editions Autrement, 2001). *Pièces détachées: Une anthologie de la poésie française aujourd'hui,* ed. Jean-Michel Espitallier (Paris: Pocket, 2000).

Pierre Alféri 1963–

PARIS, FRANCE

A poet, essayist, and translator, Alféri has frequently collaborated with the visual artists Suzanne Doppelt and Jacques Julien. With Doppelt he founded the literary review *Détail*. He also founded *La Revue de littérature générale* with Olivier Cadiot. Recently he has begun producing films with the musician Rodolphe Burger, of the group Kat Onoma. In these performances, Alféri reads text as Burger plays the guitar, against a montage of flickering Hollywood films. Principal works: *Les Allures naturelles*, 1991; *Le Chemin familier du poisson combatif*, 1992; *Kub or*, 1994; *Sentimentale journée*, 1997; *La Berceuse de Broadway*, 2001.

Quand rien n'entraîne rien

1.

quand rien n'entraîne rien
ne s'agite au-dehors l'inertie
se fait agitation entraînement en vue
de rien mais d'un rien qui se fait
obstacle et le moindre contact
inverse le sens de la marche (ignorant
qu'on l'observe à travers deux fenêtres, un inconnu
s'habille, se déshabille, s'assied, se lève, décroche, repose
le combiné) : d'abord l'incohérence
de particules en suspension
puis la période. Un geste quotidien
filmé en vidéo
un geste rejoué, son aire
parcourue en tous sens comme un pas
de *breakdance* dont l'endroit n'est plus
que l'envers de l'envers, est déjà
autre chose : une forme
cristalline impassible.

2.

à la différence du kaléidoscope
où s'agitent des éclats
de verre teinté, le tomascope
pour paver le champ d'hexagones
y découpe un triangle
qu'il renverse
par-dessus chacun des côtés.
Un détail déplié
dont les bords deviennent des axes
de symétrie.

3.

en deçà d'une certaine allure
l'équilibre est rompu. Le bruit de la pièce
sur la tranche en fin de course virant pile
ou face, tournoyant sur l'arête
bruit qui hésite bruit
qui se concentre et qui renonce
est reconnaissable entre tous
comme le souffle du saphir quand le bras

When Nothing Entices Nothing

1.
when nothing entices nothing
stirs beyond inertia
becomes agitation impulse aiming at
nothing but a nothing in the
way and the slightest contact
reverses the directional flow (ignorant
of being observed through two windows, a stranger
dresses, undresses, sits, gets up, lifts up, sets down
the receiver): first the incoherence
of suspended particles
then the period. An ordinary movement
filmed in video
a gesture replayed, its space
run through in every direction like
a break-dance whose surface is only
the other side of the reverse, is already
something else: a form
impassive crystalline.

2.
unlike the kaleidoscope
where tinted glass
slivers shake, the tomascope
paves a field of hexagons
by cutting triangles
it reverses
over each side.
An unfolded detail
whose edges become axes
of symmetry.

3.
just this side of a certain pace
the equilibrium is broken. The sound of the piece
on its edge reaching the end turning tales
or heads, spinning on the tangent
sound that hesitates to sound
that concentrates and that renounces
is recognizable anywhere
like the gasp of the needle when the arm

se précipite vers le centre et le disque
s'immobilise. Alors
il ne s'agit pas de reprendre
de la vitesse mais de poser le bras
la tête sur l'appui pour voir
la contagion s'étendre
tomber tout ce qui bouge : corps incassables
des films muets (brimbalement
des images, indolence
de la bande-son).

4.
le mouvement sans contrainte
est un état (quasi solide —
le va-et-vient le même
au même endroit le plaque
l'astique) et ce qui reste
un pavement.

Bibliothèque

oui ça se fait aussi bien
qu'un musée le livre au pas
de course humer l'antique
chiffon l'encaustique au vol
dans ses plumes pour rabattre
au premier soupir des tranches
son caquet claquer la porte

Choriste

la première seconde elle
en rappelle une autre puis
elle-même à la seconde
le chœur en noir et les bras
croisés dans le dos de l'air
pincé qui s'engouffre dans
de l'air son tour est joué

rushes to the center and the record
holds still. Then
it's not a matter of starting up
the speed again but of placing the arm
the head on the fulcrum to see
contagion spread
to drop everything that moves: unbreakable bodies
in silent films (wobbling
images, indolent
sound track).

4.
unconstrained movement
is a state (quasisolid—
the back and forth the same
to the same place polish it
burnish it) and what remains
a pavement.

—CHET WIENER

Library

yes it can be done just like
a museum the book on
the run just sniff the age-old
rags the wood polish that flies
in your face and you shut it
up at the first sigh of the
spine and then you slam the door

—COLE SWENSEN

Choirist

the first second she reminds
you of someone else then of
herself the second second
the choir in black with their
arms crossed in back with the pinched
air that rushes out into
the air she has done her bit

—COLE SWENSEN

Retour en Tunisie
(extraits)

XIV

Sonnent
les criées
        au matin des émules prospères
        Sur les quais
        Nos pas comme des caisses vides
        Résonnent dans le secret malhabile

        Les voiles ramènent nos troubles bleutés

XV

Se déversent
dans nos journées
        Empreintes de mimosas en fleurs
        Les eaux croupies comme des sanglots
        Figés dans les lueurs d'attache
        Allégresse volée à la litanie

        L'ami dédiait des bergamotes sur la route

Tahar Bekri 1951–

GABÈS, TUNISIA

A poet, essayist, and literary critic, Bekri is not only one of the leading Maghrebian writers but also a specialist on Maghrebian literature. His work is marked by its revolutionary impulses and the author's search for and evocation of an *ailleurs,* an "elsewhere." Bekri was twice arrested and finally sent into political exile (1976–1989) for his militant action for democracy and justice in his country. In 1976 he settled in Paris. He writes in both French and Arabic. Principal works: *Le Laboureur du soleil,* 1983, 1991; *Le Chant du roi errant,* 1985; *Le Coeur rompu aux océans,* 1988; *Poèmes à Selma,* 1989, 1996 (in Arabic); *Marcher sur l'oubli,* 1991; *La Sève des jours,* 1991; *Les Chapelets d'attache,* 1993; *Journal de neige et de feu,* 1997 (in Arabic); *Les Songes impatients,* 1997.

Return to Tunisia

XIV

Sounding
  the criée
        in the morning the welloff rivals
        On the wharves
        Our steps like empty crates
        Resound in the unskilled secret

        Sails bring back our bluetinged troubles

XV

Spilling
  into our days
        Traces of flowering mimosas
        The waters stagnant as sobs
        Snared in the gleams of moorings
        Happiness stolen in litany

        The friend set aside some pears on the way

XVI

Ouvertes
aux rouge-gorges
dans les cercles pourpres
Les saisons révèlent à l'olivier
Leurs secrets
Livrés à la terre de ses rires neuve

Les flots répondent à l'appel du torrent

XVII

Au seuil
de l'ultime
course trébuchent nos chevaux sobres
Haltes de fortune
Et cantabiles à rebours
Les joutes perdent nos visages fauves

Au loin les souvenirs rongent leurs mors

XVIII

Et nous
tressons
de nos rayons orphelins
Des aubades
Qui percent l'étrange naufrage
Aux portes de la mer éplorée

L'eau vêtue de nos embruns obscurs

XIX

Au baptême
de la douleur
la clameur enlise nos rivages frêles
Et les paupières assoiffées de rivières

XVI

Open
to the redbreasts
          in crimson circles
          Seasons reveal to the olive tree
          Their secrets
          Given over to the earth new with its laughter

          Water answers the call of the torrent

XVII

At the threshold
  of the ultimate
          race our sober horses stumble
          Waystations of luck
          And cantabiles backwards
          The joustings lose our tawny faces

          In the distance memories champ at their bit

XVIII

And we
   weave
          from our orphaned shelves
          Dawning songs
          Piercing the strange shipwreck
          At the doors of the despairing sea

          Water clothed with our dark spray

XIX

In the baptism
   of grief
          the clamor mires down our frail shores
          And the thirsting eyelids of rivers

Nous avivons ébranlés les eaux dormantes
Là-bas. La présence étreint ses voix de sel

Dans la flamme des distances le poème fraternel !

Pourquoi je deviens un saint

J'avais installé sous l'arbre une sorte d'auvent fait de planches sous lequel étaient
dressés une table et un lit de corde qui me servaient à venir travailler l'été face au
canal de dérivation qui descendait du lac et à surveiller en même temps les lignes
de fond tendues à l'endroit où l'eau douce rencontrait l'eau salée et où pullulait
une sorte d'anguille blanche dont je capturais les alevins que je faisais grandir.

Plus de ciel
plus de pluie
je restais là à regarder puis travailler surveiller le canal qui fait une sorte de boucle
autour de l'arbre l'eau circulant en spirale et je pouvais voir les poissons tourner
autour des lignes.

We quicken the sleeping waters shaken
Over there. Presence enfolds its salt voices

In the distant flame the fraternal poem.

—MARY ANN CAWS

Olivier Cadiot 1956–
PARIS, FRANCE

In addition to poetry and novels, Cadiot has written librettos and plays. He cofounded the *Revue de littérature générale* with fellow poet Pierre Alféri. Like Alféri, he has also worked extensively with the musician Rodolphe Burger, their joint performances uniting poetry and music. Cadiot's operatic work includes a libretto for Pascal Dusapin's *Romeo and Juliet* (1989). His play *Soeurs et frères* (1993) was directed by Ludovic Lagarde, who has also directed plays by Bertolt Brecht and Anton Chekhov. Principal works: *Rouge, vert & noir*, 1989; *Futur, ancien, fugitif*, 1993; *Mes dix photos préférées*, 1994; *Le Colonel des Zouaves*, 1997; *Art Poetic*, 1999; *Retour définitif et durable de l'être aimé*, 2002.

Why I Became a Saint

Under a tree, I'd constructed a rough shed made of planks in which I'd put a table and a rope bed to use when I came to work in the summer. As it faced the main canal running down to the lake, I could keep an eye on the fishing lines dropped in at the precise point where the fresh water meets the salt water and supports a species of white eel whose young I captured and raised.

More sky
more rain
I stayed there to watch then to work to survey the canal which ran in a ring around the tree the water spiraling and I could see the fish turning around the lines.

Et je fermais les yeux
je ne voyais plus les branches ni le ciel
et je pouvais rester là
surveiller + travailler.

Le soir je devais continuer à faire le plan de l'île — préparatoire à la maquette en volume — en utilisant des hachures dont l'espacement est en raison inverse de la rapidité des pentes est égal au quart de la distance entre deux courbes consécutives comme j'avais appris à le faire à***.

Tout en dessinant je me rendais compte que je devenais de plus en plus contemplatif. Ça y est aujourd'hui je suis un saint — juste avant je n'étais pas un saint — aujourd'hui *Ça y est je suis un saint.* St X. décide de devenir un saint (on l'appellera désormais St X.) Un saint ? Oui. Mais comment ? Comment le devenir ?

C'est par ennui qu'X devient un saint, par pur désœuvrement, mais ça c'est encore « pourquoi il devient un saint » pas « comment ».

Et depuis quand ? Il est certain que si l'on mesure une côte accidentée il faut savoir s'arrêter sinon on doit tenir compte de l'angle d'un caillou ou de la disposition d'un grain de sable.

LE SAINT

Dans ma cellule à écrire — relire — consulter — sur l'estrade en forme de maison surélevée — avec les hautes fenêtres de l'espace contenant — le lion arrêté sur le carrelage — le paon inactif et la perdrix absente — les oiseaux zébrant les fenêtres en haut — pâle jour autour — moi logé dans l'espace en bois ingénieux — comme rangé dans un bureau — écrivant dans un meuble — pensant dans les tiroirs — tout autour noir — le lion au fond gambadant sur le carrelage. La perdrix absente et le paon inactif.

Hep !

Hep !

Hé* bonjour* mes enfants**

(lé-zenfants)
l' le. — les petits, l', le
approchez, halte !

« cible »

And I closed my eyes
I no longer saw either branches or sky
and I could stay there
to survey + to work.

In the evening I had to continue to map the island—precursor to the scale model—using cross-hatchings whose spacing in inverse relation to the slope is equal to a quarter of the distance between two consecutive curves as I'd learned to do at***.

As I was drawing, I realized that I was becoming more and more contemplative. And that's why today I am a saint—yesterday I wasn't a saint—but today *Just like that I'm a saint.* St. X. decides to become a saint (we'll call him St. X. from now on) A saint? Yep. But how? How did he become a saint?

Through boredom X became a saint through boredom, through sheer laziness, but that's still "why he became a saint" not "how."

And since when? It's well known that if you set out to measure a rough coastline you'd better know where to stop or you'll end up having to consider the angle of every stone and the position of every grain of sand.

THE SAINT

In my cell to write—reread—consult—on a raised dais its own home—with high windows on the space containing—the lion on the flagstones poised—the peacock on hold and the partridge dazed—birds striating the windows above—pale day around—me living a space of intricate sculpted wood—writing-studio-as-coat—to write inside a desk—thinking in the drawers—a cool dark all around—with lion in the background ballet upon the flagstones. The partridge dazed and the peacock on hold.

—COLE SWENSEN

Psst!

Psst!

Eh* *bonjour** kids**

Les Kids
ze ze—little ones, ze
approach, halt!

"target"

C'est [f]FORmidable! Ah! le
[m]MIsérable! la [c]CAnaille! Oh! les [b]BANdits!—Toujours aussi
bête . . . Il prononce bbête

voir clair

clair (fort clair, bien clair, etc.)
disperser/ se disperser, ouvrir/ s'ouvrir

aussi clair, plus clair, moins clair
une douleur minuscule (. . .)

cataclysme
cataclysme

il s'ensuit,

conclusion

De visu: pour l'avoir vu
J'aime à regarder le vert
bleuâtre, grisâtre, noirâtre, rougeâtre, verdâtre, blanchâtre

quelquefois, souvent, tantôt, toujours, tard, tôt, etc.

de l'eau
le goût de l'eau
je vois des arbres
l'ombre des arbres
la fin est venue (. . .); la voilà
catastrophe/ catastrophique
en conséquence de quoi, en conséquence

This is [f]FORmidable! Ah! ze
[m]MISerable! ze [r]RIFFraff! Ug! ze [b]BANdits!—Everyday so
dumb . . . He pronounces it ddumb

to see clear

clear (clear indeed, so clear etc)
disperse/disperses, open/opens

oh so clear, more clear, less clear
a tiny pain (. . .)
(a minuscule dolor)
cataclysm
cataclysm

it follows

conclusion

By seeing: in order to have seen

I love to look at green
bluish, greyish, reddish, greenish, whitish
(*noirish*)

sometime, often, soon, everyday, late, early, etc.

of water
the taste of water
I see trees
the shadow of trees
the end is come (. . .): *voilà*
catastrophe/catastrophic
in consequence of what, in consequence

le beau ciel
                gris, natal

éternel, extrême, unique, etc.

le plus petit
le moindre
le plus mauvais
le pire

le temps écoule $\left\{\begin{array}{l}\text{la rivière}\\\text{la journée}\end{array}\right\}$

$\left\{\begin{array}{l}\text{la rivière}\\\text{la journée}\end{array}\right\}$ s'écoule

(silence.) silence de mort. (grand silence.)

Ah! (joie, douleur): ah! quel bonheur!
Ha! (surprise): ha! que dites-vous!
Oh! (crainte): oh! le monde!
Ho! (pour appeler): ho! là-bas!
Eh! (surprise): eh bien!
Hé! (pour appeler): hé! là-bas!

———————————————

the beautiful sky
grey, native

external, extreme, unique, etc.

the most little
the least
the most bad
the worst

the time flows { the river
the day }

{ the river
the day } flows

(silence.) dead silence. (grand silence.)

Ah! (joy, sadness): ah! what good news!
Ha! (surprise): ha! what you say!
Ug! (disgust): ug! the world!
Eh! (to call): eh! over there!
Oy! (chagrin): oy veh!
Oh! (to call): oh! over there!

—CHARLES BERNSTEIN AND OLIVIER CADIOT

L'Automne

Le Shogun, soucieux d'ajouter à sa gloire, avait ordonné qu'un grand concours de peinture se tînt au palais. Stimulons l'émulation, suscitons des joutes, pensait-il, que tous rivalisent pour me plaire. L'écho d'un tel tournoi, s'il est brillant, passera les frontières et les autres souverains en seront jaloux.

Des avis furent envoyés dans les villages les plus reculés, dans les monastères, dans les ermitages. Tous les peintres-poètes du royaume étaient requis au vingt-sixième jour de la quatrième lune sur les terrasses de l'Ouest. La règle édictée était d'apporter son matériel, rouleaux de papier ou de soie, pinceaux et brosses, bâtons d'encre et coupelles, et de se faire inscrire auprès du lieutenant de la garde. À l'appel de son nom, chacun devrait improviser une peinture devant le souverain, les hauts dignitaires et les juges, puis dire un poème inspiré par la peinture, qu'il en soit le commentaire ou seulement le titre. Il était loisible aux candidats de composer un poème sur-le-champ ou de faire appel à leur mémoire des anciens. Afin de comparer ce qui est comparable et de choisir le vainqueur sans risque d'erreur, un thème unique serait dévoilé au dernier moment.

Pour se préparer au concours, plusiers méthodes.

L'un s'était assis sur ses talons et avait longuement observé la montagne qui fait face à sa cabane, tentant d'y distinguer la naissance des sources, le rebond des cascades, comment les nuages enveloppent le sommet avant que le soleil n'apparaisse, de quelle couleur sont les pans coupés des rochers, du moins ceux qui

Jean Frémon 1946–

PARIS, FRANCE

An accomplished poet, novelist, art critic, and essayist, Frémon explores the meaning of lists, collections, and definitions in his writings. He has written numerous essays on contemporary artists. Currently, he directs the Galerie Lelong in Paris, a contemporary gallery representing artists such as Joan Miró and Andy Goldsworthy. Principal works: *Le Miroir, les alouettes*, 1969; *L'Origine des légendes*, 1972; *Ce qui n'a pas de visage*, 1976; *Échéance*, 1983; *Le Jardin botanique*, 1989; *Éclipses*, 1990; *Silhouettes*, 1991; *La Vraie Nature des ombres*, 2000.

Autumn

The Shogun, always on the lookout for ways to increase his glory, decided to hold a grand painting competition at the Palace. "Stimulate rivalry, incite confrontation," he thought. "In short, pit them all against each other in an effort to please me. News of such a competition, if it's a good one, will spread far beyond our borders, and all the other kings will be jealous."

So announcements were sent to the most distant villages, the most remote monasteries, and even to the huts of hermits. Every painter-poet in the kingdom was required to present himself on the West Terrace on the twenty-sixth day of the fourth moon. The edict demanded that each bring his own materials, including a roll of paper or silk, various brushes, ink sticks and inkstones, and register with the lieutenant of the guard upon arrival. When his name was called, each would then improvise a painting on the spot, before the sovereign, the high ministers and the judges, following it with a poem inspired by the painting, constituting either its commentary or its title. The painters could choose either to create their own poems or to select something from the standing body of literature. In order to ensure true improvisation and thus enable a clear choice of victor, it was decided that the theme of the works would be disclosed only at the last minute.

Each painter had his own way of preparing for the contest. One sat on his heels and minutely observed the mountain in front of his cabin, determining the precise location of the springs, memorizing the echos of the waterfalls, noting the uncanny way the clouds enveloped the summit just before dawn, the exact color of the rock faces left exposed to the sun. He studied the precise shapes of empti-

ne sont pas dans l'ombre, la forme des intervalles entre les arbres, les allées et venues des pêcheurs au bord du lac et l'échelle respective des êtres et des choses.

L'autre s'était exercé pendant des heures chaque jour afin de retrouver dans son poignet le délié qui lui permettait de tenir le pinceau sans rigidité ni faiblesse afin que les noirs ne soient pas bouchés et que les couleurs brillent de tout leur éclat.

Un troisième emprunta à la bibliothèque du palais un album de modèles et, ayant passé de l'huile sur du papier de riz afin qu'il fût translucide, il s'employa à reporter le plus fidèlement qu'il pût les contours des images des maîtres anciens.

Au lieu de se préparer, Hokusai donnait du grain à ses poulets et s'asseyait à l'ombre d'un grand arbre au bord de la rivière Tatsuta pour rêvasser.

Au jour dit, tous se rassemblèrent, les dames de la cour portant leurs plus beaux atours, les dignitaires prenant l'air important comme ils savent le faire, les juges s'efforçant de ne rien laisser paraître de leur humeur. Précédé des tambours et des cithares, le souverain franchit les neuf enceintes et prit place entouré des majordomes. C'est alors que le directeur adjoint aux rites dévoila le thème du concours : l'automne.

Celui qui s'était préparé en observant le réel pensa : je sais, pour l'avoir vu, qu'à l'automne les sources rejaillissent, que les nuages qui coiffent la montagne sont blancs, que les grottes et cavités apparaissent dans les rochers parce que les feuilles des arbres sont moins nombreuses et les fourrés moins fournis.

Celui qui avait exercé son poignet pensa : les couleurs doivent rester transparentes pour garder vie, même si la vie en automne a la splendeur fragile du déclin, l'encre doit se rétracter sur le papier comme la sève dans le moindre brin d'herbe, d'apparents inachèvements dans la composition seront comme les feuilles manquantes des arbres ou les trouées entre les amas de nuages, pour cela, il convient que le pinceau ne fasse qu'effleurer le papier et ne revienne jamais en arrière.

Celui qui s'était adonné à la copie des anciens tentait de se remémorer comment les uns et les autres avaient exprimé la calme tristesse de la saison, de quelle couleur il convenait de peindre la lune, si l'on voyait plutôt des grues ou des passereaux, il est sûr qu'il n'y avait plus de grillons ni de libellules au dessus de l'étang.

ness that reign between trees and the comings and goings of the fisherman on the lake, with particular attention to the relative order of beings and things.

Another exercised for several hours a day in order to keep his wrist supple enough to hold the brush without a trace of stiffness or weakness, thus ensuring that the blacks would not go flat and the colors would ring with all their brilliancy.

A third borrowed a book of models from the Palace library, made some tracing paper by painting rice paper with oil, and diligently copied the works of the ancient masters, following their sweeping contours as faithfully as he could.

For his preparation, Hokusai fed his chickens and sat in the shade of a large tree on the banks of the Tatsuta River, daydreaming.

On the stated day, everyone gathered—the women of the court dressed in their finest, the dignitaries adopting the important air they adopt so well, the judges making sure that none of their natural sense of humor showed. Preceded by drums and cythars, the sovereign crossed the nine thresholds and took his place, surrounded by his highest ministers. Only then did the Director of Rites reveal the competition's theme: Autumn.

The one who'd prepared himself by closely observing reality thought, "Ah, autumn, now that's something I know well because I've seen it—the springs surge up, the mountain is coiffed in white clouds, and crevices and grottoes appear in the rocks because there are fewer leaves on the trees and the undergrowth is sparser."

He who had exercised his wrist thought, "The colors must be kept transparent to keep them alive; even if autumn has the fragile splendor of decline, the ink must sink deep down into the paper like the life force does in the slightest blade of grass. The apparent gaps in the composition will echo the leaves missing from the trees and the openings between the banks of clouds. In order to capture that properly, the brush must just graze lightly across the surface, never retracing its path."

And the one who had given himself up to copying the ancients tried to remember exactly how various earlier painters had evoked the calm melancholy of the season, what precise color the moon should be, and whether it should be populated with sparrows or cranes. Certainly, there would be no crickets or dragonflies still hanging around the pond.

Hokusai arrive le dernier, un panier à la main et un rouleau sous le bras. Il déploie le papier sur le gazon ras de la terrasse de l'Ouest, place un poids à chaque angle. Dans une coupelle, il dilue de l'encre bleue, il ajoute de l'eau en abondance afin que la solution reste fluide et transparente. Il pose la coupelle sur le bord du papier.

Dans un bol qu'il garde près de lui, il verse un peu d'encre rouge de la sorte qu'on utilise pour les sceaux qui garantissent les documents officiels.

De son panier, il tire un poulet qui avait les pattes liées et qui néanmoins se débattait avec énergie. Le tenant fermement par les ailes, il lui trempe les pattes dans l'encre rouge.

D'un coup de pied, il renverse la coupelle d'encre bleue, le liquide se répand sur le papier et s'échappe dans l'herbe. Avec son canif, il tranche les entraves de l'animal qui se sauve en courant tout le long du rouleau, laissant derrière lui une traînée d'empreintes brillantes.

Hokusai se prosterna devant le shogun et dit:

> C'est l'automne
> les feuilles de l'érable
> glissent au fil de l'eau.

Après avoir consulté les juges, le souverain dit: «Comment vous nommez-vous et comment se nomme votre poulet? Assurément l'un de vous deux mérite la palme, mais je ne sais pas encore lequel l'emportera.»

Hokusai répondit, c'est du moins ce qu'on raconte: «Seigneur, dans tous les royaumes voisins il y a des paysans qui élèvent des poulets. Un seul souverain a pour humble sujet un vieillard fou de dessin qu'on nommait autrefois Hokusai.»

Hokusai arrived last, a basket in his hand and a roll of paper under his arm. He unrolled a length across the grass beside the West Terrace and anchored it down with a weight at each corner. He then mixed some blue ink in a little cup, adding a lot of water to keep it fluid and transparent, and placed it beside the paper.

He poured some red ink, the sort used for the seals of official documents, into another bowl at his side. From his basket, he drew out a chicken, flapping and squawking, ready for a fight, even though its legs were bound. Holding the bird firmly, he dipped its feet into the red ink. Then with a little kick, he overturned the cup of blue ink, spilling it across the paper and into the grass. With a flick of his knife, he cut the cords, freeing the bird, who set off across the paper, leaving behind her a brilliant trail of red.

Hokusai bowed low before the Shogun, saying,

> Autumn, the
> maple leaves
> glide downstream.

The sovereign turned to consult his judges and then asked, "What's your name, and what's your chicken's name? One of you has certainly won, but I haven't yet decided which."

Hokusai (it is said) replied, "Sire, in every kingdom around, there are peasants who raise chickens, but only one sovereign has for a humble subject an old man mad about drawing named Hokusai."

—COLE SWENSEN

Quand il n'y a plus rien à attendre (extraits)

Quand il n'y a plus rien à attendre
La poursuite d'un état
Cette chose ou une autre
Il est l'heure mais ce n'est plus
Le moment

Le coeur rincé
L'envie de rire
Le sens d'un mot

Quand la réponse est dans le titre
Un seul revers
Ou coup du sort

Si tu venais à manquer simplement une marche
                           Par exemple
J'ai contrôlé une insomnie de trois heures à six heures
Agitée par un vin nommé "Sang des pierres"
Un Vaqueyras bu doucement dans le cri des martinets

Liliane Giraudon 1946–

FRANCE

A poet and novelist, Giraudon is also a contributor to and cofounder and editor of many reviews. She was on the editorial board of the journals *Action poétique* (1977–1980) and *Impressions du sud* (1985–1993). She cofounded the journal *Banana Split* (1980–1990) with Jean-Jacques Viton. In 1982, with Viton and several others, she began *Quatuor manicle*, and in 1992 her journal *If* appeared. Giraudon organized a festival series entitled "Rencontres internationales de poésie contemporaine," which was held in Cogolin, France, in 1984, 1985, and 1986. She currently lives in Marseilles. Principal works: *Je marche ou je m'endors*, 1982; *La Réserve*, 1984; *Divagation des chiens*, 1988; *Pallaksch, Pallaksch*, 1990; *Les Animaux font toujours l'amour de la même manière*, 1995; *Anne n'est pas Suzanne*, 1998; *Parking des filles*, 1998.

When There's Nothing Left to Wait For

When there's nothing left to wait for
Tracking a state of being
That thing or another
It's time but no longer
The moment

The heart rinsed out
Wanting to laugh
The meaning of a word

When the answer is in the title
A single reversal
Or a stroke of fate

If by chance you were simply to miss a step
                                For example
I mastered my insomnia from three to six A.M.
Worked up by a wine called "Sang des pierres"
A Vaqueyras slowly drunk near the cry of swifts

A deux pas de la Sorgue
                          Une femme disait
J'ai un petit carnet avec la liste des amis morts
Quand j'éprouve le besoin
De l'ouvrir
                          Chaque mot
L'expression d'une existence entière
L'un d'eux m'appelle

Pourquoi les femmes appellent-elles
Plus souvent que les hommes
Le mot est le nom du lieu d'où nous parlons

———————————

Close by the river Sorgue
                        A woman said
I've got a small notebook with a list of my dead friends
When I feel like
Opening it
                        Each word
The expression of a whole life
One of them calls out to me

Why do women call out
More often than men
The word is the name of the place we're speaking from

—SERGE GAVRONSKY

Guy Goffette 1947–
JAMOIGNE, BELGIUM

Goffette, a poet, literary critic, and editor, has always followed his idiosyncratic interest in a wide range of pursuits. Between 1980 and 1987 he published the review *Triangle* with a group of fellow poets. Since 1983 he has directed the publishing house L'Apprentypographe, which is dedicated to publishing small handmade books by authors such as Umberto Saba and Michel Butor. Goffette has contributed to the *Nouvelle revue française* and has translated a comprehensive collection of African American music, including the blues and gospel. He is currently an editor at Gallimard. Principal works: *Éloges pour une cuisine de province*, 1988; *Mariana, Portugaise*, 1991; *La Vie promise*, 1991; *Le Pêcheur d'eau*, 1995; *Verlaine d'ardoise et de pluie*, 1996; *L'Ami du jars*, 1997; *Elle, par bonheur, et toujours nue*, 1998; *Partance et autres lieux*, 2000; *Un manteau de fortune: Poèmes*, 2001.

Max Jacob

Priez pour le petit saltimbanque à croix
jaune, qui enviait le crapaud, priez

pour lui qui fut ange aux jours de défaite et
bête au laboratoire de l'échanson.

Cyprien là, Max ici, pitre qui crâne
comme un oeuf sous le chapeau et pleure sans,

pleure sang et eau les cent plaies du Seigneur
et puis change de peau, noir à Paris, blanc

à Saint-Benoît et arc-en-ciel à Drancy
pour célébrer la messe de l'Arlequin

qui ouvre le paradis. Priez pour Max,
roi de Boétie et prince des poètes

qui tant pria pour nous, repentant qu'un sein
peut toujours en cacher un autre, que sous

le masque une seule vérité se terre,
la même: «Nous allons mourir tout à l'heure».

Le Relèvement d'Icare: Envoi

Je me souviens comme l'enfant tire sa mère
par le bras, à gauche à droite: un vrai petit
cheval de cirque, et comme elle

continuait sa marche, fière et sourde statue
dont la tête coupée dans un autre temps
avait roulée parmi les fruits, les légumes,

dans le panier accroché à sa main
avec les projets, les amours, les mille et une
nuits d'attente rangés sur l'étagère invisible

Max Jacob

Pray for the little acrobat with the yellow
cross, who envied a toad, pray

for him, an angel on days of defeat and
the cupbearer's laboratory animal

Cyprien there, Max here, clown who's bold
as an egg beneath his hat and weeps when bald

weeps blood and water all the Saviour's wounds
and then switches skins, black in Paris, white

in St-Benoît, a rainbow at Drancy
to celebrate the harlequin's mass

which opens Paradise. Pray for Max
king of Boeotia and prince of poets

who prayed so much for us, repeating that one breast
may stand in for another one, that beneath

the mask there's only one truth hidden
the same one: "We're going to die in a while."

—MARILYN HACKER

The Raising of Icarus: Envoi

I remember how the child was tugging his mother
by the arm, from left to right, a real
little circus horse, and how she

continued walking, a proud, deaf statue
whose head, cut off in another era
had rolled amidst the fruits and vegetables

into the basket hooked over her arm
with the plans, the loves, the thousand and one
nights of waiting, stacked on an unseen shelf

qu'elle comptait, recomptait des lèvres.
Et lui qui tirait et sa mère résistait, sachant bien
de quelle valeur sont les ailes

confectionnées dans l'ombre avec des bouts
de ficelle et des plumes d'édredon,
et de combien leur poids dépasse un espoir

d'homme dans la balance des vents,
elle qui, tant et tant de fois déjà,
derrière les persiennes de sa chambre,

enfanta Icare en criant.

---

that she counted over, barely moving her lips.
And he pulled and his mother resisted, knowing
very well what wings are worth

cobbled in the shade out of bits
of string and feathers from a comforter
and by how much they outweigh a man's

hope on the winds' scales,
she who already, how many times over,
behind the drawn blinds of her bedroom,

gave birth to Icarus screaming.

—MARILYN HACKER

Michel Houellebecq 1958–
RÉUNION, FRANCE

One of the best-known and most controversial of contemporary novelists, Houellebecq has professed disgust for almost all the leading movements in France since the 1960s. He has written passionately against psychoanalysis, against the breed of socialism defined by the student uprisings, and against the bureaucracy of the French university system. Sexual liberation and materialism, he believes, have led to an unraveling of modern society and account for the violence and despair that characterize it. Houellebecq has served as an administrative secretary in the Assemblée nationale. In addition to being an internationally known novelist, he is a best-selling poet in France. Principal works: *La Poursuite du bonheur*, 1991; *Rester vivant: Méthode*, 1991; *Extensions du domaine de la lutte*, 1994; *Le Sens du combat*, 1996; *Renaissance*, 1999.

Dans l'air limpide

Certains disent : regardez ce qui se passe en coulisse.

Comme c'est beau, toute cette machinerie qui fonctionne !

Toutes ces inhibitions, ces fantasmes, ces désirs réfléchis sur leur propre histoire. Toute cette technologie de l'attirance. Comme c'est beau !

Hélas j'aime passionnément, et depuis toujours, ces moments où plus rien ne fonctionne. Ces états de désarticulation du système global, qui laissent présager un destin plutôt qu'un instant, qui laissent entrevoir une éternité par ailleurs niée. Il passe, le génie de l'espèce. Il est difficile de fonder une éthique de vie sur des présupposés aussi exceptionnels, je le sais bien. Mais nous sommes là, justement, pour les cas difficiles. Nous sommes maintenant dans la vie comme sur des mesas californiennes, vertigineuses plates-formes séparées par le vide ; le plus proche voisin est à quelques centaines de mètres mais reste encore visible, dans l'air limpide (et l'impossibilité d'une réunification se lit sur tous les visages). Nous sommes maintenant dans la vie comme des singes à l'opéra, qui grognent et s'agitent en cadence. Tout en haut, une mélodie passe.

In the Limpid Air

Some say: look at what's happening behind the scenes.

How lovely, all this machinery working!

All these inhibitions, these phantasms, these desires reflected upon their own history. All this technology of the seductive. How lovely!

Alas, I have always loved, with great passion, these moments where nothing works any more. These states of disarticulation of the global system, which presage a fate rather than a moment, which suggest an eternity elsewhere denied. The genius of the species passes on. It is difficult to found an ethic of life on such exceptional presuppositions, I know. But we are here, precisely for difficult cases. We are now living as if on mesas in California, dizzying platforms separated by the void; the nearest neighbor is a hundred meters away, but remains visible anyway, in the limpid air (and you can read the impossibility of any reunification on every face). Now we are living like monkeys at the opera, mumbling and moving about in unison. Up there somewhere, a melody passes by.

—MARY ANN CAWS

Franck André Jamme 1947–
CLERMONT-FERRAND, FRANCE

Jamme has published widely, and produced several limited editions of poetry illustrated by such artists as Olivier Debré and Zao Wou Ki. His work has been praised by Henri Michaux and René Char, who asked him to oversee publication of Char's complete works in the Bibliothèque de la Pléiade (1983). Jamme, who lives with the painter and poet Valérie-Catherine Richez, works in both Burgundy and Paris. He currently serves as a consulting curator for contemporary tantrical Dusol Indian art. John Ashbery recently translated his *Récitation de l'oubli* into English. The poets appeared together on the French television show *Canapé* to discuss what makes a poet modern. Principal works: *L'Ombre des biens à venir,* 1981; *Absence de résidence et pratique du songe,* 1985; *La Récitation de l'oubli,* 1986; *Pour les simples,* 1987; *Bois de lune,* 1990;

Extraits de La Vie des scarabées
(extraits)

Et le paon repartait se pavaner seul dans le parc.

Ou bien un geste, simple : il traçait une diagonale sur les choses. Sur toutes les choses. Celles de son esprit, celles de ses yeux, celles de ses mains. C'était curieux, tout à coup : plus de dessus, plus de dessous, plus de haut ni de bas.

« Ne l'oublie pas, ta parole est dans ton dos, toujours passée, perdue dès que prononcée, à l'instant tranchée de toi-même. Mais elle repousse, regarde, chaque fois. Une vraie queue de lézard. Il n'oubliait pas. »

Le rêve, un matin peut-être : plus ce chahut des pensées.

Il se demandait s'il existait des pendules qui relâchaient un peu le mouvement quand on les appelait par leur nom.

Même une simple inflexion de la voix pouvait tout transformer, non ?

Il chantait ses listes : « L'arbre qui devine, la violence de l'illusion, la très savante machinerie des intérêts, ce qui enfermait, ce qui délivrait. »

Car ce qu'il cherchait encore, ce devait être aussi une parole indifférenciée, qui en aurait perdu son maître, son auteur — une aiguille de foin dans le foin.

Et le paon repartait se pavaner seul dans le parc, sous le regard de rien.

Le rêve, peut-être un soir : juste une sorte de grand sourire venant planer quelques secondes sur l'apaisement absolu.

Et puis la lumière, surtout. Qui s'amusait vraiment de l'air. Qui semblait, lui, constamment rire d'elle. Ce qui faisait que l'on ne pouvait jamais décider lequel des deux était le plus souple, le plus joueur. Même si la lumière, surtout.

Quand une larme roulait sur sa joue. Enfin.

578

De la multiplication des brèches et des obstacles, 1993; *Un diamant sans étonne-ment*, 1998; *L'Avantage de la parole*, 1999; *Encore une attaque silencieuse*, 1999; *Nouveaux exercises*, 2002.

Extracts from the Life of a Beetle

And the peacock, once again, started to strut about the park, alone.

Or rather a simple gesture: he drew a diagonal line across things. Across all things. Those of his mind, of his eyes, of his hands. Strangely, all of a sudden: no more up or down, no more high or low.

"Don't forget, your speech is behind you, always past, lost upon being uttered, at the very moment it is severed from you. But look, it grows back, each time. A real lizard's tail." He didn't forget.

Dream, one morning maybe: an end to this uproar of thoughts.

He wondered whether there were clocks which would tick a little slower when called by name.

Even a simple vocal inflection could change everything, couldn't it?

He sang out his lists: "Guessing tree, violence of illusion, clever machinery of interests, what imprisoned, what freed."

For what he still sought also had to be an undifferentiated speech, which had lost its master, its author—a needle of hay in a haystack.

And the peacock, once again, started to strut about the park, alone, unobserved.

Dream, maybe one evening: just a sort of big smile coming to hang, briefly, over the absolute appeasement.

And then, especially, the light. Which was actually making fun of the air. The air which appeared to laugh at it. Which prevented you from deciding which of the two was more supple, more playful. Even if, especially, the light.

When a tear rolled down his cheek. At last.

L'averse, dans le jardin, avait cessé. Ils étaient encore là, imperturbables :

— Il vaudrait mieux quoi, selon toi, maintenant ?

À vrai dire, j'hésite beaucoup.

La Récitation de l'oubli

Des yeux, puis une bouche. Et des taches, soudain, qui brouillaient ce visage, le ciel était bientôt criblé de mouches d'or. Je luttais, elle sentait, elle disait : « Si au fond rien n'apparaissait, ni ne disparaissait ? Tout voit, tout parle. »

Je soufflais, je ne savais plus, je soufflais. J'avançais au cœur de la force, c'était tout. « Tu verras un jour l'embrasure », disait-elle. « Ta désobéissance, anguille dans le sang du monde ; ta volonté, presque un désir. »

Chemin de l'est, pierreux, qui monte et qui demande ! Là-haut, l'ermite gardait le col, elle savait son histoire. Qu'il venait des plateaux du nord, du pays où sur le chapeau frise le duvet d'aigle ; qu'il animait les peaux et la vieille chanson. Il lui avait montré sa langue, un soir : « C'est sans appui que l'on profère. Tout vient par le ravissement. »

Elle disait : « Tu t'abandonnes et te recueilles. Ecoute, tu respires. Tu frôles parfois la racine — à peine, je le sais, mais je l'ai déjà vue trembler. Il n'y a rien derrière les choses, il y a seulement les choses. Qui se multiplient, et encore, et indéfiniment. Alors ? »

Et je me demandais : « Que fais-tu là, sur cette route, ton visage à la main — qui se mélange dans ses pas, pousse une pierre, comme ça, en pousse une autre ? Tandis qu'un seul trait rouge, sur l'ocre de la terre. Mur dormant d'énergie et de sang, de peur et de puissance. D'autres épreuves. T'es-tu trouvé, l'enfant ? T'es-tu perdu ? ».

Tu viens souvent

Tu viens souvent avec ton oiseau sur le poing. Enfin, on le voit. Tu viens et tu attends. Lui ne te ressemble pas, s'impatiente assez vite, gratte le gant de son maître, commence à y planter ses serres. Alors s'il s'agite de trop sous sa coiffe de

The downpour, in the garden, had stopped falling. They were still there,
unperturbed:

—What do you think would be best now?

To be honest, I'm really not sure.

—MICHAEL TWEED

The Recitation of Forgetting

Eyes, then a mouth. And spots, suddenly, that cloud this face, soon the sky was pitted with gold flies. I wrestled, she felt it, she said: "If, ultimately, nothing appears nor disappears? Everything sees, everything speaks."

I breathed out, I didn't know any more, I breathed out. I advanced toward the core of strength, that was all. "You'll see a doorway some day," she said. "Your disobedience, needle in the world's blood; your will, almost a desire."

Road of the east, stony, that climbs and exacts! Up there, the hermit kept watch over the pass, she knew his story. That he came from the northern plateaus, from the country where the eagle's down curls on the hat; that he brought to life the drum skins and the old song. He had stuck out his native tongue at her, one evening: "It's without any support that one utters. Everything comes to pass through enchantment."

She said: "You abandon yourself and you observe a few moments of silence. Listen, you're breathing. Sometimes you graze the root—barely, I know, but I've already seen it tremble. There is nothing behind things, there are only things. Which multiply, still, and indefinitely. So?"

And I wondered: "What are you doing there, on this highway, your face in your hand—that is muddled with its own footsteps, pushes a stone, like that, then pushes another. While a single red line, against the earth's ocher. Sleeping wall of energy and blood, of fear and force. Other trials. Did you find yourself, child? Did you lose yourself?"

—JOHN ASHBERY

Often You Come

Often you come with your bird on your wrist. That is, it would seem so. You come and you wait. He doesn't resemble you, loses patience quickly, scratches the glove of his master, starts to sink his claws in. When he grows too nervous under

cuir, c'est qu'il a senti une brèche et tu n'as plus le choix: tu lui ôtes son masque, desserres le fil de sa patte et le voilà parti. La moindre chose qui brillait ne fait jamais long feu. Et tu sais avec sûreté ce qu'il repère et tue, car il te le ramène. Mais ce qu'il a vraiment vu, là-bas, la chose hurlant de vie et de lumière, toujours tu la méconnaîtras: tu ne pourras jamais que décrire la prise qu'il dépose à l'instant à tes pieds—qui marmonne encore, c'est vrai, mais déjà de l'autre berge. En somme, tu es un aveugle. Ta chasse, une simple cueillette. Et pourtant, cet oiseau, tu n'as pas le plus petit souvenir de son bruissement dans l'air, ni de la courbe de son vol. Pour la raison qu'il est en toi. Tu n'as jamais pu repérer précisément où, mais tout cela se passe en toi.

La Mise au monde

1

Patience des anges endormis entre les caissons bleus du ciel. Patience des dieux au-dessus du larmier, à l'angle obtus des étoiles et de la terre . . .

his leather headpiece, it means he has felt an opening, and you don't have any choice: you take off his mask, undo the wire from his foot, and there he is, off. The least thing shining somewhere won't last long. And you know quite surely what he finds and kills, for he brings it back to you. But what he really saw over there, that thing shouting with life and light, you'll always see it wrong: you can only describe the prey he lays down right now at your feet—still murmuring, true, but already from the other shore. In short, you are blind. Your hunt, just a simple gathering. And yet, this bird, you don't have the slightest memory of his rustling through the air, nor the curve of his flight. Because he is in you. You have never been able to find exactly where, but it all happens in you.

—MARY ANN CAWS

Jean-Michel Maulpoix 1952–
MONTBÉLIARD, FRANCE

Maulpoix is a poet, essayist, and literary critic. He has notably written on fellow poets Henri Michaux, Jacques Réda, and René Char. Additionally, he has produced several general essays on poetry. In 1993 he cofounded the Centre de recherche sur la création poétique with Yves Charnet. Currently, Maulpoix teaches modern and contemporary poetry at the École normale supérieure de Fontenay Saint-Cloud and at the Sorbonne Paris VII. He also directs and edits the journal *Le Nouveau Recueil,* published by Champ Vallon. Principal works: *Portraits d'un éphémère,* 1990; *Une histoire de bleu,* 1992; *L'Écrivain imaginaire,* 1994; *La Poésie malgré tout,* 1996; *Domaine public,* 1998; *La Poésie comme l'amour,* 1998; *L'Instinct du ciel,* 2003.

The Giving Birth

1.

Patience of angels sleeping amid the sky's blue casings. Patience of gods above the dripstone, at the obtuse angle formed by stars and earth . . .

Que savons-nous de la fenêtre bleue par où la nuit montre tout à coup son visage de faïence? Lorsque mourir cogne à la vitre, la chambre est un coffret odorant de bois clair.

Tête lourde, comme un oeuf saturé sur la paume, j'écris à coups de coeur des mots somnambuliques. Ainsi des heures dans l'encre et la neige, des semaines de fougères et de givre infusant au bol bleuté de la chambre.
Un peu d'eau noire dans l'oeil du monde, et l'envie de se laisser glisser sous l'écorce du chant jusqu'à perdre l'idée de chair qui nous protège.

Mourir cisèle nos serrures et disperse des fleurs entre les digues, les baignades, les reins cambrés et les lavandes lointaines, criant victoire de ses mains blanches envoûtées de mouchoirs et de tumultes. Coque éblouie sous le gréement!

Ainsi résonne le coeur engorgé d'amour trouble qui bat sous la chemise de chair, tandis que le tilleul éclôt devant la fenêtre, recoloré comme un bateau neuf après une semaine de soleil et de bourrasques.
Un grand pavois de feuilles siffle dans les haubans!

2

Je rêve d'un poème en pluie sur les corolles, fécondant de ses étamines d'or une inflorescence de coeurs étoilés, faisant éclore d'autres planètes odorantes et soyeuses. Je marche dans le pré aviné sous l'averse parmi des fumées peintes.
Les pétales d'encre ont le goût de l'âme après l'amour.

Tandis que le printemps s'exclame, je vais sur la neige au fond du monde, frôlant le coeur fissible au plus bas de l'oeil et de l'os. L'encre alors cristallise et chante, blanche sonore de sel et d'acide entre les lèvres vitrifiantes de l'angoisse.

Toutes joies dévalées d'un trait, la mort abonde dans le sens de naître. Nous attendons dans le silence, paumes tièdes et bras ballants, ainsi que la jeune femme au bord du lit, le coeur en équilibre dans la nacelle de chair.

Bientôt un autre se relève, tirant les mailles du linceul, saluant la patience des dieux et la mer traversée de pollens. Des mots en ombelle lui couvrent le front.

3

Le bleu du ciel élance des oiseaux. D'impossibles semailles de chair et des voix inouïes. L'arbre a repris son souffle. Peau tiède, tissu doux, infusion verte du corps rêvé.
Dans l'âme épaisse de l'herbe, écrire naît à son chant.

What do we know of the blue window through which night suddenly shows its earthen face? When dying raps at the window, the room is a fragrant casket of light wood.

Feeling heavy-headed, like a saturated egg on the palm, heart pounding out a sleepwalker's words. Hours in ink and snow, weeks of ferns and hoarfrost fusing with the room's bluish bowl.
A little black water in the world's eye, and a longing to let oneself slip under song's husk, until one loses the idea of a protective skin.

Dying carves our latches and scatters flowers between the dikes, the baths, the arched backs and faraway lavender, shouting victory with its white hands bewitched by handkerchiefs and commotion. Dazzled hull beneath the rigging!

So echoes the heart engorged with muddled love, beating in its shirt of skin, while the linden blossoms outside the window, color restored like a new boat after a week of sun and gales.
A great bulwark of leaves whistles in the stays.

2.

I dream of a poem falling like rain on the corollas, its golden stamens fertilizing an inflorescence of spangled hearts, making other silky and sweet-smelling planets burst into bloom. I walk beneath the downpour in the drunken field, through painted vapors.
The ink petals have the same taste as the soul after love.

While spring cries out, I go off over snow to world's end, brushing past the fissionable heart at the lowest point of eye and bone. Then does the ink crystallize and sing, resonant white of salt and acid between the vitrifying lips of dread.

All joys downed in one stroke; death concords with birth. We wait in silence, palms moist and arms hanging limp, like the young woman on the edge of the bed, heart rocking in its little boat of flesh.

Soon another rises, pulling the stitches on the shroud, hailing the patience of gods and the pollen-crossed sea. Words like parasols cover his forehead.

3.

Birds thrust out from the sky's blue. Impossible seedings of flesh and unheard-of voices. The tree has caught its breath. Warm skin, soft fabric, green infusion of the body in dreams.
In the thick soul of grass, writing is born to its song.

Il fait un autre monde en boule dans le ventre des araignées et des fleurs. Des oeufs gris craquent. Des fables de plumes se disputent. Moisson de venins et de rires. Tant de meurtres féconds au bord d'un aquarium de larmes. La claire douleur où transparaît la joie.

Voici le poème revenu sur les épaules des anges. Au bout du long chemin d'images incroyables. Pâle au sortir de la mine de neige.
Voici le mot qui fut le soc et la cognée. Voici la plume d'or. Et soudain sur le tronc un long cortège de filles noires portant la graine dans leurs bras!

Arbre tressé de songes, linges et voix, tout l'amour à l'oeuvre dans les chambres des oiseaux . . .
Celui qui s'est assis dans l'herbe s'efforce de ne pas y croire. Chasseur toujours et menacé. Avide, scrutant l'obscur. Pourtant le coeur à neuf, prêt à cesser de battre.

It makes another world, curled up in the womb of arachnids and flowers. Gray eggs crack. Feather legends clash. Harvest of venom and laughter. So many fertile murders beside an aquarium of tears. Clear pain through which one glimpses joy.

Here is the poem brought back on the shoulders of angels. At the end of a long path filled with incredible images. Pale as it leaves the snow mine.

Here is the word that was the ploughshare and the felling ax. Here is the golden feather. And suddenly on the trunk a long procession of black-skinned girls carrying seed in their arms!

Tree woven from dreams, sheets and voices, all of love at work in the bird-chambers . . .

He who has sat in the grass tries not to believe in it. Hunter always, always threatened. Eager, peering into the dark. And yet the renewed heart, ready to stop beating.

—MARK POLIZZOTTI

Robert Melançon 1947–
MONTREAL, CANADA

A poet, translator, and scholar of French Renaissance literature, Melançon is also a renowned literary critic and translator. He received his M.A. and doctorate from the University François Rabelais in Tours and became a full professor at the University of Montreal in 1984. Melançon possesses a great knowledge of Canadian poetry and has translated the work of Earle Birney, one of the country's best-known poets. In the 1970s he published a bimonthly poetry chronicle in Le Devoir. He has done work for En toutes lettres on Radio-Canada since 1986. From 1974 to 1982 he was associated with the literary review Études françaises and from 1977 to 1985 with Liberté. Principal works: Inscriptions, 1978; Peintre aveugle, 1979; Territoire, 1981; Le Dessinateur, 2001.

Le Début de l'été

L'aurore se dissoudra
dans le bleu où tournera
le soleil. Tu écoutes
les rumeurs de l'espace qui s'ébauche,
tu parcours des yeux l'arc visible,
les saccades de la clarté rose
que fouille le vent. Voici
juin : une lyre d'herbe.

Éveil

Le rêve du fleuve
se dissipe à peine.
J'émerge de sa lumière
sans ombre comme un nageur
de l'étreinte de l'eau.
Je me penche à la fenêtre
et l'étrangeté
du matin me surprend.
Dans la rue sans bruit coule
l'aube, cette eau sans rive.

Beginning of Summer

Dawn will dissolve
in the blue where the sun
turns. You listen
to hints of space taking shape,
your eyes rove over the visible
arc and shock of the rosy light
sifted by wind. This is
June: a grass harp.

—PHILIP STRATFORD

Wakening

The dream of the river
is scarcely dispersed.
I emerge from its shadowless
light like a swimmer
from the water's embrace.
I lean out the window
and the strangeness
of the morning surprises me.
Into the street noiselessly spills
the dawn, a shoreless sea.

—PHILIP STRATFORD

Pascalle Monnier 1958–

BORDEAUX, FRANCE

Monnier has published articles and poems in the reviews *Banana Split*, *Action poétique*, *Les Lettres françaises*, and *La Métaphore*. She currently lives in Paris. During 1992 and 1993, she was a writer-in-residence at the Villa Medici in Rome. She collaborated on a new translation of the Bible for Éditions Bayard. Monnier also works frequently with visual artists. John

L'Été

1

Bon, c'est la chaleur.
Tu vois le tableau : fenêtres ouvertes, les premières mouches et aussi les bruits de
    motocyclettes
et le vent tiède avec des pointes de fraîcheur, les odeurs fraîches et pas encore
    l'été
(herbe coupée, bêtes crevant de chaud, huiles solaires, flaques de mazout, pizza
    brûlée).
Bouche contre bouche, jambes tordues, bras enlacés, mains collées, langues
    molles
(«*nous ne faisons, en cet instant, mon amour, sais-tu, qu'un, qu'un, qu'un!!!*»
autrement dit cri de désespoir, d'enthousiasme & de jouissance).
Tu vois le tableau.

L'Été

2

Ce sont les premiers beaux jours.
Les premiers beaux jours.
Les beaux jours reviennent.
L'arbre lentement va se couvrir de feuilles.
L'arbre va noircir, carboniser sous nos yeux.
La lumière sera blanche. Les arbres seront noirs sur le blanc de la lumière.
Des fleurs rouges vont sortir de terre.
L'herbe sera verte, puis jaune.
Le ciel sera très bleu le matin, très blanc à midi, très bleu le soir
et noir, noir!!! la nuit.
L'air va s'épaissir, devenir très épais, lent et lourd à déplacer.
C'est pour cela que les branches s'agiteront lentement,
très lentement.
Ralentir.
Le ralentissement.
La douceur.
La lenteur.
Nous marcherons très lentement.
L'air sera doux, mou, lourd.

Ashbery has translated much of her work into English. Principal works: *Les Pirates de la Havane*, 1986; *La Règne de Filostrate*, 1990; *Bayart*, 1995.

Summer

1

Good, it's hot.
You get the picture: windows wide open, the first flies and, in the background, motorcycle noise
and a warm wind tipped with cold, the cool smells and not quite summer
(fresh-cut grass, dogs exhausted in the heat, sun-tan lotion, oil stains, broiling pizza).
Mouth against mouth, legs intertwined, arms interlaced, hands embraced, tongues soft
(*"we make, at this moment, my love, don't you see, just one just one just one!!!"*
in other words: cry of despair, delight, desire).
You get the picture.

—COLE SWENSEN

Summer

2

These are the first fine days.
The first fine days.
The fine days have returned.
The trees will slowly be covered with leaves.
The trees will grow black, carbonize before your eyes.
The light will be white. The trees will be black against the white of the light.
Red flowers will spring from the earth.
The grass will be green, then gold.
In the morning, the sky will be so blue, so white at noon, so blue toward dusk
and black, black!!! at night.
The air will get heavier, grow very heavy, very slow and only lazily move.
And so the branches will move slowly,
very slowly.
To slow down.
The slowing down.
They slow down
softening.
We walk so slowly.
The air will be sweet, damp, heavy.

D'une grande lourdeur.
Lever le bras sera lent et difficile.
Les ombres, autour de nous, se déplaceront.
Elles seront grandes et très noires.
Très sombres.
Nous serons entourés de nos ombres.
Accompagnés de nos ombres.
L'ombre autour de l'arbre sera petite et claire le matin,
grande et sombre le soir.
L'arbre aura son ombre.
Les branches en s'agitant feront déplacer l'ombre des branches.
L'air sera dur, lourd, lent et les odeurs flotteront autour de nous.
Nous ne bougerons quasiment plus.
Nous regarderons.
Les branches qui s'agitent et font bouger les ombres.
L'ombre claire du matin et l'ombre noire du soir.
Le ciel sera bleu le matin, blanc à midi, bleu à nouveau puis noir,
très noir.
Les arbres aussi seront noirs.
Il n'y aura plus de vert.
Les fleurs rouges sortiront de terre.
Plus de douceur, plus d'odeurs, de la lenteur.

L'Hiver

1

C'est l'hiver. Humide et froid. Blanc ou gris.
Le brouillard et les nuages.
Des lignes grises au-dessus d'autres lignes grises,
des nuages blancs sur un ciel blanc
et des clochers presque noirs sur le ciel blanc.
Les rivières fumantes, des gouttelettes d'eau,
les odeurs des feuilles entassées et humides,
l'odeur tiède des feuilles pourrissantes,
une vague odeur de chien et le roucoulement des pigeons aussi.
L'odeur des chiens boueux et l'odeur des flaques de boue.
L'eau grise des flaques boueuses. La brume vert anis.
Une odeur d'humidité et un ciel blanc. Le froid.

A great weight.
An arm will rise only slowly, rarely.
The shadows around us will shift.
They will be big and very black.
Very dark.
We'll be surrounded by our shadows.
Escorted by our shadows.
In the mornings, the shadow around the tree will be small and bright,
evenings, great and dark.
The tree will cast shade.
When the branches sway, they will shift the shadows of the branches.
The air will be hard, heavy, slow and the scents around us will float.
We'll barely be moving.
We'll watch.
The branches that sway and sweep through the shadows.
The bright shadow of morning and black shadow of evening.
Mornings, the sky will be blue, white at noon, then again blue, then black,
very black.
The trees too will be black.
There will be no more green.
Red flowers will spring from the soil.
No more softness, no more scent, slowness.

—COLE SWENSEN

Winter

1

It's winter. Humid and cold. White or grey.
Fog and clouds.
Grey lines above grey lines,
White clouds against a white sky
And steeples nearly black against a white sky.
Steaming rivers, drops of water,
The smell of leaves bunched up and humid,
Lukewarm smell of rotting leaves,
The vague smell of a dog and also the cooing of pigeons.
The smell of muddied dogs and the smell of puddles of mud.
The grey water of muddied puddles. The fog smells of aniseed.
The smell of humidity and a white sky. The cold.

—SERGE GAVRONSKY

Mon Pouchkine

Un idiot neutre n'est pas toujours un artiste
pensa-t-il, en glissant une fois de plus de son siège
(Pouchkine lui-même avait du mal à se tenir sur une chaise*)

Oui, faisons des propositions! dit-il
la nuque encore rouge. Elle avait tapé contre le
samovar.
— Mais la proposition, en tant que ligne
strictement délimitée, est un vers, dit un ami
en se grattant. Et son bonnet se déplaçait.

Décidément quel désastre! encore un jour
sans une idée (a day = an idea) Et quelle poésie,
mais quelle poésie, pour 1835?
Là-dessus, Pouchkine remit ses caoutchoucs
(la neige tombait)

    * selon Kharms

Nathalie Quintane 1964–

PARIS, FRANCE

Quintane, primarily a poet, writes in a deceptively simple style. Her first works were published in avant-garde reviews including *Doc(k)s*, *If, Java, Nioques, Perpendiculaire*, and *La Revue de littérature générale*. She now resides in Digne-les-Bains, near the Côte d'Azur. Quintane has also produced fiction for French radio (France Culture), participated in the Deauville Film Festival, and written a play. Principal works: *Chaussures*, 1997; *Remarques*, 1997; *Début: Autobiographie*, 1999; *Mortinsteinck*, 1999; *Champagne-les-Marais*, 2001; *Saint-Tropez—Une Américaine*, 2001.

My Pushkin

A plain old dope isn't always an artist
thought he, sliding off his seat again
(Pushkin himself could barely stay seated*)

OK, so let's propose something! said he
the nape of his neck still red. He'd knocked it on
the samovar.
—But the proposal, such a limited
line, is just a verse, said a friend
scratching himself. And his cap fell to one side.

Really what a disaster! one more idea-less
day (un jour = une idée) And what poetry,
but what poetry, for 1835?
Thereupon, Pushkin put his galoshes back on
(the snow kept on falling)

* according to Kharms

—MARY ANN CAWS

Petite âme
(extraits)

« Pense au bateau qui s'éloigne du quai, qui se sépare lentement de la terre, et à cette eau noire, vivante, qui vient cogner en vagues profondes entre lui et ta stupeur d'*être là*.

« Souviens-toi du visage sans bouche, de la cendre passée sur le visage sans bouche. De son énigme vive.

« Pense à la connaissance. Jusqu'où aller pour s'éprouver ? Jusqu'à disparaître au fond de ton œil ? Une de tes voix murmure que le danger rôde sur ces routes-là. — Mais sinon, indemne, où serais-tu ? Plantée en terre, portant éternellement le même visage . . .

« Songe à la maladresse de ta quête. Sommeil, sommeil . . . Il n'y a pas de vrai, mais, un coup après l'autre, une image qui naît dans la pierre et se défait.

« Pense à la terre. Tes pieds dessus ; et d'autres continuent leur chemin par dessous. Jamais rien ne s'arrête, au fond, sinon l'entêtante rumeur qui a empêché d'être.

« Rappelle-toi ce rêve où brusquement tu étais trois : à la place de tes deux mains deux visages frémissants parlaient. Chacun contait l'une de tes vies. Et l'un de toi disait : "Mais . . . combien étiez-vous donc dans le nid ! ? "

596

Valérie-Catherine Richez 1947–

PARIS, FRANCE

A writer and painter, Valérie-Catherine Richez has been publishing in journals since 1986. She created and ran the poetry magazine *Tout est suspect* and has illustrated many limited editions of poems, by other poets and herself. She is the author of *Faits d'ombre*, 1993; *Lieux de rein* and *Petite âme*, 1998; *Échappées*, 2000; *Des yeux de nuit*, 2001; *Corps secrets* and *La Vitesse du sang*, 2002; and *L'Étoile enterrée*, 2004.

Little Soul

"Think of the boat departing from the quay, slowly leaving the shore, and of this dark living water, which comes to crash in waves between it and your astonishment at being there.

"Remember the mouthless face, the ash which settled on the mouthless face. Its intense mystery.

"Think about knowledge. How far would you go to test yourself? Until disappearing into your eye? One of your voices whispers that danger lurks on these roads.—But if not, unscathed, where would you be? Planted in the earth, always wearing the same face . . .

"Ponder the clumsiness of your quest. Sleep, sleep . . . There is no truth, but, blow upon blow, an image which emerges from the stone, then crumbles.

"Think of the earth. Your feet upon it; and others continuing their path below. Nothing ever stops, really, except the persistent murmur which has been prevented from being.

"Recall that dream in which you were suddenly three: instead of your two hands two trembling faces were talking. Each described one of your lives. And one of you said: 'But . . . then how many of you were there in the nest!?'

«Pense à ces yeux des mages. A leurs doigts secs qui dorment sur les choses comme si les choses étaient faites de vent. Comme si les choses n'existaient qu'évidées. Et regarde comme ils fixent au-delà de ton front à travers le temps. Ils ne perçoivent de ton être que ce qui vit de toi, il y a mille ans — en ce moment.»

Sentiers de lumière
(extraits)

j'ai dormi trois siècles sur un lit de rochers
j'ai vu des choses oubliées des hommes
j'ai mesuré la distance qui sépare le ciel de la terre
j'ai lu les lignes de la main j'ai rendu les oracles
une voix qui n'était pas la mienne a parlé par ma bouche
j'ai disparu dans une ville elle-même disparue
des cavaliers en armes ont envahi nos plaines
nous sommes restés dans l'attente d'autres barbares
la mer s'est retirée des portes de ma ville
je me suis concilié les fleuves de la terre

"Think of those wise men's eyes. Of their sinewy fingers which dozed on things as if they were made of wind. As if things were merely hollow. And look how they stare beyond your face across the centuries. They see only the living part of your being, a thousand years ago—but right now."

—MICHAEL TWEED

Amina Saïd 1953–
TUNIS, TUNISIA

Saïd is a poet who was educated in languages and literature at the Sorbonne. She often gives public readings of her poems accompanied by the musician Daniel Yvon. She is involved in literary gatherings in France and abroad, and her work has been anthologized many times. She currently lives in France. Saïd has won many prizes, including the Prix Jean-Malrieu (1989) and the Prix Charles-Vildrac de la Société des gens des lettres (1994). She additionally serves as a member of the jury for the Max-Pol Fouchet poetry prize. Principal works: *Feu d'oiseaux*, 1989; *Marcher sur la terre*, 1994; *Gisements de lumière*, 1998; *De décembre à la mer*, 2001.

Paths of Light

I've slept three centuries on a bed of rocks
I've seen things men have forgotten
I've measured the distance between sky and earth
I've read the lines on a hand I've delivered oracles
a voice not mine has spoken by my mouth
I've disappeared in a town itself disappeared
armed horsemen have invaded our plains
we remained awaiting more barbarians
the sea has withdrawn from the doors of my town
I've reconciled myself to the streams of the earth

j'ai orné le jour du tatouage de mes rêves
mon visage a vu mon autre visage
je n'ai pas entendu la voix qui m'appelait
la main qui me cherchait ne m'a pas trouvée
je suis née plusieurs fois de chaque étoile
je suis morte autant de fois du soleil des jours
j'ai pris très tôt des bateaux pour nulle part
j'ai demandé une chambre dans la patrie des autres
je n'avais rien accompli avant nos adieux
j'ai habité le couchant le levant et l'espace du vent
j'étais cette étrangère qu'accompagnait le soir
deux fois étrangère entre nord et sud
j'ai gravé des oiseaux tristes sur des pierres grises
j'ai dessiné ces pierres et les ai habitées
j'ai construit des radeaux où il n'y avait pas d'océans
j'ai dressé des tentes où n'étaient nuls déserts
des caravanes m'ont conduite vers un rêve d'orient
mes calligraphies ont voyagé sur le dos des nuages
je me suis souvenue de la neige des amandiers
j'ai suivi la route aérienne des oiseaux
jusqu'au mont de la lune aux duvets des naissances
j'ai appris et oublié toutes les langues de la terre
j'ai fait un grand feu de toutes les patries
j'ai bu quelques soirs au flacon de l'oubli
j'ai cherché mon étoile dans le lit des étoiles
j'ai gardé ton amour au creux de ma paume
j'ai tissé un tapis avec la laine du souvenir
j'ai déplié le monde sous l'arche des commencements
j'ai pansé les plaies du crépuscule
j'ai mis en gerbes mes saisons pour les offrir à la vie
j'ai compté les arbres qui me séparent de toi
nous étions deux sur cette terre nous voilà seuls
j'ai serré une ceinture de mots autour de ma taille
j'ai recouvert d'un linceul l'illusion des miroirs
j'ai cultivé le silence comme une plante rare
lueur après lueur j'ai déchiffré la nuit
la mort un temps m'a courtisée

. . .

j'ai fait mes premiers pas dans le limon des fleuves
on m'a ensablée vive sous un amas de dunes
on a obstrué la caverne — que mon sommeil s'éternise

I've decorated the day with the tattoos of my dreams
my face has seen my other face
I've not heard the voice calling me
the hand seeking me hasn't found me
I've been born several times from each star
I've died as often from the sun of days
I've taken early boats to nowhere
I've asked for a room in another's homeland
I'd accomplished nothing before our farewells
I've lived in the sunset the sunrise and the space of winds
I was this stranger accompanied by the evening
twice a stranger between north and south
I've engraved sad birds on gray stones
I've drawn these stones and lived in them
I've constructed rafts where there were no oceans
I've raised tents where there were no deserts
caravans have led me toward an eastern dream
my calligraphies have traveled on the back of clouds
I remembered the snow of almond trees
I've followed the airy path of birds
up to the lunar mount at the eiderdowns of births
I've learned and forgotten all the languages of earth
I've made a great fire of all homelands
I've drunk on some evenings at the flask of forgetting
I've sought my star in the bed of stars
I've kept your love in the hollow of my palm
I've woven a carpet with the wool of memory
I've unfolded the world under the arch of beginnings
I've bandaged the twilight's wounds
I've put my seasons in sheaves to offer them to life
I've counted the trees separating you from me
we were two on this earth we there alone
I have tightened a word belt around my waist
covered with a winding sheet the illusion of mirrors
cultivated silence like a rare plant
gleam after gleam I have deciphered the night
death has courted me for a time

                            . . .

I took my first steps in the river loam
they buried me living under a heap of sand
they closed off the cave—that my sleep makes eternal

on a exilé mon corps à l'intérieur de mon corps
on a effacé mon nom de tous les registres
jusqu'aux épousailles des deux rives
j'ai porté en moi le vide comme la bouche d'un noyé
décembre a disparu derrière l'horizon
j'ai appelé — seul le silence était attentif
j'ai vu les siècles s'égarer jusqu'à nous
le grenadier refleurissait entre les stèles
ma ville changeait de maîtres comme de parure
ma terre: un nuage en marge du levant
pourquoi chercher un lieu quand nous sommes le lieu
mon ombre a gravi un long chemin jusqu'à moi
un jour je suis entrée dans la maison de la langue
j'ai niché deux oiseaux à la place de cœur
j'ai traversé le miroir du poème et il m'a traversée
je me suis fiée à l'éclair de la parole
j'ai déposé un amour insoumis dans le printemps des arbres
et délivré mes mains pour que s'envolent les colombes

La Terre

portait le ciel en tête
né d'un désir de lumière
l'oiseau portait son chant

les pierres sacrées
empruntaient leur forme
au soleil à la lune

et toujours la terre
portait le ciel en tête

puis vint l'homme
sa détresse extrême

autour de son cri
la gangue du silence
dans son regard plus qu'ailleurs
la mort

they exiled my body inside my own body
they struck my name from all the records
until the wedding of the two banks
I've borne a gap in myself like a drowned man's mouth
December has disappeared behind the horizon
I've called—only silence paid any heed
I've seen the centuries lost before ours
the pomegranate tree reflowered among the tombstones
my town was changing leaders and my earth
its ornament: a cloud at the side of the sunrise
why seek a place when we are the place
my shadow has climbed a long path toward me
one day I entered the house of language
I've set two birds in the place of my heart
I've crossed the mirror of the poem and it has crossed me
I've entrusted myself to the flash of the word
I've set down a rebellious love in the springtime of trees
and freed my hands so the doves would fly off

—MARY ANN CAWS

The Earth

carried sky first
born from a longing for light
the bird carried his cry

the holy stones
borrowed their form
from the sun the moon

and still the earth
carried the sky first

then came man
his extreme distress

around his cry
the matrix of silence
in his look more than anywhere
death

car tout finit
par être ce qu'il contemple

———————————————

67 mots d'une voyelle et d'une consonne

Le terrain se rétrécit. Hier, une lettre encore est arrivée à la fin. Elle va manquer. La pénurie continue. Il en manque toujours une. Cela devient difficile. Un paquet de mots en moins. Et toute une façon de pouvoir parler et penser comme ça en moins, je ne sais pas même exactement ce qui va manquer et les paroles qui manquent déjà pour le dire, je ne pourrai plus le dire, je ne sais pas quelle sera la prochaine lettre qui va venir à manquer. La pénurie. L'accroissement de la restriction du terrain qui s'amenuise.

JOIE JOIE JOIE JOIE JOIE JOIE PUISE JOIE JOIE VIENT DE LA HAUT
JOIE JOIE JOIE JOIE JOIE JOIE JOIE JOIE JOIE JOIE JOIE PUISE JOIE

for everything ends
as what it contemplates

—MARY ANN CAWS

———————————

Christophe Tarkos 1964–
MARSEILLES, FRANCE

T arkos has published more than twenty-five volumes of poetry. He gives poetry performances regularly across Europe and collaborates frequently with other French artists, writers, and composers such as Katalin Molnar, Pascal Doury, and Eryck Abecassis. In contrast to the sparse but dense writing characteristic of his time, his is instead discursive and comedic. Tarkos is interested in the distortions and the malleability of language, as characterized by his coined term *worddoh*. His work has appeared in the reviews *Nioques* and *Action poétique*. Principal works: *Le Damier*, 1995; *L'Oiseau vole*, 1995; *Ma langue est poétique*, 1996; *Oui*, 1996; *Processe*, 1996; *Le Train*, 1996; *Caisses*, 1997; *Farine Aloou*, 1997; *La Bâton*, 1998; *L'Argent*, 1999; *La Cage*, 1999; *Le Signe*, 1999.

67 Words with One Vowel and One Consonant

The plot shrinks. Yesterday, another letter ended. It'll be missed. Poverty continues. There's always one missing. It gets hard. One pack of words less. And a whole way of speaking and thinking this way less, I don't know exactly what'll be missing and the words already missing to say it, I can't say it anymore, I don't know what letter's the next to be missing. Poverty. The growth of the restriction of the thinning plot.

JOY JOY JOY JOY JOY JOY PLUMB JOY JOY COME FROM ON HIGH
JOY JOY JOY JOY JOY JOY JOY JOY JOY JOY JOY PLUMB JOY

JOIE VIENT DE LA HAUT JOIE JOIE JOIE JOIE JOIE JOIE JOIE JOIE JOIE
JOIE JOIE PUISE JOIE JOIE VIENT DE LA HAUT JOIE JOIE JOIE JOIE
JOIE JOIE JOIE JOIE JOIE JOIE JOIE PUISE JOIE JOIE VIENT DE LA
HAUT JOIE JOIE JOIE JOIE JOIE

La restriction : un léger mouvement de perte de pieds aux poids. Où mettre les pieds. Ne plus manquer de sol. Mettre les mains, mettre des pieds. Dit que ni par ceci, ni qu'est-ce que cela. Que tu ne peux. Cela ne se fait pas de cette façon, cela se fait de cet endroit à cet endroit en marchant.

Automate d'états finis (l.m.) finite state automaton l'automate d'états est un ensemble de noeuds représentant des états et des arcs qui relient ces noeuds

Et puis progressivement, c'est progressivement, mais il n'y a pas d'autre mouvement.

Pour passer de l'acre au square foot multiplier par
43560

Le territoire se rétrécit dangereusement. Le champ et les aliments manquent.

───────────────

JOY COME FROM ON HIGH JOY JOY JOY JOY JOY JOY JOY JOY JOY
JOY JOY PLUMB JOY JOY COME FROM ON HIGH JOY JOY JOY JOY
JOY JOY JOY JOY JOY JOY JOY PLUMB JOY JOY COME FROM ON
HIGH JOY JOY JOY JOY JOY

Restriction: a light movement of loss from feet to weight. Where to
put the feet. No longer bottomless. Put hands, put feet. Say that not
by this, not by what's that. That you can't. It's not done this way, it's
done this place to this place by walking.

Finite state automaton (l.m.) Finite state automaton Finite state automaton is a set of
nodes representing states and the arcs that link these nodes

And then progressively, it is progressively, but there's no other movement.

To go from acre to square foot multiply by
43560

The plot is dangerously shrinking. The field and the nutrients missing.
—STACY DORIS

André Velter 1945–
SIGNY L'ABBAYE, FRANCE

A poet, journalist, and essayist, Velter began his studies at the Sorbonne
in philosophy but soon turned to modern history. In 1963 Velter moved
to Paris, where he met fellow poet and sometime-collaborator Serge
Sautreau. The two were first published in the review *Les Temps modernes* in 1965.
Velter and Sautreau went on to participate in gatherings organized by the review,
which included such participants as Georges Perec, Annie Le Brun, and Marcel
Bénabou. Jean-Paul Sartre, Simone de Beauvoir, and Bernard Pingaud helped

Je chante ma femme

Je chante ma femme de l'autre rive
comme un rôdeur survivant
qui a jeté son âme au vent
sans plus de soleil à poursuivre.

Il est des signes dans ma mémoire
jamais entrevus jusqu'ici
au cœur fatal d'une folie
improvisant toute l'histoire

des amants de l'amour extrême
qui sont partout où l'on s'égare
armés de foudroyants poèmes . . .

et je me refuse à ce monde
qui ne sait quelle clarté se fonde
sur le chaos de ton départ.

L'Autre

Tu es celui
Et tu es moi
Qui s'est guéri
Par la lumière

Tu es cela
D'or et de fée
Vivant réel
Sous le soleil

Tu es ici
Autre départ
Le jeu cruel

Velter's *Aisha* to be published in 1966. The book featured a preface by Alain Jouffroy. Principal works: *Ce qui murmure de loin*, 1985; *L'Arbre seul*, 1990; *Auto-portraits*, 1991; *Du Gange à Zanzibar*, 1993; *Ouvrir le chant*, 1994; *Passage en force*, 1994; *Le Haut-Pays*, 1995; *Le Septième Sonnet*, 1998; *Zingaro suite équestre*, 1998; *L'Amour extrême*, 2000; *La Vie en dansant*, 2000.

My Wife I Sing

My wife I sing from the other shore
like a prowler surviving
soul tossed to the sky's wing
no sun to pursue any more.

In my memory are signs
I've never before witnessed
in the dead heart of madness
inventing the lifelines

where we all lose our direction
are extreme love's believers
dazzling poems our protection . . .

this world I'm now leaving
that can't see light glowing
on the chaos of your going.

—ROSEMARY LLOYD

The Other One

You are the one
You are myself
Who is cured
By light

You are the thing
Of gold and magic
Living real
Under the sun

You are here
Another leaving
The cruel game

Absent dès l'aube
Tu es sans toi —
Mais le soleil

———————————

ANDRÉ VELTER

Absent from dawn
You are without you—
But the sun

—MARY ANN CAWS

Select Bibliography

Apollinaire, Guillaume. *Selected Writings*. Ed. and trans. Roger Shattuck. New York: New Directions, 1971.

Auster, Paul, ed. *The Random House Book of Twentieth-Century French Poetry, with Translations by American and British Poets*. New York: Random House, 1982.

Beckett, Samuel. *Collected Poems in French and English*. New York: Grove, 1977.

Bonnefoy, Yves. *Ce qui fut sans lumière*. Trans. John Naughton. Chicago: Chicago University Press, 1991.

———. *Poems*. Trans. Richard Pevear. New York: Random House, 1985.

Bouchet, André du. *The Uninhabited: Selected Poems of André du Bouchet*. Ed. and trans. Paul Auster. New York: Living Hand, 1976.

Burine, Claude de. *Words Have Frozen Over*. Ed. and trans. Martin Sorrell. Todmorden, U.K.: Arc, 2001.

Caws, Mary Ann, ed. *Surrealist Love Poems*. London: Tate Publishing, 2001.

Cendrars, Blaise. *Complete Poems*. Ed. and trans. Ron Padgett. Berkeley: University of California Press, 1992.

Césaire, Aimé. *The Collected Poetry of Aimé Césaire*. Ed. and trans. Clayton Eshleman and Annette Smith. Berkeley: University of California Press, 1983.

Char, René. *Selected Poems*. Ed. and trans. Mary Ann Caws and Tina Jolas. New York: New Directions, 1992.

Chénieux, Jacqueline, ed. *Il y aura une fois: Une anthologie du surréalisme*. Paris: Gallimard, 2002.

Décaudin, Michel, ed. *Anthologie de la poésie française du XXᵉ siècle*. Vol. 1. Paris: Poésie/Gallimard, 2000.

Deguy, Michel. *Donnant/Donnant*. Ed. and trans. Clayton Eshleman. Berkeley: University of California Press, 1984.

Depestre, René. *A Rainbow for the Christian West*. Ed. and trans. Joan Dayan. Amherst: University of Massachusetts Press, 1977.

Doris, Stacy, Phillip Foss, and Emmanuel Hocquard, eds. *Violence of the White Page*. Santa Fe: Tyuonyi, 1991.

Dupin, Jacques. *Fits and Starts*. Ed. and trans. Paul Auster. New York: Living Hand, 1976.

——. *Selected Poems*. Trans. Paul Auster, Stephen Romer, and David Shapiro. Wake Forest: Wake Forest University Press, 1992.

Espitallier, Jean-Michel, ed. *Pièces détachées: Une anthologie de la poésie française aujourd'hui*. Paris: Pocket, 2000.

Gavronsky, Serge, ed. and trans. *Six Contemporary French Women Poets: Theory, Practice, and Pleasures*. Carbondale: Southern Illinois University Press, 1997.

Gille, Vincent, ed. *Anthologie amoureuse du surréalisme*. Paris: Syllepse, 2001.

Guillevic, Eugène. *Selected Poems*. Ed. and trans. Denise Levertov. New York: New Directions, 1968.

Hacker, Marilyn, and John Taylor, eds. *Poetry: Contemporary French Poetry in Translation*. A Special Double Issue. October–November 2000.

Hocquard, Emmanuel. *A Test of Solitude*. Trans. Rosmarie Waldrop. Providence: Burning Deck, 2000.

Hollier, Denis, ed. *A New History of French Literature*. Cambridge: Harvard University Press, 1989.

Jabès, Edmond. *The Book of Yukel: Return to the Book*. Trans. Rosmarie Waldrop. Middletown: Wesleyan University Press, 1977.

——. *If There Were Anywhere but Desert: Selected Poems*. Ed. and trans. Keith Waldrop. New York: Station Hill Press, 1988.

Jaccottet, Philippe. *Under Clouded Skies and Beauregard*. Ed. and trans. Mark Treharne and David Constantine. Newcastle-upon-Tyne: Bloodaxe Books, 1994.

Jacob, Max. *Hesitant Fire: Selected Prose of Max Jacob*. Ed. and trans. Moishe Black and Maria Green. Lincoln: University of Nebraska Press, 1991.

Linkhorn, Renée, and Judy Cockran, eds. *Belgian Women Poets: An Anthology*. New York: Peter Lang, 2000.

Malroux, Claire. *Edge*. Ed. and trans. Marilyn Hacker. Winston-Salem: Wake Forest University Press, 1996.

——. *A Long-Gone Sun*. Ed. and trans. Marilyn Hacker. Riverdale-on-Hudson: Sheep Meadow, 2000.

Melançon, Robert. *Blind Painting*. Trans. Philip Stratford. Montreal: Signal Editions, 1988.

Para, Jean-Baptiste, ed. *Anthologie de la poésie française du XXe siècle*. Vol. 2. Paris: Poésie/Gallimard, 2000.

Penrose, Valentine. *Écrits d'une femme surréaliste*. Ed. Georgiana Colville. Paris: Éditions Joelle Losfeld, 2001.

Péret, Benjamin. *Death to the Pigs and Other Writings: Selected Writings of Benjamin Péret*. Trans. Rachel Stella. Lincoln: University of Nebraska Press, 1986.

Perse, St.-John. *Collected Poems*. Trans. W. H. Auden, Hugh Chisholm, Denis

Devlin, T. S. Eliot, Robert Fitzgerald, Wallace Fowlie, Richard Howard, and Louise Varèse. Bollingen Series. Princeton: Princeton University Press, 1971.

——. *Song for an Equinox.* Trans. Richard Howard. Bollingen Series. Princeton: Princeton University Press, 1977.

Ponge, Francis. *The Nature of Things.* Trans. Lee Fahnestock. New York: Red Dust, 1995.

Portugal, Anne. *Nude.* Trans. Norma Cole. Berkeley: Kelsey Street Press, 2001.

Preminger, Alex, and T. V. F. Brogan, with Frank J. Warnke, O. B. Hardison, Jr., and Earl Miner. *The New Princeton Encyclopedia of Poetry and Poetics.* Princeton: Princeton University Press, 1993.

Queneau, Raymond. *Pounding the Pavement; Beating the Bush; and Other Pataphysical Poems.* Trans. Teo Savory. Greensboro: Unicorn Press, 1985.

Reverdy, Pierre. *Roof Slates and Other Poems.* Ed. and trans. Mary Ann Caws and Patricia Terry. Boston: Northeastern University Press, 1981.

——. *Selected Poems.* Ed. and trans. John Ashbery, Mary Ann Caws, and Patricia Terry. Winston-Salem: Wake Forest University Press, 1991.

Risset, Jacqueline. *The Translation Begins.* Trans. Jennifer Moxley. Providence: Burning Deck Press, 1996.

Romer, Stephen, ed. *Twentieth-Century French Poems.* London: Faber and Faber, 2002.

Roubaud, Jacques. *Quelque chose noir.* Trans. Rosmarie Waldrop. New York: Dalkey Archive, 1990.

Smith, Frank, and Christophe Fauchon. *Zigzag poésie: Formes et mouvements: L'Effervescence.* Paris: Éditions Autrement, 2001.

Sorrell, Martin, ed. and trans. *Elles.* Exeter: Exeter University Press, 1995.

——. *Modern French Poetry.* London: Forest Books, 1992.

Tardieu, Jean. *The River Underground: Selected Poems and Prose.* Ed. and trans. David Kelley. Newcastle-upon-Tyne: Bloodaxe Books, 1991.

Tarkos, Christophe. *Ma langue est poétique: Selected Work.* Ed. and trans. Stacy Doris and Chet Wiener. New York: Roof Books, 2000.

Taylor, Simon Watson, and Edward Lucie-Smith, ed. and trans. *French Poetry Today: A Bilingual Anthology.* New York: Schocken, 1971.

Terry, Patricia, and Serge Gavronsky, ed. and trans. *Modern French Poetry: A Bilingual Anthology.* New York: Columbia University Press, 1975.

Tzara, Tristan. *Approximate Man and Other Writings.* Ed. and trans. Mary Ann Caws. Detroit: Wayne State University Press, 1978.

Velter, André. *Orphée Studio: Poésie d'aujourd'hui à voix haute.* Paris: Gallimard, 1999.

Acknowledgments

The editor has made every reasonable effort to secure permissions. If any errors should be noticed, please contact Mary Ann Caws care of Yale University Press. Corrections will follow in subsequent editions.

Anne-Marie Albiach

Excerpts from "Le Chemin de l'ermitage," from *Le Genre humain*, © P.O.L., 1986. Reprinted by permission of P.O.L.

"The Hermitage Road," trans. by Keith Waldrop, from *Oblek* 8 (1990). Reprinted by permission of Keith Waldrop.

Pierre Alféri

"Quand rien n'entraîne rien," excerpts from *Les Allures naturelles* (I–IV), © P.O.L., 1991; "Bibliothèque," "Choriste," from *Kub or*, © P.O.L., 1994. Reprinted by permission of P.O.L.

"When Nothing Entices Nothing," excerpts from *Les Allures naturelles* (I–IV), trans. by Chet Wiener, from *Violence of the White Page*, 1991. Reprinted by permission of Chet Wiener. "Choirist," trans. by Cole Swensen, from *Sites* #1, 1999. Reprinted by permission of Cole Swensen. "Library," trans. by Cole Swensen. Printed by permission of Cole Swensen.

Guillaume Apollinaire

"Zone," "L'Adieu," "Miroir," from *Alcools*, © Éditions Gallimard, 1920; "Les Fenêtres," "Toujours," "La Petite Auto," from *Calligrammes*, © Éditions Gallimard, 1925. Reprinted by permission of Éditions Gallimard.

"Zone," "The Farewell," "Windows," "Mirror," trans. by Roger Shattuck, from *Guillaume Apollinaire: Selected Writings*, © New Directions Publishing Corporation, 1971. Reprinted by permission of New Directions Publishing Corporation. "Always," trans. by Mary Ann Caws and Patricia Terry. Printed by permission of Mary Ann Caws and Patricia Terry. "The Little Car," trans. by Ron Padgett, from *The Random House Book of Twentieth Century French Poetry*, © Random House, Inc., 1982. Reprinted by permission of Ron Padgett.

Louis Aragon

"Pièce à grand spectacle," from *Les Destinées de la poésie, Le Mouvement perpétuel,* © Éditions Gallimard, 1925; "Parti pris," from *Feu de joie,* © Éditions Gallimard, 1920; "L'Étreinte," from *L'Homme seul,* © Éditions Gallimard, 1973. Reprinted by permission of Éditions Gallimard.

"Big Spectacular Play," "Partial," trans. by Mary Ann Caws. Printed by permission of Mary Ann Caws. "The Embrace," trans. by Edward Lucie-Smith, from *French Poetry Today: A Bilingual Anthology,* © Random House UK, Inc., 1971. Reprinted from Random House UK, Inc., and Edward Lucie-Smith.

Antonin Artaud

Excerpts from *Le Pèse-nerfs;* "L'Amour sans trêve," from *L'Ombilic des limbes,* © Éditions Gallimard, 1925. Reprinted by permission of Éditions Gallimard.

Excerpts from "The Nerve Meter," trans. by Mary Ann Caws and Patricia Terry. Printed by permission of Mary Ann Caws and Patricia Terry. "Love with No Letup," trans. by Mary Ann Caws. Printed by permission of Mary Ann Caws.

Marie-Claire Bancquart

"Contrefable d'Orphée," "Retour d'Ulysse," "Je marche . . . ," from *Sans lieu sinon l'attente,* © Éditions Obsidiane, 1991. Reprinted by permission of Éditions Obsidiane.

"Counterfable of Orpheus," trans. by Martin Sorrell, from *Modern French Poetry,* © Forest Books, 1992. Reprinted by permission of Forest Books. "Return of Ulysses," trans. by Martin Sorrell, from *Elles,* © University of Exeter Press, 1995. Reprinted by permission of University of Exeter Press. "I Walk . . . ," trans. by Mary Ann Caws. Printed by permission of Mary Ann Caws.

Silvia Baron Supervielle

"Ici l'heure," from *Après le pas,* © Éditions Arfuyen, 1997. Reprinted by permission of Éditions Arfuyen.

"Here Time," trans. by Rosemary Lloyd. Printed by permission of Rosemary Lloyd.

Georges Bataille

"La Nuit est ma nudité," "Je rêvais de toucher," from *Archangélique et autres poèmes,* © Mercure de France, 1967. Reprinted by permission of Mercure de France.

"Night Is My Nudity," "I Dreamed of Touching," trans. by Rosemary Lloyd. Printed by permission of Rosemary Lloyd.

Samuel Beckett

"Musique de l'indifférence," "Dieppe," "Je suis," "Que ferais-je," from *Samuel Beckett: Collected Poems in English and French,* © Beckett Estate, 2002. Reprinted by permission of Calder Publications, Ltd.

"Music of Indifference," trans. by Mary Ann Caws. Printed by permission of Mary Ann Caws. "Dieppe," "My Way," "What Would I Do," trans. by Samuel Beckett, from *Samuel*

618

Beckett: Collected Poems in English and French, © Beckett Estate, 2002. Reprinted by permission of Calder Publications, Ltd.

Tahar Bekri

Excerpts from "Retour en Tunisie," from *Chapelets d'attache,* © L'Harmattan, 1989–1991. Reprinted by permission of L'Harmattan.

Excerpts from "Return to Tunisia," trans. by Mary Ann Caws. Printed by permission of Mary Ann Caws.

Yves Bonnefoy

"Le Livre . . . ," "Une voix," from *Pierre écrite,* © Mercure de France, 1965; "A la voix . . . ," from *Hier régnant désert,* © Mercure de France, 1965; "La Neige," "La Tâche . . . ," from *Ce qui fut sans lumière,* © Mercure de France, 1987. Reprinted by permission of Mercure de France.

"The Book . . . ," trans. by Richard Pevear, from *Yves Bonnefoy: Poems 1959–1975,* © Random House, Inc., 1985. Reprinted by permission of Random House, Inc. "A Voice," trans. by Hoyt Rogers, *Harvard Review,* 1995. Reprinted by permission of Hoyt Rogers. "The Voice . . . ," trans. by Mary Ann Caws. Printed by permission of Mary Ann Caws. "The Snow," "The Task of Hope," trans. by John Naughton, from *In the Shadow's Light,* © University of Chicago Press, 1991. Reprinted by permission of University of Chicago Press.

André du Bouchet

"Pierre ou eau," from *Axiomes,* © Mercure de France, 1986; "La Lumière . . . ," from *L'Inhabité,* © Mercure de France, 1968; "Fraction," from *Où le soleil,* © Mercure de France, 1968. Reprinted by permission of Mercure de France.

"Stone or Water," trans. by Hoyt Rogers, from *Poetry,* 2000. Reprinted by permission of Hoyt Rogers. "The Light . . . ," trans. by Paul Auster, from *The Uninhabited: Selected Poems of André du Bouchet,* © Living Hand, 1976. Reprinted by permission of Paul Auster. "Fraction," trans. by Mary Ann Caws. Printed by permission of Mary Ann Caws.

André Breton

"Le Corset mystère," "Vigilance," "Toujours pour . . . ," "On me dit . . . ," "L'Union libre," "Sur la route . . . ," from *Poèmes,* © Éditions Gallimard, 1948. Reprinted by permission of Éditions Gallimard.

"The Mystery Corset," "Vigilance," "Always for . . . ," "They Tell Me . . . ," "On the Road . . . ," trans. by Mary Ann Caws. Printed by permission of Mary Ann Caws. "Free Union," trans. by Mary Ann Caws and Patricia Terry, from *Surrealist Love Poems,* © Tate Publishing, 2001. Reprinted by permission of Mary Ann Caws and Patricia Terry.

Martine Broda

"Je lave," "Je voulais . . . ," from *Grand Jour,* © Éditions Belin, 1994. Reprinted from Éditions Belin.

"I Wash," "I Wanted . . . ," trans. by Mary Ann Caws. Printed by permission of Mary Ann Caws.

ACKNOWLEDGMENTS

Nicole Brossard

"Je veux . . . ," from *Anthologie 80,* © Le Castor Astral, 1981. Reprinted by permission of Le Castor Astral.
"I Want . . . ," trans. by Marilyn Hacker. Printed by permission of Marilyn Hacker.

Claude de Burine

"Te saluer," from *Le Passager* © La Bartarelle, 1993, "Mais quand j'aurai," from *L'Arbre aux oiseaux,* © Arc Publications, 2001. Reprinted by permission of Arc Publications.
"Greet You," "But When I Have," trans. by Martin Sorrell, from *Words Have Frozen Over,* © Arc Publications, 2001. Reprinted by permission of Arc Publications.

Olivier Cadiot

"Pourquoi je . . . ," from *Futur, ancien, fugitif,* © P.O.L., 1993. Reprinted by permission of P.O.L. Excerpts from "Hep!" from *Rouge, vert & noir,* © Potes and Poets Press, 1989. Reprinted by permission of Potes and Poets Press.
"Why I . . . ," trans. by Cole Swensen, from *Future, Former, Fugitive.* Reprinted by permission of Cole Swensen. Excerpts from "Psst!" from *Red, Green & Black,* trans. by Charles Bernstein and Olivier Cadiot, © Potes and Poets Press, 1990. Reprinted by permission of Potes and Poets Press, with thanks to Charles Bernstein and Olivier Cadiot.

Claude Cahun

"La Sadique Judith," from *Il y aura une fois,* © Jean-Michel Place, 2002. Reprinted by permission of Jean-Michel Place.
"Sadistic Judith," trans. by Mary Ann Caws. Printed by permission of Mary Ann Caws.

Blaise Cendrars

Excerpts from "Prose du Transsibérien . . . ," "Journal," "Ma danse," "Lettre," from *Dix-neuf poèmes élastiques,* © Éditions Gallimard, 1967. Reprinted by permission of Éditions Gallimard.
Excerpts from "The Prose of the Trans-Siberian . . . ," "Newspaper," "My Dance," "Letter," trans. by Ron Padgett, from *Blaise Cendrars: Complete Poems,* © University of California Press, 1992. Reprinted by permission of University of California Press and Ron Padgett.

Aimé Césaire

"Le Cristal automatique," from *Les Armes miraculeuses,* © Éditions Gallimard, 1946. Reprinted by permission of Éditions Gallimard. "An neuf," from *Aimé Césaire: La Poésie,* © Éditions du Seuil, 1994. Reprinted by permission of Éditions du Seuil.
"The Automatic Crystal," trans. by Mary Ann Caws and Patricia Terry. Printed by permission of Mary Ann Caws and Patricia Terry. "New Year," trans. by Clayton Eshleman and Annette Smith, from *The Collected Poetry of Aimé Césaire,* © University of California Press, 1983. Reprinted by permission of University of California Press.

René Char

"Redonnez-leur . . . ," "Le Martinet," from *Fureur et mystère*, © Éditions Gallimard, 1948; "Toute vie . . . ," from *Les Matinaux*, © Éditions Gallimard, 1950; "Le Mortel Partenaire," "Vers l'arbre-frère . . . ," "La Chambre dans l'espace," from *La Parole en archipel*, © Éditions Gallimard, 1962; "Lutteurs," "Lied du figuier," from *Le Nu perdu*, © Éditions Gallimard, 1971. Reprinted by permission of Éditions Gallimard.

"Restore to Them . . . ," trans. by Mary Ann Caws; "The Mortal Partner," trans. by Nancy Kline; "To Friend-Tree . . . ," trans. by William Carlos Williams; "Lied of the Fig Tree," trans. by Gustaf Sobin, from *René Char: Selected Poems*, © New Directions Publishing Corporation, 1992. Reprinted by permission of New Directions Publishing Corporation. "Fighters," trans. by Thomas Merton, from *The Collected Poems of Thomas Merton*, © New Directions Publishing Corporation, 1997. Reprinted by permission of New Directions Publishing Corporation and Trustees of the Merton Legacy Trust. "The Swift," trans. by Patricia Terry, from *Lightning: The Poetry of René Char*, © Northeastern University Press, 1997. Reprinted by permission of Patricia Terry. "Every Life . . . ," trans. by James Wright, "Room in Space," trans. by W. S. Merwin, from *The Random House Book of Twentieth Century French Poetry*, © Random House, Inc., 1982. Reprinted by permission of James Wright and W. S. Merwin.

Malcolm de Chazal

Excerpts from "Sens plastique (1947)," "Sens plastique (1948)," from *Sens plastique*, © Éditions Gallimard, 1947–1948. "La Logique," from *Poèmes*, © Éditions Gallimard, 1968. Reprinted by permission of Éditions Gallimard.

Excerpts from "Plastic Sense (1947)," "Plastic Sense (1948)," "Logic," trans. by Mary Ann Caws. Printed by permission of Mary Ann Caws.

Andrée Chedid

"Épreuves du poète," "Regarder l'enfance," from *Épreuves du vivant*, © Éditions Gallimard, 2002. Reprinted by permission of Éditions Gallimard.

"Trials of the Poet," "Looking at Childhood," trans. by Rosemary Lloyd. Printed by permission of Rosemary Lloyd.

Paul Claudel

"Octobre," "Tristesse de l'eau," from *Connaissance de l'Est*, © Mercure de France, 1974. Reprinted by permission of Mercure de France.

"October," "The Sadness of Water," trans. by James Lawler. Printed by permission of James Lawler.

Jean Cocteau

"Jeune fille endormie," from *Jean Cocteau: Opéra: Oeuvres poétiques, 1925–1927*, © Stock, 1959. Reprinted by permission of the Comité Jean Cocteau.

"Young Girl Sleeping," trans. Alfred Corn. Printed by permission of Alfred Corn.

ACKNOWLEDGMENTS

Bernard Collin

"Perpétuel *voyez* physique," 17/5, from *Perpétuel* voyez *physique,* © Éditions Ivrea, 1996. Reprinted by permission of Éditions Ivrea.
"Perpetual *Look* Physics," 17/5, trans. by Mary Ann Caws. Printed by permission of Mary Ann Caws.

Danielle Collobert

"Je temps de quoi," "Dont le soleil," from *Survie,* © Orange Export, Ltd., 1978. Reprinted from Orange Export, Ltd.
"I Time of What," "For Which the Sun," trans. by Michael Tweed. Printed by permission of Michael Tweed.

Léon-Gontran Damas

"Solde," "Par la fenêtre . . . ," from *Névralgies,* © Éditions Gallimard, 1972. Reprinted by permission of Éditions Gallimard.
"On Sale," "Through the Half-Opened Window," trans. by Mary Ann Caws. Printed by permission of Mary Ann Caws.

René Daumal

"Je parle dans tous les âges," from *Anthologie de la poésie française du XXe siècle,* © Éditions Gallimard, 2000; "Le Mot et la mouche," from *Le Contre-ciel,* © Éditions Gallimard, 2000. Reprinted by permission of Éditions Gallimard.
"I Speak in All Ages," trans. by Mary Ann Caws. Printed by permission of Mary Ann Caws. "Poetry and Thought," trans. by Michael Wood, from *The Random House Book of Twentieth Century French Poetry,* © Random House Inc., 1982. Reprinted by permission of Michael Wood.

Michel Deguy

"O la grande apposition du monde," from *Poèmes de la presqu-île,* © Éditions Gallimard, 1962; "Quai gris," from *Oui dire,* © Éditions Gallimard, 1966; "Qui quoi," "Le Mur . . . ," "Ici souvent je suis," from *Tombeau de Du Bellay,* © Éditions Gallimard, 1973; "La Ballade," from *Donnant donnant,* © Éditions Gallimard, 1981. Reprinted by permission of Éditions Gallimard.
"O Great Apposition of the World," "Grey Pier," "Who What," "The Wall . . . ," "Here Often I Am," "The Ballad," trans. by Clayton Eshleman, from *Given, Giving,* © University of California Press, 1984. Reprinted by permission of University of California Press.

René Depestre

"Romancero d'une petite lampe," from *Un arc-en-ciel pour l'Occident chrétien,* © L'Harmattan, 1967. Reprinted by permission of L'Harmattan.
"Ballad of a Little Lamp," trans. by Joan Dayan, from *A Rainbow for the Christian West,* © University of Massachusetts Press, 1977. Reprinted by permission of University of Massachusetts Press.

622

Robert Desnos

"Notre paire," "Comme," "Non l'amour . . . ," "Si tu savais," "Jamais d'autre que toi," "J'ai tant . . . ," from *Domaine public,* © Éditions Gallimard, 1953. Reprinted by permission of Éditions Gallimard.

"Hour Farther," "Like," trans. by Martin Sorrell, from *Modern French Poetry,* © Forest Books, 1992. Reprinted by permission of Forest Books. "No, Love Is Not Dead," "If You Knew," "Never Anyone but You," "I've Dreamt of You So Often," trans. by Mary Ann Caws. Printed by permission of Mary Ann Caws.

Mohammed Dib

"A un voyageur," from *Formulaires (Poèmes),* © Éditions du Seuil, 1970. Reprinted by permission of Éditions du Seuil.

"To a Voyager," trans. by Ronnie Scharfman. Printed by permission of Ronnie Scharfman.

Jacques Dupin

"Même si . . . ," "J'ai cru rejoindre . . . ," from *Lichens,* © Éditions Gallimard, 1958; "Commencer . . . ," "Il y a," "Il respire . . . ," "Il m'est interdit," from *Moraines,* © Éditions Gallimard, 1969. Reprinted by permission of Éditions Gallimard. "Quand il est impossible," from *Écart,* © P.O.L., 2000. Reprinted by permission of P.O.L.

"Even If . . . ," "I Am Forbidden," trans. by Paul Auster, from *Jacques Dupin: Selected Poems,* © Bloodaxe Books, 1992. Reprinted by permission of Bloodaxe Books. "Begin Like Tearing," "There Exists," "At Instants I Thought," "He Breathes . . . ," trans. by Stephen Romer. Printed by permission of Stephen Romer. "When It Is Impossible," trans. by Mary Ann Caws. Printed by permission of Mary Ann Caws.

Paul Éluard

"L'Amoureuse," from *Mourir de ne pas mourir,* © Éditions Gallimard, 1924; "Je te l'ai dit," "La Terre . . . ," from *L'Amour la poésie,* © Éditions Gallimard, 1929; "Le Diamant . . . ," "Elle est," from *Capitale de la douleur,* © Éditions Gallimard, 1926; excerpt from "Nuits partagées," from *La Vie immédiate,* © Éditions Gallimard, 1932. Reprinted by permission of Éditions Gallimard. "D'un . . . ," from *Corps mémorable,* © Seghers, 1947. Reprinted by permission of Seghers.

"Loving," "I've Told You," "The Diamond . . . ," "She Exists," "The Earth Is Blue . . . ," excerpt from "Shared Nights," "Of One . . . ," trans. by Mary Ann Caws. Printed by permission of Mary Ann Caws.

Claude Esteban

"Le Soir venu," from *Quelqu'un commence à parler dans une chambre,* © Éditions Gallimard, 1995. Reprinted by permission of Éditions Gallimard.

"Once Evening's Fallen," trans. by Rosemary Lloyd. Printed by permission of Rosemary Lloyd.

ACKNOWLEDGMENTS

Marie Étienne

"Cauchemars," from *Anatolie,* © Éditions Gallimard, 1997. Reprinted by permission of Éditions Gallimard.
"Nightmares," trans. by Marilyn Hacker. Printed by permission of Marilyn Hacker.

Léon-Paul Fargue

"Une odeur nocturne . . . ," from *Poésies,* © Éditions Gallimard, 1963. Reprinted by permission of Éditions Gallimard.
"A Fragrance of Night . . . ," trans. by Wallace Stevens, from *The Random House Book of Twentieth Century French Poetry,* © Random House, Inc., 1982. Reprinted by permission of Random House, Inc.

Jean Follain

"Églogue," "Félicité," "La Pomme rouge," "Quincaillerie," from *Territoires,* © Éditions Gallimard, 1953. Reprinted by permission of Éditions Gallimard.
"Eclogue," "Bliss," trans. by Stephen Romer. Printed by permission of Stephen Romer. "The Red Apple," trans. by Serge Gavronsky, from *Modern French Poetry,* © Columbia University Press, 1975. Reprinted by permission of Columbia University Press. "Hardware Store," trans. by Marilyn Hacker. Printed by permission of Marilyn Hacker.

Louis-René des Forêts

"Il n'est que temps," from *Poèmes de Samuel Wood,* © Éditions Fata Morgana, 1988. Reprinted by permission of Éditions Fata Morgana.
"It Is High Time," trans. by John Naughton, from *Modern Poetry in Translation* 8 (1995). Reprinted by permission of John Naughton.

Dominique Fourcade

"Ensembles," from *Le Sujet monotype,* © P.O.L., 1997. Reprinted by permission of P.O.L.
"Ensembles," trans. by Cole Swensen. Printed by permission of Cole Swensen.

Jean Frémon

"L'Automne," from *La Vraie Nature des ombres,* © P.O.L., 2000. Reprinted by permission of P.O.L.
"Autumn," trans. by Cole Swensen. Printed by permission of Cole Swensen.

André Frénaud

"Toast en réponse," "Les Paroles . . . ," from *Depuis toujours déjà,* © Éditions Gallimard, 1984; "La Création de soi," from *Les Rois mages,* © Éditions Gallimard, 1977. Reprinted by permission of Éditions Gallimard.

"Toast in Response," trans. by Mary Ann Caws. Printed by permission of Mary Ann Caws. "Self-Creation," "The Words . . . ," trans. by Michael Sheringham. Printed by permission of Michael Sheringham.

Jacques Garelli

"Démesure de la poésie," from *Prendre appui,* © Mercure de France, 1968. Reprinted by permission of Encre Marine, Jacques Garelli, and Mercure de France.
"Excess of Poetry," trans. by Mary Ann Caws. Printed by permission of Mary Ann Caws.

Lorand Gaspar

"Joueur de flûte," "Minoen récent I (Aiguières d'Hagia . . .)," from *Égée, Judée,* © Éditions Gallimard, 1980. Reprinted by permission of Éditions Gallimard.
"Flute Player," "Late Minoan I (Ewers of . . .)," trans. by Ronnie Scharfman. Printed by permission of Ronnie Scharfman.

Liliane Giraudon

Excerpt from "Quand il n'y . . . ," from *Les Animaux font toujours l'amour de la même manière,* © P.O.L. Reprinted by permission of P.O.L., 1995.
Excerpt from "When There's Nothing . . . ," trans. by Serge Gavronsky, from *Six Contemporary French Women Poets: Theory, Practice, and Pleasures,* © Southern Illinois University Press, 1997. Reprinted by permission of Southern Illinois University Press.

Édouard Glissant

"Pour Mycéa," from *Pays rêvé, pays réel,* © Éditions Gallimard, 1985. Reprinted by permission of Éditions Gallimard.
"For Mycea," trans. by Brent Hayes Edwards, from *Poetry* 177, no. 1 (October–November 2000): 52–55. Reprinted by permission of Brent Hayes Edwards.

Guy Goffette

"Max Jacob," "Le Relèvement d'Icare: Envoi," from *Un Manteau de fortune: Poèmes,* © Éditions Gallimard. Reprinted by permission of Éditions Gallimard.
"Max Jacob," "The Raising of Icarus: Envoi," trans. by Marilyn Hacker. Printed by permission of Marilyn Hacker.

Michelle Grangaud

"Isidore Ducasse . . . ," from *Formes de l'anagramme,* © Éditions Gallimard, 1995. Reprinted by permission of Éditions Gallimard.
"Michelle Grangaud . . . ," by Paul Lloyd and Rosemary Lloyd, "Isidore Ducasse . . . ," trans. by Paul Lloyd and Rosemary Lloyd. Printed by permission of Paul Lloyd and Rosemary Lloyd.

Jean Grosjean

"L'Aïeul," "Désert à l'essai," from *Cantilènes,* © Éditions Gallimard, 1998. Reprinted by permission of Éditions Gallimard.

"The Ancestor," "Trial Desert," trans. by Mary Ann Caws and Patricia Terry. Printed by permission of Mary Ann Caws and Patricia Terry.

Eugène Guillevic

"Quand il eut regardé," "Je ne parle pas," from *Exécutoire,* © Éditions Gallimard, 1947. Reprinted by permission of Éditions Gallimard.

"When He'd Looked Hard," trans. by Hoyt Rogers. Printed by permission of Hoyt Rogers. "I Don't Speak," trans. by Denise Levertov, from *Guillevic: Selected Poems,* © New Directions Publishing Corporation, 1968. Reprinted by permission of New Directions Publishing Corporation.

Anne Hébert

"Je suis la terre . . . ," from *Poèmes,* © Éditions du Seuil, 1960. Reprinted by permission by Éditions du Seuil. "Terre originelle," from *Poètes d'aujourd'hui,* © Seghers, 1969. Reprinted by permission of Seghers.

"I Am Earth and Water," trans. by Marilyn Hacker. Printed by permission of Marilyn Hacker. "Earth at Its Origin," trans. by Mary Ann Caws. Printed by permission of Mary Ann Caws.

Emmanuel Hocquard

Excerpts from "À Noël" (I, II, III, XXV), from *Un test de solitude,* © P.O.L., 1998. "Trois leçons de morale," from *Les Dernières Nouvelles,* © P.O.L., 1979. Reprinted by permission of P.O.L.

Excerpts from "At Christmas" (I, II, III, XXV), trans. by Rosmarie Waldrop, from *A Test of Solitude,* © Burning Deck Press, 1998. Reprinted by permission of Burning Deck Press. "Three Moral Tales," trans. by Michael Palmer, from *The Random House Book of Twentieth Century French Poetry,* © Random House, Inc., 1982. Reprinted by permission of Michael Palmer.

Michel Houellebecq

"Dans l'air limpide," from *Le Sens du combat,* © Éditions Gallimard, 1996. Reprinted by permission of Éditions Gallimard.

"In the Limpid Air," trans. by Mary Ann Caws. Printed by permission of Mary Ann Caws.

Radovan Ivsic

"Mavena," from *Collection S,* leaflet series, © Éditions Maintenant, 1972. Reprinted by permission of Radovan Ivsic.

"Mavena," trans. by Mary Ann Caws. Printed by permission of Mary Ann Caws.

Edmond Jabès

"Le Miroir et le mouchoir," from *Le Livre de Yukel*, © Éditions Gallimard, 1964; "Soleilland," from *Je bâtis ma demeure: Poèmes, 1953–1957*, © Éditions Gallimard, 1959. Reprinted by permission of Éditions Gallimard.

"Mirror and Scarf," trans. by Rosmarie Waldrop, from *The Book of Yukel: Return to the Book*, © Wesleyan University Press, 1977. Reprinted by permission of Wesleyan University Press. "Sunland," trans. by Keith Waldrop, from *If There Were Anywhere but Desert: Selected Poems*, © Station Hill Press, 1988. Reprinted by permission of Keith Waldrop.

Philippe Jaccottet

"Sérénité," from *Airs*, © Éditions Gallimard, 1967; "Sur les pas de la lune," from *L'Ignorant*, © Éditions Gallimard, 1958; "Je me redresse avec effort," from *Chant d'en bas*, © Éditions Gallimard, 1974; "Pensées sous les nuages," from *Pensées sous les nuages*, © Éditions Gallimard, 1983. Reprinted by permission of Éditions Gallimard.

"Serenity," trans. by Martin Sorrell, from *Modern French Poetry*, © Forest Books, 1992. Reprinted by permission of Forest Books. "In the Steps of the Moon," trans. by Edward Lucie-Smith, from *French Poetry Today: A Bilingual Anthology*, © Random House UK, Inc., 1971. Reprinted from Random House UK, Inc., and Edward Lucie-Smith. "With Effort, I Sit up and Look Outside," trans. by Hoyt Rogers. Printed by permission of Hoyt Rogers. "Clouded Skies," trans. by Mark Treharne and David Constantine, from *Under Clouded Skies*, © Bloodaxe Books, 1994. Reprinted by permission of Bloodaxe Books.

Max Jacob

"La Rue Ravignan," "Mauvais caractère," "Réunion," "Un œuf," from *Le Cornet à dés*, © Éditions Gallimard, 1917; "La Révélation," "Visitation," from *La Défense de Tartufe* [sic], © Éditions Gallimard, 1964. Reprinted by permission of Éditions Gallimard.

"The Rue Ravignan," trans. by John Ashbery, from *The Random House Book of Twentieth Century French Poetry*, © Random House, 1982. Reprinted by permission of Georges Borchardt, Inc., and John Ashbery. "The Revelation," "Visitation," trans. by Moishe Black and Maria Green, from *Hesitant Fire: Selected Prose of Max Jacob*, © University of Nebraska Press, 1991. Reprinted by permission of University of Nebraska Press. "Shady Soul," "Meeting," "An Egg," trans. by Mary Ann Caws. Printed by permission of Mary Ann Caws.

Franck André Jamme

Excerpts from *Extraits de la vie des scarabées*, © Editions Melville, 2004; excerpts from *La Récitation de l'oubli*, © Éditions Fata Morgana, 1986; "Tu viens souvent," from *Bois de lune*, © Éditions Fata Morgana, 1990. Reprinted by permission of Franck André Jamme and Éditions Fata Morgana.

Excerpts from *Extracts from the Life of a Beetle*, trans. by Michael Tweed. Printed by permission of Michael Tweed. "The Recitation of Forgetting," trans. by John Ashbery, © John Ashbery, 2002. Reprinted by permission of Georges Borchardt, Inc., and John Ashbery. "Often You Come," trans. by Mary Ann Caws. Printed by permission of Mary Ann Caws.

ACKNOWLEDGMENTS

Pierre-Albert Jourdan

"Parle . . . ," "Prière," from *Le Bonjour et l'adieu,* © Mercure de France, 1991. Reprinted by permission of Mercure de France.

"Speak . . . ," "Prayer," trans. by Mary Ann Caws. Printed by permission of Mary Ann Caws.

Pierre-Jean Jouve

"Lamentations . . . ," from *Sueur de sang,* © Mercure de France, 1955. Reprinted by permission of Mercure de France. "De plus . . . ," from *Les Noces,* © Éditions Gallimard, 1966; "Après le déluge," from *Le Père de la terre,* © Éditions Gallimard, 1930. Reprinted by permission of Éditions Gallimard.

"Lament . . . ," trans. by Keith Waldrop. Printed by permission of Keith Waldrop. "More and More Woman," trans. by Mary Ann Caws. Printed by permission of Mary Ann Caws. "After the Deluge," trans. by Lee Fahnestock. Printed by permission of Lee Fahnestock.

Hédi Kaddour

"Le Chauffeur," from *Jamais une ombre simple,* © Éditions Gallimard, 1994; "Variations," from *La Fin des vendanges,* © Éditions Gallimard, 1989. Reprinted by permission of Éditions Gallimard.

"The Bus Driver," trans. by Marilyn Hacker, from *Prairie Schooner.* Reprinted by permission of Marilyn Hacker. "Variations," trans. by Marilyn Hacker, from *Verse,* 2000. Reprinted by permission of Marilyn Hacker.

Vénus Khoury-Ghata

"Elle lançait . . . ," from *Anthologie personnelle,* © Actes Sud, 1997. Reprinted by permission of Vénus Khoury-Ghata. "L'Automne précéda . . . ," from *Elle dit,* © Éditions Balland, 1999. Reprinted by permission of Éditions Balland.

"She Used to Throw . . . ," "Autumn Preceded . . . ," trans. by Marilyn Hacker. Printed by permission of Marilyn Hacker.

Greta Knutson

"Pêche lunaire," from *Lunaires,* © Éditions Flammarion, 1985. Reprinted from Éditions Flammarion.

"Moon Fishing," trans. by Mary Ann Caws. Printed by permission of Mary Ann Caws.

Abdellatif Laâbi

"Le Portrait du père," from *Gare du Nord # 3* (1998), ed. by Alice Notley and Douglas Oliver. Reprinted by permission of Alice Notley and Douglas Oliver. "Demain sera . . . ," from *Le Spleen de Casablanca,* © Éditions de la Différence, 1996. Reprinted by permission of Éditions de la Différence.

"The Portrait of the Father," "Tomorrow Will Be . . . ," trans. by Pierre Joris. Printed by permission of Pierre Joris.

628

Valery Larbaud

"Ode," "Le Don de soi-même," from *Poèmes par un riche amateur, ou oeuvres françaises de M. Barnabooth,* © Éditions Gallimard, 1908. Reprinted by permission of Éditions Gallimard.

"Ode," "The Gift of Oneself," trans. by Mary Ann Caws and Patricia Terry. Printed by permission of Mary Ann Caws and Patricia Terry.

Annie Le Brun

"Des rites," "Des fêtes," from *Sur-le-champ,* © Jean-Michel Place, 1967. Reprinted by permission of Annie Le Brun.

"Rituals," "Festivals," trans. by Mary Ann Caws. Printed by permission of Mary Ann Caws.

Michel Leiris

"Vertical," "Avare," from *Autres lancers,* © Éditions Gallimard, 1969; "Maldonne," from *Haut mal,* © Éditions Gallimard, 1943. Reprinted by permission of Éditions Gallimard.

"Vertical," "Miserly," trans. by Cole Swensen. Printed by permission of Cole Swensen. "Misdeal," trans. by Keith Waldrop. Printed by permission of Keith Waldrop.

Claire Lejeune

"Illettrée," from *Mémoire de rien: Le Pourpre, La Geste, Elle,* © Éditions Labor, 1994; "Où donc," "La Mort, j'en parle," from *Belgian Women Poets: An Anthology,* © Peter Lang, 2000. Reprinted by permission of Peter Lang.

"Illiterate," trans. by Mary Ann Caws. Printed by permission of Mary Ann Caws. "So Where?" "Death, I Speak of It," trans. by Renée Linkhorn and Judy Cockran, from *Belgian Women Poets: An Anthology,* © Peter Lang, 2000. Reprinted by permission of Peter Lang.

Gherasim Luca

"Ma déraison d'être," "La Fin du monde . . . ," from *Poésies complètes,* © José Corti, 1990. Reprinted by permission of José Corti.

"My Folly of Being," trans. by Michael Tweed. Printed by permission of Michael Tweed. "The End of the World . . . ," trans. by Mary Ann Caws. Printed by permission of Mary Ann Caws.

Dora Maar

"Si l'attendrissant souvenir," "Les Grandes Constructions," from *Les Vies de Dora Maar,* © Thames and Hudson, 2000. Reprinted by permission of Thames and Hudson.

"If the Touching Memory," "These Tall Constructions," trans. by Mary Ann Caws, from *Picasso's Weeping Woman: The Life and Art of Dora Maar,* © Little Brown/Bulfinch, 2000. Reprinted by permission of Mary Ann Caws.

629

ACKNOWLEDGMENTS

Claire Malroux

"Rendez-vous . . . ," from *Suspens,* © Le Castor Astral, 2001; "Il y a la guerre . . . ,"
"Toutes les haleines," from *Soleil de jadis,* © Le Castor Astral, 1998. Reprinted by permission of Le Castor Astral.
"Appointment . . . ," "There's War . . . ," trans. by Marilyn Hacker, from *A Long-Gone Sun,* © Sheep Meadow Press, 2000. Reprinted by permission of Sheep Meadow Press.
"Every Breath," trans. by Marilyn Hacker, from *Edge,* © Wake Forest University Press, 1996. Reprinted by permission of Wake Forest University Press.

Joyce Mansour

"Je veux . . . ," from *Territoires,* © Éditions Gallimard, 1953. Reprinted by permission of Cyrille Mansour. "Papier d'argent," "Rappelle-toi," "L'Orage tire . . . ," from *Joyce Mansour: Prose et poésie,* © Actes Sud, 1991. Reprinted by permission of Cyrille Mansour.
"I Want . . . ," trans. by Mary Ann Caws. Printed by permission of Mary Ann Caws.
"Tinfoil," trans. by Martin Sorrell, from *Modern French Poetry,* © Forest Books, 1992.
Reprinted by permission of Forest Books. "Remember," "The Storm Sketches . . . ," trans. by Mary Ann Caws, from *Surrealist Love Poems,* © University of Chicago Press, 2002. Reprinted by permission of Mary Ann Caws.

Robert Marteau

"Je consens que tout s'efface," from *Liturgie,* © Champ Vallon, 1992. Reprinted by permission of Champ Vallon.
"I Consent That Everything Vanishes," trans. by John Montague, from *Poetry,* 2000. Reprinted by permission of John Montague.

Jean-Michel Maulpoix

"Le Mise au monde," from *Une histoire de bleu,* © Mercure de France, 1992. Reprinted by permission of Jean-Michel Maulpoix and Mercure de France.
"The Giving Birth," trans. by Mark Polizzotti. Printed by permission of Mark Polizzotti.

Abdelwahab Meddeb

"Sur des traces oubliées," "Je prends le chemin," from *Tombeau d'Ibn Arabi,* © Éditions Fata Morgana, 1995. Reprinted by permission of Éditions Fata Morgana.
"On Forgotten Tracks," "I Take the Path," trans. by Charlotte Mandell, from *Notus 12,* © Other Wind Press, 1993. Reprinted by permission of Charlotte Mandell.

Robert Melançon

"Le Début de l'été," "Éveil," from *Blind Painting,* © Signal Editions, Véhicule Press, 1986. Reprinted by permission of Signal Editions, Véhicule Press.
"Beginning of Summer," "Wakening," trans. by Philip Stratford, from *Blind Painting,* © Signal Editions, 1985. Reprinted from Véhicule Press.

Henri Michaux

"Avenir," from *Lointain intérieur,* © Éditions Gallimard, 1938; "Mes statues," from *Épreuves, exorcismes,* © Éditions Gallimard, 1946; excerpts from "Tranches de savoir," from *Face aux verrous,* © Éditions Gallimard, 1950. Reprinted by permission of Éditions Gallimard.

"Future," "My Statues," trans. by Mary Ann Caws and Patricia Terry. Printed by permission of Mary Ann Caws and Patricia Terry. Excerpts from "Slices of Knowledge," trans. by Rosemary Lloyd. Printed by permission of Rosemary Lloyd.

Gaston Miron

Excerpts from "La Marche . . . ," from *L'Homme rapaillé,* © Éditions Typo, 1998. Reprinted by permission of Éditions Typo and M. Beaudet and E. Miron.

Excerpts from "The Walk . . . ," trans. by Mary Ann Caws. Printed by permission of Mary Ann Caws.

Pascalle Monnier

"L'Été 1: Bon . . . ," "L'Été 2: Ce sont . . . ," "Hiver 1" from *Bayart,* © P.O.L., 1995. Reprinted by permission of P.O.L.

"Summer 1: Good . . . ," "Summer 2: These are . . . ," trans. by Cole Swensen, from *Provincetown Arts,* 2001. Reprinted by permission of Cole Swensen. "Winter 1," trans. by Serge Gavronsky. Printed by permission of Serge Gavronsky.

Bernard Noël

"Portrait," from *La Rumeur de l'air,* © Éditions Fata Morgana, 1986; "Angers," from *Le Reste du voyage,* © Éditions Fata Morgana, 1997. Reprinted by permission of Éditions Fata Morgana.

"Portrait," trans. by Michael Tweed. Printed by permission of Michael Tweed. "Angers," trans. by Rosemary Lloyd. Printed by permission of Rosemary Lloyd.

Meret Oppenheim

"Rêve à Barcelone," from *Poèmes et carnets,* © Éditeur Christian Bourgois, 1993. Reprinted by permission of Éditeur Christian Bourgois.

"Dream in Barcelona," trans. by Mary Ann Caws. Printed by permission of Mary Ann Caws.

Valentine Penrose

"La Pluie retrouvant," "À mes carreaux," from *Valentine Penrose: Écrits d'une femme surréaliste,* © Éditions Joëlle Losfeld, 2001. Reprinted by permission of Mme J. Devise and Éditions Joëlle Losfeld.

"The Rain Finding Once More," "At My Windows," trans. by Mary Ann Caws. Printed by permission of Mary Ann Caws.

631

Benjamin Péret

"Allo," "Clin d'œil," "Source," from *Jeu sublime*, 1936, © José Corti, 1971; "Où es-tu," from *Feu central*, 1947, © José Corti, 1995. Reprinted by permission of José Corti.

"Hello," "Wink," "Fountain," trans. by Mary Ann Caws, from *Surrealist Love Poems*, © Tate Publishing, 2001. Reprinted by permission of Mary Ann Caws. "Where Are You" trans. by Rachel Stella, from *Death to the Pigs and Other Writings: Selected Writings of Benjamin Péret*, © University of Nebraska Press, 1986. Reprinted by permission of University of Nebraska Press.

Anne Perrier

"Toutes les choses de la terre," from *Oeuvre poétique*, © L'Escampette, 1996. Reprinted by permission of L'Escampette.

"All Earth's Things," trans. by Mary Ann Caws. Printed by permission of Mary Ann Caws.

Saint-John Perse

"Chanson: Il naissait un poulain," "Chanson: Mon cheval arrêté," from *Anabase*, © Éditions Gallimard, 1924; "Nocturne," from *Chant pour un équinoxe*, © Éditions Gallimard, 1975. Reprinted by permission of Éditions Gallimard.

"Song: A Colt Was Foaled," "Song: I Have Halted My Horse," trans. by T. S. Eliot, from *St.-John Perse: Collected Poems*, © Princeton University Press, 1971; "Nocturne," trans. by Richard Howard, from *Song for an Equinox*, © Princeton University Press, 1977. Reprinted by permission of Princeton University Press.

Pablo Picasso

"Ses grosses cuisses," from "De la Celestina à Dora Maar" (exhibition), © Estate of Pablo Picasso, Artist Rights Society, 2003. Reprinted by permission of Artist Rights Society.

"Her Great Thighs," trans. by Mary Ann Caws, from *Picasso's Weeping Woman: The Life and Art of Dora Maar*, © Little Brown/Bulfinch, 2000. Reprinted by permission of Mary Ann Caws.

Marcelin Pleynet

"Dans la lumière du jour," from *Provisoires amants des nègres*, © Éditions du Seuil, 1962. Reprinted by permission of Éditions du Seuil.

"In the Daylight," trans. by Mary Ann Caws. Printed by permission of Mary Ann Caws.

Francis Ponge

"Les Plaisirs . . . ," "Les Mûres," "L'Huître," "Les Arbres se défont . . . ," from *Le Parti-pris des choses*, © Éditions Gallimard, 1942; "L'Ardoise," from *Le Nouveau Recueil*, © Éditions Gallimard, 1967. Reprinted by permission of Éditions Gallimard.

"The Pleasures . . . ," "Trees That Come Undone . . . ," trans. by Lee Fahnestock, from *The Nature of Things*, © Red Dust, 1995, 2000. Reprinted by permission of Lee Fahnestock and Red Dust. "Blackberries," "The Oyster," trans. by Serge Gavronsky, from *Modern French Poetry*, © Columbia University Press, 1975. Reprinted by permission of Columbia Univer-

sity Press. "Slate," trans. by Simon Watson Taylor, from *French Poetry Today: A Bilingual Anthology*, © Random House UK, Inc., 1971. Reprinted from Random House UK, Inc., and Simon Watson Taylor.

Anne Portugal

"Vu de ce côté-ci: De l'horizon," "Vu de ce côté ci: Il y avait," "Chaque case," from *Nu*, © P.O.L., 1988. Reprinted by permission of P.O.L.

"Seen from over Here: From the Horizon," "Seen from over Here: There Was," "Every Shack," trans. by Norma Cole, from *Nude*, © Kelsey Street Press, 2001. Reprinted by permission of Norma Cole and Kelsey Street Press.

Catherine Pozzi

"Nyx," from *Poèmes*, © Éditions Gallimard, 1959. Reprinted by permission of Éditions Gallimard.

"Nyx," trans. by Mary Ann Caws. Printed by permission of Mary Ann Caws.

Gisèle Prassinos

"Qualités d'apôtre," "Poème amoureux," from *Trouver sans chercher*, © Éditions Flammarion, 1975. Reprinted from Éditions Flammarion.

"Apostle Qualities," "Loving Poem," trans. by Mary Ann Caws. Printed by permission of Mary Ann Caws.

Jacques Prévert

"Barbara," from *Paroles*, © Éditions Gallimard, 1949. Reprinted by permission of Éditions Gallimard.

"Barbara," trans. by Martin Sorrell, from *Modern French Poetry*, © Forest Books, 1992. Reprinted by permission of Forest Books.

Raymond Queneau

"Renfort [1], [2]," from *Les Ziaux*, © Éditions Gallimard, 1943; "Je crains pas . . . ," from *L'Instant fatal*, © Éditions Gallimard, 1946; "Pour nourrir . . . ," from *Battre la campagne*, © Éditions Gallimard, 1968. Reprinted by permission of Éditions Gallimard.

"Reinforcements [I]," trans. by Keith Waldrop, from *Prism International*, 1971. Reprinted by permission of Keith Waldrop. "Reinforcements [II]," trans. by Keith Waldrop. Printed by permission of Keith Waldrop. "That Don't Scare Me," trans. by Keith Waldrop, from *A Windmill near Calvary*, © University of Michigan Press, 1986. Reprinted by permission of Keith Waldrop. "The Nourishment . . . ," trans. by Teo Savory, from *Raymond Queneau: Pounding the Pavement; Beating the Bush; and Other Pataphysical Poems*, © Unicorn Press, 1985. Reprinted from Unicorn Press.

Nathalie Quintane

"Mon Pouchkine," from *Poèmes*, © P.O.L., 1999. Reprinted by permission of P.O.L.

"My Pushkin," trans. by Mary Ann Caws. Printed by permission of Mary Ann Caws.

Jacques Réda

"Distance de l'automne," "Amen," from *Amen*, © Éditions Gallimard, 1968. Reprinted by permission of Éditions Gallimard.
"Autumn Distance," "Amen," trans. by Stephen Romer. Printed by permission of Stephen Romer.

Pierre Reverdy

"Dans les champs . . . ," from *Les Ardoises du toit*, © Éditions Gallimard, 1918; "La Trame," "Souffle," "Plus lourd," "Ça," ". . . S'entre-bâille," from *La Liberté des mers*, © Éditions Gallimard, 1959; "La Tête pleine de beauté," from *Flaques de verre*, © Éditions Gallimard, 1929. Reprinted by permission of Éditions Gallimard.
"In the Fields . . . ," trans. by Patricia Terry, "The Head Filled with Beauty," trans. by Mary Ann Caws, from *Roof Slates and Other Poems*, © Northeastern University Press, 1981. Reprinted by permission of Northeastern University Press. "The Web," "Breath," trans. by Mary Ann Caws and Patricia Terry, "Heavier," "That," ". . . Is Ajar," trans. by John Ashbery, from *Pierre Reverdy: Selected Poems*, © Wake Forest University Press, 1991. Reprinted by permission of Wake Forest University Press.

Valérie-Catherine Richez

Excerpts from "Petite âme," © Éditions Unes, 1998. Reprinted by permission of Valérie-Catherine Richez.
Excerpts from "Little Soul," trans. by Michael Tweed. Printed by permission of Michael Tweed.

Jacqueline Risset

"M. S. [Maurice Scève] 1544," from *La Traduction commence*, © Éditeur Christian Bourgois, 1978. Reprinted by permission of Éditeur Christian Bourgois.
"M. S. 1544," trans. by Jennifer Moxley, from *The Translation Begins*, © Burning Deck Press, 1996. Reprinted by permission of Burning Deck Press.

Jacques Roubaud

"Méditation . . . ," "Lumière . . . ," "Dans cet arbre," from *Quelque chose noir*, Éditions Gallimard, 1986. Reprinted by permission of Éditions Gallimard. "Une glace de," "Partout les," from *Traduire, Journal, Nous*, 1990. Reprinted by permission of Jacques Roubaud. "Il pleut," "Le Passé," "Certaine manière je," from *La Forme d'une ville change plus vite hélas que le coeur des hommes*, © Éditions Gallimard, 1999. Reprinted by permission of Éditions Gallimard.
"Meditation . . . ," "Light . . . ," "In This Tree," trans. by Rosmarie Waldrop, from *Something Black*, Dalkey Archive, 1999. Reprinted by permission of Dalkey Archive and Rosmarie Waldrop. "It Is Raining," "The Past," trans. by Richard Sieburth and Françoise Gramet, from *Painted Lady*. Reprinted by permission of Richard Sieburth and Françoise Gramet. "Ice In," "Everywhere the," "A Way I," trans. by Jacques Roubaud, from *Traduire, Journal, Nous*, 1990. Reprinted by permission of Jacques Roubaud.

Paul de Roux

"Labeur du jour," "Encore le froid," from *Poèmes de l'aube,* © Éditions Gallimard, 1990. Reprinted by permission of Éditions Gallimard.

"The Day's Labor," "The Cold Again," trans. by Stephen Romer, from *Poetry/Chicago* (Special French Poetry Issue), 2000–2001. Reprinted by permission of Stephen Romer.

Saint-Pol Roux

"La Volière," from S. Henry, Camaret, 1892. "Lever de soleil," from *La Rose et les épines du chemin,* 1900. Reprinted by permission of La Rougerie.

"The Aviary," trans. by Robin Magowan. Printed by permission of Robin Magowan. "Sunrise," trans. by Mary Ann Caws. Printed by permission of Mary Ann Caws.

Claude Royet-Journoud

"Localité," from *Les Natures invisibles,* © Éditions Gallimard, 1997. Reprinted by permission of Éditions Gallimard.

"Locality," trans. by Keith Waldrop, from *Exact Change Yearbook,* 1995. Reprinted by permission of Keith Waldrop.

Amina Saïd

Excerpts from "Sentiers de lumière," from *Duelle,* no. 3, 2000. Reprinted by permission of Association Duelle. "La Terre," from *Gisements de lumière,* © Éditions de la Différence, 1998. Reprinted from Éditions de la Différence.

Excerpts from "Paths of Light," "The Earth," trans. by Mary Ann Caws. Printed by permission of Mary Ann Caws.

Victor Segalen

"Édit funéraire," "Par respect," "Éloge du jade," "Trahison fidèle," from *Stèles,* © Éditions Gallimard, 1912. Reprinted by permission of Éditions Gallimard.

"Funerary Edict," "Out of Respect," trans. by Mary Ann Caws and Patricia Terry. Printed by permission of Mary Ann Caws and Patricia Terry. "In Praise of Jade," "Faithful Betrayal," trans. by Timothy Billings and Christopher Bush. Printed by permission of Timothy Billings and Christopher Bush.

Léopold Sédar Senghor

"Prière aux masques," from *Chants d'ombre,* © Éditions du Seuil, 1945; "Le Salut du jeune soleil," from *Lettres d'hivernage,* © Éditions du Seuil, 1973. Reprinted by permission of Éditions du Seuil.

"Prayer to the Masks," "The Young Sun's Greeting," trans. by Hoyt Rogers. Printed by permission of Hoyt Rogers.

Philippe Soupault

"Georgia," "Horizon," from *Georgia,* © Les Cahiers libres, 1926. Reprinted by permission of Christine Chemetoff-Soupault. "Cinéma-palace," "Chanson pour des . . . ," from

Georgia Épitaphes Chansons, © Éditions Gallimard, 1984. Reprinted by permission of Christine Chemetoff-Soupault.

"Georgia," "Horizon," trans. by Mary Ann Caws and Patricia Terry, from *Surrealist Love Poems,* Tate Publishing, 2001. Reprinted by permission of Mary Ann Caws and Patricia Terry. "Movie-house," "Song for Ghosts . . . ," trans. by Mary Ann Caws. Printed by permission of Mary Ann Caws.

Jude Stéfan

"Viande de . . . ," "Emma Zola . . . ," from *Laures,* © Éditions Gallimard, 1984; "Harengs . . . ," from *Cyprès,* © Éditions Gallimard, 1967. Reprinted by permission of Éditions Gallimard.

"Butcher's Meat . . . ," "Emma Zola . . . ," trans. by Marilyn Hacker. Printed by permission of Marilyn Hacker. "Herrings . . . ," trans. by Edward Lucie-Smith, from *French Poetry Today: A Bilingual Anthology,* © Random House UK, Inc., 1971. Reprinted from Random House UK, Inc., and Edward Lucie-Smith.

Salah Stétié

"Le Jardin de l'un," from *Fièvre et guérison de l'icône,* © Éditions Gallimard, 1998. Reprinted by permission of Éditions Gallimard.

"The Garden of the One," trans. by Marilyn Hacker. Printed by permission of Marilyn Hacker.

Jules Supervielle

"Un poète," "Le Regret de la terre," from *Les Amis inconnus,* © Éditions Gallimard, 1934. Reprinted by permission of Éditions Gallimard.

"A Poet," "Regretting the Earth," trans. by Patricia Terry, from *Modern French Poetry,* © Columbia University Press, 1975. Reprinted by permission of Columbia University Press.

Jean Tardieu

"La Mouche . . . ," from *Le Fleuve caché,* © Éditions Gallimard, 1933; "Les Jours," "La Seine de Paris," from *Le Témoin invisible,* © Éditions Gallimard, 1943; "Cézanne," from *Figures,* © Éditions Gallimard, 1944. Reprinted by permission of Alix Turolla Tardieu and Éditions Gallimard.

"The Fly . . . ," "Days," "The Seine in Paris," "Cézanne," trans. by David Kelley, from *Jean Tardieu: The River Underground: Selected Poems and Prose,* © Bloodaxe Books, 1991. Reprinted by permission of Bloodaxe Books.

Christophe Tarkos

"67 mots d'une voyelle . . . ," from *Le Livre des carrés de terre,* © Les Contemporains Favoris, 2000. Reprinted by permission of Stacy Doris and Roof Editions.

"67 Words with One Vowel . . . ," trans. by Stacy Doris, from *Christophe Tarkos: Ma langue est poétique: Selected Work,* © Roof Books, 2000. Reprinted by permission of the Segue Foundation, Roof Editions, and Stacy Doris.

Habib Tengour

"Secrète . . . ," excerpts from "Au Pays . . . ," from *Po&sie,* no. 80, © Éditions Belin, 1987. Reprinted by permission of Habib Tengour.
"Secret . . . ," trans. by Mary Ann Caws. Printed by permission of Mary Ann Caws. Excerpts from "In the Country . . . ," trans. by Marilyn Hacker. Printed by permission of Marilyn Hacker.

Tristan Tzara

"Le Géant . . . ," from *Vingt-cinq poémes,* © J. Heuberger, 1918; "Le Dompteur de lions . . . ," "Réalités cosmiques . . . ," from *L'Homme approximatif,* © Éditions Gallimard, 1968; "La Mort . . . ," from *De nos oiseaux,* © Éditions kra, 1929; "Le Cheval," from *Miennes,* © Coractèves, 1955.
"White Giant . . . ," "The Lion Tamer Remembers," "Cosmic Realities . . . ," "The Death . . . ," "The Horse," trans. by Mary Ann Caws, from *Tristan Tzara: Approximate Man and Other Writings,* © Mary Ann Caws, 1995. Reprinted by permission of Mary Ann Caws.

Paul Valéry

"La Fileuse," from *Album de vers anciens,* © Éditions Gallimard, 1920; "Le Rameur," "Le Cimetière marin," from *Charmes ou poèmes,* © Éditions Gallimard, 1922. Reprinted by permission of Éditions Gallimard.
"The Spinner," trans. by Grace Schulman. Printed by permission of Grace Schulman. "The Oarsman," trans. by Mary Ann Caws and Patricia Terry. Printed by permission of Mary Ann Caws and Patricia Terry. "The Seaside Cemetery," trans. by Derek Mahon, from *The Recorder: Journal of the American Irish Historical Society,* © American Irish Historical Society, Fall 2001. Reprinted by permission of Christopher Cahill and Derek Mahon.

André Velter

"Je chante ma femme," "L'Autre," from *Du Gange à Zanzibar,* © Éditions Gallimard, 1993. Reprinted by permission of Éditions Gallimard.
"My Wife I Sing," trans. by Rosemary Lloyd. Printed by permission of Rosemary Lloyd. "The Other One," trans. by Mary Ann Caws. Printed by permission of Mary Ann Caws.

Franck Venaille

"Éloge . . . ," "Maintenant," from *Papiers d'identité,* © Éditions Oswald, 1966. Reprinted by permission of Éditions Oswald.
"In Praise . . . ," "Now," trans. by Mary Ann Caws. Printed by permission of Mary Ann Caws.

Boris Vian

"Un jour," "Pourquoi que je vis," from *Je voudrais pas crever,* © Jean-Jacques Pauvert, 1962. Reprinted by permission of Jean-Jacques Pauvert.
"One Day," "What for Do I Live Then," trans. by Rosemary Lloyd. Printed by permission of Rosemary Lloyd.

ACKNOWLEDGMENTS

Renée Vivien

"La Rançon," from *Évocations,* © Éditions Gallimard, 1903. Reprinted by permission of Éditions Gallimard.
"The Ransom," trans. by Mary Ann Caws. Printed by permission of Mary Ann Caws.

Marguerite Yourcenar

"Épitaphe . . . ," "Journaux quotidiens," "Poème pour une poupée . . . ," from *Feux,* © Éditions Gallimard, 1974. Reprinted by permission of Éditions Gallimard.
"Epitaph . . . ," "Daily Papers," "Poem for a Doll . . . ," trans. by Martin Sorrell, from *Elles,* © University of Exeter Press, 1995. Reprinted by permission of University of Exeter Press.

Index of Poets

Index of Titles

Index of Translators